murach's
MVS TSO
PART 2 commands,
CLIST & REXX

Doug Lowe

MIKE MURACH & ASSOCIATES, INC.
(800) 221-5528 • (559) 440-9071 • Fax: (559) 440-0963
murachbooks@murach.com • www.murach.com

Development team

Author:	Doug Lowe
Writer/editor:	Anne Prince
Editor:	Sheila Lynch
New cover design:	Zylka Design

Books in the new Murach series

Murach's Mainframe COBOL

Murach's OS/390 and z/OS JCL

Murach's CICS for the COBOL Programmer

Murach's CICS Desk Reference

Murach's DB2 for the COBOL Programmer

Murach's Java SE 6

Murach's Java Servlets and JSP

Murach's VB 2005

Murach's ASP.NET 2.0 Web Programming with VB 2005

Murach's C# 2005

Murach's ASP.NET 2.0 Web Programming with C# 2005

Murach's SQL Server 2005 for Developers

Books in the Murach Classic series

MVS TSO: Concepts and ISPF

MVS TSO: CLIST and REXX

ISBN-10: 0-911625-57-7
ISBN-13: 978-0-911625-57-8
20 19 18 17 16 15 14 13 12 11 10 9 8 7 6

MURACH

Dear reader,

We've designated this book as a Murach Classic because it was originally published in 1991, and the content is still the same (only the cover has changed). Yet it's still the quickest and best way to learn how to use TSO commands…and how to write and use CLIST and REXX procedures that incorporate those commands…on an IBM mainframe.

Without this book, most programmers have to learn TSO, CLIST, and REXX on their own. Yet the code is far from intuitive. And the documentation that's available is often heavy on details, but doesn't present those details in terms of the tasks you actually want to do. That's why this book continues to sell year after year.

But haven't the software products been enhanced since 1991? Yes, they have. But because all IBM mainframe software is upwards-compatible, the essential skills are still the same...and it's the essential skills that this book focuses on. Once you master those skills, you'll be able to learn the enhancements on your own.

Beyond that, equipment references and the appearance of the computer screens in the book examples will probably differ at least slightly from what you see on the job. But mainframe programmers are used to dealing with bigger problems than those. So I don't think the differences will stop you from quickly learning the essential concepts and skills.

In short, please accept this book for what it is: a classic Murach book with a new cover. The good news is that it has taught thousands of programmers how to use TSO for everyday program-development tasks...and it can do the same for you.

Have a great day!

Mike Murach, Publisher

P. S. Please don't confuse the books in this Classic series with our new series of Murach books. Our new Murach books have been completely re-engineered for current subjects like Java, VB.NET, and SQL, as well as for the latest releases of mainframe subjects like CICS, OS/390 JCL, and DB2.

Contents

Preface

This book is the second of a two-part revision of my 1984 book, *MVS TSO*. *MVS TSO, Part 1* shows you how to use IBM's standard platform for program development under TSO, ISPF/PDF. This book teaches you how to use TSO commands directly. It also shows you how to combine those commands into procedures using both of TSO's procedure facilities: CLIST and REXX. And it shows you how to create CLIST and REXX procedures for two types of applications that are especially useful to ISPF users: edit macros and ISPF dialogs.

If you're an ISPF user, you owe it to yourself to learn how to use the TSO commands presented in this book and how to create CLIST or REXX procedures. Although ISPF/PDF provides most of the functions you need for common program development tasks, some essential tasks can only be accomplished using TSO commands. And, as you become more proficient with TSO and ISPF/PDF, you'll want to combine commands into procedures so you can perform routine tasks with ease. With this book in hand, you'll have no problem learning these essential skills.

Why this book is effective

I believe this book is effective for the same two reasons the first edition remained successful for six years. First, I spent a great deal of time planning the content and organization of this book. I have found that although most technical books today are easy to read, few of them are effective. The reason is simple: poor planning. They usually cover every possible aspect of a subject without regard to what's useful and what's not. And they present information in a sequence that often defies logical explanation. So for this book, I spent more time planning than I did writing. As in the first edition, I've focused on a practical subset of TSO commands and procedure facilities that let you do almost everything you'll ever need to do. And I've made every effort to ensure that each element of that subset is presented as clearly and logically as possible.

Second, I've placed a heavy emphasis on illustration in this book. Most technical books today simply don't have enough illustrations, and the illustrations they do include are often trivial or unrealistic. I believe the illustrations are at least as important as the text. As a result, I've included over two hundred of them in this book. You'll find illustrations that present command formats, show examples of how commands are used, show examples of CLIST and REXX procedures, and show how ISPF edit macros and dialogs operate. These illustrations not only help you learn new skills, but also serve as handy references later on.

Who this book is for

This book is for anyone who uses TSO. That includes both beginning and experienced programmers, application and system programmers, operators, and college students learning programming subjects. The only prerequisite is a basic knowledge of ISPF/PDF, enough so that you can access the TSO Command option to enter TSO commands and edit library members that contain CLIST or REXX procedures. If you aren't familiar with ISPF/PDF, I suggest you get a copy of the first part of this series, *MVS TSO, Part 1: Concepts and ISPF.*

MVS, TSO, and ISPF come in many different versions. There are three basic versions of the MVS operating system in use today: MVS/370, MVS/XA, and MVS/ESA. In addition, MVS must be used with a Job Entry Subsystem, either JES2 or JES3. And there are several releases of TSO in common use today. This book applies to all of these software versions. Whenever I introduce a feature that's unique to a particular software version, I'll be sure to point it out. Otherwise, you can assume that everything you learn in this book will work properly on any MVS system. (All of the examples were tested under MVS/ESA with TSO/E version 2.)

How to use this book

I organized this book in the most logical sequence for an experienced ISPF/PDF user who wants to learn how to use TSO commands and procedures. So the most logical way to read it is to start with chapter 1 and read each chapter in sequence. However, you don't have to follow this sequence to get the maximum benefit from this book. There are several alternate study plans you might follow, depending on your unique needs.

The chapters in section 1 present TSO commands and should be read in sequence. However, only chapters 1 and 2 present information that is required for the rest of the book. As a result, once you've read chapters 1 and 2, you can skip ahead to the other sections. Then, you can return to chapters 3 and 4 when you wish.

Sections 2 and 3 show you how to create and use CLIST and REXX procedures. Because these sections are independent of one another, you can read them in any order you wish. In other words, the REXX chapters do not assume that you've read the CLIST chapters. Within the sections, however, the chapters are organized sequentially. So you should read chapter 5 before you read chapter 6, and you should read chapter 7 before you read chapter 8.

Section 4 includes two chapters that present advanced CLIST and REXX applications. These chapters are independent of one another, so you can read them in any order you wish. Both chapters, however, assume a basic familiarity with either CLIST or REXX procedures. So you should read the chapters in section 2 or 3 before you read either of the chapters in section 4.

Conclusion

I'm confident this book will be a valuable addition to your technical bookshelf. It will not only teach you how to use TSO effectively, but it will also serve as a desk reference you'll consult frequently once you've mastered the fundamentals.

As always, I'd appreciate your comments, criticisms, and suggestions. I'm especially interested in any TSO, CLIST, or REXX techniques you may have discovered that I didn't include in this book. So please feel free to use the postage-paid comment form at the back of this book. I hope to hear from you soon.

Doug Lowe
Fresno, California
January, 1991

TSO commands

If you're an experienced TSO user, you know that the most efficient way to get your work done is by using ISPF/PDF for as many functions as possible. However, there are some TSO functions that are best performed by native TSO commands rather than via ISPF/PDF. And there are a few essential TSO functions that simply can't be done via ISPF/PDF, such as allocating data sets that will be processed by an application program or sending a message to another TSO user. To perform these functions, you have to use native TSO commands. In addition, if you want to develop CLIST or REXX procedures, you have to know how to use native TSO commands as well.

If you haven't used TSO commands before, you should read chapter 1 first. It explains the syntax requirements for TSO commands, shows you how to use a few basic commands, and presents an overview of the commands presented in chapters 2, 3, and 4. Because those chapters are independent of one another, you can read them in any order you wish once you've finished chapter 1.

Chapter 1

An introduction to TSO commands

When TSO was developed, the most common type of computer terminals were teletype-like devices that displayed or printed output and accepted keyboard input one line at a time. The terminal user controlled TSO by issuing commands that performed such basic functions as editing files, listing available file names, and deleting and renaming files. Today, those functions are usually done under TSO using ISPF/PDF to take advantage of the full-screen capabilities of 3270 terminals. However, TSO still retains its command-line orientation, and there are still many TSO functions that are best done with commands rather than with ISPF/PDF.

This chapter presents a general introduction to TSO commands. It consists of two topics. In topic 1, I'll present an overview of the most useful TSO commands, show you the syntax rules you must follow when coding them, and show you how to enter them from the standard TSO READY prompt or from ISPF. In addition, I'll show you how to use a few simple commands.

In topic 2, I'll show you how to use an optional TSO command environment called the session manager. The session manager is designed to take advantage of the 3270 terminal's full-screen features while still retaining TSO's line-by-line orientation. Since you don't have to use the session manager to use TSO commands, you can skip this topic for now and come back to it later.

Topic 1   Basic TSO commands and coding rules

Before you can learn the details of using specific TSO commands, you need a general understanding of the functions provided by TSO commands. First, you'll learn how to start a TSO session so you can use TSO commands. Then, you'll learn the rules you must follow to use TSO commands, and the techniques you use to enter them. This topic gives you that required background information. Along the way, you'll learn a few simple but useful TSO commands.

TSO COMMANDS: AN OVERVIEW

Figure 1-1 lists 27 TSO commands. Although TSO provides many more commands, these are the ones you'll probably use most often. Once you master these commands, you should have no trouble learning how to use other commands from the IBM manuals, if necessary.

I've divided the commands in figure 1-1 into five categories: session management, basic data set management, data set allocation, foreground program development, and background job. This isn't how the commands are classified in the IBM manual (they're described in alphabetical order with no classification at all). But I think this classification makes sense.

Session management commands

Session management commands are designed to help you control your TSO session. Obviously, this group includes the LOGON and LOGOFF commands, which let you start and end a session. I also include the HELP command in this category, because it provides information on how to use other TSO commands, and I include the SEND and LISTBC commands, because they let you send and

Session management commands

LOGON	Start a terminal session.
LOGOFF	End a terminal session.
HELP	Display explanatory information.
SEND	Send a message to another user.
LISTBC	Display broadcast messages.

Basic data set management commands

LISTCAT	List catalog entries.
LISTDS	List data set information.
RENAME	Change the name of a data set.
DELETE	Scratch a data set.
LIST	Display the contents of a data set or member.
COPY	Reproduce a data set or member.
SMCOPY	Reproduce a data set or member.
PRINTDS	Print the contents of a data set or member.
EDIT	Modify the contents of a data set or member.

Figure 1-1   TSO commands you'll use most often (not including CLIST or REXX commands) (part 1 of 2)

receive messages to and from other TSO users. Later in this topic, I'll describe the LOGON, LOGOFF, HELP, and SEND commands.

Basic data set management commands

Basic data set management commands perform routine functions like copying or renaming files. The first four commands in this category don't need much explanation here. The LISTCAT command lists cataloged data sets; the LISTDS command lists information for specific data sets; the RENAME command changes the name of a data set; and the DELETE command deletes a data set.

The next two commands both provide essential functions: the LIST command displays the contents of a data set at your terminal,

Data set allocation commands

ALLOCATE	Allocate a data set.
FREE	Free an allocated data set.
LISTALC	List data sets currently allocated.

Foreground program development commands

COBOL	Compile a COBOL program.
LINK	Link-edit a compiled program.
CALL	Execute a link-edited program.
LOADGO	Link-edit and execute a compiled program.
TESTCOB	Test a COBOL program.
COBTEST	Test a COBOL II program.

Background job commands

SUBMIT	Submit a job for background processing.
STATUS	Display the current status of submitted jobs.
OUTPUT	Obtain output from background jobs.
CANCEL	Cancel a submitted job.

Figure 1-1   TSO commands you'll use most often (not including CLIST or REXX commands) (part 2 of 2)

and the COPY command reproduces a data set. However, they're *not* a part of standard TSO. Instead, they're licensed separately from IBM as part of the *TSO Data Set Utilities* package. As a result, you'll have to check to see if they're available at your installation or if you'll be using other commands for these functions. For example, if you don't have the Data Set Utilities package, you can copy a file using the SMCOPY command.

The next command, PRINTDS, prints a data set at an on-line printer. And the last command listed in this group, EDIT, is TSO's general purpose editor. In most installations, however, EDIT is *not* used as a general purpose editor. That's because there are a variety of other editors available, including ISPF's editor, that provide substantially better features. However, EDIT is sometimes helpful when you're using a CLIST.

I'll describe all the basic data set management commands except EDIT in detail in topic 1 of the next chapter. Then, I'll describe the EDIT command in topic 2.

Data set allocation commands

Data set allocation commands let you allocate and deallocate data sets. If you're familiar with MVS JCL, you'll soon realize that the ALLOCATE command provides nearly the same functions as the DD statement. You use it to create new data sets or to define existing data sets for programs you run under TSO. The FREE command deallocates a data set that was previously allocated with an ALLOCATE command. And the LISTALC command lists the names of all data sets currently allocated to you.

Quite frankly, it's difficult to understand the concept of data set allocation if you haven't had much MVS or TSO experience. So if you're confused about the allocation commands right now, don't worry. Everything will make sense when I describe these commands in topic 3 of chapter 2.

Foreground program development commands

Foreground program development commands help you compile and test programs. The COBOL command compiles source programs using various COBOL compilers. The LINK command link-edits a compiled program to produce a load module you can execute using the CALL command. The LOADGO command does essentially the same thing as the LINK and CALL commands, but it doesn't create a permanent load module. And the TESTCOB and COBTEST commands help you debug COBOL and COBOL II programs. I cover these commands in chapter 3.

Background job commands

Background job commands let you manage batch jobs in a background region. First, you use the SUBMIT command to initiate a background job. Then, you use the STATUS command to monitor

TSO command	ISPF option
Session management	
LOGON	None
LOGOFF	X followed by LOGOFF
HELP	T (tutorial) or Help key
SEND	None
LISTBC	None
Basic data set management	
LISTCAT	3.4 (DSLIST utility)
LISTDS	3.2 (data set utility) or 3.4 (DSLIST utility)
RENAME	3.2 (data set utility) or 3.4 (DSLIST utility)
DELETE	3.2 (data set utility) or 3.4 (DSLIST utility)
LIST	1 (browse)
COPY	3.3 (move/copy utility)
SMCOPY	3.3 (move/copy utility)
PRINTDS	3.6 (hardcopy utility)
EDIT	2 (edit)

Figure 1-2   A comparison of TSO commands and ISPF options (part 1 of 2)

the job's progress. When the job has completed, you use the OUTPUT command to retrieve its output. And you can use the CANCEL command to remove the job from the system. I cover background job commands in chapter 4.

TSO commands compared with ISPF options

If you're familiar with ISPF, you've probably been comparing the TSO commands with their equivalent ISPF options. Figure 1-2 lists the equivalent ISPF options for the TSO commands in figure 1-1. Here, you can see that the main area of variation is in the allocation commands. The term *allocate* has a slightly different meaning

TSO command	ISPF option
Data set allocation	
ALLOCATE	3.2 (data set utility—not exactly the same function)
FREE	None
LISTALC	None
Foreground program development	
COBOL	4.2A (foreground COBOL)
LINK	4.7 (foreground link-edit)
CALL	None
LOADGO	None
TESTCOB	4.10A (COBOL interactive debugger)
COBTEST	4.10 (COBOL II interactive debugger)
Background jobs	
SUBMIT	5 (background processing) SUBMIT command of 2 (edit)
STATUS	3.8 (outlist utility)
OUTPUT	3.8 (outlist utility)
CANCEL	3.8 (outlist utility)

Figure 1-2   A comparison of TSO commands and ISPF options (part 2 of 2)

under TSO than it does under ISPF. That's why there aren't equivalent ISPF options for the FREE and LISTALC commands. But even though it provides for fewer functions, the ISPF allocate option is considerably easier to use than the ALLOCATE command.

I also want to stress that the ISPF browse and edit options are a dramatic improvement over the TSO LIST and EDIT commands. And the ISPF utilities, especially option 3.4, let you manage data sets and libraries without remembering complicated command syntax. As a result, although it's important that you know how to use the TSO commands, you should use ISPF instead whenever you can.

HOW TO START AND END A TSO SESSION

Before you can begin using TSO, you need to start a TSO session. At some installations, you can do that by entering your user-id and password in the appropriate fields on a logon screen. If your installation doesn't provide a logon screen, you start your TSO session by entering a LOGON command.

The basic format of the LOGON command is this:

```
LOGON user-id/password
```

For example, if your user-id is TSO0001 and your password is DAL, you enter the LOGON command like this:

```
LOGON TSO0001/DAL
```

If you omit the parameters and enter just the word LOGON, TSO prompts you for the missing information.

You may also be required to specify an account number on your LOGON command. If so, you code it following the password like this:

```
LOGON TSO0001/DAL ACCT(1234)
```

Here, the account number is 1234.

In response to your LOGON command, TSO may display a number of messages, called *notices*. Usually, it's a good idea to scan these messages. But if you want, you can suppress the notices by specifying NONOTICE on your LOGON command, like this:

```
LOGON TSO0001/DAL NONOTICE
```

To end a TSO session, you enter the LOGOFF command. The format of the LOGOFF command is simple:

```
LOGOFF
```

HOW TO USE TSO COMMANDS

Before you can learn the specifics of how to use individual TSO commands, you need to learn the syntax rules that apply to all TSO commands. In addition, you need to know how TSO responds to your commands with mode messages, prompts, and error messages. And finally, you need to know about two systems that affect how you enter TSO commands: ISPF and the TSO session manager.

TSO command syntax

When you code a TSO command, you must follow a few rules. To begin with, all TSO commands follow this pattern:

```
command-name  operands
```

The *command-name* field identifies the TSO function you want to invoke. The *operands* (sometimes called *parameters*) provide information specific to each command.

You code TSO command operands in free form (that is, without worrying about what column they start in), separating them with commas or spaces. Some of the operands are *positional operands*. The location of a positional operand within a command is significant to its meaning. For example, consider this TSO command:

```
RENAME TEST.COBOL TEST1.COBOL
```

This command changes the name of the file identified by the first operand (TEST.COBOL) to the file name specified in the second operand (TEST1.COBOL). Obviously, the operand order is important in this command.

Other operands are *keyword operands*. Keyword operands don't depend on their position within a command for their meaning. Instead, TSO recognizes keyword operands wherever they appear within a command. To illustrate, consider this command:

```
FREE ALL HOLD
```

Here, TSO recognizes two keywords: ALL and HOLD (FREE is the command name). The presence of these keywords affects how the command is processed; if you omit either one, the command is processed differently. But the order of the keywords isn't important. So the command

```
FREE HOLD ALL
```

has the same meaning.

Many keyword operands require that you supply a value within parentheses, like this:

```
DDNAME(OUTDD)
```

Here, TSO recognizes the keyword DDNAME and associates the value OUTDD with it. Some keyword operands require two or more values within the parentheses, separated by commas or spaces, as in this example:

```
SPACE(100 50)
```

Within the keyword operand, the *suboperands* are positional.

Command and keyword abbreviations As you gain experience with TSO, you'll find that many of the command and keyword combinations you use frequently require more keystrokes than seem necessary. Fortunately, TSO lets you abbreviate commands and keywords liberally.

To begin with, many TSO command names have an abbreviated form. For example, you can specify DEL as the command name for the DELETE command. Figure 1-3 gives the abbreviated form for each of the commands in figure 1-1.

As for keyword operands, TSO lets you abbreviate them by specifying only as many characters as are necessary to distinguish the keyword from other keywords within the same command. For example, all these are valid abbreviations for the LISTALC command's STATUS operand:

```
STATUS
STATU
STAT
STA
ST
```

But S isn't acceptable because it could be confused with the SYSNAMES operand.

Since the minimum abbreviation for any keyword operand depends on the other operands available for the same command, they're often difficult to remember. As a result, I suggest you avoid using excessive abbreviation until you become proficient with the TSO commands.

How to continue a TSO command on another line If a command requires so many operands that you can't code it in the 80 columns of a single terminal line, you must continue it to the next line. To do that, just keep typing when you reach the end of the line. The cursor will wrap around to the beginning of the next line, and TSO will process the command properly.

If you want to break a long command before the end of the line, you can use either a plus sign (+) or a hyphen (-) as a continuation character, like this:

```
ALLOCATE DSNAME(TEST.COBOL) DDNAME(SYSUT2) +
NEW CATALOG SPACE(100 10) CYLINDERS DIR(10)
```

Here, the plus sign means the command continues on the next line. (When you include a multi-line command in a CLIST or REXX

Full command name	Abbreviation
LOGON	
LOGOFF	
HELP	H
SEND	SE
LISTBC	LISTB
LISTCAT	LISTC
LISTDS	LISTD
RENAME	REN
DELETE	DEL
LIST	
COPY	
SMCOPY	SMC
PRINTDS	PR
EDIT	E
ALLOCATE	ALLOC
FREE	
LISTALC	LISTA
COBOL	
LINK	
CALL	
LOADGO	LOAD
TESTCOB	
COBTEST	
SUBMIT	SUB
STATUS	ST
OUTPUT	OUT
CANCEL	

Figure 1-3   Abbreviations for TSO commands

Type	Meaning
ASM	Assembler language source code
CLIST	CLIST procedure
CNTL	JCL job stream used for batch job facility
COBOL	COBOL source code
DATA	Uppercase text data
EXEC	REXX procedure
FORT	FORTRAN source code
LOAD	Executable program module
OBJ	Object module
PLI	PL/I source code
TEXT	Upper and lowercase text data

Figure 1-4   Common data set types

procedure, you must use a continuation character. I present CLIST and REXX procedures in sections 2 and 3.)

TSO data sets   As you use TSO, you will need to create and modify data sets. For example, when you edit a program source file, you modify a member of a partitioned data set.

TSO uses standard MVS data set naming conventions, but adds some conventions of its own. Normally, TSO names any data set you create or modify in a TSO session according to these conventions. As you will see in a moment, however, these conventions are *not* absolute requirements.

In TSO, a data set name generally follows this format:

```
user-id.name.type
```

User-id is the TSO user identification number assigned to each user. *Name* is the name you create to identify the data set. And *type* is one of the values in figure 1-4 used to identify the type of data stored in the data set.

To illustrate this naming convention, suppose your user-id is TSO0001 and you want to create a COBOL source library named

SOURCE. In this case, TSO0001.SOURCE.COBOL is the TSO data set name.

Normally, TSO supplies the user-id component of a data set name. For example, you can refer to TSO0001.SOURCE.COBOL simply as SOURCE.COBOL. TSO automatically adds your user-id to the name.

Incidentally, you can qualify the name component of a TSO data set name. For example, you can create a data set name like this:

```
TSO0001.SOURCE.TEST.COBOL
```

Here, the name component of the data set name is SOURCE.TEST. The only restriction on this kind of qualification is that the total length of the data set name, including the periods used to separate its components, can't be longer than 44 characters. That's because the TSO data set name must conform to MVS naming requirements.

You specify partitioned data set members in the usual way: enclose the member name in parentheses following the data set name. For example, in the data set name

```
TSO0001.SOURCE.COBOL(MKTG1200)
```

the member name is MKTG1200. To access this data set, specify the data set name as SOURCE.COBOL(MKTG1200). (Remember, TSO automatically adds the user-id.)

Remember that these conventions are just that: conventions. They are not absolute requirements of MVS or TSO. In fact, TSO allows you to bypass these conventions by specifying a data set name in apostrophes, using any format you desire. As a result, you can refer to a data set named CUSTOMER.MASTER like this:

```
'CUSTOMER.MASTER'
```

When you use apostrophes like this, TSO doesn't add the user-id component to the data set name.

The HELP command   If you forget the syntax of a command, you can use the HELP command to refresh your memory. If you enter the word HELP by itself, TSO displays a summary of all its available commands. If you enter HELP followed by a command name, TSO provides an explanation of that command, including the command's syntax and an explanation of each of its operands.

System responses

During a TSO session, TSO displays short messages at your terminal. These messages fall into four categories: mode messages, prompts, informational messages, and broadcast messages.

Mode messages   The *mode messages* tell you that TSO is ready to accept a command. The most common mode message is this:

> READY

When you see this at your terminal, it means TSO is waiting for you to enter a command. Other mode messages appear when you enter a command that has its own set of subcommands, such as the EDIT command. For example, this mode message,

> EDIT

means TSO is waiting for you to enter an EDIT subcommand. I'll describe EDIT and other subcommands later in this book.

Prompts   If you enter a command that has an error in it, or if you omit a required operand, TSO responds with a *prompt* that describes the problem and asks you to enter the operand again. For example, the LIST command requires a data set name. Suppose you enter the command without a data set name, like this:

> LIST

Then, TSO responds with a message asking you to enter a data set name. Prompts are easy to identify because they always end with a question mark.

Informational messages   Many of TSO's messages simply provide information about the progress of a command's execution. These *informational messages* may or may not be important to you. Usually, they indicate that all is well. Sometimes, however, an informational message may indicate a problem that requires your attention.

Broadcast messages   *Broadcast messages* are created by a system operator or another TSO user. In general, you'll receive a set of broadcast messages when you log on. These messages may inform you of important events like scheduled interruptions in your

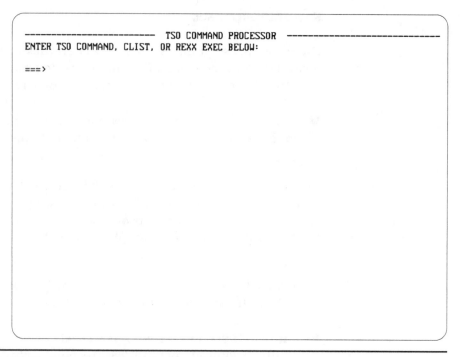

```
------------------------- TSO COMMAND PROCESSOR -------------------------------
ENTER TSO COMMAND, CLIST, OR REXX EXEC BELOW:

===>
```

Figure 1-5   ISPF's TSO command processor panel

system's availability. So it's a good idea to check them briefly. You can redisplay them at any time by entering a LISTBC command.

How to use TSO commands from ISPF

When you use ISPF, you invoke most of the commonly used TSO functions via menu selections. As a result, you don't use TSO commands on a day-by-day basis. But you will want to use them in certain situations.

There are three ways to enter a TSO command from ISPF. First, you can select option 6 from the primary option menu. Then, ISPF displays the command entry panel shown in figure 1-5. Here, you can enter any TSO command. You return to ISPF by pressing the End key, PF3/15.

Second, you can enter a TSO command in the command area of any ISPF panel, provided you prefix the command with the word TSO. For example, if you enter the command

    TSO LISTALC STATUS

The SEND command

```
SEND 'message'  {USER(user-id)}   [LOGON]
                {OPERATOR(n)  }
```

Explanation

message	The text of the message you want to send, enclosed in apostrophes. The message can be up to 115 characters long.
user-id	The user to whom you want the message sent.
n	The system operator to whom you want the message sent.
LOGON	Specifies that if the user isn't logged on, the message should be displayed the next time the user logs on.

Figure 1-6   The SEND command

in the command area of an ISPF panel, ISPF will pass the LISTALC command to TSO to be processed.

Third, you can enter a TSO command as a line command on a data set or member list panel for the data set utility, option 3.4. You'll find a detailed description of how to do this in *Part 1: Concepts and ISPF.*

How to send messages to other users

TSO lets you communicate with other users by sending messages to them and receiving messages from them. To send a message to another user, you use the SEND command. The format for this command is shown in figure 1-6. For example, to send the message "Do you have a copy of MKTG1200?" to a user named APRINCE, you enter this command:

```
SEND 'DO YOU HAVE A COPY OF MKTG1200?' USER(APRINCE)
```

If APRINCE is logged on, the message is displayed immediately. Otherwise, you're notified that the message can't be sent.

If you want the message to be delivered as soon as the user logs on, include the LOGON keyword, like this:

```
SEND 'DO YOU HAVE A COPY OF MKTG1200?' USER(APRINCE) LOGON
```

In this example, if APRINCE is logged on, the message is displayed immediately. Otherwise, the message is displayed the next time APRINCE logs on.

You can also send a message to a system operator, if you know the operator's routing code. For example, to send a message to operator 7, use this command:

```
SEND 'PLEASE MOUNT THE FFA TAPE' OPERATOR(7)
```

Before you can send a message like this one, you have to find out the proper routing codes for your system operators.

DISCUSSION

One question you might be asking right now is, if ISPF is so much easier to use, why should I bother learning TSO commands at all? There are two reasons. First, TSO commands provide some functions that simply aren't available using ISPF. For example, ISPF doesn't provide a way to send messages to other users or to allocate a data set so it can be processed by a program.

Second, TSO commands are useful in CLIST and REXX procedures, which let you automate routine or complex tasks. You'll learn about CLIST and REXX procedures in sections 2 and 3 of this book.

In the next topic of this chapter, you'll learn how to use the TSO session manager, which is designed to make the full-screen capabilities of the 3270 easier to use. Although the session manager doesn't fundamentally change the line-by-line nature of TSO, it does provide some substantial benefits. If you plan on working extensively in TSO line mode and the session manager is available at your installation, you should read that topic. Otherwise, feel free to move directly to chapter 2.

Terms

allocate	keyword operand
notice	suboperand
command name	mode message
operand	prompt
parameter	informational message
positional operand	broadcast message

Objectives

1. Briefly describe five categories of TSO commands.

2. Describe the rules for creating TSO commands.

3. Describe these types of TSO system responses:
   a. mode messages
   b. prompts
   c. informational messages
   d. broadcast messages

4. Describe how to invoke a TSO command from ISPF.

Topic 2   The TSO session manager

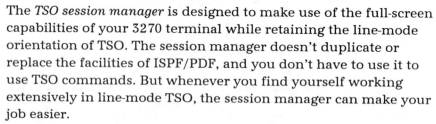

The *TSO session manager* is designed to make use of the full-screen capabilities of your 3270 terminal while retaining the line-mode orientation of TSO. The session manager doesn't duplicate or replace the facilities of ISPF/PDF, and you don't have to use it to use TSO commands. But whenever you find yourself working extensively in line-mode TSO, the session manager can make your job easier.

Although the session manager is an integral part of TSO, it must be activated by your logon procedure for you to use it. If the session manager is not active when you log on to TSO, you'll have to contact your TSO system administrator to find out how to log on using the session manager.

Streams and windows

To act as an interface between native TSO and the user, the session manager uses special data sets called *streams*. Quite simply, each record in a stream represents one line sent to or received from a terminal. As a session manager user, you communicate with streams; you can look at information in them or add information to them. The session manager, in turn, communicates with TSO via the streams; it presents commands one line at a time from a stream and stores TSO's output in a stream.

To illustrate, figure 1-7 shows how two of the session manager's streams work together. (Although there are many other streams, these are the only two I'll describe in this chapter.) One stream, called the *TSOIN stream*, receives commands you enter at your terminal and in turn passes them on to TSO. The other, called the *TSOOUT stream*, receives TSO's output and passes it on to your terminal. In addition, each time you enter a command into the TSOIN stream, it's copied directly to the TSOOUT stream. As a result, the TSOOUT stream contains TSO output intermixed with

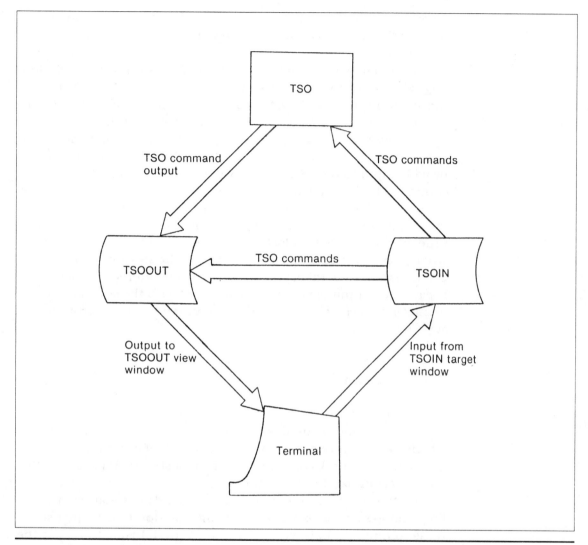

Figure 1-7   How the session manager uses the TSOIN and TSOOUT streams

your commands. In short, the TSOOUT stream is an exact image of
the terminal screen for a non-session manager TSO session.

So far, this is probably very confusing. What puts it all together
is the idea of windows. Under the session manager, a *window* is a
part of your terminal's screen that's linked to one of the session
manager's streams. For example, one part of your terminal screen
is used as a window that views the TSOOUT stream. That way,

whenever TSO adds information to the TSOOUT stream, you can
see it in the screen window that views that stream.

Similarly, some portions of your terminal's screen are used as
windows that provide input to a stream. For example, one window
might be linked to the TSOIN stream. When you enter a TSO
command in that window, the command is passed on to the TSOIN
stream, which in turn passes the command on to TSO.

A window can double as both input and output. For example, a
window might display the contents of the TSOOUT stream and
provide input to the TSOIN stream. That way, you can enter a
command and receive the command's output in the same window.

A major benefit of streams and windows is that all the activity
for a TSO session is saved in the streams and can be recalled at any
time. In contrast, data is lost once it's removed from the screen
when you're working under TSO without the session manager.
Under native TSO, then, you often have to reenter a command
because its output is no longer displayed. With the session
manager, you can simply recall the command's output from the
stream where it was saved.

Commands and PF keys

The session manager provides a command language of its own.
The most commonly used commands are the scrolling commands,
which let you move a window from one part of a stream to
another. That's how you recall data from a stream. I'll describe the
scrolling commands later in this topic.

Another set of session manager commands lets you redefine
the windows and streams you're using. You don't normally use
these commands, however, at least not at first. Instead, you use the
arrangement of streams and windows supplied by IBM, called the
default format.

You can associate session manager commands with PF keys, so
each command is invoked when you press its PF key. This makes
common session manager commands easy to use. Figure 1-8 shows
the PF key assignments that are in effect when you first enter the
session manager. In this topic, I'll explain the PF key functions that
are shaded. The others, though sometimes useful, represent functions that are beyond the scope of this book.

Key	Function
PF1/13	Print screen snapshots.
PF2/14	Change scroll amount.
PF3/15	Enter command.
PF4/16	Take screen snapshot.
PF5/17	Find text.
PF6/18	Change CURRENT window.
PF7/19	Scroll up.
PF8/20	Scroll down.
PF9/21	Scroll up max.
PF10/22	Scroll left.
PF11/23	Scroll right.
PF12/24	Scroll down max.

Figure 1-8   PF key functions under the session manager

The default screen format

Figure 1-9 shows a typical session manager display. Although it's not apparent, this display actually consists of eleven windows. Here, however, I'll describe only the four windows labeled in figure 1-10. (The seven windows that aren't labeled in figure 1-10 contain headings and other constant data.)

The *MAIN window* takes up most of the display screen: 19 full lines. It displays the contents of the TSOOUT stream. When you use one of the scrolling commands I'll describe in a moment, it's the MAIN window that is scrolled. (You can scroll other windows, but you usually don't.)

The *CURRENT window* is smaller than the MAIN window; it's only two lines of 62 characters each. It displays the last two lines of the TSOOUT stream. So when you scroll the TSOOUT stream in the MAIN window, the most recent information in the TSOOUT stream is still shown in the CURRENT window.

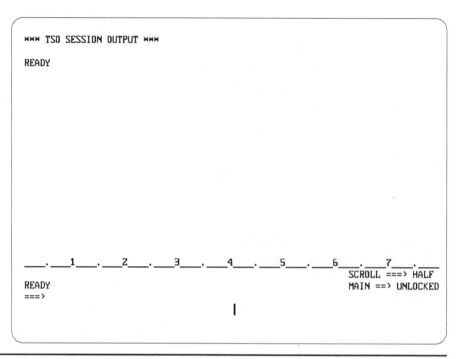

Figure 1-9   The session manager screen format

The *ENTRY window* is tied to the TSOIN stream. As you can see
in figure 1-10, this window begins right after the arrow (===>) near
the lower left corner of the screen. It's here that you normally
enter your TSO commands.

You use the next window in figure 1-10, the *PASSWORD window*,
only when TSO prompts you for a password. This window is tied
to the TSOIN stream just like the ENTRY window, but data isn't
displayed as it's entered. In other words, no characters appear on
the screen when you enter a password; the cursor simply moves
across the window as though you were entering spaces.

Besides the ENTRY and PASSWORD windows, the MAIN and
CURRENT windows are also tied to the TSOIN stream for input. So
although those windows normally display data from the TSOOUT
stream, any data you enter in them is sent to the TSOIN stream
and processed by TSO as a command.

One common use of the MAIN window as input is when you're
entering several commands that vary only slightly. In this case,
you enter the first command in the ENTRY window. After the

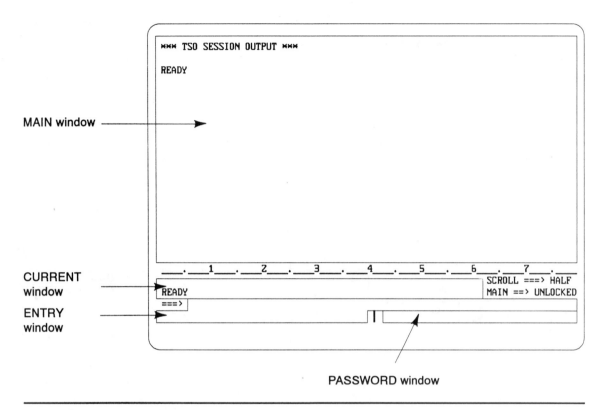

Figure 1-10   Major windows on the session manager screen

command is processed, it's displayed in the MAIN window along with the command's output. To enter the second command, move the cursor to the command in the MAIN window, make any changes necessary by typing over the command and using the Insert and Delete keys, and press the Enter key. The command is sent to the TSOIN stream and processed again by TSO.

In fact, any line you change in the MAIN or CURRENT window is sent to the TSOIN stream. So if you modify four lines in the MAIN window, four lines are sent to TSOIN.

To illustrate how you use the default screen windows to enter TSO commands, consider figure 1-11. In part 1, I enter a simple TSO command, LISTCAT, in the ENTRY window. Part 2 of this figure shows how the screen appears after TSO processes the LISTCAT command. The output from the command is displayed in the MAIN window. And the last two lines displayed in the MAIN window are also displayed in the CURRENT window.

Part 1:

Enter the command

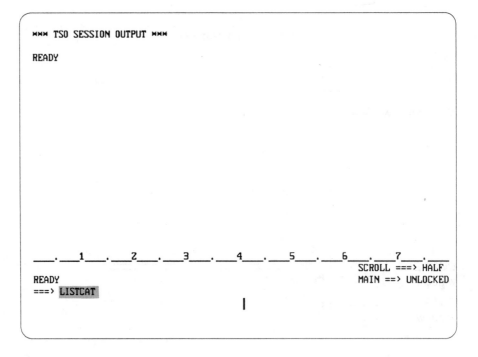

```
*** TSO SESSION OUTPUT ***

READY




                                                                        


___. ___1___. ___2___. ___3___. ___4___. ___5___. ___6___. ___7___. ___
                                                   SCROLL ===> HALF
READY                                              MAIN ==> UNLOCKED
===> LISTCAT
                              |
```

Part 2:

The resulting output

```
*** TSO SESSION OUTPUT ***

READY
LISTCAT
IN CATALOG: CATALOG. ICFCAT1.VTS0001
DLOWE.COPY.COBOL
DLOWE.ISPPROF
DLOWE.MKTG1Z00.LINKLIST
DLOWE.MKTG1Z00.LIST
DLOWE.TEST.CLIST
DLOWE.TEST.CNTL
DLOWE.TEST.COBOL
DLOWE.TEST.LOAD
DLOWE.TEST.OBJ
READY



___. ___1___. ___2___. ___3___. ___4___. ___5___. ___6___. ___7___. ___
DLOWE.TEST.OBJ                                     SCROLL ===> HALF
READY                                              MAIN ==> UNLOCKED
===>
                              |
```

Figure 1-11   Entering a TSO command under the session manager

Value	Meaning
HALF	Move the screen window half a page.
PAGE	Move the screen window a full page.
n	Move the screen window *n* lines or columns.
MAX	Move the screen window to the top, bottom, left, or right margin.

Note: Scroll amounts are set by entering the correct value in the ENTRY window and pressing the PF2/14 key.

Figure 1-12   SCROLL values

How to scroll a window

Under the default screen format, the MAIN window displays 19 lines of 79 columns each. During a TSO session, the TSOOUT stream collects more than 19 lines after you enter just one or two commands. So the MAIN window generally displays just a portion of the TSOOUT stream's records. In addition, the records in the TSOOUT stream may be longer than 79 characters. To display TSOOUT records other than the ones currently shown, or to show data beyond the first 79 columns of each record, you use *scrolling*.

If you're familiar with ISPF, you'll have no trouble learning how to scroll a session manager window. Referring back to figure 1-8, you can see that the session manager uses the same scrolling PF key assignments as ISPF: the PF7/19 and PF8/20 keys scroll up and down, while the PF10/22 and PF11/23 keys scroll left and right. In addition, the session manager provides two scrolling keys that aren't available under ISPF: the PF9/21 and PF12/24 keys, which scroll to the top and bottom of the stream.

Also, like ISPF, the session manager uses scroll amount values to indicate how far the scrolling keys scroll the stream. The current scroll amount is shown in the SCROLL field near the bottom right corner of the screen. To change the scroll amount value, type the new scroll amount in the ENTRY window and press the PF2/14 key. Figure 1-12 lists the valid scroll amount values for the session manager. They're the same as the scroll amount values you can use under ISPF, except that DATA isn't valid with the session manager.

To illustrate the effect of scrolling a stream window, figure 1-13 shows a half-page scroll during a TSO session. To set up this display, I entered an OUTPUT command that caused many pages of output to be written to the TSOOUT stream. Then, I used scrolling commands to move backwards in the stream to the point shown in part 1 of figure 1-13. Notice that the SCROLL field indicates that the scroll value is HALF. When I press the PF8/20 key, the display moves up 9 lines, as shown in part 2. If I press the PF7/19 key at this point, the screen returns to the display in part 1.

Locked and unlocked windows   Before I go on, let me explain the difference between an unlocked window and a locked window. When a window is *unlocked*, it's scrolled automatically by the session manager so the most current data in the stream is always displayed. When you enter the session manager, both the MAIN and the CURRENT windows are unlocked. So as you enter TSO commands, both windows are automatically scrolled so they display the most recent entries in the TSOOUT stream. Once you use a scrolling key, however, the MAIN window is *locked*. That means it's not automatically scrolled as entries are added to the TSOOUT stream. Instead, the window moves only in response to your scrolling commands.

Now that you know about locked and unlocked windows, you'll understand why the default screen format provides two windows to view the TSOOUT stream: MAIN and CURRENT. Since the MAIN window can become locked when you enter a scrolling command, the CURRENT window remains unlocked throughout your TSO session. Thus, the CURRENT window *always* displays the two most current lines from the TSOOUT stream, even when the MAIN window is locked.

The status of the MAIN window is shown in the MAIN field near the bottom right corner of the screen, beneath the scroll amount field. In figure 1-11, the MAIN window is unlocked because I haven't used any scrolling keys. But in figure 1-13, the MAIN window is locked. To unlock the MAIN window once it's locked, use the PF12/24 key to move the window to the end of the stream. Then, the status of the MAIN window returns to UNLOCKED.

Part 1:

Before the scroll

```
PP 5668-958 REL. 2.0, 09/08/86, IBM VS COBOL II.                              DATE
  000001  000100 IDENTIFICATION DIVISION.
  000002  000200*
  000003  000300 PROGRAM-ID.     MKTG1200.
  000004  000400*
  000005  000500 ENVIRONMENT DIVISION.
  000006  000600*
  000007  000700 CONFIGURATION SECTION.
  000008  000800*
  000009  000900 INPUT-OUTPUT SECTION.
  000010  001000*
  000011  001100 FILE-CONTROL.
  000012  001200     SELECT CUSTMST  ASSIGN TO AS-CUSTMST.
  000013  001300     SELECT SALESMN  ASSIGN TO SALESMN
  000014  001400                     ORGANIZATION IS INDEXED
  000015  001500                     ACCESS IS RANDOM
  000016  001600                     RECORD KEY IS SM-SALESMAN-KEY.
  000017  001700     SELECT SALESRPT ASSIGN TO SALESRPT.
  000018  001800
____.___1___.___2___.___3___.___4___.___5___.___6___.___7____.____
                                            SCROLL ===> HALF
READY                                       MAIN ==>  LOCKED
===>
                                    I
```

Part 2:

After the scroll

```
  000010  001000*
  000011  001100 FILE-CONTROL.
  000012  001200     SELECT CUSTMST  ASSIGN TO AS-CUSTMAST.
  000013  001300     SELECT SALESMN  ASSIGN TO SALESMN
  000014  001400                     ORGANIZATION IS INDEXED
  000015  001500                     ACCESS IS RANDOM
  000016  001600                     RECORD KEY IS SM-SALESMAN-KEY.
  000017  001700     SELECT SALESRPT ASSIGN TO SALESRPT.
  000018  001800*
  000019  001900 DATA DIVISION.
  000020  002000*
  000021  002100 FILE SECTION.
  000022  002200*
  000023  002300 FD  CUSTMST
  000024  002400     RECORD CONTAINS 42 CHARACTERS.
  000025  002500*
  000026  002600 COPY CUSTMAST.
  000027C 000100 01  CUSTOMER-MASTER-RECORD.
  000028C 000200*
____.___1___.___2___.___3___.___4___.___5___.___6___.___7____.____
                                            SCROLL ===> HALF
READY                                       MAIN ==>  LOCKED
===>
                                    I
```

Figure 1-13   Effect of a half page scroll

How to find text

Sometimes, you need to scroll the MAIN window repeatedly to display a certain portion of the TSOOUT stream. For example, in figure 1-13, I had to scroll through several hundred lines of text before I came to the start of my compiler listing. If the part of the TSOOUT stream you're looking for contains a unique series of characters, you can use a find operation to scroll directly to it. A find operation searches backwards through the TSOOUT stream. So if the text you want to find is past your current location in the stream, you should first use the PF12/24 key to scroll to the end of the stream.

To start a find operation, enter the text string you want to locate in the ENTRY window, and press the PF5/17 key. Then, the session manager scrolls the window backwards until it finds the specified text. If the text string contains any spaces, commas, or parentheses, you must enclose it in apostrophes, like this:

```
'PIC (X)'
```

And if the text contains apostrophes, double them, like this:

```
'VALUE ''SALES REPORT''.'
```

Here, the text string for the find operation is VALUE 'SALES REPORT'.

Discussion

I've presented only a small subset of the session manager's capabilities in this topic. The IBM manual, *TSO/E Command Reference*, describes more than 20 session manager commands. Some of these allow you to change PF key assignments. So if you use a certain command repeatedly, you can assign it to a PF key and press only the one key whenever you want to enter that command. Many of the other session manager commands let you change the default screen format. For example, you can divide the screen in half, into two large windows, and scroll through each one separately.

At this point, I just want you to realize that the session manager is both powerful and flexible. The default key assignments and screen format I've presented in this topic are adequate for most applications. But as you gain experience with the session manager, you may want to experiment with its capabilities.

Terms

TSO session manager
stream
TSOIN stream
TSOOUT stream
window
default format
MAIN window
CURRENT window
ENTRY window
PASSWORD window
scrolling
unlocked window
locked window

Objectives

1. Describe how the session manager uses streams and windows as an interface between a user and TSO.

2. Describe the function of these windows:
   a. MAIN
   b. CURRENT
   c. ENTRY
   d. PASSWORD

3. Under the session manager, (1) scroll through a data set and (2) use a find operation to locate specific text.

Chapter 2

Data set management and allocation commands

In this chapter, I'll present the TSO commands you use to manage data sets. This chapter consists of three topics. Topic 1 describes the basic data set management commands. These commands let you list catalog and data set information and rename, delete, copy, list, or print data sets or members. Topic 2 describes the TSO EDIT command. You use it to create or change a sequential data set or library member. And topic 3 describes the TSO commands you use to allocate data sets.

Topic 1   Data set management commands

In this topic, I'll describe eight basic data set management commands: LISTCAT, LISTDS, RENAME, DELETE, COPY, SMCOPY, LIST, and PRINTDS. These commands let you perform basic data set management functions like listing catalog entries, changing data set names, and displaying or printing the contents of a data set.

Keep in mind as you read this chapter that most of these functions are better performed using the ISPF utilities. In particular, the data set utility, option 3.4, can do almost all of the functions these commands provide, and more. So you'll probably use these commands most in CLIST or REXX procedures, or when ISPF isn't available.

How to list catalog entries

Figure 2-1 gives the format of the LISTCAT command, used to list entries in an MVS catalog. The LISTCAT operands let you control the number of entries displayed (LEVEL and ENTRIES) and the amount of information displayed for each entry (NAME, HISTORY, VOLUME, and ALL). Figure 2-2 gives five examples of how these operands are used.

Example 1 in figure 2-2 shows a LISTCAT command with no operands. When you enter this command, LISTCAT displays a list of all cataloged data sets that are prefixed with your user-id. Figure 2-3 shows output that's typical of this type of LISTCAT command.

If you want to list catalog entries for a specific data set or group of data sets, you can code an ENTRIES or LEVEL operand. Both have similar functions but different coding requirements. For the ENTRIES operand, you supply one or more data set names. TSO supplies your user-id as the high-level qualifier for each data set name you supply, unless you enclose the name in apostrophes.

The LISTCAT command

```
LISTCAT  [ {ENTRIES(data-set-names)}  ]
           {LEVEL(level)          }

         [ {NAME   }  ]
           {HISTORY }
           {VOLUME  }
           {ALL     }
```

Explanation

ENTRIES   Specifies the data set names to be listed. If more than one name is specified, they must be separated by commas or spaces. You can use an asterisk (*) for one of the levels in a data set name; in that case, more than one data set may be listed.

LEVEL   Specifies one or more levels of qualification for the data sets to be listed. For example, if you specify LEVEL(DLOWE.TEST), any data set starting with DLOWE.TEST is listed.

NAME   Specifies what information to list for each catalog entry. NAME says to list the
HISTORY   data set name and entry type. HISTORY says to list the data set name, entry
VOLUME   type, owner-id, creation date, and expiration date. VOLUME says to list
ALL   HISTORY information plus the vol-ser and device type. And ALL says to list all catalog fields. NAME is the default.

Figure 2-1   The LISTCAT command

Example 2 in figure 2-2 shows a LISTCAT command that specifies a data set in the ENTRIES operand. Here, the catalog entry for the data set TEST.COBOL (prefixed by your user-id) is listed. The VOLUME operand tells LISTCAT to list creation and expiration date and volume information in addition to the file name.

Within a data set name specified in an ENTRIES operand, you can replace one of the qualifiers with an asterisk. Then, the name is a *generic data set name*. That means the name may refer to more than one data set. For example, the ENTRIES operand in example 3 looks like this:

```
ENTRIES(TEST.*)
```

Here, TSO lists any data set name with your user-id as its first qualifier, TEST as its second qualifier, and *any* value as its third qualifier.

Example 1

```
LISTCAT
```

Example 2

```
LISTCAT ENTRIES (TEST.COBOL) VOLUME
```

Example 3

```
LISTCAT ENTRIES(TEST.*)
```

Example 4

```
LISTCAT ENTRIES(TEST.COBOL TEST.OBJ TEST.LOAD) VOLUME
```

Example 5

```
LISTCAT LEVEL(DLOWE.TEST)
```

Figure 2-2   LISTCAT examples

You can specify more than one data set name in an ENTRIES operand, as in example 4:

```
ENTRIES(TEST.COBOL TEST.OBJ TEST.LOAD)
```

Here, TSO lists the catalog entries for three data sets.

The LEVEL operand is similar to the ENTRIES operand, with two significant differences. First, the LEVEL operand does *not* add your user-id as the high-level qualifier of a data set. Second, you specify one or more levels of qualification in a LEVEL operand, rather than a complete data set name. To illustrate, consider the LEVEL operand in example 5 of figure 2-2:

```
LEVEL(DLOWE.TEST)
```

For this LISTCAT command, TSO lists any data set starting with DLOWE.TEST, whether the data set name has two, three, or more levels in its name. In contrast, if you specify a two-level data set

```
READY
LISTCAT
IN CATALOG:CATALOG.ICFCAT1.VTS0001
DLOWE.COPY.COBOL
DLOWE.CUSTMAST.DATA
DLOWE.MKTG1200.LINKLIST
DLOWE.MKTG1200.LIST
DLOWE.SALESMAN.DATA
DLOWE.SUBPROG.LOAD
DLOWE.SYSDATE.LINKLIST
DLOWE.SYSDATE.LIST
DLOWE.SYSTIME.LINKLIST
DLOWE.SYSTIME.LIST
DLOWE.TEST.CNTL
DLOWE.TEST.COBOL
DLOWE.TEST.LOAD
DLOWE.TEST.OBJ
DLOWE.TESTMKTG.COBOL
```

Figure 2-3   Typical LISTCAT command output

name in an ENTRIES operand, only data sets with names of two levels are listed, even if one of the levels is an asterisk.

To illustrate the differences between the ENTRIES and LEVEL operands, figure 2-4 shows which of five data set names TSO lists for each of four ENTRIES and LEVEL operands. The first ENTRIES operand lists the three data sets whose names consist of three levels, with the second level named TEST. The second ENTRIES operand lists the two data sets whose names consist of three levels, with the third level named COBOL. The first LEVEL operand lists the data sets whose names have DLOWE and TEST as their first and second qualifiers, regardless of how many levels of qualification the name contains.

The last LEVEL operand is a special case. Here, I code my user-id as the LEVEL. As a result, all my data sets are listed. You never have to code a LEVEL operand like this, however, because if you don't code a LEVEL operand or an ENTRIES operand, TSO supplies your user-id as the default LEVEL.

I usually use the LEVEL operand rather than ENTRIES. Since LEVEL doesn't require that you specify all levels of qualification in a data set name, it's more useful when you're trying to remember a data set name you've forgotten. The ENTRIES operand is

Catalog data set name	ENTRIES (TEST.*)	ENTRIES (*.COBOL)	LEVEL (DLOWE.TEST)	LEVEL (DLOWE)
DLOWE.TEST.COBOL	X	X	X	X
DLOWE.TEST.OBJ	X		X	X
DLOWE.TEST.LOAD	X		X	X
DLOWE.TEST.CM.DATA			X	X
DLOWE.COPY.COBOL		X		X

Figure 2-4   Effect of various ENTRIES and LEVEL parameters in the LISTCAT command (shows what data sets are listed)

especially useful when you want to list catalog information for a specific data set.

As for the other operands, HISTORY and VOLUME are useful if you want to know a file's creation and expiration dates or the volume a file is stored on. ALL displays complete information about each file, which takes many display lines. ALL provides too much information for most purposes, so you probably won't use it often.

How to list data set information

Figure 2-5 shows the format of the LISTDS command, used to list information about one or more data sets. You can see how to use this command and its operands in the examples in figure 2-6.

Example 1 in figure 2-6 shows the simplest form of the LISTDS command. As a result of this command, TSO displays the record format, logical record size, block size, data set organization, and volume serial number for DLOWE.TEST.COBOL.

Example 2 shows a more complex LISTDS command. Here, TSO lists information for three data sets: DLOWE.TEST.COBOL, DLOWE.TEST.OBJ, and DLOWE.TEST.LOAD. Notice that if you specify more than one data set, you must enclose the list of data sets in parentheses.

Example 3 shows how you can use an asterisk in a data set name. Here, I want to list all data sets whose names consist of three

---

The LISTDS command

```
LISTDS    (data-set-names)

          [MEMBERS]

          [HISTORY]

          [STATUS]

          [LEVEL]
```

Explanation

data-set-names	A list of data set names to be listed. If only one data set is specified, the parentheses aren't needed. You can replace one or more levels of qualification with an asterisk (*). In that case, more than one data set may be listed.
MEMBERS	List the member names for a partitioned data set.
HISTORY	List the creation and expiration dates and the owner-id.
STATUS	List the ddname associated with the data set as well as the data set's disposition (KEEP, DELETE, CATLG, or UNCATLG).
LEVEL	List the high-level qualifiers rather than the fully-qualified data set names. Thus, any data sets whose high-level qualifiers match those specified in the data-set-names area are listed.

Figure 2-5   The LISTDS command

qualifiers, with the second level named TEST (the first corresponds to my user-id).

Example 4 shows how to achieve a similar result using the LEVEL operand. Here, I want to list data set information for all data sets whose names begin with DLOWE.TEST, regardless of how many qualifiers are in the name. For the LISTDS command, the LEVEL operand has the same effect as it does for the LISTCAT command, although its syntax is different.

Example 5 shows how to code the other LISTDS operands. MEMBERS tells TSO to list the names of each member of a partitioned data set. HISTORY tells TSO to list the file's creation date, expiration date, and security information. And STATUS tells TSO to list the data set's allocation information. (I'll explain data set allocation in topic 3 of this chapter.)

Example 1

```
LISTDS TEST.COBOL
```

Example 2

```
LISTDS (TEST.COBOL TEST.OBJ TEST.LOAD)
```

Example 3

```
LISTDS TEST.*
```

Example 4

```
LISTDS TEST LEVEL
```

Example 5

```
LISTDS TEST MEMBERS HISTORY STATUS LEVEL
```

Figure 2-6   LISTDS examples

Figure 2-7 shows the output generated by three LISTDS commands. Example 1 shows the standard LISTDS information, example 2 shows a list of member names, and example 3 shows STATUS and HISTORY information.

How to rename a data set

You use the RENAME command to change the name of a data set or a member of a partitioned data set. As you can see in figure 2-8, the format of the RENAME command is simple. You specify two data set names: the name of the data set whose name you want to change and the new name for the data set. When you enter the RENAME command, be sure the new name you specify doesn't already exist. If it does, you get an error message and TSO doesn't rename the data set.

```
Example 1

LISTDS TEST.COBOL
 DLOWE.TEST.COBOL
 --RECFM-LRECL-BLKSIZE-DSORG
   FB     80    3120    PO
 --VOLUMES--
   TSO003


Example 2

LISTDS TEST.COBOL MEMBERS
 DLOWE.TEST.COBOL
 --RECFM-LRECL-BLKSIZE-DSORG
   FB     80    3120    PO
 --VOLUMES--
   TSO003
 --MEMBERS--
   MKTG1100
   MKTG1200
   MKTG1300
   MKTG1400


Example 3

LISTDS TEST.COBOL STATUS HISTORY
 DLOWE.TEST.COBOL
 --RECFM-LRECL-BLKSIZE-DSORG-CREATED---EXPIRES---SECURITY--DDNAME---DISP
   FB     80    3120    PO    1990.059  00.000     NONE    SYS00008 KEEP
 --VOLUMES--
   TSO003
```

Figure 2-7   Typical LISTDS command output

Example 1 in figure 2-9 shows a basic RENAME command. Here, I renamed a data set named DLOWE.TEST.COBOL to DLOWE.ARTEST.COBOL.

Example 2 in figure 2-9 shows how you can use generic data set names in a RENAME command. Here, TSO changes only the second-level qualifier of each affected data set. For example, suppose you have these three data sets:

```
DLOWE.TEST.COBOL
DLOWE.TEST.OBJ
DLOWE.TEST.LOAD
```

The RENAME command

```
RENAME old-name new-name [ALIAS]
```

Explanation

old-name	The name of an existing data set or member of a partitioned data set. You can replace one or more levels of qualification with an asterisk (*).
new-name	The new name of the data set or PDS member. You can replace one or more levels of qualification with an asterisk (*). When you rename a member, you can specify just the new member name in parentheses, omitting the PDS name.
ALIAS	Valid only when you rename a member of a PDS; specifies that the new name is an alias of the old member.

Figure 2-8   The RENAME command

TSO renames the data sets to:

```
DLOWE.ARTEST.COBOL
DLOWE.ARTEST.OBJ
DLOWE.ARTEST.LOAD
```

Whenever you use generic data set names in a RENAME command, the asterisks must be in the same position for both data set names.

To change the name of a partitioned data set member, you specify the complete PDS and member name for the first operand. For the second operand, however, you can omit the name of the PDS and supply just the new member name in parentheses. Example 3 in figure 2-9 shows how to do this. Here, I renamed a member named REORDLST to ORDLST2.

The ALIAS operand is valid only when you rename a PDS member. It says that instead of changing the name of the member, you want to create a second name, called an *alias*, for the same member. Example 4 in figure 2-9 shows how to create an alias for a PDS member. After you execute this command, you can refer to the member as REORDLST or ORDLST2.

Under normal circumstances, there's no reason to create a member alias. But there are special circumstances where it's desirable to have a member alias. For example, suppose you create a command procedure (CLIST) that compiles a COBOL program. The member name for the procedure is COMPILE, but you want to let

Example 1

```
RENAME TEST.COBOL ARTEST.COBOL
```

Example 2

```
RENAME TEST.* ARTEST.*
```

Example 3

```
RENAME TEST.COBOL(REORDLST) (ORDLST2)
```

Example 4

```
RENAME TEST.COBOL(REORDLST) (ORDLST2) ALIAS
```

Figure 2-9   RENAME examples

users abbreviate the command as COMP. So, you leave the member in the CLIST library under its original name: COMPILE. Then, you create a member name alias: COMP. Now, whether you specify COMPILE or COMP, TSO invokes the same CLIST.

How to delete a data set

Figure 2-10 gives the format of the DELETE command, used to delete data sets. And figure 2-11 gives four examples that show how to use the DELETE command. In the first example, I delete a single data set. Example 2 shows how to delete a list of data sets. And example 3 shows how to delete any data sets that conform to a generic data set name.

The PURGE operand, used in example 4 in figure 2-11, says to bypass expiration date checking. Normally, TSO won't let you delete a data set unless its expiration date has passed. (A data set's *expiration date* indicates when the data set is no longer needed.) If you specify PURGE on a DELETE command, TSO deletes the data set even if its expiration date hasn't passed. Of course, you should be careful about how you use the PURGE operand. Otherwise, you may accidentally delete important data sets.

The DELETE command

```
DELETE (data-set-names) [PURGE]
```

Explanation

data-set-names   Specifies a list of data set names to be scratched. If you specify only one data set name, you can omit the parentheses. One level of qualification (not the highest) can be an asterisk; in that case, more than one data set may be scratched.

PURGE   Scratch the data set even if its expiration date has *not* passed.

Figure 2-10   The DELETE command

Example 1

```
DELETE TEST.COBOL
```

Example 2

```
DELETE (TEST.COBOL TEST.OBJ TEST.LOAD)
```

Example 3

```
DELETE TEST.*
```

Example 4

```
DELETE TEST.* PURGE
```

Figure 2-11   DELETE examples

How to copy a data set

Standard TSO does not provide a straightforward way to copy data sets. However, if your installation has installed an optional package of TSO commands called the TSO Data Set Utilities, you can use the COPY command to copy a data set. Alternatively, you

---

The COPY command

```
COPY   old-data-set-name   new-data-set-name
```

Explanation

old-data-set-name   Specifies the name of an existing data set or PDS member.

new-data-set-name   Specifies the name of the new data set or PDS member where the old
                           data set is copied.

Figure 2-12   The COPY command

can use the SMCOPY command if your version of TSO/E supports it. SMCOPY was designed for use under the session manager, but you can use it to copy data sets whether or not you use the session manager.

How to use the COPY command   The format of the COPY command is shown in figure 2-12. The operation of the COPY command is simple. You specify two data set names, and the first data set is copied to the second data set. If the second data set doesn't already exist, COPY automatically creates it, using the attributes of the first data set.

To illustrate, consider this COPY command:

```
COPY TEST.COBOL ARTEST.COBOL
```

Here, TSO copies a data set named DLOWE.TEST.COBOL to DLOWE.ARTEST.COBOL (assuming DLOWE is the user-id).

If the copy operation involves partitioned data sets, the second data set can be an existing library. In that case, members are copied one by one from the first data set to the second. If there are members that exist in both libraries, they too are copied, so the original versions in the second library are lost.

How to use the SMCOPY command   The SMCOPY command is designed to be used under the session manager to copy data between session manager streams and data sets. However, you can use it separately from the session manager to copy one data set to another.

The SMCOPY command

```
SMCOPY   FROMDATASET(data-set-name) TODATASET(data-set-name)

         [NOTRANS]
```

Explanation

FROMDATASET	Specifies the name of an existing data set or PDS member. FROMDATASET can be abbreviated FDS.
TODATASET	Specifies the name of the new data set or PDS member where the old data set is copied. TODATASET can be abbreviated TDS.
NOTRANS	Species that SMCOPY is *not* to make any changes to the data as it is copied. Should always be used when copying data sets.

Figure 2-13   The SMCOPY command

Figure 2-13 shows the syntax of the SMCOPY command when used to copy data sets. As you can see, the SMCOPY command's syntax isn't as straightforward as the COPY command's. But it performs the same function. And, like the COPY command, the SMCOPY command uses the attributes of the original data set to create the new data set, if it doesn't already exist.

Notice the NOTRANS parameter, which specifies that the data set should not be changed in any way as it is copied. If you omit this parameter, SMCOPY automatically converts all characters in the data set to uppercase, and substitutes spaces for any unprintable characters. This is because SMCOPY's primary function is to copy data to and from session manager streams, which ordinarily contain only uppercase letters and shouldn't contain unprintable characters. As a result, you should always specify NOTRANS when you use SMCOPY to copy data sets.

Here's an example of the SMCOPY command:

```
SMCOPY FDS(USER1.COBOL(MKTG1200)) +
       TDS(USER2.COBOL(MKTG1200)) NOTRANS
```

Here, the MKTG1200 member of the DLOWE.USER1.COBOL library is copied to the DLOWE.USER2.COBOL library (assuming DLOWE is the user-id).

The LIST command

```
LIST    data-set-name
```

Explanation

data-set-name   The name of the data set or PDS member to be listed.

Figure 2-14   The LIST command

How to list a data set

Like the COPY command, the LIST command is part of the TSO
Data Set Utilities, so it may not be available at your installation.
Instead, your installation may have created its own version of the
LIST command. Or it may use some other technique for listing
data sets.

In any event, figure 2-14 gives the basic format of the LIST
command. On it, you supply the name of the data set you want to
list. Then, the LIST command displays the contents of the data set
at your terminal. For example, if you enter the command

```
LIST TEST.COBOL(MKTG1200)
```

the member named MKTG1200 in TEST.COBOL is listed at your
terminal.

How to print a data set

To print a data set, you use the PRINTDS command. This causes
the contents of the specified data set to be spooled to the JES
output queue. Then, JES prints the data set according to specifications you make on the PRINTDS command.

Before I present the details of using the PRINTDS command, I
want to point out the differences between the PRINTDS command
and an older TSO command called DSPRINT. As I mentioned,
PRINTDS uses the output processing facilities of JES to print a data
set. In contrast, DSPRINT manages its own output processing, so it
can't print data sets on JES printers. I'll cover only the PRINTDS
command in this book.

Figure 2-15 gives the format of the PRINTDS command. Although it has several operands, only the first one is required. It tells PRINTDS the name of the data set you want to print. Although you can't use an asterisk to create a generic name, you can enter a list of names in the DSNAME/DATASET operand.

How to handle line numbers   The NUM, SNUM, and NONUM operands tell PRINTDS how to handle line numbers in the data set. If you say NUM, PRINTDS looks for line numbers in the position you specify. For example,

```
NUM(73,8)
```

means the line numbers start in position 73 and are 8 bytes long. The line numbers are printed in the first columns of each print line even if they're located in the middle or at the end of the records in the data set.

The SNUM operand tells PRINTDS that the data set contains line numbers in the position you specify, but that you don't want to print the line numbers. And the NONUM operand tells PRINTDS to do no special line number processing. If your data set contains line numbers and you specify NONUM, PRINTDS prints the line numbers along with the rest of the data in the records.

How to print a range of lines   The LINES operand tells PRINTDS that you don't want to print all the records in the data set. Instead, you want to print a subset of the file identified by the line numbers you provide in the LINES operand. If you provide just one line number, the listing begins at the number you specify and continues to the end of the file. For example, if you say LINES(1000), the listing starts at line 1000. If you specify two numbers separated by a colon, the listing starts at the first line number and ends at the second. Thus, to print lines 1000 through 2000, you would say LINES(1000:2000).

When you use the LINES operand, the line numbers you specify refer to either the line numbers that occur in the file or relative line numbers. If you specify the NUM or SNUM operand, PRINTDS uses the line numbers in the file. If you specify NONUM or let it default, PRINTDS uses relative line numbers.

How to format the output   The next eleven PRINTDS operands shown in figure 2-15 let you control the format of the printed

The PRINTDS command

```
PRINTDS        {DSNAME(data-set-names) }
               {DATASET(data-set-names)}

               {NUM(location,length) }
           [   {SNUM(location,length)} ]
               {NONUM                 }

           [ LINES(start[:end]) ]

           [ COLUMNS(start[:end]) ]

               {SINGLE}
           [   {DOUBLE}  ]
               {TRIPLE}
               {CCHAR }

               {FOLD(width)    }
           [   {TRUNCATE(width)} ]

           [ PAGELEN(lines) ]

           [ TMARGIN(lines) ]

           [ BMARGIN(lines) ]

           [ COPIES(nnn) ]

               {MEMBERS  }
           [   {DIRECTORY} ]
               {ALL      }

               {CLASS(output-class) }
           [   {SYSOUT(output-class)} ]

               {HOLD  }
           [   {NOHOLD} ]
```

Explanation

DSNAME   The name of the data set to be printed.
DATASET

NUM   Defines how line numbers are to be printed. NUM says that line numbers are
SNUM   contained in the position indicated by location and length and should be
NONUM   printed at the start of each print line. SNUM means that the line numbers are
               contained in the specified position, but should not be printed. NONUM means
               that no special line-number processing is to be done. If line numbers are
               present, they are printed just as if they were data. NONUM is the default.

Figure 2-15   The PRINTDS command (part 1 of 2)

Explanation (continued)

LINES	Specifies the starting and ending line numbers for the records to be printed. If you omit LINES, all the records in the data set are printed. If you omit the ending line number, the end of the file is assumed. You must specify NUM or SNUM if you specify LINES.
COLUMNS	Specifies the starting and ending column numbers for the records to be printed. If you omit COLUMNS, all the columns in each record are printed. If you omit the ending column number, the right hand column of the record is assumed. You can specify up to 32 pairs of columns by separating them with commas.
SINGLE DOUBLE TRIPLE CCHAR	Specifies how the printed lines are to be spaced. SINGLE means to single-space the listing. DOUBLE means to double-space the listing. TRIPLE means to triple-space the listing. CCHAR means to use the control characters in the file to determine spacing. CCHAR is meaningful only if the file contains printer control characters. CCHAR is the default if the data set contains printer control characters. Otherwise, there is no default.
FOLD TRUNCATE	Specifies what to do with records that are too long to be printed on a single line. FOLD says to continue the record on the next print line. TRUNCATE says to ignore the remainder of the record. There is no default for this operand.
PAGELEN	Specifies the number of lines to be printed on each page of the output listing. The default is 60.
TMARGIN	Specifies the number of lines to be left blank at the top of each page of the output listing. The default is 0.
BMARGIN	Specifies the number of lines to be left blank at the bottom of each page of the output listing. The default is 0.
COPIES	Specifies the number of copies of the output listing to be printed. The default is 1.
MEMBERS DIRECTORY ALL	Specifies the information to be printed for a partitioned data set. MEMBERS says to print the contents of each member in the data set. DIRECTORY says to print only the directory information for the data set. ALL says to print both the directory information and the content of each member in the data set. These operands have no effect on a sequential data set or a specific member of a partitioned data set. ALL is the default.
CLASS SYSOUT	Specifies the output class to be used by JES for printing the data set. If neither of these operands are specified, your default class is used.
HOLD NOHOLD	Specifies whether the output is to be held in the JES held output queue (HOLD) or made available for printing immediately (NOHOLD). NOHOLD is the default.

Figure 2-15   The PRINTDS command (part 2 of 2)

output. If you want just a straight listing of the file, you can ignore all of these operands.

To control the columns in the file that are printed, use the COLUMNS operand. If you specify a single column number, the listing begins at the column you specify and continues to the last column. For example, if you enter COLUMNS(7) for a file that contains 80 characters, PRINTDS prints columns 7 through 80. If you specify two column numbers separated by a colon, the listing begins at the first column number and ends at the second. So, to print columns 7 through 72, you enter COLUMNS(7:72). Note that you can enter up to 32 pairs of columns separated with commas.

The SINGLE, DOUBLE, TRIPLE and CCHAR operands tell PRINTDS how to space the output listing. SINGLE, DOUBLE, and TRIPLE tell PRINTDS to single-, double-, or triple-space the output and to suppress any blank lines that occur in the file. CCHAR tells PRINTDS to use printer control characters in the file to control printer spacing. So if the data set contains printer control characters, you should use the CCHAR operand.

The FOLD and TRUNCATE operands tell PRINTDS what to do if the data set's records are longer than the printer's line length. If you say FOLD, PRINTDS prints the number of characters you specify for the line length on one print line and continues the record on the next print line. If you say TRUNCATE, PRINTDS prints only the number of characters you specify for the line length. The line length you specify must be no greater than the actual printer line length. You should specify one of these operands if the records are longer than the printer line length because there is no default.

The PAGELEN operand determines the number of lines PRINTDS prints on a page. The default is 60. You can also specify the number of blank lines at the top and bottom of each page using the TMARGIN and BMARGIN operands.

The COPIES operand determines the number of copies of the data set PRINTDS prints. The number you specify on this operand must be between 1 and 255. The default is 1.

How to print partitioned data set information   Three PRINTDS operands, MEMBERS, DIRECTORY, and ALL, control how PRINTDS handles a partitioned data set if you don't list a specific member in the DATASET operand. If you specify MEMBERS, PRINTDS prints the contents of each member of a partitioned data set. If you specify DIRECTORY, PRINTDS prints a list of all the members in the partitioned data set's directory. If you specify ALL, PRINTDS prints both the directory and the members. PRINTDS ignores these operands if you code them for a sequential data set or for a specific member of a partitioned data set.

How to direct PRINTDS output   Because PRINTDS uses JES to handle its output, you can control the final disposition of the output by specifying an output class. To do that, you use the CLASS or SYSOUT operand. If you don't specify either of these operands, JES uses the default output class.

You can also determine whether PRINTDS output is held in the JES held output queue or is immediately made available for printing. To do that, specify HOLD or NOHOLD. NOHOLD is the default.

PRINTDS Examples   Figure 2-16 gives four examples of the PRINTDS command to print a member named MKTG1200 in a partitioned data set named DLOWE.TEST.COBOL. In example 1, I supply just the data set and member name. That causes PRINTDS to print the member using its default format. In example 2, I code the NUM operand to tell PRINTDS that the line numbers are 6 bytes long and start in column 1. I also specify that I want two copies of the output. In example 3, I again supply the NUM operand and tell PRINTDS to print only lines 2100 through 4000. And in example 4, I tell PRINTDS to double-space the listing and to hold the output.

Discussion

In this topic, I've presented a set of TSO commands you'll probably use daily as you manipulate data sets. Unfortunately, it's impossible to present all of the commands you'll use frequently because each installation adds its own commands or tailors the existing commands to suit its own needs. For example, your installation may have added commands to compress a library or list data set space allocation information. So you'll have to find out from your supervisor what additional TSO commands are available to you.

Example 1

```
PRINTDS DSNAME(TEST.COBOL(MKTG1200))
```

Example 2

```
PRINTDS DSNAME(TEST.COBOL(MKTG1200)) NUM(1,6) COPIES(2)
```

Example 3

```
PRINTDS DSNAME(TEST.COBOL(MKTG1200)) NUM(1,6) LINES(2100:4000)
```

Example 4

```
PRINTDS DSNAME(TEST.COBOL(MKTG1200)) DOUBLE HOLD
```

Figure 2-16   Examples of the PRINTDS command

Terms

generic data set name
alias
expiration date

Objective

Use the following commands for data set management:
- a. LISTCAT
- b. LISTDS
- c. RENAME
- d. DELETE
- e. COPY or SMCOPY
- f. LIST
- g. PRINTDS

Topic 2 How to use the TSO EDIT command

The EDIT command used to be the main text editor under TSO. Since the introduction of the 3270, however, most installations have replaced EDIT with ISPF, or have extended it to provide similar capabilities. Still, there are occasions when you'll want to use EDIT for simple editing functions.

Figure 2-17 gives the format of the EDIT command. The only required operands are library, member, and type. EDIT combines the current user-id with these operands to form the complete data set name. To illustrate, suppose you enter this EDIT command:

```
EDIT TEST(MKTG1200) COBOL
```

Here, the complete data set name (assuming DLOWE is the user-id) is DLOWE.TEST.COBOL(MKTG1200).

You can use the OLD and NEW operands to specify whether you're editing an existing data set (OLD) or creating a new one (NEW). You don't need to specify either of these operands, however, because EDIT assumes OLD for existing members and NEW for non-existent members. Still, it's common practice to include one of these operands. That way, you get an error message if you attempt to create a member that already exists.

Besides specifying whether you're editing a new or old member, the NEW and OLD operands control what mode EDIT initially enters. When you specify NEW, EDIT enters *input mode*. In input mode, you can enter data directly into your member. When you specify OLD, EDIT enters *edit mode*. In edit mode, you can enter a variety of EDIT subcommands that let you manipulate the data in your member.

Input mode

As I just said, input mode lets you enter data directly into your member. You just key in the data one line at a time, pressing the Enter key after each line. Each time you do this, EDIT adds the line

---

The EDIT command

```
EDIT   library(member)   type   [{OLD }]
                                 {NEW }
```

Explanation

library(member)	The library and member to be edited.
type	The type qualifier to be added to the user-id, library, and member to form the complete data set name.
OLD NEW	If you say OLD, EDIT assumes you're editing an existing member and enters edit mode. If you say NEW, EDIT assumes you're editing a new member and enters input mode. If you omit this operand, EDIT assumes OLD for existing members and NEW for new members.

Figure 2-17   The EDIT command

---

to the end of your member. When you finish adding lines, you enter a null line by pressing the Enter key without keying in any data first. Then, EDIT enters edit mode without adding the null line to your member.

Most of the members you edit will contain line numbers that identify each line of text. In input mode, EDIT automatically supplies those line numbers, starting with 10 and counting up in increments of 10 (10, 20, 30, and so on). As a result, you don't have to worry about line numbers in input mode.

Figure 2-18 shows a brief editing session using input mode. Here, I enter an EDIT command to edit a new member named MKTG1200 in TEST.COBOL. Since the member is new, EDIT enters input mode, displaying these prompts:

```
INPUT
00010
```

The first prompt tells you EDIT is in input mode. The second prompt is the line number for the first line of text in the member.

In this example, I entered text on lines 10 through 70, and a null line on line 80. Although you can't tell by looking at figure 2-18, EDIT did *not* add line 80 to the member. Instead, it entered edit mode, as indicated by the EDIT message.

```
 READY
EDIT TEST(MKTG1200) COBOL NEW
 INPUT
 00010  IDENTIFICATION DIVISION.
 00020 *
 00030  PROGRAM-ID.  MKTG1200.
 00040 *
 00050  ENVIRONMENT DIVISION.
 00060 *
 00070  INPUT-OUTPUT SECTION.
 00080
 EDIT
```

Figure 2-18   Using EDIT in input mode

Edit mode

In edit mode, EDIT doesn't prompt you for input. Instead, it lets you enter data lines or *EDIT subcommands* directly, so you can make changes to your member.

To insert or replace a single line in a member, you simply enter a line number followed by text. If the line already exists in the member, it's replaced. Otherwise, it's inserted. To delete a single line, you enter just the line number with no text.

To illustrate, look at figure 2-19. The top part of the figure shows a portion of a member that contains several errors. The middle part of the figure shows an editing session where I replace line 30, insert line 45, and delete line 60. The bottom part of the figure shows the member after the editing session.

While this technique is fine for changing a line or two at a time, you'll want to use the EDIT subcommands for more extensive editing. There are 33 EDIT subcommands in all, but in this

---

The MKTG1200 member before editing

```
00010  IDENTIFICATION DIVISION.
00020 *
00030  PORGRAM-ID.  MKTG1200.
00040 *
00050 *
00060      MOVE CM-CUSTOMER-NUMBER TO CL-CUSTOMER-NO.
00070  INPUT-OUTPUT SECTION.
```

The editing session

```
EDIT TEST(MKTG1200) COBOL OLD
 EDIT
00030  PROGRAM-ID.  MKTG1200.
00045  ENVIRONMENT DIVISION.
00060
```

The MKTG1200 member after editing

```
00010  IDENTIFICATION DIVISION.
00020 *
00030  PROGRAM-ID.  MKTG1200.
00040 *
00045  ENVIRONMENT DIVISION.
00050 *
00070  INPUT-OUTPUT SECTION.
```

Figure 2-19   Using the insert/replace/delete function

book, I cover only the ones shown in figure 2-20. Once you learn these subcommands, you'll be able to handle most of your editing requirements. And you'll have no trouble learning the more advanced editing subcommands from the IBM manual.

Most of the EDIT subcommands require that you identify the line or lines the subcommand affects. Normally, you just supply one or more line numbers. That's called *line-number editing*.

Another technique, called *context editing*, uses a pointer called the *current line pointer* to indicate the line you want to process. You indicate the current line pointer in an EDIT subcommand by coding an asterisk rather than a line number. For example, the subcommand

```
DELETE 1000
```

says to delete line 1000. But the subcommand

    DELETE *

says to delete the line indicated by the current line pointer.

Before you issue a command that uses the current line pointer, you need to be sure the pointer is on the line you want to process. In most cases, the current line pointer points to the last line you referred to. For example, if the last command you issued inserted a line into the member, the current line pointer points to the inserted line.

To move the current line pointer, use one of the last four subcommands in figure 2-20, TOP, BOTTOM, UP, or DOWN. These subcommands move the current line pointer to the top or bottom of the member, or up or down one or more lines in the member.

How to insert more than one line

To add several lines at a time to your member, use the INPUT subcommand. When you issue an INPUT subcommand, EDIT returns to input mode. But instead of adding lines to the end of your member, it adds lines following the line you specify in the subcommand. For example, if you enter the subcommand

    INPUT 4000

EDIT inserts lines following line 4000. And

    INPUT *

enters input mode at the location indicated by the current line pointer. If you enter the INPUT subcommand with no operands, EDIT enters input mode at the end of the data set.

When you use the INPUT subcommand, you have to make sure there are enough unused line numbers to accommodate the lines you're adding. Otherwise, EDIT displays an error message and returns to edit mode when you run out of line numbers. Any lines you add before that happens, however, remain in the member.

You can provide enough line numbers in one of two ways. First, before you issue the INPUT subcommand, you can renumber your member using a large increment, like 100. I'll show you how to do that later on. Second, you can specify a small increment on the INPUT subcommand itself. For example, the subcommand

    INPUT 2210 1

Subcommand	Function
`INPUT line-number [increment]`	Enters input mode so you can insert one or more lines following *line-number*. When *increment* is coded, it becomes the increment value for the new line numbers.
`DELETE [{start-line [end-line] / * [count]}]`	Deletes the range of lines specified. If you specify an asterisk as the start-line, deletes *count* lines beginning with the current line.
`FIND text-string`	Locates the first occurrence of *text-string*, starting from the current line.
`CHANGE   start-line [end-line] old-string new-string [ALL]`	Changes *old-string* to *new-string* within the specified range of lines. ALL says to change all occurrences of *old-string*; otherwise, only the first occurrence is changed.
`LIST [{start-line [end-line] / * [count]}]`	Lists the range of lines specified. If you specify an asterisk as the start-line, lists *count* lines beginning with the current line.
`RENUM [new-first-line] [increment]`	Resequences line numbers. The new line numbers start with *new-first-line* and are incremented according to *increment*. The default for either operand is 10.
`END {SAVE / NOSAVE}`	Ends the editing session. SAVE says to rewrite the member with the changes made during the editing session; NOSAVE means the changes aren't kept.
`TOP`	Moves the current line pointer to the first line in the data set.
`BOTTOM`	Moves the current line pointer to the last line in the data set.
`UP [count]`	Moves the current line pointer up *count* number of lines. The default is 1.
`DOWN [count]`	Moves the current line pointer down *count* number of lines. The default is 1.

Figure 2-20   Some EDIT subcommands

adds lines following line 2210, numbering the new lines in increments of one. As a result, the first new line will be 2211.

How to delete more than one line

To delete more than one line from your member, you use the DELETE subcommand. On it, you specify two line numbers, like this:

```
DELETE 100 500
```

Here, EDIT deletes all lines between, and including, lines 100 and 500.

If you specify an asterisk for the first line number, EDIT begins with the current line and deletes the number of lines you specify as the second line number. In other words, if you enter

```
DELETE * 10
```

EDIT deletes ten lines beginning with the current line.

As you can see from the format in figure 2-20, you can also use the DELETE subcommand to delete a single line by omitting the end-line operand. But it's easier to use the delete function as shown in figure 2-19 for a single line deletion.

How to find text

The FIND subcommand searches forward from the current line position to find the first occurrence of the text string you specify. If you want to search the entire file, and the current line pointer isn't on the first line in the member, use a TOP subcommand before you use the FIND subcommand.

You can enter the string in one of two ways. First, you can enclose the string in apostrophes, like this:

```
FIND 'PROCEDURE'
```

Alternatively, you can precede the string with a *delimiter character*, like this:

```
FIND /PROCEDURE
```

The delimiter can be any character other than a number, apostrophe, semicolon, comma, parenthesis, or asterisk. Notice that you do not have to repeat the delimiter at the end of the string.

If the first character of the text string is an asterisk, don't use a slash as the delimiter. The combination of a slash and an asterisk marks the beginning of a CLIST or REXX comment, so TSO won't correctly interpret any text string that begins with a slash followed by an asterisk. (You'll learn how to code CLIST comments in chapter 5, and REXX comments in chapter 7.)

How to change text

You use the CHANGE subcommand to change text within your member. On it, you specify one or two line numbers. If you specify just one, the change affects only that one line; if you specify two, the change affects each line between and including those two lines.

Following the line numbers, you specify two text strings. The first one is the existing text string, the one you want to change. The second one is the new string, the string that replaces the first string. Note that the strings don't have to be the same length; EDIT makes any necessary adjustments if they're not.

Just like the FIND subcommand, there are two ways you can code the text strings in a CHANGE subcommand. First, you can enclose both of them in apostrophes, like this:

```
CHANGE 30 'POR' 'PRO'
```

Here, the string POR is changed to PRO in line 30.

Second, you can use a delimiter to separate the text strings. If you do, you must code the delimiter before each text string. You can also code it after the second text string, but it's not required. To illustrate, consider this CHANGE subcommand:

```
CHANGE 30 /POR/PRO
```

Here again, POR is changed to PRO in line 30. The delimiter is a slash.

If you want to change every occurrence of a string in the line or lines you specify, you must code ALL on the CHANGE subcommand. Otherwise, EDIT changes only the first occurrence of the string. For example, to change the line

```
50   SUBTRACT CM-SALES-LAST-YTD FROM CM-SALES-THIS-YTD
```

to

```
50   SUBTRACT CMR-SALES-LAST-YTD FROM CMR-SALES-THIS-YTD
```

you have to code this:

```
CHANGE 50 /CM-/CMR-/ ALL
```

Without ALL, the result is:

```
50   SUBTRACT CMR-SALES-LAST-YTD FROM CM-SALES-THIS-YTD
```

Notice that if you specify ALL, you have to code a delimiter after the second text string.

How to list lines

The LIST subcommand lets you list lines from your member. If you enter LIST without any operands, EDIT lists the entire member. If you code one line number, EDIT lists that line. And if you code two line numbers, EDIT lists a range of lines.

As with the DELETE subcommand, LIST treats the second number as a count if you specify an asterisk for the first line number. So the command

```
LIST * 10
```

lists 10 lines starting with the current line.

If your installation doesn't have the LIST command, you can use the LIST subcommand of EDIT to list your data sets. It's a little awkward, but it works.

How to renumber a member

Sometimes, when you've made many changes to a member, you find that the line numbers seem almost random. In some places, you have large gaps, while in other places you have lines numbered in small increments. In a case like this, you can use the RENUM subcommand to resequence your line numbers in fixed increments.

If you enter RENUM with no operands, your member is renumbered starting with 10 using an increment of 10. You can change those defaults by specifying a starting line number and an increment on your RENUM command. For example, if you code

```
RENUM 1000 100
```

your member is renumbered starting with 1000 and using an increment of 100. As a result, your lines are numbered 1000, 1100, 1200, and so on.

How to end an editing session

You use the END subcommand to end an editing session. If you code

```
END SAVE
```

EDIT saves any changes you made to your member. If you code

```
END NOSAVE
```

your changes are lost. Normally, you'll code END SAVE.

Terms

input mode
edit mode
EDIT subcommands
line-number editing
context editing
current line pointer
delimiter character

Objective

Use the EDIT command and the subcommands described in this
topic to make basic changes to a data set or member.

Topic 3   Data set allocation commands

Whenever a program running under MVS needs to process a file, it must first *allocate* the file. Then, when the program finishes, the file is *deallocated*. During a typical TSO session, several dozen files are allocated and deallocated. Most of these allocations take place automatically. For example, when you edit a file using ISPF, ISPF automatically allocates the file for you. Similarly, when you copy a file using the COPY or SMCOPY command, TSO allocates the old and new files automatically.

TSO provides several commands that let you control file allocation. In this topic, I cover three of them: ALLOCATE, FREE, and LISTALC. The ALLOCATE command lets you directly allocate a data set. The FREE command lets you deallocate a data set. And the LISTALC command lets you display a list of all data sets currently allocated to your TSO session.

THE ALLOCATE COMMAND

The ALLOCATE command allocates a new or existing data set. One of its main functions is to associate *ddnames*, which are the names programs use to refer to files, with *data set names*, which are the names of actual data sets on disk or tape. Other functions of the ALLOCATE command include specifying whether the file should be kept or deleted when it is deallocated, whether the file is required for exclusive access or can be shared with other users, and, for new files only, the file characteristics and space requirements. If you're familiar with MVS JCL, you'll see right away that the ALLOCATE command is analogous to the JCL DD statement. In fact, most ALLOCATE operands have equivalent DD statement operands.

In some cases, you use an ALLOCATE command to prepare a data set for processing by a program you'll run in foreground mode. For example, you may want to run the IEBCOPY utility program to compress a partitioned data set. Or, you may want to run an application program you've written in COBOL or some other language. Before you run the program, you must issue a series of ALLOCATE commands to associate the data sets used by the program with the specific ddnames required by that program. In the case of IEBCOPY, for example, the required ddnames are SYSPRINT, SYSIN, SYSUT3, and SYSUT4.

Sometimes, though, you don't intend to invoke a foreground program to process an existing data set. Instead, you want to create a new data set. In this case, you again use the ALLOCATE command, but you don't have to specify a ddname at all. TSO assigns a system-generated ddname to the data set, and you don't need to know what it is.

The ALLOCATE command has a relatively simple format when it's used to relate an existing data set to a specific ddname. So I'll explain that usage first. Then, I'll show you how to use the ALLO-CATE command to create a new data set. After that, I'll describe three alternate forms of the ALLOCATE command.

Before I present the ALLOCATE command, you should realize that the operands you code on it depend on whether or not the file you're allocating is managed by SMS. The difference in the oper-ands you code is most significant for new files. As I present the various operands, I'll tell you if their use is affected by SMS.

How to associate an existing data set with a ddname

Figure 2-21 shows the basic format for the ALLOCATE command when used to associate an existing data set with a ddname. The DSNAME operand gives the data set's name. As usual, TSO adds your user-id to the beginning of the data set name unless you enclose it in apostrophes. If the data set is cataloged, the DSNAME operand completely identifies the file. But if it's not cataloged, you'll have to supply the UNIT and VOLUME operands as well. I'll describe those operands in a moment.

The DDNAME operand supplies the ddname for the data set. For a system utility program, you can find out what ddnames are required by reading appropriate system documentation. For a COBOL application program, the ddname is the name you supply in the ASSIGN clause of the file's SELECT statement. For example, suppose your COBOL program contains this statement:

```
SELECT CUSTMAST ASSIGN TO AS-CUSTMST
```

In this case, you must use an ALLOCATE command to allocate a data set for the ddname CUSTMST.

If you want, you can say DATASET instead of DSNAME and FILE instead of DDNAME. The alternate terms have the same meaning. As a result, these two ALLOCATE commands have identical meanings:

```
ALLOCATE DSNAME(CUSTMAST.DATA) DDNAME(CUSTMST)
ALLOCATE DATASET(CUSTMAST.DATA) FILE(CUSTMST)
```

I prefer to use DSNAME and DDNAME because those terms correspond to the equivalent parameters used on a JCL DD statement.

Status values   You specify OLD, SHR, or MOD to define the file's *status*. If you say OLD, you're telling TSO that you want exclusive control over an existing data set. If another foreground or background program tries to access the same file, it has to wait until you're finished.

When you code SHR, you're telling TSO that you don't want exclusive control over the file. (SHR means share, so more than one program or user can access the file at the same time.) You should code SHR when you access a file of general interest, such as a program library, unless you're updating that file.

When you code MOD, you're telling TSO that you want to *extend* an existing file. That means that when your program performs output operations on the file, it adds the new records after any existing records.

Disposition values   The four *disposition* operands, KEEP, DELETE, CATALOG, and UNCATALOG, tell TSO what to do with the file when you're finished processing it. That is, when you issue a FREE command, which I'll describe later in this topic, or when you log off. KEEP means, naturally, to keep the file. If the file is cataloged, it remains cataloged. KEEP is the default if you don't specify a disposition.

DELETE tells TSO to delete the file. This includes removing the catalog entry if the file is cataloged. Any request to retrieve a file after you delete it causes an error.

CATALOG tells TSO to create a catalog entry for the file. Once a file is cataloged, you can retrieve it without specifying UNIT and VOLUME operands on the ALLOCATE command. Since you usually catalog files when you create them, you won't code CATALOG very often for existing files. And, if the file is managed

The ALLOCATE command

```
ALLOCATE        (DSNAME(data-set-name) )
                (DATASET(data-set-name))

                (DDNAME(ddname))
                (FILE(ddname)  )

           [ (OLD)
             {SHR} ]
             (MOD)

           [ (KEEP      )
             (DELETE    )
             (CATALOG   ) ]
             (UNCATALOG )

           [ UNIT(device) ]

           [ VOLUME(volume-serial-number) ]
```

Explanation

DSNAME DATASET	The data set name for the data set to be allocated.
DDNAME FILE	The ddname to be associated with the data set.
OLD SHR MOD	The status of the data set. OLD means you want exclusive control of the data set. SHR means you want shared access to the data set. And MOD means you want to extend a data set. OLD is the default.
KEEP DELETE CATALOG UNCATALOG	The disposition of the data set. KEEP means you want to keep the data set as it is. DELETE means you want to delete the data set. CATALOG means you want to create a catalog entry for the file. UNCATALOG means you want to keep the data set but remove it from the catalog. The disposition is not processed until the data set is deallocated when you issue a FREE command or log off. KEEP is the default.
UNIT	The device or device type for the file. Not required for a cataloged data set.
VOLUME	The volume serial number for the volume that contains the file. Not required for a cataloged data set.

Figure 2-21   The ALLOCATE command for existing data sets

by SMS, you'll never need to code CATALOG for an existing file because SMS files are automatically cataloged when they're created.

UNCATALOG tells TSO that the file is cataloged and you want to remove its entry from the catalog. When a file is uncataloged, the file itself is not deleted. However, you must include UNIT and VOLUME operands on any future ALLOCATE commands for the file to completely identify it. Because all data sets used under TSO should be cataloged, you probably won't use this option often. UNCATALOG isn't valid for files managed by SMS because they must be cataloged.

The location of the file   If you're accessing a file that isn't cataloged, you have to tell TSO where the file resides. You use two ALLOCATE operands to do this. The UNIT operand tells TSO the type of device where the file resides. And the VOLUME operand tells TSO the specific serial number of the volume that contains the file. Since SMS files are always cataloged, you'll never need to codes these operands for them.

For the UNIT operand, you can specify a specific device type, such as 3380. So if you code UNIT(3380), the data set must reside on a 3380-type disk. Typically, though, you'll specify a *group name* that includes all devices of a particular kind. Each installation defines its own group names, so you'll have to check with your supervisor to find out what group names you can use. Usually, names like TAPE and SYSDA are used to indicate the standard tape and disk devices. So if you code UNIT(SYSDA), the file can reside on any disk device belonging to the SYSDA category.

The VOLUME operand gives the volume serial number of the specific volume containing the file. For example, if you code VOLUME(TSO001), TSO looks on the volume named TSO001 to locate the file. If that volume isn't mounted on the system when you issue the ALLOCATE command, the system instructs an operator to mount it.

Examples of allocating existing data sets   Figure 2-22 gives three examples of ALLOCATE commands for existing data sets. Example 1 associates a data set named DLOWE.TEST.COBOL (assuming DLOWE is the user-id) with a ddname of SYSUT1. Then, any program that accesses a data set using that ddname processes DLOWE.TEST.COBOL. This ALLOCATE command is the same whether or not the file is managed by SMS.

```
Example 1

ALLOCATE DSNAME(TEST.COBOL) DDNAME(SYSUT1)


Example 2

ALLOCATE DSNAME(TEST.DATA) DDNAME(CUSTMST) MOD


Example 3

ALLOCATE DSNAME('AR.DAILY.TRANS') DDNAME(ARTRANS) UNIT(TAPE) +
VOLUME(MMA010)
```

Figure 2-22   Examples of ALLOCATE commands for existing data sets

Example 2 associates a data set named DLOWE.TEST.DATA with a ddname of CUSTMST. Here, the status is MOD. So any new records added to this data set are placed at the end of the file. Again, this command is the same whether or not the file is managed by SMS.

Example 3 shows how to allocate an uncataloged data set. Here, a file named AR.DAILY.TRANS on a TAPE volume labeled MMA010 is associated with a ddname of ARTRANS. Since most, if not all, of the direct-access data sets you process will be cataloged, you use this form of the ALLOCATE command mostly for tape data sets. You don't use this format for SMS files, however, because they must be cataloged.

How to create a new data set

Figure 2-23 gives an expanded format for the ALLOCATE command that lets you create new data sets. Some of the operands in figure 2-23 (DSNAME, DDNAME, UNIT, and VOLUME) you already know. The other operands supply information required to create a data set, like how much space to allocate to the file, when the file can be deleted, and the specific characteristics of the file. Again, the operands you code depend on whether the file is managed by SMS.

The ALLOCATE command

```
ALLOCATE        ⎰DSNAME(data-set-name)⎱
                ⎱DDNAME(ddname)        ⎰

                ⎧KEEP    ⎫
           [   ⎨CATALOG ⎬  ]
                ⎩DELETE  ⎭

           [ UNIT(device) ]

           [ VOLUME(volume-serial-number) ]

           [ SPACE(primary secondary) ]

                ⎧BLOCK(block-length)⎫
           [   ⎨TRACKS             ⎬  ]
                ⎩CYLINDERS          ⎭

           [ DIR(directory-space) ]

                ⎰EXPDT(expiration-date) ⎱
           [   ⎱RETPD(retention-period)⎰  ]

           [ DSORG(organization) ]

           [ RECFM(record-format) ]

           [ LRECL(record-length) ]

           [ BLKSIZE(block-size) ]

           [ DATACLAS(data-class) ]

           [ STORCLAS(storage-class) ]

           [ MGMTCLAS(management-class) ]

           [ LIKE(model-data-set-name) ]
```

Explanation

DSNAME	Specifies the name of the data set to be created.
DDNAME	The ddname associated with the file. If omitted, TSO generates a default ddname.
KEEP CATALOG DELETE	The disposition of the data set. KEEP means you want to retain the data set. CATALOG means you want to retain the data set and create a catalog entry for it. And DELETE means you want to delete the data set when you're through with it. CATALOG is the default.

Figure 2-23 The ALLOCATE command for new data sets (part 1 of 2)

Explanation (continued)

UNIT	Identifies the device type. May be a specific device (like 3380) or a device class (like SYSDA). If omitted, MVS chooses a device based on your profile, normally SYSDA.
VOLUME	Specifies the volume serial number of the volume that will contain the file. If omitted, your default volume is used.
SPACE	Specifies the amount of space to be allocated to the data set. Space is in units of tracks, cylinders, or blocks, depending on how you code other options in the ALLOCATE command. Primary allocation is allocated initially. When additional space is needed, extents are allocated using the secondary allocation.
BLOCKS TRACKS CYLINDERS	Defines the unit of measure for SPACE. If you say BLOCKS, space is allocated in blocks using the block-length you specify. If you say TRACKS, space is allocated in tracks. If you say CYLINDERS, space is allocated in cylinders. If you omit BLOCKS, TRACKS, and CYLINDERS, space is allocated in blocks, using the block-length you specify in the BLKSIZE operand.
DIR	Specifies the number of 256-byte directory blocks to be allocated for a partitioned data set.
EXPDT	Defines the date when the file can be deleted. The date is specified in the form yyddd, where yy is the year and ddd is the day within the year. So 90001 is January 1, 1990.
RETPD	An alternative to EXPDT; RETPD defines the expiration date as a retention period. After the specified number of days have elapsed, the file can be scratched.
DSORG	Specifies the data set's organization: PS for sequential files, PO for partitioned data sets.
RECFM	Defines the record format. Specify RECFM(F) for fixed-length, unblocked records. Use RECFM(F,B) for fixed-length, blocked records.
LRECL	Defines the file's record length in bytes.
BLKSIZE	Defines the file's block size in bytes.
DATACLAS	The data class that contains the data set characteristics you want to assign to the file. Used only with SMS.
STORCLAS	The storage class that contains the performance and availability characteristics you want to assign to the file. Used only with SMS.
MGMTCLAS	The management class that contains the migration and backup characteristics you want to assign to the file. Used only with SMS.
LIKE	Specifies a data set name where other ALLOCATE operands are derived. All the operands listed here (other than DSNAME) can be derived from a model data set.

Figure 2-23 The ALLOCATE command for new data sets (part 2 of 2)

One important point before I go on: the DDNAME operand in figure 2-23 is optional. If you're going to process the data set using a foreground program, you should specify a ddname in the DDNAME operand. But if you're creating a file that you're not going to process with a foreground program, you can omit it. Then, TSO assigns a ddname for you, but you don't have to know what it is.

Disposition values   You already know how to code disposition values when you allocate an existing data set. When you allocate a new data set, you must supply a disposition value to tell MVS whether or not the data set is permanent. If you say CATALOG, or let the disposition default to CATALOG by coding nothing, MVS creates a catalog entry so you can retrieve the data set later without specifying unit and volume information. If you say KEEP, MVS retains the data set but doesn't create a catalog entry for it unless the file is managed by SMS. In that case, the file is cataloged automatically. If you say DELETE, MVS removes the data set when you free it.

How to allocate space to a file   When you create a data set, you must tell TSO how much space to allocate to the file. To do this, you tell TSO three things: (1) how many units of space to allocate, (2) how big each unit is, and (3) how much space to allocate to the directory (required for partitioned data sets only).

You use the SPACE operand to specify how many units of space to allocate to a file. You specify space in both primary and secondary allocations. The *primary allocation* is the amount of space that is initially allocated to the file. It's the first number you code in a SPACE operand, and it should represent the total amount of space you expect to need for the file.

The *secondary allocation* provides for additional space beyond the primary allocation. When a file grows beyond the amount of space the primary allocation provides, MVS makes the secondary allocation. If that still isn't enough space, MVS makes the secondary allocation again. MVS can make up to 15 secondary allocations before the file runs out of space.

To illustrate, suppose you code this SPACE operand:

```
SPACE(10 5)
```

Here, ten units are allocated initially. The secondary allocation is five units. So, this file can grow to a maximum of 85 units (ten units of primary allocation plus 15 secondary allocations of five units each).

The next set of operands, BLOCK, TRACKS, and CYLINDERS, defines the size of each unit of allocated space. If you say BLOCK, MVS allocates space using the block length you specify. If you say TRACKS, MVS allocates space in terms of direct-access tracks. If you say CYLINDERS, MVS allocates whole cylinders of space. If you omit all three operands, MVS allocates space using the block size you specify in the BLKSIZE operand, which I'll discuss later.

Note that the operand you code can have a dramatic effect on how much space MVS allocates to your file. For example, if you say

    SPACE(10 10) TRACKS

MVS assigns ten tracks to your file. But if you say

    SPACE(10 10) CYLINDERS

MVS assigns ten cylinders. On a 3380, that's 15 times as much space as ten tracks.

You use the last space allocation operand, DIR, when you create a partitioned data set. It says how many directory blocks to allocate for the file. Each directory block is 256 bytes long and can hold entries for several members. Under normal circumstances, each directory block can hold 21 directory entries. So if you expect the library to contain a maximum of about 200 members, allocate 10 directory blocks. If you edit members in the library with the ISPF editor and STAT=ON is specified in your profile, ISPF will use additional space in the directory to store statistics. In that case, you should allow only six directory entries per block. Thus, you should allocate about 35 directory blocks for a library with 200 members and statistics. Finally, if the library will contain load modules, each directory holds only four member entries. So for a 200-member load library, you should allocate 50 directory blocks.

A common but aggravating problem when using TSO is running out of directory space in a partitioned data set. Since directory blocks don't require much space, it's best to allocate much more directory space than you think you'll need.

How to specify an expiration date   A file's *expiration date* specifies when the file is no longer needed and can be deleted. In the first topic of this chapter, you saw how the DELETE command checks the expiration date before it deletes a file, and you saw how you can override the expiration date check to delete the file even if the expiration date hasn't arrived. In addition, some installations automatically delete all data sets whose expiration dates have passed. In such an installation, you can expect that any data set you create today will be gone tomorrow, unless you explicitly assign an expiration date. (Since SMS sets the expiration date for you, you don't need to code this operand for SMS-managed files.)

You use one of two ALLOCATE operands to assign an expiration date. The EXPDT operand assigns a specific date as the expiration date. You specify this date in the form *yyddd*, where *yy* is the year and *ddd* is the day within the year. So 90001 is January 1, 1990, and 90365 is December 31, 1990.

Quite frankly, I have trouble remembering the relative day within the year for a date like July 23, especially if it's a leap year. So I find it's usually easier to use the RETPD operand. This operand assigns a *retention period* to the file. So if you specify RETPD(30), the file's expiration date will be 30 days from the day you allocate it.

How to specify a file's characteristics   When you create a new data set, you must specify the file's characteristics. In particular, you must specify: the file's organization (usually, sequential or partitioned); the format of the file's records (variable or fixed, blocked or unblocked); the length of the file's records; and the length of each block of records. (These operands aren't required if the file you're allocating is managed by SMS.)

You use the DSORG operand to define the file's organization. If you specify DSORG(PS), the file is sequential. If you specify DSORG(PO), the file is a partitioned data set.

The RECFM operand identifies the format of the file's records. Although there are many possible combinations of record format characteristics you can code, you'll usually code the RECFM operand like this:

```
RECFM(F,B)
```

Here, the records are fixed-length and blocked. Other common record formats are: RECFM(F) for fixed-length, unblocked records; RECFM(V,B) for variable-length, blocked records; and RECFM(V) for variable-length, unblocked records.

The LRECL operand defines the logical record length for the file. For 80-byte records, such as COBOL source records, specify LRECL(80). For variable-length records, specify the longest possible record length plus four bytes for a system record-count field.

Block size	Blocks/ track	Records/ track	Percent usage
47440	1	593	98.90
23440	2	586	97.73
15440	3	579	96.56
11440	4	572	95.40
9040	5	565	94.23
7440	6	558	93.06
6320	7	553	92.23
5440	8	544	90.73
4800	9	540	90.06

Figure 2-24   Optimum block sizes for 80-byte records on a 3380 device

The BLKSIZE operand defines the size of each block of records. Because each type of direct-access device has different characteristics, a block size that is efficient for one type of device may waste a great deal of space on a different device type. For example, suppose you want to allocate a source library that will contain 10,000 80-byte records. You choose a block size of 3120; that's 39 80-byte records in each block. If the disk device is a 3350, you'll use about 97% of the available space on each track. That's an efficient utilization of disk space. However, the same file on a 3380 device will use only 84% of the available disk space. That's not an efficient utilization of disk space.

Determining the best block size for a file of any given record length on any given device type is a complex task. Figure 2-24 lists the block sizes that use disk space most efficiently for files with 80-byte records stored on a 3380 disk device. If you select one of these values, you'll know you're not wasting disk space.

Figure 2-24 also shows the number of records per track for each block size listed. So, if you select a block size of 9040, 565 records are stored in each track. To determine the number of tracks to allocate for a data set, just divide the number of records per track for the block size you select into the number of records in the file and round the result up. For example, a 10,000-record data set with a block size of 9040 requires 18 tracks (10,000 / 565 = 17.7).

How to allocate an SMS file   You've probably noticed that many of the operands I've presented so far aren't required for SMS-managed files. Instead of coding these operands, you can specify three types of classes to define the data set requirements: data class, storage class, and management class. As a result, if you use SMS at your installation, you need to find out what classes you should use.

The three operands you can code on the ALLOCATE command to specify the three SMS classes are DATACLAS, STORCLAS, and MGMTCLAS. If you code DATACLAS, MVS assigns the characteristics of the data class you specify to the file. These characteristics include record organization, record format, record length, space, and expiration date. If you omit the DATACLAS operand, MVS uses the default data class defined by the system administrator.

Whether you specify a data class or use the default class, you can override the characteristics of the class by coding the appropriate operands. The data class value you're most likely to override is the space allocation. As a result, you'll probably want to include the SPACE operand on ALLOCATE commands for SMS files.

You rarely code the STORCLAS or MGMTCLAS operands. The storage class defines performance and availability characteristics and the management class defines characteristics related to the migration and backup of the file. If you omit these operands, MVS uses the default classes.

How to model a data set after an existing file   Another way to simplify the coding required for an ALLOCATE command is by using the LIKE operand to model a new data set after an existing one. Although you can use the LIKE operand for SMS-managed files, you usually won't need to. For these files, it makes more sense to specify the classes you want to use.

When you specify the name of an existing file in a LIKE operand, MVS looks to that file for information you don't specify in the ALLOCATE command. If you code a LIKE operand, you can omit any of the operands I've discussed in this section except the data set name. Then, MVS obtains the values for the operands from the data set label for the file you specify. You can change one or more operand values by coding those operands.

Using a model data set can be a real time-saver, particularly if you don't remember the optimum block size for a particular blocking factor and device type. Be careful, though, about modeling a small data set after a very large one. If you don't over-

Example 1

```
ALLOCATE DSNAME(CUSTMAST.DATA) SPACE(10 5) TRACKS DSORG(PS) +
RECFM(F,B) LRECL(42) BLKSIZE(4200)
```

Example 2

```
ALLOCATE DSNAME(CUSTMAST.DATA) DDNAME(CUSTMST) SPACE(10 5) +
TRACKS DSORG(PS) RECFM(F,B) LRECL(42) BLKSIZE(4200)
```

Example 3

```
ALLOCATE DSNAME(TEST.COBOL) SPACE(100 50) TRACKS DIR(10) +
DSORG(PO) RECFM(F,B) LRECL(80) BLKSIZE(6160) RETPD(60)
```

Example 4

```
ALLOCATE DSNAME(TEST.COBOL) DATACLAS(P)
```

Example 5

```
ALLOCATE DSNAME(TEST.COBOL) LIKE('SAMP.TEST.COBOL') +
UNIT(SYSDA) VOLUME(TS0001)
```

Figure 2-25   Examples of creating new data sets

ride the space allocation values, you'll allocate too much space to your file.

Examples of creating data sets   Figure 2-25 gives four examples of ALLOCATE commands for creating data sets. Example 1 creates a sequential data set (DSORG(PS)), and names it DLOWE.CUST-MAST.DATA. This example assigns 10 tracks of primary space to the file and 5 tracks of secondary space. The file consists of fixed-length, blocked records. The record length is 42 bytes, and the block size is 4200 bytes.

The ALLOCATE command in example 2 creates the same data set as the ALLOCATE command in example 1, except example 2 associates a ddname (CUSTMST) with the newly-created data set. Then, I can run a foreground program to load records into the file.

The ALLOCATE command in example 1 assigns a system-generated ddname to the new file.

Example 3 creates a partitioned data set (DSORG(PO)) named DLOWE.TEST.COBOL. This file has 100 tracks of primary space and a secondary allocation of 50 tracks. This example allocates 10 directory blocks, so the library can hold a maximum of 210 source members without statistics. The 80-byte records are fixed-length and blocked (6160 bytes per block), and the file expires in 60 days.

Example 4 uses SMS to create the same partitioned data set as example 3. Here, the data class P is assigned to the data set. So MVS uses the characteristics assigned to data class P to allocate the data set. Since this example doesn't specify a storage or management class, SMS uses its defaults.

Example 5 creates a new data set, modeled after an existing data set named SAMP.TEST.COBOL. All the data set characteristics and space allocation operands are obtained from the data set label for the model file. The new file is placed on a direct-access device (SYSDA) on a volume named TSO001.

Other ALLOCATE command formats

Besides the formats presented in figures 2-21 and 2-23, you can code the ALLOCATE command using one of several other formats. Figure 2-26 shows three commonly used ALLOCATE command formats. You use these formats when your foreground program has special processing requirements.

You use format 1 in figure 2-26 when you want to receive input from or direct output to your terminal. The asterisk in the DSNAME operand simply means you want to use your terminal as the data set. This form of the ALLOCATE command is particularly useful when you're testing programs. For input files, you can supply test data interactively, and for output files, you can view program results immediately.

You use format 2 in figure 2-26 to simulate the presence of a file without actually processing the file. To do this, you code DUMMY instead of a DSNAME operand. Then, when your program tries to read a record from that file, an end-of-file indication is passed to your program. And when your program tries to write a record to the DUMMY file, no data is transferred. This form of the ALLOCATE command is also useful when testing a program.

Format 1

```
ALLOCATE   DSNAME(*)
           DDNAME(ddname)
```

Format 2

```
ALLOCATE   DUMMY
           DDNAME(ddname)
```

Format 3

```
ALLOCATE   DDNAME(ddname)
           SYSOUT(class)
         [ {HOLD  } ]
           {NOHOLD }
         [ DEST(station-id) ]
```

Explanation

DSNAME	An asterisk as the data set name means your terminal is used as a data set for input or output.
DUMMY	A data set is to be simulated. No actual I/O is done.
DDNAME	The ddname for the data set.
SYSOUT	Directs output to JES2/JES3 using the specified SYSOUT class. Output is not actually released for processing by JES2/JES3 until you deallocate the data set by issuing a FREE command or by logging off.
HOLD NOHOLD	HOLD means the data set is held in the SYSOUT queue until released by an operator or TSO user. NOHOLD means the output is *not* held but is released for processing. This parameter overrides the default specified for the SYSOUT class.
DEST	Specifies the installation-defined station-id for a remote site where the output is routed.

Figure 2-26   Alternate formats for the ALLOCATE command

(Incidentally, you can achieve exactly the same effect by coding a data set name of NULLFILE in the DSNAME operand.)

You use format 3 in figure 2-26 to direct program output to a SYSOUT queue. Here, you specify the ddname for the file and a

---

Example 1

```
ALLOCATE DSNAME(*) DDNAME(REORDLST)
```

Example 2

```
ALLOCATE DUMMY DDNAME(CUSTMST)
```

Example 3

```
ALLOCATE DDNAME(SALESRPT) SYSOUT(X)
```

Example 4

```
ALLOCATE DDNAME(SALESRPT) SYSOUT(A) DEST(RMT200)
```

Figure 2-27   Examples of alternate ALLOCATE command formats

SYSOUT class. The output from your program is directed to a SYSOUT queue for processing by JES2/JES3 according to the SYSOUT class. Normally, you can specify SYSOUT(A) to direct the output to a system printer. But if you direct the output to a held SYSOUT class, or if you code HOLD on the ALLOCATE command, the output is retained in the output queue. You can retrieve it later using the OUTPUT command, which I'll describe in chapter 4. Or, you can route it to a different output class by using the FREE command, which I'll explain in a moment.

If you want to route SYSOUT data to a remote printer, such as a 2780/3780 station, you can code the DEST operand on the ALLO-CATE command. Here, you enter the installation-defined station-id for the remote printer you want to use. Then, when that station signs on to the system, the output is delivered to it.

Examples of other ALLOCATE formats   Figure 2-27 gives four examples of ALLOCATE commands following the formats presented in figure 2-26. In example 1, I assign my terminal as the file for ddname REORDLST. In example 2, I assign ddname CUSTMST to a DUMMY file. Example 3 routes output directed to ddname SALESRPT to SYSOUT class X. And example 4 routes output directed to ddname SALESRPT to a remote site named RMT200, using SYSOUT class A.

OTHER DATA SET ALLOCATION COMMANDS

In addition to the ALLOCATE command, TSO provides several other commands you can use to manage data set allocation. Now, I'll describe two of them: FREE and LISTALC. The others aren't used often, so I don't cover them in this book.

The FREE command

You use the FREE command to deallocate data sets you allocated with an ALLOCATE command. Why would you want to deallocate a data set? Mainly because the disposition you specified on the ALLOCATE command, CATALOG, KEEP, DELETE, or UNCAT-ALOG, isn't actually processed until you deallocate the data set. Similarly, SYSOUT data isn't actually released to JES2/JES3 until you deallocate it. Normally, all your data sets are implicitly deallocated when you end your terminal session by entering a LOGOFF command. The FREE command lets you deallocate your data sets without logging off.

Figure 2-28 gives the format of the FREE command. Its operands fall into three categories: (1) those that identify the data sets to deallocate; (2) those that change the final disposition of a data set; and (3) those that change the routing for a SYSOUT data set.

How to identify the data sets to free   You code ALL, DSNAME, or DDNAME to identify the data sets you want to deallocate. If you say ALL, all the data sets currently allocated to you are freed. If you want to deallocate specific data sets, you use DSNAME or DDNAME. The DSNAME operand lets you list one or more data sets by name. The DDNAME operand lets you list one or more ddnames. Either way, the effect is the same: the data sets you specify are deallocated.

How to change the disposition of a data set   When you free a data set, the disposition assigned to it when it was allocated is processed. However, you can change that disposition by specifying KEEP, DELETE, CATALOG, or UNCATALOG on the FREE command. These operands have the same meanings as they do for the ALLOCATE command. When used here, they override the corresponding operands entered on the ALLOCATE commands for the files you're freeing.

The FREE command

```
FREE      {ALL                      }
          {DSNAME(data-set-names)   }
          {DDNAME(ddnames)          }


       [  {KEEP      }  ]
          {CATALOG   }
          {UNCATALOG }
          {DELETE    }


       [ SYSOUT(class) ]


       [  {HOLD   }  ]
          {NOHOLD }


       [ DEST(station-id) ]
```

Explanation

ALL DSNAME DDNAME	Identifies the data sets to be freed. ALL means to free all allocated data sets. DSNAME means to free the named data sets. DDNAME means to free the data sets allocated under the specified ddnames.
KEEP CATALOG UNCATALOG DELETE	Overrides the disposition specified when you allocated the data set. KEEP means to retain the data set. CATALOG means to retain the data set and create a catalog entry for it. UNCATALOG means to retain the data set but remove it from the catalog. And DELETE means to delete the data set.
SYSOUT	Reroutes SYSOUT output to the specified class.
HOLD NOHOLD	Overrides the HOLD/NOHOLD operand you specified when you allocated the data set. HOLD means to keep the data set in the SYSOUT queue until released by an operator or TSO user. NOHOLD means to release the data set from the queue.
DEST	Routes the output to the specified remote station.

Figure 2-28   The FREE command

How to change SYSOUT routing   You can also change the final routing of a SYSOUT data set by specifying SYSOUT, HOLD/NO-HOLD, or DEST on a FREE command. Again, these operands mean the same thing here as they do in an ALLOCATE command. Bear in mind, though, that you can't specify any of these operands unless you assigned the file to SYSOUT when you allocated it.

```
Example 1

FREE ALL


Example 2

FREE DSNAME(TEST.COBOL TEST.OBJ TEST.LOAD)


Example 3

FREE DDNAME(CUSTMST)


Example 4

FREE DDNAME(CUSTMST) DELETE


Example 5

FREE DDNAME(SALESRPT) SYSOUT(A) DEST(RMT200)
```

Figure 2-29   Examples of the FREE command

Examples of FREE commands   Figure 2-29 gives five examples of the FREE command. Example 1 frees all data sets previously allocated. Example 2 frees three data sets: DLOWE.TEST. COBOL, DLOWE.TEST.OBJ, and DLOWE.TEST.LOAD. Example 3 frees one data set identified by the ddname CUSTMST. Example 4 frees the same data set as example 3, but changes its final disposition to DELETE. As a result, MVS deletes this data set even if its ALLO-CATE command said to keep or catalog it.

Example 5 in figure 2-29 frees a SYSOUT data set and changes its output routing. Here, the SYSOUT class is changed to A and DEST is specified so the output is routed to a remote site named RMT200. Any corresponding operands on the original ALLOCATE command for this data set are overridden.

The LISTALC command

```
LISTALC [STATUS]

        [HISTORY]

        [MEMBERS]

        [SYSNAMES]
```

Explanation

STATUS	List the ddname and disposition for each allocated data set.
HISTORY	List the creation date, expiration date, and owner-id for each allocated data set.
MEMBERS	List the member names for each allocated partitioned data set.
SYSNAMES	List complete names of data sets whose names were generated by the system, such as SYSOUT data sets.

Figure 2-30   The LISTALC command

The LISTALC command

Figure 2-30 shows the format of the LISTALC command. This command displays the name and other information for each data set currently allocated to you. If you enter LISTALC with no operands, TSO lists only the names of the data sets. If you code one or more of the four operands, TSO lists additional information.

If you say STATUS, TSO lists the ddname and disposition for each data set currently allocated. If you say HISTORY, TSO also lists the file's creation and expiration dates and owner-id. MEMBERS causes TSO to list the member names for each allocated partitioned data set. Finally, SYSNAMES lists the names of system-generated files like SYSOUT data sets.

Figure 2-31 shows an example of LISTALC output. Most of the data sets listed here are allocated automatically when you log on.

```
READY
LISTALC
SYS4.ISR.V3R1M0.ISRPLIB
SYS4.ISP.V3R1M0.ISPPLIB
SYS4.ISF.V1R1M0.ISFPLIB
SYS4.ISR.V3R1M0.ISRMLIB
SYS4.ISP.V3R1M0.ISPMLIB
SYS4.ISR.V3R1M0.ISRSLIB
SYS4.ISP.V3R1M0.ISPSLIB
SYS4.ISR.V3R1M0.ISRTLIB
SYS4.ISP.V3R1M0.ISPTLIB
SYS4.ISF.V1R1M0.ISFTLIB
SYS4.ISR.V3R1M0.ISRCLIB
SYS1.CMDPROC
TERMFILE
TERMFILE
TERMFILE
TERMFILE
TERMFILE
DLOWE.ISPPROF
DLOWE.CUSTMAST.DATA
DLOWE.SALESMAN.DATA
READY
```

Figure 2-31   Typical LISTALC output

DISCUSSION

In this topic, I've presented just a small subset of the ALLOCATE command's operands. IBM's TSO manual describes many more that let you define additional options for disk and tape data sets. Still, the ALLOCATE operands I presented here should be all you need to allocate most types of data sets. And if you master the material in this topic, you'll have no trouble understanding the TSO manual when you need to use additional operands.

One important point worth remembering here is that you use the ALLOCATE command to define non-VSAM data sets only. To create a VSAM data set, you use IDCAMS' DEFINE command. Since VSAM file creation is beyond the scope of this book, I don't cover the DEFINE command here. Instead, I suggest you get a copy of my book, *VSAM Access Methods Services and Application Programming*, available from Mike Murach & Associates, Inc.

Terms

allocate
deallocate
ddname
data set name
status
extend a file
disposition
group name
primary allocation
secondary allocation
expiration date
retention period

Objective

Use the ALLOCATE, FREE, and LISTALC commands to manage
data set allocation.

Chapter 3

Foreground program development commands

Because ISPF/PDF is designed primarily as an application development environment, it provides menu selections that let you compile, link-edit, and test programs written in a variety of IBM programming languages in foreground mode. In this chapter, you'll learn how to use the equivalent TSO commands. In most cases, the only reason for using these commands is to put them into a CLIST or REXX procedure to make program development even easier than using the ISPF/PDF foreground options.

HOW TO COMPILE, LINK-EDIT, AND EXECUTE A COBOL PROGRAM

In this section, I'll show you how to use standard TSO features to compile, link-edit, and execute a COBOL program using either the OS/VS COBOL compiler or the VS COBOL II compiler. The procedures for compiling a COBOL program depend on the compiler you use. To compile a program using OS/VS COBOL, you use a program called the *COBOL Prompter*, which allocates certain required data sets and invokes the compiler. When you use the VS COBOL II compiler, however, you have to allocate those data sets yourself. Once you compile the program, the procedures you use to link-edit and execute the program are essentially the same regardless of the compiler you use.

Data sets used for developing COBOL programs

Before I go on, I want to point out that developing programs under TSO requires a variety of libraries and data sets. Figure 3-1 shows the data sets I use in this chapter. These names should serve as examples for the names you use for your own program development data sets.

Usually, you have at least two source libraries: a test library that contains versions of programs under development, and a COPY library that contains members included via COPY statements. You maintain the members in these libraries with an editor like ISPF's edit option.

All the foreground compilers place the compiled version of a program, called an *object module*, in an *object library*. In general, the object library's name is patterned after the source library's name with OBJ as the type qualifier. Thus, if the source library is DLOWE.TEST.COBOL, the object library should be named DLOWE.TEST.OBJ.

The output listing generated by a compiler is placed in a sequential data set. Usually, the type qualifier for the listing data set is LIST.

The OS/VS COBOL compiler can also create a *symbolic debugging file*. It's used by the OS/VS COBOL interactive debugger to obtain symbolic information, such as data names and statement numbers, when you debug your program. The type qualifier for this data set is usually SYM. With VS COBOL II, the symbolic debugging information is stored in the object module, so a separate debugging file isn't required.

The linkage editor places its output, called a *load module*, in a *load library*. Again, the load library name is patterned after the source library name with LOAD as the type qualifier. As a result, DLOWE.TEST.LOAD is a valid load library name. The output listing from the linkage editor, like the output from the compilers, is placed in a sequential data set using LINKLIST as the type qualifier.

The last data set listed in figure 3-1 is the loader listing. The *loader* is similar to the linkage editor, but instead of creating a load module, it directly executes the program. It is often used for

DLOWE.TEST.COBOL	COBOL source library for programs under development
DLOWE.TEST.COPY	COBOL COPY library
DLOWE.TEST.OBJ	Object library for the compiled versions of programs in the COBOL source library
DLOWE.TEST.LOAD	Load library for the link-edited versions of programs in the object library
DLOWE.TEST.SYM	Symbolic debugging library (OS/VS COBOL only)
DLOWE.member.LIST	COBOL compiler listing
DLOWE.member.LINKLIST	Linkage-editor listing
DLOWE.member.LOADLIST	Loader listing

Figure 3-1   Data sets used for COBOL program development

testing purposes. The loader listing is placed in a sequential data set with LOADLIST as the type qualifier.

Now, I'll show you how you use these files as you develop a program in foreground mode.

How to compile a program written in OS/VS COBOL: The COBOL command

To compile an OS/VS COBOL program, you use the COBOL command. Figure 3-2 gives its format. As you can see, the COBOL command has a number of operands. The only required operand is the data set name that supplies the source program as input to the compiler.

The LOAD operand tells COBOL where to put the object program. If you omit the LOAD operand, COBOL creates the object program as a member in a library whose name is the same as the input library's, but whose type qualifier is OBJ. The member name for the source and object program is the same. So if the source member named MKTG1200 is in the source library named DLOWE.TEST.COBOL, TSO stores the object program in a library named DLOWE.TEST.OBJ with the member named MKTG1200. Because this is usually what you want, you normally won't code the LOAD operand. If you don't want COBOL to create an object

---

The COBOL command

```
COBOL     data-set-name

          [ {LOAD(object-module-name)} ]
            {NOLOAD                   }

            {PRINT(print-file-name)}
          [ {PRINT(*)              } ]
            {NOPRINT               }

          [ {LIB(library-names)} ]
            {NOLIB             }

          [ options ]
```

Explanation

data-set-name	The COBOL source program. Usually a member of a partitioned data set.
LOAD	Specifies an alternate location for the object program.
NOLOAD	Specifies that no object program should be created.
PRINT	Specifies an alternate location for the print file. An asterisk (*) directs print output to the terminal.
NOPRINT	Specifies that no print file should be created.
LIB	Provides a list of libraries that are searched for COPY members. The libraries are searched in the order you list them.
NOLIB	Says that the source program contains no COPY statements. NOLIB is the default.
options	One or more of the compiler options listed in figure 3-3.

Figure 3-2   The COBOL command

module, say NOLOAD. Incidentally, don't be confused by the LOAD operand; the compiler output is an object module, not a load module.

The PRINT operand specifies the name of the file that will contain the generated compiler listing. If you omit PRINT, the COBOL prompter creates a sequential data set using the input library name with a type qualifier of LIST. For example, for the MKTG1200 program, the COBOL prompter creates a data set named DLOWE.MKTG1200.LIST. If you want the compiler output to go to your terminal, code an asterisk (*) as the print file name. And if you want to suppress compiler output, say NOPRINT.

Option	Meaning
SOURCE NOSOURCE	Print the source listing.
DMAP NODMAP	Print a Data Division map.
PMAP NOPMAP	Print a complete Procedure Division map.
CLIST NOCLIST	Print a condensed Procedure Division map. CLIST can't be used with PMAP.
VERB NOVERB	Print procedure names and verb names on the Procedure Division map; meaningful only when you code CLIST or PMAP.
XREF NOXREF	Print a cross-reference listing.
SXREF NOSXREF	Print a cross-reference listing sorted into alphabetical order.
APOST QUOTE	Indicates whether apostrophes (') or quotes (") are used to mark non-numeric literals.
BUF(n)	Specifies how much buffer space to allow. You can specify n as an integer or use K to represent units of 1024 bytes. Thus, BUF(2048) and BUF(2K) are the same.
TERM NOTERM	Display status information and error messages at the TSO terminal.
TEST NOTEST	Create a symbolic debugging file so the program can be tested using the interactive COBOL debugger.

Figure 3-3   Common OS/VS COBOL compiler options

If you use a COPY statement in your COBOL program, you define the library containing the COPY member with a LIB operand. In the LIB operand, you can specify more than one library. In that case, TSO searches the libraries in the order you list them to locate the member being copied.

In addition to the operands listed in figure 3-2, you can supply one or more *compiler options* that control other aspects of the compiler's operation. Figure 3-3 lists some of the more commonly used compiler options. I've indicated the IBM-supplied default settings for these options by underlining them. However, your installation may have changed those defaults, so you need to check with your supervisor about what options you should use.

```
Example 1

COBOL TEST.COBOL(MKTG1200)


Example 2

COBOL TEST.COBOL(MKTG1200) LIB(TEST.COPY) TEST


Example 3

COBOL TEST.COBOL(MKTG1200) DMAP CLIST XREF
```

Figure 3-4   Examples of the COBOL command

The options you choose that deal with compiler output, like SOURCE and DMAP, affect the PRINT operand on the COBOL command. If none of those options are active, no print file is created even if you specify PRINT. Also, note that you use another compiler option, TERM, to say whether status information and error messages are sent to the terminal. TERM works independently of PRINT.

Figure 3-4 shows three examples of the COBOL command. Example 1 shows its simplest form. This example specifies just a data set name for the source program. All the other operands assume their default settings.

In example 2, I specify a LIB operand and the TEST option. In this case, any COPY statements in the COBOL program retrieve members from TEST.COPY, the copy library I specify. And since I include the TEST option, the compiler will create a symbolic debugging file so I can test the program using the interactive COBOL debugger.

Example 3 shows how to code options that create additional compiler output. Here, the compiler listing will include a Data Division map (DMAP), a condensed Procedure Division listing (CLIST), and a cross-reference listing of data names (XREF), in addition to the source listing.

ddname	Explanation
SYSIN	Data set that contains the source program used as input to the compiler.
SYSLIB	Library containing members to be copied into the source program during compilation.
SYSPRINT	Data set where output listings and messages from the compiler are written.
SYSTERM	Used to display diagnostics and progress messages issued by the compiler at the terminal.
SYSLIN	Object module created by the compiler that's used as input to the linkage editor.
SYSUT1	Work data set required by the compiler.
SYSUT2	Work data set required by the compiler.
SYSUT3	Work data set required by the compiler.
SYSUT4	Work data set required by the compiler.
SYSUT5	Work data set required by the compiler if COPY statements are present in the source program.

Figure 3-5   ddnames for data sets used to compile VS COBOL II programs

How to compile a program written in VS COBOL II

Before you can execute the VS COBOL II compiler under TSO, you need to allocate the required data sets. To do that, you use the ALLOCATE command you learned in chapter 2. Figure 3-5 presents the data sets you can allocate.

To illustrate, consider the sample ALLOCATE commands for data sets used by the VS COBOL II compiler in figure 3-6. Here, the first two ALLOCATE commands are for the two input data sets. The first data set, SYSIN, is the source program (in this case, MKTG1200). The second data set, SYSLIB, is the COPY library DLOWE.TEST.COPY.

The next two commands allocate SYSPRINT and SYSTERM, which route any output from the compiler to a print file and your terminal. Following these commands is the ALLOCATE command for the object module to be created by the compiler (SYSLIN). Usually, you want to give this data set the same name as the source file except for the type qualifier, which should be OBJ.

The next five ALLOCATE commands provide for the required work files. Notice that these ALLOCATE commands specify only a

```
ALLOCATE  DDNAME(SYSIN)  DSNAME(TEST.COBOL(MKTG1200))
ALLOCATE  DDNAME(SYSLIB)  DSNAME(TEST.COPY)
ALLOCATE  DDNAME(SYSPRINT)  DSNAME(*)
ALLOCATE  DDNAME(SYSTERM)  DSNAME(*)
ALLOCATE  DDNAME(SYSLIN)  DSNAME(TEST.OBJ(MKTG1200))  OLD
ALLOCATE  DDNAME(SYSUT1)  CYLINDERS  SPACE(1,1)
ALLOCATE  DDNAME(SYSUT2)  CYLINDERS  SPACE(1,1)
ALLOCATE  DDNAME(SYSUT3)  CYLINDERS  SPACE(1,1)
ALLOCATE  DDNAME(SYSUT4)  CYLINDERS  SPACE(1,1)
ALLOCATE  DDNAME(SYSUT5)  CYLINDERS  SPACE(1,1)
CALL  'SYS1.COB2COMP(IGYCRCTL)'  'OBJECT,TERMINAL,APOST,LIB,TEST'
```

Figure 3-6   Sample commands for compiling a VS COBOL II program

ddname and space requirements; you don't have to specify a data set name for a work file.

After you allocate all the required data sets, you use the CALL command to invoke the compiler. Figure 3-7 presents the format of the CALL command. On it, you specify the program you want to execute. In the parameter string, you list any compiler options you want in effect.

The last command in figure 3-6 illustrates the CALL command for executing the VS COBOL II compiler. Here, the program is named IGYCRCTL and is stored in the library SYS1.COB2COMP. I also specify five compiler options: OBJECT, TERMINAL, APOST, LIB, and TEST. Figure 3-8 presents some of the most commonly used compiler options for VS COBOL II. The IBM default settings are underlined, but your installation defaults may be different. So be sure to check with your supervisor about what options to use.

How to link-edit a program: The LINK command

Before you can execute a compiled program, you must *link-edit* it. When you link-edit a program, the program is combined with any subprograms you invoke using CALL statements and with any compiler subroutines to form a load module that's ready to be executed by MVS.

You use the LINK command to invoke the linkage editor from TSO. Figure 3-9 gives the format of this command. Here, the first data set name specifies the input to the linkage editor, usually an

---

The CALL command

```
CALL data-set-name
     ['parameter-string']
```

Explanation

data-set-name   The name of the load module to be executed. If the type qualifier is LOAD, you can omit it since LOAD is the default.

'parameter-string'   A parameter string that's passed to the program.

Figure 3-7   The CALL command

Option	Meaning
SOURCE NOSOURCE	Print the source listing.
MAP NOMAP	Print a Data Division map.
LIST NOLIST	Print a Procedure Division map.
OFFSET NOOFFSET	Print a condensed Procedure Division map.
XREF NOXREF	Print a sorted cross-reference listing.
APOST QUOTE	Indicates whether apostrophes (') or quotes (") are used to mark non-numeric literals.
BUFSIZE(n)	Specifies how much buffer space to allow. You can specify n as an integer or use K to represent units of 1024 bytes. Thus, BUFSIZE(2048) and BUFSIZE(2K) are the same.
TERMINAL NOTERMINAL	Display status information and error messages at the TSO terminal.
LIB NOLIB	Allow the use of COPY statements in the source program.
TEST NOTEST	Create symbolic debugging information so the program can be tested using the VS COBOL II interactive debugger.

Figure 3-8   Common VS COBOL II compiler options

The LINK command

```
LINK       data-set-name

      [ LOAD(load-module-name) ]

        (PRINT(print-file-name))
      [ {PRINT(*)                } ]
        (NOPRINT                 )

      [ LIB(library-name) ]

      [ COBLIB ]
```

Explanation

data-set-name	The program to be link-edited.
LOAD	Specifies an alternate location for the load module.
PRINT	Specifies an alternate location for the print file. An asterisk (*) directs print output to the terminal.
NOPRINT	Specifies that no print file should be created.
LIB	Supplies one or more subprogram libraries used to retrieve called subprograms. The libraries are searched in the order you list them.
COBLIB	Specifies that the OS/VS COBOL subroutine library (SYS1.COBLIB) should be used to retrieve compiler subroutines. Doesn't apply to VS COBOL II.

Figure 3-9   The LINK command

object module previously created by a language translator. The LOAD operand tells the linkage editor where to put the link-edited load module. Usually, you omit this operand, so the linkage editor places the load module in a LOAD library with the same name as the object module. For example, if you link-edit a program named MKTG1200 in the library DLOWE.TEST.OBJ, the linkage editor places the load module in the library DLOWE.TEST.LOAD with the same member name, MKTG1200.

The PRINT operand tells how to handle the link listing. If you omit this operand, the linkage editor writes the link listing to a LINKLIST data set. For example, if the object program is named MKTG1200, the linkage editor gives the listing the name DLOWE.MKTG1200.LINKLIST. If you code a print file name, the linkage editor writes the listing to the file you specify. If you code PRINT(*), the linkage editor sends the listing directly to your

---

Example 1 (OS/VS COBOL)

```
LINK TEST.OBJ(MKTG1200) COBLIB
```

Example 2 (VS COBOL II)

```
ALLOCATE DDNAME(SYSLIB) DSNAME('SYS1.COB2LIB') SHR
LINK TEST.OBJ(MKTG1200)
```

Figure 3-10   Examples of the LINK command

terminal. And if you say NOPRINT, the linkage editor suppresses the listing.

If your program invokes subprograms via a CALL statement or its equivalent, you have to supply the name of the object library that contains the subprograms with a LIB operand. If you specify more than one library in a LIB operand, they're searched in the order you list them.

The last operand, COBLIB, says that the program also invokes subprograms contained in a system subroutine library named SYS1.COBLIB. You must code COBLIB when you link-edit an OS/VS COBOL program, but the COBLIB operand doesn't apply to VS COBOL II programs. Instead, you should issue an ALLOCATE command to allocate the VS COBOL II subroutine library (named SYS1.COB2LIB) to the ddname SYSLIB before you use the LINK command.

Figure 3-10 presents two link-edit operations. In the first example, I link-edit an OS/VS COBOL program named MKTG1200 that's in a library named TEST.OBJ. In example 2, I link-edit a VS COBOL II program named MKTG1200. Notice that I allocate SYS1.COB2LIB before I use the LINK command.

How to execute a program: The CALL command

Once you link-edit your program, you can execute it in foreground mode by issuing a CALL command. I presented the format of this command in figure 3-7. But before you issue a CALL command, you must issue an ALLOCATE command for each data set processed by your program.

For example, suppose you want to run a program named
MKTG1200 that's in a load library named DLOWE.TEST.LOAD,
and that requires three data sets: CUSTMST, SALESMN, and
SALESRPT. To invoke this program, you could enter these four
TSO commands:

```
ALLOCATE DSNAME(CUSTMAST.DATA) DDNAME(CUSTMST)
ALLOCATE DSNAME(SALESMAN.DATA) DDNAME(SALESMN)
ALLOCATE DSNAME(*) DDNAME(SALESRPT)
CALL TEST(MKTG1200)
```

The CALL command assumes LOAD is the qualifier for the load
library. And since I allocate the output file (SALESRPT) to the
terminal, TSO displays the program's output.

If your program requires run-time parameters, you supply
them in apostrophes following the name of the load module. For
example, suppose you code a CALL command like this:

```
CALL TEST(MKTG1200) 'JANUARY'
```

Here, the word JANUARY is passed to MKTG1200 as a parameter.
Since most COBOL programs don't use parameters, you won't
specify a parameter string often.

How to link-edit and execute a program:
The LOADGO command

The LOADGO command, whose format is shown in figure 3-11,
combines the functions of the LINK and CALL commands. The
input to the LOADGO command is an object module created by a
compiler. LOADGO link-edits the object module and loads and
executes the result. The main difference between the LOADGO
command and the LINK and CALL commands is that the LOADGO
command does *not* create a permanent load module in a load
library. Although the LOADGO command link-edits the object
program before executing it, it doesn't use the system linkage
editor to do this. Instead, it uses the loader to link-edit, load, and
execute the program.

The PRINT operand of the LOADGO command specifies what
to do with the loader's listing. If you omit this operand, the loader
writes the listing to a LOADLIST file. Otherwise, the loader writes
the listing to the file you specify. If you specify an asterisk (*), the
loader sends the listing to your terminal. And if you say NOPRINT,
the loader suppresses the listing.

The LOADGO command

```
LOADGO      data-set-name

            [ 'parameter-string' ]

              (PRINT(print-file-name))
            [ {PRINT(*)              } ]
              (NOPRINT               )

            [ LIB(library-name) ]

            [ COBLIB ]
```

Explanation

data-set-name	The program to be link-edited.
parameter-string	A parameter string that's passed to your program.
PRINT	Specifies an alternate location for the print file. An asterisk (*) directs print output to the terminal.
NOPRINT	Specifies that no print file should be created.
LIB	Supplies one or more subprogram libraries used to retrieve called subprograms. The libraries are searched in the order you list them.
COBLIB	Specifies that the OS/VS COBOL subroutine library (SYS1.COBLIB) should be used to retrieve compiler subroutines. Doesn't apply to VS COBOL II.

Figure 3-11　　The LOADGO command

The LIB operand defines the subprogram libraries used to locate the subprograms your program calls. And COBLIB tells LOADGO to use the standard OS/VS COBOL subroutine library (SYS1.COBLIB) in addition to the libraries you specify in the LIB operand. For VS COBOL II programs, you allocate the COBOL II subroutine library with the ddname SYSLIB before you execute LOADGO, just like you do when you use the linkage editor.

To illustrate the LOADGO command, suppose you issue this command:

```
LOADGO TEST.OBJ(MKTG1200) COBLIB
```

Here, the COBOL member MKTG1200 in TEST.OBJ is link-edited using SYS1.COBLIB for compiler subroutines. If the link-edit is successful, the program is loaded into storage and executed. For your program to execute properly, of course, you must issue the

appropriate ALLOCATE commands for the data sets your program
processes.

In some cases, the LOADGO command may save you some
time because you don't have to link-edit and execute your program
separately. In general, though, I recommend you use the LINK and
CALL commands rather than the LOADGO command for two
reasons. First, it's more efficient to create a load module with the
LINK command if you're going to execute your program more than
once between compilations. And second, your program has to be
processed by the LINK command if you want to debug it using the
interactive COBOL or COBOL II debugger.

HOW TO INVOKE THE INTERACTIVE COBOL DEBUGGERS UNDER TSO

IBM supplies an interactive debugger for each of its COBOL
compilers. For OS/VS COBOL, the debugger is called TESTCOB; for
VS COBOL II, the debugger is called COBTEST. In *MVS TSO Part 1*, I
showed you how to use these debuggers under ISPF. Although
these debuggers operate similarly under TSO, there are some differences you need to know about. In particular, you need to know
how to invoke these debuggers from TSO. That's what I'll show
you to do here. I won't show you how to debug programs here,
though. If you want to learn how to use these debuggers, refer to
Part 1: Concepts and ISPF.

How to invoke the OS/VS COBOL interactive debugger

There are two things you have to do to invoke the OS COBOL interactive debugger under TSO. First, you allocate the files you'll use
during the debugging session. Second, you issue the TESTCOB
command to execute the debugger. Figure 3-12 shows a typical
sequence of commands to invoke TESTCOB. (For clarity, I omitted
the READY prompts that TSO displays after each command.)

The first two ALLOCATE commands in figure 3-12 are required
by TESTCOB. The first allocates the load library that contains the
program using the ddname LOADLIB. Notice that it allocates the
entire library, not just the load member. The second ALLOCATE

```
ALLOCATE DSNAME(TEST.LOAD) DDNAME(LOADLIB)
ALLOCATE DSNAME(TEST.SYM(MKTG1200)) DDNAME(SYMDD)
ALLOCATE DSNAME(CUSTOMER.DATA) DDNAME(CUSTMST)
ALLOCATE DSNAME(SALESMAN.DATA) DDNAME(SALESMN)
ALLOCATE DDNAME(SALESRPT) SYSOUT(A)
TESTCOB (MKTG1200:SYMDD) LOAD(MKTG1200:LOADLIB)
```

Figure 3-12   Invoking the OS COBOL interactive debugger

command allocates the symbolic debugging file produced when
you compile a program, using the ddname SYMDD.

The next three ALLOCATE commands allocate files used by the
program being debugged. In this case, the MKTG1200 program
uses three data files with ddnames CUSTMST, SALESMN, and
SALESRPT.

If you want to keep output from your TESTCOB session so you
can print or display it later, you need to code another ALLOCATE
command to assign a ddname to the print file. For example, you
might issue this command:

```
ALLOCATE DSNAME(MKTG1200.TESTLIST) DDNAME(LISTDD)
```

In this case, output is written to DLOWE.MKTG1200.TESTLIST.
You can also direct output to a SYSOUT queue by coding the ALLO-
CATE command like this:

```
ALLOCATE DDNAME(LISTDD) SYSOUT(A)
```

As you'll see in a minute, you code the ddname for the print file on
the TESTCOB command that executes the debugger.

After you allocate all the required files, you issue a TESTCOB
command to execute the debugger. Figure 3-13 gives the format of
the TESTCOB command. On it, you must specify: (1) the program-
id for the program you're debugging; (2) the ddname you previously allocated to the symbolic debug file; (3) the member name
for the program you're debugging; and (4) the ddname you
previously allocated to the load library containing the program.

The last command in figure 3-12 is the TESTCOB command.
This command says that MKTG1200 is the name of the program I
want to execute (taken from the PROGRAM-ID paragraph in the
COBOL source program), SYMDD is the debug file, MKTG1200 is
the load member name, and LOADLIB is the load library.

The TESTCOB command

```
TESTCOB    (program-id:ddname1)

           LOAD(member:ddname2)

           [PRINT(ddname3)]

           [PARM('parameter-string')]
```

Explanation

program-id	The name from the PROGRAM-ID paragraph of the program to be debugged.
ddname1	The ddname allocated to the symbolic debug file.
LOAD	Says that *member* identifies the name of the load module for the file and *ddname2* is the ddname allocated to the load library that contains the member.
PRINT	Routes output from the debug session to the device or file allocated to *ddname3*.
PARM	Specifies a parameter string that's passed to the program.

Note: If you want to debug more than one program (for example, a main program and one or more subprograms), you can repeat the program-id:ddname group, separating each group with a comma.

Figure 3-13 The TESTCOB command

If you think this format for the TESTCOB command seems complicated and confusing, you're right. Unfortunately, there's nothing you can do about it (except possibly code a CLIST or REXX procedure to simplify the required entries). So don't let the complicated format bother you.

If you allocate a print file for output from your TESTCOB session, you must specify a PRINT operand on the TESTCOB command to identify the print file. For example, if you code an ALLOCATE command that assigns the ddname LISTDD to the print file, you specify PRINT(LISTDD) on the TESTCOB command. Then, TESTCOB writes output to the print file associated with LISTDD.

If your program requires execution-time parameters, you specify them in the PARM operand. For example, suppose you code this PARM operand:

```
PARM('JANUARY')
```

```
ALLOCATE DSNAME(TEST.LOAD) DDNAME(LOADLIB)
ALLOCATE DSNAME(TEST.SYM(MKTG1200)) DDNAME(SYMDD1)
ALLOCATE DSNAME(SUBPROG.SYM(SYSDATE)) DDNAME(SYMDD2)
ALLOCATE DSNAME(SUBPROG.SYM(SYSTIME)) DDNAME(SYMDD3)
ALLOCATE DSNAME(CUSTOMER.DATA) DDNAME(CUSTMST)
ALLOCATE DSNAME(SALESMAN.DATA) DDNAME(SALESMN)
ALLOCATE DDNAME(SALESRPT) SYSOUT(A)
TESTCOB (MKTG1200:SYMDD1,SYSDATE:SYMDD2,SYSTIME:SYSDD3)
LOAD(MKTG1200:LOADLIB)
```

Figure 3-14   Invoking TESTCOB to debug a main program and two subprograms

Then, the word JANUARY is passed to your program as a parameter. Since most COBOL programs don't use execution-time parameters, you won't use the PARM operand often.

After you enter the TESTCOB command, the interactive debugger displays this mode message:

    TESTCOB

That means it's waiting for you to enter a command to direct your debugging session.

The example in figure 3-12 illustrates how to invoke TESTCOB only for a main program. If the program contains any subprograms you want to debug, you have to specify their names on the TESTCOB command along with the name of the main program. But first, you have to allocate each subprogram to a SYM file. For example, suppose you're debugging a program named MKTG1200 that calls two subprograms: SYSDATE and SYSTIME. Figure 3-14 shows the commands necessary to allocate the data sets and invoke TESTCOB. As you can see, you specify a list of program-ids and ddnames for the programs you're debugging. But you still specify a single load module, since the main program and the subprograms are link-edited together to create the load module.

How to invoke the VS COBOL II interactive debugger

The procedure for invoking COBTEST, the VS COBOL II interactive debugger, is similar to the procedure for invoking the OS/VS COBOL interactive debugger. It's somewhat simplified, however, because the VS COBOL II compiler stores the symbolic data required for debugging in the object module. As a result, you don't

```
ALLOCATE DSNAME(TEST.LOAD) DDNAME(LOADLIB)
ALLOCATE DSNAME(CUSTOMER.DATA) DDNAME(CUSTMST)
ALLOCATE DSNAME(SALESMAN.DATA) DDNAME(SALESMN)
ALLOCATE DDNAME(SALESRPT) SYSOUT(A)
COBTEST LOAD(MKTG1200:LOADLIB)
```

Figure 3-15   Invoking the VS COBOL II interactive debugger

have to allocate separate symbolic debugging files for the programs and subprograms you're executing. Figure 3-15 shows a typical sequence of commands to invoke COBTEST.

Before I go on, I want you to understand that when you execute the VS COBOL II debugger from TSO, you're executing it in interactive line mode. So it doesn't have the full-screen capabilities that it does when you execute it from ISPF. In particular, you can't display the source listing as you execute a program. However, you can still perform many of the same operations you can perform in full-screen mode.

There is only one ALLOCATE command you have to issue before you can execute COBTEST. That command assigns a ddname to the data set that contains the load module you want to execute. The first ALLOCATE command in figure 3-15 shows an example of this assignment. This command assigns the ddname LOADLIB to the data set named DLOWE.TEST.LOAD.

If you plan to create printed output during your debugging session, you need to allocate a data set associated with the ddname SYSDBOUT. For example, to direct the output to a SYSOUT queue, you issue this command:

```
ALLOCATE DDNAME(SYSDBOUT) SYSOUT(A)
```

Or, to direct the output to a sequential file, issue this command:

```
ALLOCATE DSNAME(MKTG1200.TESTLIST) DDNAME(SYSDBOUT)
```

If the program you're debugging uses any data files, you need to allocate those files as well. For example, the MKTG1200 program uses three files with ddnames CUSTMST, SALESMN, and SALESRPT. As you can see in figure 3-15, I coded an ALLOCATE command for each of these files.

To execute COBTEST, you issue the COBTEST command. Its format, shown in figure 3-16, is similar to the format of the TESTCOB command. You specify the load member in the LOAD

The COBTEST command

```
COBTEST    LOAD(member:ddname)
           [PARM('parameter-string')]
```

Explanation

LOAD   Says that member identifies the name of the load module for the file and
                ddname is the ddname allocated to the load library that contains the members.

PARM   Specifies a parameter string that's passed to the program.

Figure 3-16 The COBTEST command

operand and list any run-time parameters in the PARM operand.
After you enter the COBTEST command, the interactive debugger
displays this mode message:

```
COBTEST
```

That means it's waiting for you to enter a command to direct your
debugging session.

DISCUSSION

Because many of the procedures I've described in this chapter
require you to enter a series of allocate commands followed by a
CALL, LINK or other command, I recommend you create a simple
CLIST or REXX procedure that contains the required commands.
Then, you can compile, link-edit or test a program by entering one
simple command. I'll show you how to create and use CLIST and
REXX procedures in sections 2 and 3.

Terms

COBOL prompter
object module
object library
symbolic debugging file
load module

load library
loader
compiler option
link-edit

Objectives

1. Compile, link-edit, and execute an OS/VS COBOL or VS COBOL II program.

2. Invoke the OS/VS COBOL or VS COBOL II debugger to debug a COBOL program.

Chapter 4

Background job commands

As you know, MVS provides two basic types of processing: foreground and background. Foreground processing lets you interact directly with the computer via a terminal. In contrast, background processing does not interact with a terminal. So you can't control background processing with the TSO commands this book teaches. Instead, you control background processing using Job Control Language statements, or JCL.

Foreground processing under TSO provides many advantages over background processing, but background processing is often more appropriate for many common tasks. For example, although you can compile and link-edit programs using the foreground commands I presented in chapter 3, it ties up your terminal so you can't do other work until the compile and link-edit finishes. If you perform the same task using background processing, you can use your terminal to perform other foreground tasks while the compile and link-edit executes separately in background mode.

The life cycle of a job

Figure 4-1 describes the life cycle of a typical background job under MVS. First, a system operator or a TSO user submits a job for execution. Once a job is submitted for execution, the job entry

1. The job is submitted for execution by a system operator or a TSO user.
2. The job waits in a job queue.
3. The job is selected for execution by JES.
4. The job executes.
5. The job output is collected and held in a SYSOUT queue.
6. The job output is routed to its final destination and removed from the SYSOUT queue.

Figure 4-1   The life cycle of a background job

subsystem (JES2 or JES3) places it in a job queue, where it waits until an MVS component called an *initiator* is available to execute it. How long it waits in the job queue depends on a number of factors, including its storage and I/O device requirements and the job class assigned to it when it's submitted.

Every job submitted for execution under MVS must have a *job name*. You specify this name, which is one to eight characters in length, in the JCL for the job. Under TSO, a job name must be your user-id followed by a single character. Thus, DLOWEA is a valid job name for user DLOWE.

When you refer to a job you've submitted, you usually use its job name. However, MVS doesn't require you to use unique job names. As a result, it's perfectly acceptable to submit two jobs with the same job name. MVS assigns a unique *job-id* to each job as it's submitted. So if you submit more than one job with the same job name, you must use the job-id rather than the job name to identify each job.

When an initiator becomes available for your job, JES2/JES3 assigns the job for execution. As your job executes, MVS generates informational messages that are collected in the job output and stored in a SYSOUT queue. In addition, programs executed by the job's steps can generate output that's written to a SYSOUT queue. So the job output from a single job can consist of multiple SYSOUT data sets. Later in this chapter, I'll show you how to display all or part of the SYSOUT data for a job. Data in a SYSOUT queue is held there until it's printed at a local or remote printer, copied to a data set, or deleted.

Each data set written to a SYSOUT queue is assigned a one-character *SYSOUT class* that determines how MVS prints the output. Each SYSOUT class is normally associated with a printer or a group of printers. Typically, SYSOUT class A is used for the installation's main printer or printers. Other SYSOUT classes may be assigned to specific printers or other devices.

If a SYSOUT class isn't associated with a printer or other device, it's called a *reserved class*. MVS holds any output written to a reserved class in the SYSOUT queue until an operator (1) directs it to a specific printer, (2) directs it to another SYSOUT class, or (3) deletes it. At my installation, class X is defined as a reserved class.

When you submit a background job from TSO, you usually want to direct the output to a reserved class. Then, you can examine the output at your terminal to determine if you should print it or delete it.

As a TSO user, you need to know how to do four things before you can effectively manage background jobs. First, you need to know how to use the SUBMIT command to submit a job for background processing. Second, you need to know how to use the CANCEL command to delete a job you submit. Third, you need to know how to use the STATUS command to monitor the status of a job you submit so you can see if it's waiting for execution, executing, or waiting for its output to print. And fourth, you need to know how to use the OUTPUT command to retrieve the output for a job that's completed.

The SUBMIT command

Figure 4-2 shows the format of the SUBMIT command. The operation of the SUBMIT command is simple: the data set or member you specify is submitted as a background job. SUBMIT assumes that the type qualifier for any data set you specify is CNTL. So if you issue the SUBMIT command

```
SUBMIT JOB1
```

TSO submits the data in DLOWE.JOB1.CNTL as a background job (assuming DLOWE is the user-id). If you want to specify a fully-qualified data set name, enclose it in apostrophes.

The data set or member you specify must contain valid job-control statements for the job to execute properly. However, if the data set doesn't contain a JOB statement, TSO generates one for

---

The SUBMIT command

```
SUBMIT data-set-name [JOBCHAR(character)]
```

Explanation

data-set-name   The name of the data set or member to be submitted for background
                processing. If you specify more than one data set or member, separate the
                names with commas and enclose the entire list in parentheses.

character   A single letter or digit that's appended to your user-id to form a job name if the
                job stream doesn't contain a JOB statement.

Figure 4-2   The SUBMIT command

---

you using your user-id and account information. TSO prompts you
for the single character it adds to your user-id for the job name. Or,
you can supply the job character on the SUBMIT command by specifying the JOBCHAR parameter, like this:

```
SUBMIT JOB1 JOBCHAR(A)
```

If you want, you can code more than one job in a single data set
or member. To do this, code all the JCL and data for the first job.
Then, code the JOB statement and additional JCL and data for the
second job. For example, if a data set or member contains three
JOB statements, TSO submits three separate jobs when you specify
that data set or member in a SUBMIT command.

You can also specify more than one data set or member in a
SUBMIT command by separating the names with commas and
enclosing the entire list in parentheses. In that case, the data sets
or members are treated as if they were a continuous stream of JCL
and data.

To illustrate, suppose you create two data sets. The first,
DLOWE.JCL.CNTL, contains JCL statements to execute a program.
The second, DLOWE.DATA.CNTL, contains data that's processed by
the program. To submit this job for background processing, issue
this SUBMIT command:

```
SUBMIT (JCL,DATA)
```

Then, MVS processes the two data sets in sequence to create a
single job.

The CANCEL command

```
CANCEL      {job-name              }
            {job-name(job-id)      }

          [ {PURGE   }  ]
            {NOPURGE }
```

Explanation

job-name	Specifies one or more jobs to be cancelled. If you specify more than one job, you must separate the job names with commas and enclose the entire list in parentheses. If more than one job exists with the same name, you must specify the job-id in parentheses.
PURGE NOPURGE	PURGE means to remove the job's output from the SYSOUT queue. NOPURGE means that the job should be cancelled if it's executing, but the output should *not* be removed from the job queue. NOPURGE is the default.

Figure 4-3   The CANCEL command

The CANCEL command

You use the CANCEL command to remove from the job queue a job that you submitted using the SUBMIT command. If you code the CANCEL command for a job the hasn't executed yet, MVS removes it from the job queue. If the job is currently executing, MVS terminates it.

Figure 4-3 gives the format of the CANCEL command. As you can see, you must specify a job name. And if more than one job in the job queue has the same job name, you must specify a job-id to uniquely identify the job you want to cancel. (You can find out what the job-id is by entering a STATUS command, which I'll describe next.)

The PURGE/NOPURGE operand determines the disposition of the job output. If you specify PURGE on a CANCEL command, MVS deletes all the job's output from the SYSOUT queue. If you specify NOPURGE or let it default, MVS terminates the job if it's executing, but doesn't delete its output. As a result, you can examine the output using an OUTPUT command (as I'll describe in a minute) or delete it using a CANCEL command with the PURGE operand.

The STATUS command

$$\text{STATUS} \quad \texttt{[} \left\{ \begin{array}{l} \texttt{job-name} \\ \texttt{job-name(job-id)} \end{array} \right\} \texttt{]}$$

Explanation

job-name	The name of the job whose status is listed. If you specify more than one job, you must separate the job names with commas and enclose the entire list in parentheses. If there's more than one job with the same name, you must supply the job-id in parentheses. If you don't specify a job name, all of your jobs are listed.

Figure 4-4   The STATUS command

To illustrate the CANCEL command, suppose you enter:

```
CANCEL DLOWEA(JOB0403) PURGE
```

Here, JOB0403 is the job-id for the job I want to cancel; the job name is DLOWEA. Since I specify PURGE, MVS deletes any job output.

The STATUS command

A submitted job has one of three possible status conditions: (1) waiting for execution; (2) executing; or (3) finished executing with output waiting on the SYSOUT queue. The STATUS command, shown in figure 4-4, tells you the current status of one or more of your jobs. It identifies the jobs by listing both their job names and their job-ids.

If you enter just the word STATUS with no operands, TSO displays the status of each job you submitted. You can limit the output to one or more jobs by specifying one or more job names with or without job-ids. Then, TSO displays the status of the jobs you specify. To specify more than one job, separate the job names with commas and enclose the list in parentheses, like this:

```
STATUS (DLOWEA,DLOWEB)
```

Here, TSO lists the status of all the jobs with the names DLOWEA and DLOWEB.

The OUTPUT command

```
OUTPUT     {job-name              }
           {job-name(job-id)      }

      [ NEWCLASS(class-name) ]

      [ DEST(station-id) ]

      [ {HOLD   } ]
        {NOHOLD }

      [ CLASS(class-names) ]

      [ DELETE ]

      [ PAUSE ]
```

Explanation

job-name	The name of the job whose output is displayed. If you specify more than one job, you must separate the job names with commas and enclose the entire list in parentheses. If there's more than one job with the same name, you must supply the job-id in parentheses.
NEWCLASS	Changes the output's SYSOUT class.
DEST	Changes the output's destination.
HOLD NOHOLD	Changes the output's HOLD status. HOLD means the output should remain in the SYSOUT queue until you release it for printing. NOHOLD means that held output should be released for printing.
CLASS	Limits the affected job output so that only the output data sets in the specified classes are processed.
DELETE	Deletes the output.
PAUSE	Interrupts the display between each SYSOUT data set and allows you to enter the OUTPUT subcommands shown in figure 4-7.

Figure 4-5   The OUTPUT command

The OUTPUT command

You use the OUTPUT command to process job output. With the OUTPUT command, you can display the output at your terminal, delete it, or route it to another SYSOUT class or a remote printer.

Figure 4-5 gives a simplified format of the OUTPUT command. Although the OUTPUT command has other operands, I've presented just the ones that are most useful for program

---

Example 1

```
OUTPUT DLOWEA
```

Example 2

```
OUTPUT DLOWEA NEWCLASS(A)
```

Example 3

```
OUTPUT DLOWEA DEST(RMT193)
```

Example 4

```
OUTPUT DLOWEA NOHOLD
```

Example 5

```
OUTPUT DLOWEA CLASS(X)
```

Example 6

```
OUTPUT DLOWEA CLASS(A M X) DELETE
```

Figure 4-6   Examples of the OUTPUT command

development under TSO. Rather than discuss each OUTPUT operand separately, I'll describe them in context with the examples presented in figure 4-6.

If you specify just the job name operand on an OUTPUT command, as in example 1 of figure 4-6, TSO displays the job output at your terminal. Once the output starts displaying, you can interrupt it using the PA1 key. Then, you can enter one of several subcommands, which I'll describe in a moment.

Example 1 assumes there's only one job named DLOWEA. If more than one job has the same name, you have to enter a job-id, like this:

```
OUTPUT DLOWEA(JOB0403)
```

Here, JOB0403 uniquely identifies the job you want to display.

The OUTPUT command in example 2 doesn't display the job output at your terminal. Instead, it changes the SYSOUT class to class A. Since most installations define class A as output to the main system printer, you can use this command to print your job output.

Example 3 shows how to route job output to a remote printer. Here, MVS routes the output to a remote station identified as RMT193. When RMT193 signs on the system, the output is delivered, assuming you assigned the output to a SYSOUT class that's associated with RMT193.

In example 4, the NOHOLD operand causes MVS to release any output held for processing by JES2/JES3. (Held output is not simply spooled output. It's output that you've specified should *not* be printed until you say otherwise.) For example, if you originally directed job output to class A and specified HOLD=YES on the DD statement to hold the output, you could use an OUTPUT command like the one in example 4 to tell MVS to release the output for printing. Note, however, that if the output class you specified when you submitted the job is a reserved class, saying NOHOLD on an OUTPUT command won't cause MVS to print the output unless you change the output class as well.

Example 5 shows how to limit the displayed output to SYSOUT data of a specific class. Here, I want to display class X output at my terminal. Any job output for DLOWEA that isn't class X isn't displayed.

Example 6 shows how to delete output for three classes: A, M, and X. In this case, MVS doesn't display the data. Instead, it deletes the data from the SYSOUT queues.

OUTPUT subcommands   As I mentioned earlier, the OUTPUT command has several subcommands you can use when you're displaying the contents of SYSOUT data. Normally, when you display SYSOUT data, MVS sends the data in a continuous stream to your terminal. Under TSO, each screen of data is followed by three asterisks (***) that signal you to press the Enter key to receive the next screen of data.

You can interrupt the continuous display of SYSOUT data in one of two ways: by pressing the Attention key, PA1, or by specifying PAUSE on the OUTPUT command. If you press the PA1 key, the output is immediately interrupted, and TSO displays this mode message:

```
OUTPUT
```

The CONTINUE subcommand

CONTINUE [$\left\{ \begin{array}{l} \text{BEGIN} \\ \text{HERE} \\ \underline{\text{NEXT}} \end{array} \right\}$]

[$\left\{ \begin{array}{l} \text{PAUSE} \\ \text{NOPAUSE} \end{array} \right\}$]

The SAVE subcommand

SAVE data-set-name

The END subcommand

END

Explanation

BEGIN HERE <u>NEXT</u>	Indicates the output to be displayed: the start of the current data set (BEGIN), the data following the current location (HERE), or the start of the next SYSOUT data set (NEXT). NEXT is the default.
PAUSE NOPAUSE	Indicates whether output should be interrupted between SYSOUT data sets. Overrides the corresponding operand on the OUTPUT command.
data-set-name	The name of the data set where the output will be saved.

Figure 4-7   OUTPUT subcommands

That means TSO is waiting for an OUTPUT subcommand.

You can specify PAUSE on the OUTPUT command, like this:

OUTPUT DLOWEA PAUSE

Then, output is interrupted after each SYSOUT data set in the job output.

Once the display is interrupted, you can enter one of the OUTPUT subcommands listed in figure 4-7. You use the CONTINUE subcommand to resume the display at the current location, at the beginning of the current SYSOUT data set, or at the start of the next SYSOUT data set. You use the SAVE subcommand to copy the current SYSOUT data set to a file. And you use the END subcommand to terminate OUTPUT.

To illustrate, suppose you enter an OUTPUT command to display output from a background job. As TSO displays the job output at your terminal, you press the PA1 key to interrupt the display. TSO displays OUTPUT at your terminal, indicating it's waiting for an OUTPUT subcommand. At this point, if you enter

CONTINUE HERE

the output display continues at the point you interrupted it. If you enter

CONTINUE NEXT

the output display skips forward to the start of the next SYSOUT data set and continues displaying. If you enter

CONTINUE BEGIN

the output display skips backwards to the start of the current SYSOUT data set and continues displaying. If you enter

SAVE JOBOUT

MVS copies the current SYSOUT data set to a data set named DLOWE.JOBOUT.OUTLIST (assuming the user-id is DLOWE). And if you enter

END

the OUTPUT session is terminated, and TSO returns to READY mode.

Discussion

Because managing SYSOUT data with the OUTPUT command isn't easy, I recommend a few simple techniques to control SYSOUT data. First, minimize the amount of SYSOUT data you create. For example, when you compile a COBOL program, don't use options like DMAP, PMAP, or XREF unless you really need the output they produce. Second, use the PAUSE operand on the OUTPUT command. That way, you can interrupt the output and skip over output you don't really need. And third, use the session manager if it's available. Then you can use scrolling and find operations to locate specific parts of your output listing, as described in topic 2 of chapter 1.

If you're using ISPF, you may find that it includes features for submitting and managing background jobs that are easier to use than the commands I've presented here. In particular, both ISPF's outlist utility and SDSF are superior to the OUTPUT command for viewing SYSOUT data. So I recommend you use the outlist utility or SDSF if they're available.

Terms

initiator
job name
job-id
SYSOUT class
reserved class

Objective

Use the SUBMIT, CANCEL, STATUS, and OUTPUT commands to manage background jobs.

Section 2

CLIST

The two chapters in this section show you how to create and use
command procedures, or CLISTs. CLIST is one of two procedure
languages provided under TSO/E; the other, REXX, is covered in
section 3. Because CLIST is the older procedure language, it is
more familiar and more widely used. The REXX language has
been available under the VM operating system since the early
1980's, but didn't become available under TSO until TSO/E
Version 2 was announced.

The choice of which procedure language to use for a particular project depends on many factors, including the standards
and policies of your installation, your experience (or lack of
experience) with either of the languages, and the nature of the
project. As to which language you should learn, the answer is
simple: you should learn both.

Chapter 5

A basic subset of CLIST facilities

This chapter presents a basic subset of CLIST facilities. When you finish it, you'll be able to create and use CLIST procedures that combine the TSO commands you learned in chapters 1-4 with basic CLIST facilities like symbolic variables, built-in functions, and control statements such as GOTO, IF, SELECT, DO WHILE, and DO UNTIL.

This chapter is divided into two topics. Topic 1 presents a basic introduction to CLISTs: what they are, how you create them, how you invoke them, and how you can pass command-line parameters to a procedure. Then, in topic 2, you'll build on these fundamentals as you learn to use additional CLIST programming features.

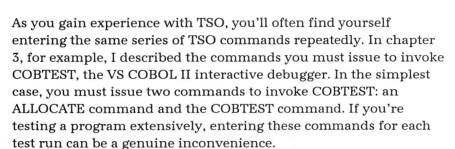

Topic 1   An introduction to CLIST procedures

As you gain experience with TSO, you'll often find yourself entering the same series of TSO commands repeatedly. In chapter 3, for example, I described the commands you must issue to invoke COBTEST, the VS COBOL II interactive debugger. In the simplest case, you must issue two commands to invoke COBTEST: an ALLOCATE command and the COBTEST command. If you're testing a program extensively, entering these commands for each test run can be a genuine inconvenience.

Under TSO, however, you can store a sequence of commands in a *command procedure*, or *CLIST*. Then, you can invoke the CLIST by name to cause TSO to execute each of its commands. As you can imagine, a CLIST can be a real time-saver.

Besides storing TSO commands together, command procedures provide facilities similar to a high-level programming language. With these facilities, you can define symbolic variables, control the flow of execution within a CLIST, and do simple terminal and file I/O.

In this topic, I present an introduction to command procedures. First, I describe how to create and invoke a simple CLIST. Then, I show you how to generalize your command procedures by using symbolic variables.

HOW TO USE A SIMPLE COMMAND PROCEDURE

To illustrate the use of command procedures, suppose you're in the process of testing and debugging a COBOL program named MKTG1200. As you proceed, you find yourself repeatedly issuing the commands to compile, link-edit, and test the program. So, you decide to store the commands in a command procedure.

Figure 5-1 shows that procedure. It contains the two TSO commands necessary to invoke the VS COBOL II interactive debugger to debug your program. I'll use this procedure as an

```
ALLOCATE DSNAME(TEST.LOAD) DDNAME(LOADLIB)
COBTEST LOAD(MKTG1200:LOADLIB)
```

Figure 5-1 A simple command procedure named MKTGTEST in the library
DLOWE.TEST.CLIST

example as I show you how to create and invoke a command procedure.

How to create a command procedure

To create a command procedure, you use a text editor, such as the
ISPF edit option or the EDIT command, to simply enter the
commands you want to include in the CLIST. Keep in mind,
however, that the commands in a CLIST execute in order. As a
result, you have to anticipate what TSO expects as you code each
procedure line. For example, to extend the CLIST in figure 5-1, you
code a COBTEST subcommand because that's what TSO expects
after a COBTEST command.

Each CLIST should be stored as a member of a partitioned data
set whose type qualifier is CLIST. When you create the CLIST
library, you should pattern it after the existing system-wide procedure library, which should have a name like SYS1.CLIST. To find
out the name of the system procedure library, use a LISTALC
command and take note of the name of the data set assigned to
SYSPROC. Then, to create a private procedure library using the
system procedure library's characteristics, use the LIKE operand
on an ALLOCATE command, like this:

```
ALLOCATE DSNAME(CLIST) LIKE('SYS1.CLIST')
```

Here, a library named DLOWE.CLIST will be created (assuming
DLOWE is the user-id) with the same characteristics as SYS1.CLIST.

Most CLIST libraries have either fixed-length records of 80
bytes each or variable-length records of up to 255 bytes. If you
need to include a line that's longer than the maximum, you can

continue it to the next line by using a + or - continuation character. For example, consider this ALLOCATE command:

```
ALLOCATE DSNAME(TEST.COBOL) DDNAME(SYSUT2) NEW CATALOG +
         SPACE(100 10) CYLINDERS DIR(20)
```

Here, the plus sign tells TSO that the command is continued to the next line. When you use a plus sign as a continuation character, leading blank spaces on the following line are ignored. So you must leave a blank space before the plus sign; otherwise, TSO won't interpret the command properly. If you use a minus sign, leading spaces on the continuation line are not ignored.

How to invoke a command procedure

To execute, or *invoke*, a command procedure, you use the EXEC command, whose format is shown in figure 5-2. As you can see, you can code the EXEC command in one of two forms: explicit and implicit.

The explicit form of the EXEC command   In the *explicit form* of the EXEC command, you specify the word EXEC followed by the name of the procedure library and member you want to execute. To invoke the CLIST in figure 5-1 this way, you would code this EXEC command:

```
EXEC TEST(MKTGTEST)
```

Since EXEC assumes that the type qualifier for the library is CLIST, you shouldn't specify that in the command. EXEC also provides the current user-id, so usually you don't have to specify that either. In fact, for a procedure library named user-id.CLIST, you can omit the library name entirely and just specify the member name, like this:

```
EXEC (MKTGTEST)
```

The implicit form of the EXEC command   In the *implicit form* of the EXEC command, you don't specify the word EXEC or the name of the library that contains the procedure. Instead, you specify just the procedure name, like this:

```
MKTGTEST
```

This command invokes the procedure named MKTGTEST. In a minute, I'll show you how to specify the library where the member is stored when you use the implicit form.

Notice that the implicit form of the EXEC command makes your command procedure look like another TSO command. In fact, it looks so similar that TSO has to search its own command libraries first to be sure it isn't a TSO command. Since you know it's not a TSO command when you enter it, type a percent sign in front of the procedure name, like this:

```
%MKTGTEST
```

The percent sign tells TSO that MKTGTEST is a command procedure, not a command, so TSO doesn't have to search its command libraries. Using a percent sign in this way can result in better execution time, since TSO will find your procedure more quickly.

As you can see in figure 5-2, both forms of the EXEC command let you pass parameters to the procedure you're invoking. Don't worry about that for now, though. I'll explain how and when to code parameters on the EXEC command later in this topic.

Library allocation for the implicit form   When you use the implicit form of the EXEC command, TSO looks in the library allocated to the ddname SYSPROC to find your procedure. As a result, before you issue an implicit EXEC command, you must allocate your command procedure library to SYSPROC with an ALLOCATE command, like this:

```
ALLOCATE DDNAME(SYSPROC) DSNAME(TEST.CLIST) SHR REUSE
```

SHR means other TSO users can allocate this procedure library as well. If you omit SHR, you have exclusive control of the procedure library. REUSE means SYSPROC is freed and reallocated if it is currently allocated. If you don't code REUSE and SYSPROC is already allocated, an error occurs.

Usually, you allocate more than one data set to SYSPROC. For example, you might allocate three procedure libraries: a system command procedure library named SYS1.CLIST; a private command procedure library named DLOWE.CLIST; and a library of command procedures being tested named DLOWE.TEST.CLIST. To allocate all three of these libraries, issue an ALLOCATE command like this:

```
ALLOCATE DDNAME(SYSPROC) +
    DSNAME('SYS1.CLIST' CLIST TEST.CLIST) SHR REUSE
```

Explicit form of the EXEC command

```
EXEC library-name(procedure-name) 'parameters'
```

Implicit form of the EXEC command

```
[%] procedure-name parameters
```

Explanation

library-name	The name of the library containing the procedure (a type qualifier of CLIST is assumed). May be omitted if the library name is user-id.CLIST.
procedure-name	The member name of the procedure to be invoked.
parameters	A list of parameter values as defined in the procedure's PROC statement. For the explicit form, the list must be enclosed in apostrophes.
%	For the implicit form, tells TSO to bypass the search of its command libraries.

Figure 5-2   The EXEC command

When you invoke a CLIST, MVS searches the libraries in the order you specify them on the ALLOCATE command. As a result, you should specify the library you use most often first. That way, you save search time.

You may run into a problem here, though. When you concatenate procedure libraries, you must follow this MVS rule: the library with the largest block size must be specified first in a list of concatenated libraries. As a result, if SYS1.CLIST has a block size of 6160 and DLOWE.TEST.CLIST has a block size of 800, you must allocate SYS1.CLIST before DLOWE.TEST.CLIST.

The easiest way around this problem is to use a model data set, like SYS1.CLIST, when you create a procedure library. That way, all your procedure libraries will have the same attributes, so you can concatenate them in any order. (IBM changed this requirement in Version 2.3 of the Data Facility Product. So if you're using Data Facility Product 2.3 or later, you can concatenate the libraries in any order you want, regardless of block size.)

At most installations, if your procedure library is named according to shop standards, it's automatically allocated when you log on. Check with your supervisor to see if that's the case at your shop. If so, you won't have to allocate your procedure library since your logon procedure allocates it for you.

If your shop uses MVS/ESA, you can also allocate your procedure library using the ALTLIB command. To do that, you must first allocate the library to the ddname SYSUEXEC, like this:

```
ALLOCATE DDNAME(SYSUEXEC) DSN(TEST.EXEC) SHR REUSE
```

Then, you activate the user libary by using an ALTLIB command like this one:

```
ALTLIB ACTIVATE USER (EXEC)
```

The advantage of allocating your procedure library this way is that you don't have to worry about overriding the system-wide procedure library. That's because the system procedure library remains allocated under the ddname SYSEXEC or SYSPROC. And when you use ALTLIB, TSO searches the SYSUEXEC library *before* it searches the system procedure library.

Figure 5-3 shows the most common forms of the ALTLIB commands for CLIST libraries. As you can see, it also includes options to deactivate a user library and to display the order that libraries are searched.

How to invoke a procedure from ISPF   Keep in mind that the examples I've shown so far assume you're invoking the CLIST from the TSO READY prompt. To allocate the procedure library and invoke a procedure from ISPF, you have to make sure ISPF knows you're issuing a TSO command rather than an ISPF command. You can do that from any ISPF panel by prefixing the command with the word TSO. Thus, to allocate a user procedure library, you would enter these two commands in the ISPF primary command area:

```
TSO ALLOCATE DDNAME(SYSUEXEC) DSN(TEST.EXEC) SHR REUSE
TSO ALTLIB ACTIVATE USER(EXEC)
```

Then, to invoke a procedure from the user library, you would enter a command like this:

```
TSO %MKTGTEST
```

Here, the procedure named MKTGTEST is invoked. You can also use ISPF's primary option 6 to enter TSO commands. When you do, you don't have to prefix the commands with the word TSO.

There are two other ways to invoke a CLIST from ISPF. The first is from a member list displayed by the data set list utility,

Command	Explanation
`ALTLIB ACTIVATE USER(EXEC)`	Activates a user exec library. Before you issue this command, use an ALLOCATE command to allocate your procedure library to the ddname SYSEXEC.
`ALTLIB DEACTIVATE USER(EXEC)`	Deactivates the user procedure library.
`ALTLIB DISPLAY`	Displays the current search order for procedure libraries.

Figure 5-3   The ALTLIB command

option 3.4. To do that, you just type the name of the procedure you want to execute next to the member name. The second is as an *edit macro* from the ISPF editor. I'll show you how to do that in chapter 9.

HOW TO GENERALIZE A COMMAND PROCEDURE

A command procedure like the one in figure 5-1 can save you considerable time while you're testing and debugging a particular program. But, as you may already realize, the procedure would be much more useful if it was generalized. In other words, if the procedure wasn't limited to a specific program, you could use it to start a test of any VS COBOL II program.

Figure 5-4 presents a procedure named COBTEST that does just that. As you can see, this procedure consists of an ALLOCATE command and a COBTEST command, just like the procedure in figure 5-1. But these commands are coded a little differently than they were before. And the procedure starts with a new statement, the PROC statement.

In addition, the EXEC command to invoke this procedure contains more information than the one for the MKTGTEST procedure did:

```
%COBTEST MKTG1200 LIBRARY(MASTER) PARM(MAY)
```

This command invokes COBTEST for a program named
MKTG1200 in a library named MASTER. In addition, it causes a
parameter (MAY) to be passed to MKTG1200.

The elements you see in the procedure's TSO commands, the
PROC statement, and the EXEC command all work together to
control the execution of COBTEST. I'm going to explain those
elements now so you'll know how to create and use general-
purpose procedures.

Symbolic variables

To make a procedure general-purpose, you use *symbolic variables*.
Basically, a symbolic variable is a name that takes on a different
value as a procedure executes. Since a symbolic variable's *real
value* can change from one execution of a procedure to the next, a
procedure can perform differently with each execution.

A symbolic variable consists of an ampersand (&) followed by
up to 31 alphanumeric characters, starting with a letter. Thus,
these are valid symbolic variables:

```
&A
&MEMBER
&MEMB1
```

while these are not:

```
&1MEMBER
&MEMBER*
&(
```

In some cases, which I'll be sure to point out, you can omit the
leading ampersand.

In figure 5-4, I used three symbolic variables in the ALLOCATE
and COBTEST commands: &LIBRARY, &MEMBER, and &PARM.
For the procedure to execute properly, I have to provide real values
for these variables in a PROC statement or on an EXEC command
that invokes the procedure. When I do that, TSO uses a process
called *symbolic substitution* to replace each symbolic variable with
its real value. I'll show you examples of this in a minute.

The command procedure

```
PROC 1 MEMBER LIBRARY(TEST) PARM()
ALLOCATE DSNAME(&LIBRARY..LOAD)_DDNAME(LOADLIB)
COBTEST LOAD(&MEMBER:LOADLIB) PARM('&PARM')
```

Invoking the procedure

```
%COBTEST MKTG1200 LIBRARY(MASTER) PARM(MAY)
```

The actual commands executed

```
ALLOCATE DSNAME(MASTER.LOAD) DDNAME(LOADLIB)
COBTEST LOAD(MKTG1200:LOADLIB) PARM('MAY')
```

Figure 5-4   A command procedure named COBTEST that uses symbolic variables

How to define symbolic variables: The PROC statement

The PROC statement is one of many procedure statements that let you control the execution of a procedure. (A *procedure statement* is executed by the procedure interpreter, as opposed to a command, which is executed by TSO.) When you use a PROC statement, it must be the first statement in your procedure. It defines the symbolic variables in the procedure and relates them to parameters coded on the EXEC command.

Figure 5-5 gives the complete format of the PROC statement. To code this statement, you enter symbolic variable names *without* the ampersands to specify positional and keyword parameters. A *positional parameter* is one TSO recognizes because of its position within a command; a *keyword parameter* is one TSO recognizes by its variable name.

As you'll see in a moment, you must code the real values for positional parameters in the EXEC command; you can also code the real values for keyword parameters there. If you want to assign a default value to a keyword parameter, you enter the default in parentheses after the variable name in the PROC statement.

Before the parameters themselves, though, you specify a count of positional parameters. In other words, you tell TSO how many of the variable names that follow should be treated as positional

---

The PROC statement

```
PROC count [positional-parms] [keyword-parm[(value)]]...
```

Explanation

count	Says how many positional parameters follow. If none follow, you must code a zero.
positional-parms	Symbolic variable names for positional parameters, without the ampersands.
keyword-parm	Symbolic variable names for keyword parameters, without the ampersands.
value	Default values assumed by keyword parameters. If a null value is to be assumed, specify ().

Figure 5-5 The PROC statement

parameters. If there are no positional parameters, you must specify zero as the count.

In figure 5-4, then, the PROC statement defines only one positional parameter, MEMBER. The other two, LIBRARY and PARM, are keyword parameters with their default values in parentheses.

How to assign real values to symbolic variables in the EXEC command

If you look back at the explicit and implicit formats of the EXEC command in figure 5-2, you'll remember that you can code a list of parameters on an EXEC command. This is where you assign real values to the symbolic variables in a PROC statement. So you have to know what the PROC statement looks like before you can code an EXEC command for a procedure.

If there are positional parameters in the PROC statement, you must code their real values in the EXEC command immediately following the procedure name. You don't code the symbolic variable names at all, just the real values. When TSO executes the command, these values are matched up, in order, with the symbolic variable names for positional parameters in the PROC statement. If you leave out a value, TSO prompts you for it. So, in figure 5-4, TSO substitutes the first parameter, MKTG1200, for the symbolic variable named &MEMBER.

If there are keyword parameters in the PROC statement, you may assign real values to them in the EXEC command. To do this, code the symbolic variable name without the ampersand (just as it is in the PROC statement). Then, code the real value in parentheses. In figure 5-4, for example, I assign a value of MASTER to the symbolic variable named &LIBRARY, and I assign a value of MAY to the symbolic variable named &PARM.

I realize this may all seem confusing right now. But I think the examples that follow will clarify: (1) how to code PROC statements; and (2) how PROC statements work together with EXEC commands.

Some examples of PROC statements and EXEC commands

Figure 5-6 presents four examples of PROC statements. For each of these examples, assume the procedure name is TEST1.

Example 1 specifies one positional parameter, named MEMBER. If you invoke the procedure with an implicit EXEC command like this:

```
%TEST1 MKTG1200
```

the real value of the symbolic variable &MEMBER is MKTG1200. Throughout the procedure, then, wherever &MEMBER appears, TSO substitutes the name MKTG1200. Remember, values are always required for positional parameters. So if you omit one when you invoke a procedure, TSO prompts you to supply a value.

Example 2 shows how to code two positional parameters, MEMBER1 and MEMBER2. Here, TSO will look for the first two parameters in the EXEC command and assign them to &MEMBER1 and &MEMBER2. So if you invoke the procedure like this:

```
%TEST1 MKTG1200 MKTGNEW
```

the real value of &MEMBER1 is MKTG1200 and the real value of &MEMBER2 is MKTGNEW.

Example 3 includes one positional parameter (MEMBER) and one keyword parameter (LIBRARY). In this example, the LIBRARY parameter has a default value of TEST. So if you don't specify LIBRARY when you invoke the procedure, TEST becomes the real value of &LIBRARY.

To illustrate, suppose you invoke the procedure like this:

```
%TEST1 MKTG1200 LIBRARY(MASTER)
```

Here, &MEMBER takes on a real value of MKTG1200, and &LIBRARY takes on a real value of MASTER. But if you omit the LIBRARY parameter, like this:

```
%TEST1 MKTG1200
```

the real value of &LIBRARY defaults to TEST. On the other hand, if you specify the keyword without a value, like this:

```
%TEST1 MKTG1200 LIBRARY
```

TSO prompts you to supply the real value for &LIBRARY.

Example 4 illustrates three points. First, there are no positional parameters, so the count is zero. Second, the LIB2 keyword has a *null default value.* So if you don't specify LIB2 when you invoke the command, no value is assigned to &LIB2; it's as though &LIB2 doesn't exist. And third, the LIB3 parameter doesn't specify a default value.

When you code a keyword parameter like LIB3 without a default value, you can't specify a real value when you invoke the procedure. Instead, the presence or absence of the keyword on the EXEC command determines the parameter's value. If you specify the keyword when you invoke the procedure, the parameter's value is set to the actual keyword name. If you omit it, the parameter's value becomes null. For example, suppose you invoke the procedure in example 4 like this:

```
%TEST1 LIB3
```

Then, the symbolic variable &LIB3 takes on a real value of LIB3. But if you omit LIB3, &LIB3 takes on a null value. Again, you can't code any other value for &LIB3 in the EXEC command.

When do you use keywords without defaults? Generally, you use them to control processing within your procedure. Many TSO commands have operands whose presence or absence determines how the command works. For example, consider the DELETE command. On it, you can say PURGE to indicate that a file should be deleted even if its expiration date hasn't passed. But if you omit PURGE, the expiration date is enforced. In a similar manner, you can code keyword operands whose presence or absence on the EXEC command determine how your procedure executes.

Example 1

```
PROC 1 MEMBER
```

Example 2

```
PROC 2 MEMBER1 MEMBER2
```

Example 3

```
PROC 1 MEMBER LIBRARY(TEST)
```

Example 4

```
PROC 0 LIB1(TEST) LIB2() LIB3
```

Figure 5-6   Examples of the PROC statement

Additional rules for coding EXEC parameters

So far, all the EXEC commands I've shown you have been pretty straightforward. But the coding rules are such that the commands can easily become complex and confusing, especially when you're using the explicit form.

First, when you use the explicit form, you must enclose the entire list of parameters in apostrophes. So these are properly coded EXEC commands:

```
EXEC (TEST1) 'MKTG1200'
EXEC (TEST1) 'MKTG1200 LIBRARY(MASTER)'
```

Second, if a keyword value contains spaces or commas, you must enclose it in apostrophes. In the implicit form, you code the value like this:

```
%COBTEST UPDAT1 PARM('DIST1,PER1')
```

If you omit the apostrophes, the comma marks the end of the value and the data past the comma is ignored.

In the explicit form, you also have to distinguish between the apostrophes that enclose the keyword value and the apostrophes that mark the beginning and end of the parameter list. So, in its explicit form, the previous EXEC command is:

```
EXEC (COBTEST) 'UPDAT1 PARM(''DIST1,PER1'')'
```

As you can see, you have to double the apostrophes that enclose the keyword value. Otherwise, the first apostrophe marks the end of the entire list of parameters.

Third, if the keyword value itself contains an apostrophe, you must double the apostrophe and enclose the entire value in apostrophes. Here's an example using the implicit form:

```
DSN('''SYS1.COB2LIB''')
```

In this example, the real value of &DSN is 'SYS1.COB2LIB'.

Of course, you're really in trouble if you try to code a value like this using the explicit form of EXEC. Since the entire list of parameters is enclosed in apostrophes, you have to double all the apostrophes again. So you would code the keyword parameter like this:

```
'DSN(''''''SYS1.COB2LIB'''''')'
```

Again, the real value of &DSN is 'SYS1.COB2LIB'.

How to use concatenation with symbolic variables

Up to now, I've shown you how to perform only the simplest type of symbolic substitution: replacing a symbolic variable with its real value. But, it becomes more complicated when you want to combine the real value of a symbolic variable with another character or the value of another symbolic variable. That process is called *concatenation*, and its rules are rather complex. Unfortunately, you need to know them well to use symbolic variables effectively.

To illustrate the rules of concatenation, figure 5-7 presents nine examples. In each of these examples, assume that the real value of &VAR1 is TEST and the real value of &VAR2 is LIST.

Example 1 doesn't look like a concatenation, but it is. Here, the characters DSN= are combined with &VAR1 to form DSN=TEST. I could have presented the examples in figure 5-7 without the leading DSN=. But since you almost always use symbolic substitution in conjunction with other TSO command text, I think it's clearer to present it as I have.

Example 2 is a more direct example of how TSO concatenates a character string with a variable. Here, the letter A is combined with

Example	As coded in CLIST	As interpreted during execution
1	DSN=&VAR1	DSN=TEST
2	DSN=A&VAR1	DSN=ATEST
3	DSN=&VAR1(&VAR2)	DSN=TEST(LIST)
4	DSN=&VAR1.A	DSN=TESTA
5	DSN=&VAR1..CLIST	DSN=TEST.CLIST
6	DSN=&VAR1&VAR2	DSN=TESTLIST
7	DSN=&VAR1..&VAR2	DSN=TEST.LIST
8	PARM=' &VAR1,&VAR2 '	PARM=' TEST,LIST '
9	DSN=&&&&&VAR1	DSN=&&TEST

Note: In each example, the real value of &VAR1 is TEST, and the real value of &VAR2 is LIST.

Figure 5-7   Examples of concatenation with symbolic variables

&VAR1 to form ATEST. Notice in this example (and in example 1) that no special coding is necessary to combine text and the real value of a symbolic variable, provided the text comes first.

Likewise, you can add text to the end of a symbolic variable as long as the text starts with a special character, as shown in example 3. Here, DSN=&VAR1(&VAR2) becomes DSN=TEST(LIST). The left parenthesis following &VAR1 causes no problem. Similarly, the right parenthesis following &VAR2 is concatenated as you would expect.

Adding text after a symbolic variable when the text begins with a letter or digit, however, is another matter. That's because TSO can't tell the start of the concatenated text from the symbolic variable name. For example, suppose you want to add the letter A to the end of a symbolic variable. If you coded

```
DSN=&VAR1A
```

TSO would look for a variable named &VAR1A.

To solve this problem, you use a period as a *delimiter* between the symbolic variable name and the concatenated text, as shown in example 4. Whenever TSO encounters a period in a symbolic variable name, it marks the end of the variable name. Any text that follows is concatenated after the variable's real value. Since the period doesn't become a part of the final text, &VAR1.A in example 4 becomes TESTA after symbolic substitution.

The use of a period as a delimiter creates an exception to the rule that you need to use a delimiter only with alphabetic and numeric characters. If you want to concatenate a period following a variable, you must code the period twice, as shown in example 5. The first period is the delimiter; the second period is concatenated after the variable. So in this example, &VAR1..CLIST becomes TEST.CLIST. As you can imagine, this type of concatenation is common when forming data set names.

Example 6 shows that you don't need a delimiter when you concatenate two variables. Here, DSN=&VAR1&VAR2 becomes DSN=TESTLIST. You can use a period as a delimiter if you want, but it's not necessary. So DSN=&VAR1.&VAR2 has the same result as example 6.

To concatenate two symbolic variables with a period in between, you still must use two periods, as shown in example 7. Here, &VAR1..&VAR2 becomes TEST.LIST.

Example 8 shows that apostrophes and commas cause no special problems. Here, PARM='&VAR1,&VAR2' becomes PARM='TEST,LIST'. I included this example because many uses of concatenation in command procedures involve apostrophes and commas.

Finally, example 9 illustrates the special problem that's introduced when you want to include an ampersand in the final substituted text. To do this, you must code two ampersands in a row. Otherwise, TSO thinks the ampersand marks the start of a symbolic variable name. For example, under standard MVS JCL, a temporary data set name starts with two ampersands. So to create such a name from a symbolic variable, you must code five consecutive ampersands, as shown in example 9. The first four are converted to two ampersands in the final text, while the fifth marks the start of the variable name. As a result, DSN=&&&&&VAR1 becomes DSN=&&TEST.

That covers most of the possibilities for symbolic substitution and simple concatenation. In the next topic, I'll introduce some new language elements and present some examples that are even more complicated. But now, look back to the CLIST in figure 5-4. If you study the symbolic variables coded in the ALLOCATE and COBTEST commands, comparing them with the final text shown at the bottom of the figure, you'll get a good idea of how symbolic variables work.

DISCUSSION

Using the command procedure facilities you've learned in this topic, you should now be able to write a generalized command procedure of considerable complexity. In the next topic, I'll present some additional command procedure facilities that will give you even more control over a procedure's execution.

Terms

command procedure
CLIST
invoke a procedure
explicit form
implicit form
symbolic variable
real value
symbolic substitution
procedure statement
positional parameter
keyword parameter
null default value
concatenation
delimiter

Objectives

1. Distinguish between explicit and implicit procedure invocation.

2. Create and invoke a simple command procedure that doesn't contain any symbolic variables.

3. Use symbolic variables and parameters to create and invoke a generalized command procedure.

Topic 2   Completing the basic subset

In this topic, I'll present a variety of command procedure facilities. In particular, I'll show you: how to use comments in a command procedure; how to write messages to the terminal; how to use advanced features of symbolic substitution, including expressions, built-in functions, and control variables; and how to control the execution of a CLIST using unconditional branching, IF-THEN-ELSE statements, SELECT statements, DO statements, and EXIT statements.

HOW TO USE COMMENTS

For simple command procedures like the ones I presented in the last topic, there's really no need to provide documentation that explains how the procedures work; their operation is self-evident. But more advanced command procedures can easily become confusing. That's when you need to use *comments* in your procedures to explain what's going on.

Coding a comment in a CLIST is easy. You begin the comment with a slash and an asterisk (/*), and you end it with an asterisk and a slash (*/). Between these delimiters, you can code any information you want, with the exception of an asterisk-slash, since that would mark the end of the comment. For example, here's a valid comment:

```
/* THIS IS A COMMENT */
```

Just how you use comments in your command procedures depends on shop standards and personal preference. It's usually a good idea to include a comment at the start of a CLIST to give the procedure's function as well as other identifying information. It's also a good idea to use comments throughout your CLIST to identify major functions.

I like to set off my comments with lines of asterisks, as shown in figure 5-8. Here, a group of seven comment lines identifies the

```
PROC 0 LIST
/*                                                                        */
/************************************************************************/
/*      PROCEDURE NAME: COMPRESF                                        */
/*      AUTHOR:         DOUG LOWE                                       */
/*      FUNCTION:       COMPRESS A PARTITIONED DATA SET                 */
/************************************************************************/
/*                                                                        */
GLOBAL GDATASET TEST
/*                                                                        */
/************************************************************************/
/*      CONTROL TEST ENVIRONMENT                                        */
/************************************************************************/
/*                                                                        */
CONTROL NOMSG
IF &TEST=TEST THEN CONTROL MSG LIST CONLIST
```

Figure 5-8   A segment of a CLIST that uses comments

procedure's name, author, and function. Later on, another group of comments indicates that the code that follows controls the procedure's test environment. Again, shop standards or personal preference may dictate a different format for comments.

You can also continue a comment to the next line using a continuation character (- or +). For example, in figure 5-8, I could have coded the first seven comment lines as a single comment by coding a continuation character at the end of the first six lines. However, I usually create a separate comment on each line to avoid the continuation characters.

If you want, you can code a comment on the same line as a command procedure statement or TSO command. For example, in figure 5-9, I placed the CONTROL TEST ENVIRONMENT comment on the same line as the CONTROL statement. Although this format uses less space, I prefer the format in figure 5-8 because it makes the comments more noticeable.

HOW TO WRITE MESSAGES TO THE TERMINAL

As a command procedure executes, you often want to send messages to the terminal user to indicate error conditions or the status of the CLIST. To do that, you use the WRITE statement.

```
PROC 0 LIST
/*                                                                      */
/**********************************************************************/
/*      PROCEDURE NAME: COMPRESF                                        */
/*      AUTHOR:         DOUG LOWE                                       */
/*      FUNCTION:       COMPRESS A PARTITIONED DATA SET                 */
/**********************************************************************/
/*                                                                      */
GLOBAL GDATASET TEST
CONTROL NOMSG                                    /* CONTROL TEST ENVIRONMENT */
IF &TEST=TEST THEN CONTROL MSG LIST CONLIST
```

Figure 5-9   Coding a comment on the same line with other text

The format of the WRITE statement is simple. Just code the word WRITE followed by the information you want to display at the terminal. Contrary to what you might expect, apostrophes or quotes are *not* used to mark the text sent to the terminal. In fact, if you use apostrophes, they're displayed along with the rest of the message.

To illustrate, consider this WRITE command:

```
WRITE AN ERROR HAS OCCURRED
```

When TSO executes this statement, the following message appears at the terminal:

```
AN ERROR HAS OCCURRED
```

Symbolic substitution takes place in a WRITE statement, so you can also include symbolic variables. For example, suppose you code a WRITE statement like this:

```
WRITE AN ERROR(&LASTCC) HAS OCCURRED
```

Assuming &LASTCC has a value of 16, this message is displayed:

```
AN ERROR(16) HAS OCCURRED
```

As I said before, you use the WRITE statement most often to display status information or error messages as your procedure executes. In addition, the WRITE statement is useful when you're testing your CLIST. For example, suppose your procedure starts with a complex PROC statement. You might follow it with a series of WRITE statements, like this:

```
PROC 1 DATASET LIST SYSOUT(X) JOBCLASS(A)
WRITE DATASET  = &DATASET
WRITE LIST     = &LIST
WRITE SYSOUT   = &SYSOUT
WRITE JOBCLASS = &JOBCLASS
```

Then, you can check the setting for each parameter before your CLIST continues. And, of course, you might use WRITE statements later in your procedure to make sure symbolic variables are set properly.

HOW TO CHANGE THE VALUE OF A SYMBOLIC VARIABLE: THE SET STATEMENT

In the last topic, I showed you how a CLIST user can set the value of a symbolic variable by entering it as a parameter on the EXEC command that invokes the procedure. Now, I'll show you another facility that lets you change a symbolic variable's value as your procedure executes: the SET statement. The SET statement is equivalent to an assignment statement in PL/I, BASIC, or FORTRAN, or a MOVE statement in COBOL.

The format of the SET statement is:

```
SET variable-name = expression
```

On the left of the equals sign, you can omit the ampersand from the variable name; TSO knows it's a variable name by its location in the SET statement.

An *expression* can be a real value, like

```
SET COUNT = 1
```

or

```
SET DATASET = SYS1.COB2LIB
```

Alternatively, an expression can be another symbolic variable:

```
SET VAR1 = &VAR2
```

Notice that on the right-hand side of the equals sign, an ampersand *is* required to identify a symbolic variable.

Note that the spaces on either side of the equals sign in a SET statement are not required. In fact, they're ignored. So the three statements

```
SET NAME=SMITH
SET NAME = SMITH
SET NAME=       SMITH
```

all have the same result: they set &NAME to SMITH. If you need to set a variable to a value that starts with a space, you'll have to use a special function, &STR, which I'll explain later in this topic.

You can assign a *null value* to a symbolic variable like this:

```
SET MIDDLE =
```

Here, &MIDDLE has no value. To illustrate how you can use a null value during symbolic substitution, suppose you code this statement:

```
WRITE &FIRST&MIDDLE&LAST
```

If &FIRST is ABC, &LAST is XYZ, and &MIDDLE is null, TSO displays this message:

```
ABCXYZ
```

Since &MIDDLE is null, nothing is substituted for it.

Arithmetic expressions   An expression in a SET statement can also be an *arithmetic expression.* An arithmetic expression is a series of symbolic variables and real values connected by *arithmetic operators*, like

```
SET COUNT = &COUNT + 1
```

or

```
SET INDEX = &COUNT * 10 + 1
```

As you can see, arithmetic expressions in a command procedure look very much like arithmetic expressions in most high-level programming languages.

Figure 5-10 lists the operators you can use in arithmetic expressions. The first four provide the standard arithmetic operations: addition, subtraction, multiplication, and division. They should present no difficulties. The last two, however, need some explanation.

The exponentiation operator (**) lets you raise a number to any power. For example, the value of 3 ** 2 is 9. CLIST doesn't support negative exponents; if you use a negative exponent, CLIST converts

Function	Operator
Addition	+
Subtraction	-
Multiplication	*
Division	/
Exponentiation	**
Remainder	//

Figure 5-10 Arithmetic operators

it to zero, yielding a value of 1 since any value raised to the power of zero is 1.

The remainder operator (//) gives the remainder resulting from a division operation. CLIST doesn't provide for fractional values; all of its numeric values are integers. As a result, the real value of 7/4 is 1, even though the exact result of the division is 1.75. To determine the remainder in that division, you code 7 // 4. Here, the real value of the expression is 3, since 7 divided by 4 is 1 with a remainder of 3.

The remainder operator is sometimes used for *modulus arithmetic*. Without going into the details of modulus arithmetic, suppose you want to convert any number to a value between zero and 11. You might code a SET statement like this:

```
SET MODVALUE = &VALUE // 12
```

Then, the real value of &MODVALUE is always between zero and 11 inclusive, since the remainder of &VALUE / 12 is never greater than 11.

Within an expression, arithmetic operations are performed according to the rules of standard algebra. In other words, exponentiation is always performed first, followed by multiplication and division, followed by addition and subtraction. Within that order, operations are performed from left to right. To illustrate, consider this expression:

```
1 + 2 * 3
```

Its real value is 7 because the multiplication (2 * 3) is performed before the addition.

You can change the standard order of evaluation by using parentheses. For example, the expression

```
(1 + 2) * 3
```

has a real value of 9 because the parentheses specify that the addition be done before the multiplication.

HOW TO USE BUILT-IN FUNCTIONS

Figure 5-11 lists six *built-in functions* that let you perform specific operations on an expression and one built-in function that operates on a data set. Each built-in function is a symbolic variable that's evaluated to a real value. You can use a built-in function anywhere you can use a symbolic variable, including in an expression.

The &DATATYPE function   You use the &DATATYPE function to determine an expression's data type: *numeric* or *character*. An expression is numeric if it consists only of digits with an optional leading sign. In that case, &DATATYPE has a real value of NUM. If an expression isn't numeric, it's character data, and &DATATYPE is CHAR.

To illustrate, suppose the real value of &VALUE is AB34. Then, the real value of &DATATYPE(&VALUE) is CHAR. On the other hand, if &VALUE is 123, &DATATYPE(&VALUE) is NUM.

The &LENGTH function   The &LENGTH function determines the number of bytes in the real value of an expression. The result of the &LENGTH function is numeric. For example,

```
&LENGTH(ABC)
```

is 3. Similarly,

```
&LENGTH(50 * 2)
```

is 3, since the result of the multiplication, 100, is a three-digit number. The length of a null value is zero.

If the expression is numeric, leading zeros aren't counted in the length. As a result, the real value of the expression

```
&LENGTH(00003)
```

is 1.

Built-in function	Use
`&DATATYPE(expression)`	Returns the data type of the expression: NUM for numeric values, CHAR for character values.
`&LENGTH(expression)`	Returns the length of the expression.
`&EVAL(expression)`	Forces the expression to be evaluated when it normally wouldn't be.
`&STR(expression)`	Suppresses the evaluation of an expression when it would normally be evaluated.
`&SUBSTR(start:end,string)`	Extracts a substring from *string* starting at *start* and ending at *end*. Both *start* and *end* have numeric values. *End* is optional; if omitted, only the character in the position specified by *start* is extracted.
`&SYSINDEX(string-1,string-2,start)`	Returns the position of *string-1* in *string-2* starting at *start*. *Start* is optional. If included, it must have a numeric value. If omitted, the search starts at the first character in *string-2*.
`&SYSDSN(data-set-name)`	Returns the value OK if the specified data set exists and is available for use. Returns one of several messages otherwise. If the data set is partitioned, you can also specify a member name.

Figure 5-11   Built-in functions

The &EVAL function   The &EVAL function causes an expression to be evaluated. For example, the real value of &EVAL(1 + 2) is 3, since the result of the expression 1 + 2 is 3.

You use &EVAL when you want to evaluate an expression even though the syntax of the CLIST statement doesn't call for an expression. For example, the statement

```
WRITE 1 + 2
```

displays the following message at the terminal:

```
1 + 2
```

That's because the WRITE statement calls for a text string and not an expression, so the expression isn't evaluated. To display the result of the expression, code the WRITE command like this:

```
WRITE &EVAL(1 + 2)
```

This command displays the result of the expression (3).

The &STR function   The &STR function is the opposite of &EVAL; it suppresses the evaluation of an expression. For example, suppose you code this:

```
&STR(1 + 2)
```

Here, the real value is 1 + 2, not 3. That's because the expression 1 + 2 is *not* evaluated. Symbolic substitution takes place within the &STR function, though. So, if &VALUE is 1, the expression

```
&STR(&VALUE + 2)
```

also reduces to 1 + 2.

You'll use the &STR function most for coding that might be confusing or even invalid without it. For example, suppose you want to test a variable to see if it's a slash (/). You couldn't code the expression

```
&CHAR = /
```

because the slash is the division operator and that makes the syntax invalid. So you must code the expression like this:

```
&CHAR = &STR(/)
```

To the &STR function, the slash has no special meaning, so the syntax is correct.

The &SUBSTR function   You use the &SUBSTR function to extract a portion of a character string. In its simplest form, you extract a single character by specifying the character's location and a symbolic variable that contains the character string, like this:

```
&SUBSTR(5,&CHAR)
```

The real value of this expression is the fifth character in &CHAR. So if &CHAR is ABCDEFG, the value is E.

You can also use a symbolic variable or an expression to indicate the character location. For example, suppose &START is 4 and &CHAR is still ABCDEFG. Then, the real value of the expression

```
&SUBSTR(&START,&CHAR)
```

is D. And

```
&SUBSTR(&START + 1,&CHAR)
```

is E.

You can extract more than one character from a string by specifying both a starting and an ending location. For example, suppose you code the SET statement

```
SET ALPHABET = ABCDEFGHIJKLMNOPQRSTUVWXYZ
```

followed by the expression

```
&SUBSTR(5:10,&ALPHABET)
```

This expression returns the fifth through the tenth characters in &ALPHABET, EFGHIJ.

If you want to extract a given number of characters starting at a particular location, you can code an expression like this:

```
&SUBSTR(&START:&START + &LEN − 1,&ALPHABET)
```

Here, the starting location is &START, while the ending location is &START plus &LEN minus 1. If &START is 5 and &LEN is 6, this expression yields the fifth through the tenth (5 + 6 - 1 is 10) characters in &ALPHABET, EFGHIJ.

The &SYSINDEX function   You use the &SYSINDEX function to locate a character string within another character string. For example, if the value of &INPUT is "DOUG,JUDY,ANNE", and value of &DELIM is a comma, you can locate the first comma in &INPUT with this function:

```
SET LOC1 = &SYSINDEX(&DELIM,&INPUT)
```

Here, the value of &LOC1 is set to 5, since the first comma is the fifth character of &INPUT.

You can also specify where you want the search for the first character string to begin in the second character string. For example, if the position of the first comma in &INPUT is in &LOC1, you can locate the second comma with this function:

```
SET LOC2 = &SYSINDEX(&DELIM,&INPUT,&LOC1+1)
```

This time, the value of LOC2 is set to 10, because the search starts at the sixth character of &INPUT.

This function is particularly useful for unstringing a group of values that are separated by a specified delimiter. Once you locate the position of each delimiter using &SYSINDEX, you can determine the length of each value, then use the &SUBSTR function to extract the values. For example, using the above illustration, once you locate the first and second delimiters, you can extract the second value using this function:

```
SET VALUE2 = &SUBSTR(&LOC1+1:&LOC2-1,&INPUT)
```

Here, the starting location is the position after the first delimiter, and the ending location is the position before the second delimiter.

The &SYSDSN function   The &SYSDSN function lets you check to see if a data set or member exists and is available for use. On this function, you specify the name of a data set like this:

```
&SYSDSN(TEST.COBOL)
```

If you specify a fully-qualified data set name, you must enclose it in apostrophes. Otherwise, TSO adds your user-id to the beginning of the data set name. If the data set is partitioned, you can also specify a member name like this:

```
&SYSDSN(TEST.COBOL(MKTG1200))
```

The &SYSDSN function returns one of several values depending on the existence and availability of the data set you specify. If the data set exists and is available for use, the value that's returned is OK. The other values are text messages that indicate why the data set isn't available.

You'll use the &SYSDSN function most often when the processing you want to perform depends on the existence of a data set. For example, if you want to allocate a data set, you might need to know if it already exists so you can allocate it appropriately. After you execute the &SYSDSN function, then, you can test the value it returns to determine what allocate command is executed. I'll show you how to do this kind of conditional processing later in this topic.

HOW TO OBTAIN SYSTEM INFORMATION USING CONTROL VARIABLES

Figure 5-12 lists 13 *control variables* that you can use in a CLIST to obtain system information. The meaning of each control variable is either self-evident or is explained later in this book, so I'm not going to describe them individually here. I just want you to be

Control variables that contain information about the user who invoked the command procedure

&SYSUID   The user-id of the current user.

&SYSPROC   The name of the logon procedure used to start the current user's terminal session.

&SYSPREF   The default prefix added to the start of data set names for the current user.

Control variables that contain information related to the command procedure's execution

&LASTCC   The condition code returned by the last TSO command or CLIST statement. Should be zero unless an error condition exists.

&MAXCC   The highest condition code encountered during a command procedure.

&SYSICMD   If the user invoked the procedure implicitly, this variable contains the name of the member invoked. Otherwise, it's blank.

&SYSNEST   Contains YES if a procedure is nested; otherwise, contains NO.

&SYSPCMD   The name of the most recently executed TSO command.

&SYSSCMD   The name of the most recently executed TSO subcommand.

Control variables that contain information used for terminal I/O

&SYSDVAL   A special register that contains information entered by a user.

&SYSDLM   Used for terminal I/O when the TERMIN statement is used.

Control variables that contain the time and date

&SYSTIME   The current time in the form hh:mm:ss (two-digit hours, minutes, and seconds).

&SYSDATE   The current date in the form mm/dd/yy (two-digit month, day, and year).

Figure 5-12   Control variables

aware that these variables exist. They're automatically maintained by the system, but you can change the value of some of them if you want.

To illustrate the use of a control variable, consider this WRITE statement:

```
WRITE JOB SUBMITTED AT &SYSTIME ON &SYSDATE
```

Here, the generated output looks something like this:

```
JOB SUBMITTED AT 13:45:20 ON 10/12/90
```

As you can see, TSO substitutes the current time for &SYSTIME and the current date for &SYSDATE.

HOW TO CONTROL A COMMAND PROCEDURE'S EXECUTION

Like other high-level languages, CLIST provides extensive facilities to control the flow of execution through the procedure. The most basic of these facilities is the GOTO statement, which lets you branch unconditionally to any point in the CLIST. CLIST also provides more advanced control facilities, including an IF-THEN-ELSE structure, a SELECT structure, and DO WHILE, DO UNTIL, and repetitive DO loops. Here, I'll show you how to use these control facilities.

The GOTO statement

To branch unconditionally to another section of a command procedure, you must do two things. First, you must establish a command procedure *label*. Second, you must code a GOTO statement that refers to that label.

A label can be up to 31 alphanumeric characters, and must start with a letter and be followed by a colon. The label identifies the TSO command or procedure statement that immediately follows it. For example, in figure 5-13, the label LOOP refers to the WRITE statement that follows it.

A GOTO statement causes a procedure to branch to a specified statement. On the GOTO statement, you code the label that identifies the statement. In figure 5-13, for example, the last statement in the procedure

```
GOTO LOOP
```

causes the procedure to branch to the statement labeled LOOP.

Now that you know how to code labels and GOTO statements, let me explain how the procedure in figure 5-13 works. The first statement assigns all the letters of the alphabet to &ALPHABET. The second statement assigns an initial value of 1 to &COUNT. The

```
SET ALPHABET = ABCDEFGHIJKLMNOPQRSTUVWXYZ
SET COUNT = 1
LOOP: WRITE LETTER &COUNT IS &SUBSTR(&COUNT,&ALPHABET)
      SET COUNT = &COUNT + 1
      GOTO LOOP
```

Figure 5-13   Using a label and a GOTO statement to create a procedure loop

third statement displays a message at the terminal using a WRITE statement. The next statement adds one to &COUNT. And the last statement branches to LOOP. If you study this procedure, you'll see that it prints the letters of the alphabet one by one. For example, the first time through the loop, it displays the message

```
LETTER 1 IS A
```

and the second time through the loop, it displays the message

```
LETTER 2 IS B
```

The procedure continues to display the letters of the alphabet until an error occurs when the value of &COUNT is greater than the length of &ALPHABET.

The IF statement

You use the IF statement when you want to perform one of two actions based on a condition that is either true or false. Figure 5-14 presents the format of the IF statement. As you can see, you code the condition you want to test as an expression. If the expression is true, the CLIST executes the statement or command associated with the THEN action. If the expression is false, the CLIST executes the statement or command associated with the ELSE action, if one is coded.

To illustrate, take a look at the command procedure in figure 5-15. This procedure performs the same function as the one in figure 5-13. The difference is that the procedure in figure 5-15 tests the value of &COUNT before it executes the GOTO statement. If the value of &COUNT is less than 27, the GOTO statement is executed. Otherwise, the procedure ends. The advantage of this procedure is that the end of the procedure is controlled. In contrast, the procedure in figure 5-13 ends when an error occurs.

The IF statement

```
IF   expression   THEN   [statement-1]

[ELSE   [statement-2]]
```

Explanation

expression   A comparative or logical expression.

statement-1   A single TSO command or procedure statement or a DO group that's executed
                 if *expression* is true.

statement-2   A single TSO command or procedure statement or a DO group that's executed
                 if *expression* is false.

Figure 5-14   The IF statement

```
SET ALPHABET = ABCDEFGHIJKLMNOPQRSTUVWXYZ
SET COUNT = 1
LOOP: WRITE LETTER &COUNT IS &SUBSTR(&COUNT,&ALPHABET)
      SET COUNT = &COUNT + 1
      IF &COUNT < 27 THEN GOTO LOOP
```

Figure 5-15   Using an IF statement to control a procedure loop

Comparative expressions   The expression in an IF statement is usually a comparison of two symbolic variables or real values in a format similar to that found in most high-level languages. For example, to test if &A is greater than 10, you could code an IF statement like this:

```
IF &A > 10 THEN WRITE &A IS GREATER THAN 10
ELSE WRITE &A IS NOT GREATER THAN 10
```

Here, the CLIST executes the first WRITE statement if &A is greater than 10; otherwise, it executes the second WRITE statement. In this example, &A > 10 is called a *comparative expression*.

Figure 5-16 lists the *comparative operators* you can use in a comparative expression. Notice that you can use the normal algebraic forms familiar to BASIC, PL/I, and COBOL, or you can use

Function	Operator	Two-letter abbreviation
Equal	=	EQ
Not equal	¬=	NE
Less than	<	LT
Greater than	>	GT
Less than or equal	<=	LE
Greater than or equal	>=	GE
Not greater than	¬>	NG
Not less than	¬<	NL

Figure 5-16 Comparative operators

the two-letter abbreviations commonly used in FORTRAN. As a result, these two expressions are equivalent:

```
&A = &B
&A EQ &B
```

Note that if you use a two-letter operator abbrevation, you *must* separate it from the rest of the expression with spaces.

Logical expressions   Using the *logical operators* shown in figure 5-17, you can combine two or more comparative expressions to form a *logical expression*. If you use the AND operator, all the comparative expressions involved must be true for the entire expression to be true. For example, the expression

```
50 < 75 AND 100 > 75
```

is true, and the expression

```
&A < &X AND &B < &X AND &C < &X
```

is true if &A, &B, and &C are all less than &X; otherwise, it's false.

If you use the OR operator, only one of the comparative expressions must be true for the entire expression to be true. For example, the expression

```
50 < 75 OR 80 < 75
```

Function	Operator	Word
And	&&	AND
Or	|	OR

Figure 5-17 Logical operators

is true because 50 is less than 75, even though 80 is not. However, the expression

```
100 < 75 OR 80 < 75
```

is false since neither 100 nor 80 is less than 75.

If an expression contains both AND and OR conditions, TSO evaluates all the ANDs from left to right, then combines them with the ORs from left to right. I recommend you avoid mixing AND and OR, however, because the resulting expressions are often very confusing. For example, try to determine what's meant by this expression:

```
&A < &X AND &B < &X OR &C < &X OR &D < &X AND &E < &X
```

Even knowing the order of evaluation TSO uses doesn't make this expression any easier to follow.

Incidentally, you can use a double ampersand (&&) rather than the word AND. And you can use a vertical bar (|) rather than the word OR. I prefer the words AND and OR because they indicate clearly what logical operation you're using. But if you prefer && and |, that's fine.

Coding rules   There are a few rules you must follow when you code an IF-THEN-ELSE structure. First, the word THEN must appear on the same logical line as the word IF. (By logical line, I mean one or more lines connected by the + or - continuation characters.) Second, you can code only *one* statement to be executed if the expression is true, and it too must be on the same line as the word IF. Third, if you use an ELSE clause, the word ELSE must be on a separate line from the word IF. And fourth, you can code only *one* statement to be executed if the expression is false, and it must be on the same line as the word ELSE. In short, the IF-THEN-ELSE structure should be coded just as shown in figure 5-14.

```
IF expression THEN  DO
        statement-1
        statement-2
        END
ELSE DO
        statement-3
        statement-4
        END
```

Figure 5-18   Using a DO group within an IF-THEN-ELSE structure

DO groups   Obviously, limiting the THEN and ELSE clauses to a single statement is a severe restriction. Fortunately, there's a facility called a *DO group* that lets you code a series of statements on separate lines that TSO treats as a single statement.

To code a DO group, enter the word DO, followed by TSO commands or procedure statements on separate lines, followed by the word END on a separate line. For example, this is a valid DO group:

```
DO
    WRITE LETTER &COUNT IS &SUBSTR(&COUNT,&ALPHABET)
    SET COUNT = &COUNT + 1
END
```

Here, TSO treats the WRITE statement and the SET statement as if they are a single statement.

You use a DO group in an IF-THEN-ELSE structure as shown in figure 5-18. Here, TSO executes statement-1 and statement-2 if the expression is true. Otherwise, it executes statement-3 and statement-4. In this example, I provided two statements for the THEN and ELSE DO groups. But there's no limit to how many statements you can code.

Figure 5-19 is an example of a DO group used in an IF statement. Here, TSO executes the WRITE statement and the SET statement together as a DO group if &COUNT is less than 27.

Notice in the examples I've given so far how I've indented the conditionally-executed statements from the main body of the procedure. That way, you can easily see the procedure's structure. In contrast, if you don't use indentation, the procedure's structure becomes obscure and often misleading.

One other point about DO groups: Make sure each END statement has a previous DO statement. The word END by itself is a

```
IF &COUNT < 27 THEN DO
    WRITE LETTER &COUNT IS &SUBSTR(&COUNT,&ALPHABET)
    SET COUNT = &COUNT + 1
    END
```

Figure 5-19   Using a DO group in an IF statement

TSO command that causes a procedure to stop executing. So although you would expect an unmatched END statement in a DO group to cause an error, it doesn't. Instead, it's executed as an END command, thus terminating your procedure with no apparent error. As you can imagine, a problem like this can take hours to isolate, unless you know to check for unmatched END statements. (By the way, you shouldn't use the END command to terminate a procedure. Instead, use the EXIT statement described later in this topic. It gives you more coding flexibility than the END command.)

Nested IF statements   Within an IF statement, or within a DO group under the control of an IF statement, you can code another IF statement. If you do, the IF statement is said to be *nested*. Within a nested IF statement, each ELSE clause is paired with the previous unpaired IF.

Since ELSE clauses are optional, you can code nested IF statements in a variety of different forms. In each case, however, you should use indentation to show the levels of nesting. In particular, you should align each ELSE clause with its corresponding IF statement so you can easily see how IF and ELSE statements are paired. But be careful. Your indentation doesn't affect how TSO interprets your CLIST. In other words, TSO always pairs an ELSE with the previous IF, regardless of what your indentation shows.

To illustrate, figure 5-20 shows some common variations for three levels of nesting. Note that in each case, the indentation corresponds to the way TSO interprets these statements.

Nested IF statements can be further complicated by the fact that the statement on an ELSE clause is optional. So, if you code just the word ELSE, you tell TSO to perform no action if the corresponding expression is false. Although you could omit the ELSE clause altogether, you don't want to do that if the IF statement is nested within another IF statement. Even though a null ELSE clause doesn't perform an action, it does mark the end of the

```
Example 1

IF expression THEN DO
    statements
    IF expression THEN DO
        statements
        IF expression THEN DO
            statements
            END
        END
    END


Example 2

IF expression THEN DO
    statements
    IF expression THEN DO
        statements
        IF expression THEN DO
            statements
            END
        ELSE DO
            statements
            END
        END
    ELSE DO
        statements
        END
    END
ELSE DO
    statements
    END


Example 3

IF expression THEN DO
    statements
    END
ELSE IF expression THEN DO
        statements
        END
    ELSE IF expression THEN DO
            statements
            END
        ELSE DO
            statements
            END
```

Figure 5-20   Some common examples of nested IF statements

```
IF expression THEN DO
    statements
    IF expression THEN DO
        statements
        IF expression THEN DO
            statements
            END
        ELSE
        END
    ELSE DO
        statements
        END
    END
```

Figure 5-21   Using a null ELSE in a nested IF statement

IF-THEN-ELSE structure. That way, TSO pairs any ELSE clauses that follow with the correct IF statement.

To illustrate how this works, consider figure 5-21. Here, I coded three levels of nested IF statements. Although only the second one requires an action for the ELSE condition, I coded a null ELSE clause for the third IF statement. Then, the following ELSE clause is correctly paired with the second IF statement. In contrast, if I had omitted the ELSE clause for the third IF statement, TSO would have paired the following ELSE clause with the third IF statement instead of with the second one as intended.

The SELECT statement

One of the limitations of the IF statement is that it lets you specify only two actions: one to take if the condition is true, the other if the condition is false. The SELECT statement lets you specify more than two possible actions to take depending on the results of a condition test. For example, suppose you want to display an error message that explains the meaning of a return code whose value can be 0, 4, 8, 12, or 16. To do this with IF statements, you would have to nest a series of them, each testing the value of the return code. With the SELECT statement, you can perform this processing with a single test.

There are two forms of the SELECT statement: simple and compound. I'll cover them both here.

The simple SELECT statement

```
SELECT

    {WHEN (expression) [statement-1]}...

    [OTHERWISE statement-2]

END
```

Explanation

expression	A comparative or logical expression.
statement-1	A single TSO command or procedure statement or a DO group that's executed if the expression is true.
statement-2	A single TSO command or procedure statement or a DO group that's executed if none of the WHEN expressions are true.

Figure 5-22 The simple SELECT statement

The simple form of the SELECT statement Figure 5-22 presents the simple form of the SELECT statement. To use this form, you code the word SELECT followed by a series of WHEN clauses. As you can see, a WHEN clause resembles an IF statement; it includes a condition test and a single statement or command that's executed if the condition is true. In addition, you can code multiple statements and commands on a WHEN clause by coding them as a DO group just like you do on an IF statement. Following the WHEN clauses, you can code an OTHERWISE clause. The statement in the OTHERWISE clause is executed if none of the conditions in the WHEN clauses are true. To complete the SELECT statement, you must code an END statement after the WHEN clauses and the optional OTHERWISE clause.

To illustrate how the simple SELECT statement works, consider figure 5-23. Here, the SELECT statement tests for the value of a return code from a DELETE command. If the return code is 4, 8, or 12, a WRITE statement displays a message on the terminal that indicates the severity of the error. If the return code is 16, a WRITE statement displays a message and the procedure is terminated with an EXIT statement. (I'll present the EXIT statement later in this topic.) I didn't code an OTHERWISE clause on this SELECT

```
SELECT
    WHEN (&RC=4)   WRITE WARNING MESSAGE ISSUED
    WHEN (&RC=8)   WRITE PROCESSING INCOMPLETE
    WHEN (&RC=12)  WRITE PROCESSING UNSUCCESSFUL
    WHEN (&RC=16)  DO
          WRITE SEVERE ERROR
          EXIT CODE(16)
          END
END
```

Figure 5-23   A simple SELECT statement that tests a return code

statement, because the WHEN clauses account for all the possible return codes from a DELETE command except zero, for which no action is required.

The compound form of the SELECT statement   Figure 5-24 presents the compound form of the SELECT statement. You use this form to simplify coding when all of the WHEN clauses test for a value of the same variable.

To use the compound SELECT statement, you don't code a condition test in each WHEN clause. Instead, you specify a simple expression, usually just a variable name, after the word SELECT. Then, in each WHEN clause, you specify another simple expression, usually a literal value. The SELECT statement compares the value of the expression in each WHEN clause with the value of the expression in the SELECT clause, and executes the first WHEN clause that yields a match.

To illustrate, example 1 in figure 5-25 shows how the compound form simplifies the coding that was required in figure 5-23. Here, the variable &RC is listed following the word SELECT. Then, each WHEN clause simply lists the value to be tested against &RC.

The compound SELECT statement also lets you specify two or more values to be tested in each WHEN clause. To do that, you simply list each value, separated by a vertical bar (|) or the word OR. Example 2 in figure 5-25 illustrates this. Here, the same message is displayed when &RC is 8 or 12.

Finally, the compound SELECT statement lets you test for a range of values by listing the beginning and ending values,

---

The compound SELECT statement

```
SELECT expression-1

    {WHEN  (expression-2) [statement-1]}...

    [OTHERWISE statement-2]

END
```

Explanation

expression-1	A variable or expression used for the test.
expression-2	A comparative or logical expression whose value is compared with the value of *expression-1*. It can be a range of values separated by a colon.
statement-1	A single TSO command or procedure statement or a DO group that's executed if the expression is true.
statement-2	A single TSO command or procedure statement or a DO group that's executed if none of the WHEN expressions are true.

Figure 5-24 The compound SELECT statement

separated by a colon. To illustrate, example 3 in figure 5-25 displays the same message for any return code between 4 and 12.

Three forms of the DO statement

Earlier in this topic, I showed you how to construct simple loops using the GOTO and IF statements. CLIST provides three forms of the DO statement that provide better control over looping: DO-WHILE, DO-UNTIL, and the repetitive DO. Figure 5-26 presents the format of these three DO-statement types.

The DO-WHILE statement   The DO-WHILE statement provides an easy way to control looping within a CLIST. With this format, the statements in the DO-WHILE structure are executed repeatedly until the expression is false. In other words, they're executed as long as the expression is true.

```
Example 1

SELECT &RC
    WHEN (4)  WRITE WARNING MESSAGE ISSUED
    WHEN (8)  WRITE PROCESSING INCOMPLETE
    WHEN (12) WRITE PROCESSING UNSUCCESSFUL
    WHEN (16) DO
        WRITE SEVERE ERROR
        EXIT CODE(16)
        END
END


Example 2

SELECT &RC
    WHEN (4)           WRITE WARNING MESSAGE ISSUED
    WHEN (8 OR 12) WRITE PROCESSING INCOMPLETE OR UNSUCCESSFUL
    WHEN (16) DO
        WRITE SEVERE ERROR
        EXIT CODE(16)
        END
END


Example 3

SELECT &RC
    WHEN (4:12) WRITE WARNING MESSAGE ISSUED
    WHEN (16) DO
        WRITE SEVERE ERROR
        EXIT CODE(16)
        END
END
```

Figure 5-25   Three compound SELECT statements that test a return code

Figure 5-27 shows how you can use a DO-WHILE structure to refine the simple loop first presented in figure 5-13. The first two statements in figure 5-27 set &ALPHABET and &COUNT. Then, the DO-WHILE statement marks the start of a DO-WHILE structure. The expression, &COUNT < 27, says that the statements in the DO-WHILE structure are to be executed over and over again as long as &COUNT is less than 27. As soon as &COUNT is *not* less than 27, however, the DO-WHILE structure ends and control falls through to the next statement in sequence. The effect of the DO-WHILE

The DO-WHILE statement

```
DO WHILE expression
    statements
END
```

The DO-UNTIL statement

```
DO UNTIL expression
    statements
END
```

The repetitive DO statement

```
DO variable = from-exp TO to-exp [BY by-exp]
    statements
END
```

Explanation

expression	A comparative or logical expression that controls the execution of the DO loop.
statements	A sequence of TSO commands or procedure statements. If coded on the DO-WHILE statement, they're executed as long as *expression* is true. If coded on the DO-UNTIL statement, they're executed as long as the condition is false. And if coded on a repetitive DO loop, they're executed until *variable* reaches the value of *to-expression*.
variable	A symbolic variable that controls the execution of the DO loop.
from-exp	Specifies the initial value of *variable*.
to-exp	Specifies the terminal value of *variable*.
by-exp	Specifies the amount that's added to *variable* each time the loop is executed. If omitted, the default is 1.

Figure 5-26   The DO-WHILE, DO-UNTIL, and repetitive DO statements

loop in figure 5-27 is that TSO displays each letter of the alphabet at the terminal.

In a DO-WHILE structure, the expression stated in the WHILE clause is evaluated *before* each execution of the loop. As a result, if the expression is false the first time, the statements in the loop aren't executed at all. Usually, that's the way you want the test to function.

```
SET ALPHABET = ABCDEFGHIJKLMNOPQRSTUVWXYZ
SET COUNT = 1
DO UNTIL &COUNT > 26
    WRITE LETTER &COUNT IS &SUBSTR(&COUNT,&ALPHABET)
    SET COUNT = &COUNT + 1
END
```

Figure 5-28   A DO-UNTIL loop

```
SET ALPHABET = ABCDEFGHIJKLMNOPQRSTUVWXYZ
SET COUNT = 1
DO WHILE &COUNT < 27
    WRITE LETTER &COUNT IS &SUBSTR(&COUNT,&ALPHABET)
    SET COUNT = &COUNT + 1
END
```

Figure 5-27   A DO-WHILE loop

The DO-UNTIL statement   The DO-UNTIL statement is similar to the DO-WHILE statement. With this format, the statements in the DO-UNTIL structure are executed until the expression is true. In other words, they're executed as long as the expression is false.

Figure 5-28 presents the loop in figure 5-13 again, this time using the DO-UNTIL statement. Notice that the only difference between this loop and the loop that uses DO-WHILE in figure 5-27 is the expression that's coded on the DO statement. For DO-UNTIL, the expression is

```
DO UNTIL &COUNT > 26
```

In a DO-UNTIL structure, the expression in the UNTIL clause is evaluated *after* each execution of the loop instead of before the loop. As a result, a DO-UNTIL loop is always executed at least once.

The repetitive DO statement   The last form of the DO statement is the repetitive DO loop. With this format, each time the loop is executed, the value of the specified variable is incremented by the value in by-expression. The initial value of the variable is the value of from-expression. The variable is incremented until it reaches the value specified by to-expression.

Figure 5-29 illustrates a repetitive DO loop. This loop performs the same function as the loops in figures 5-13, 5-27, and 5-28. In the

```
SET ALPHABET = ABCDEFGHIJKLMNOPQRSTUVWXYZ
DO &COUNT = 1 TO 26 BY 1
    WRITE LETTER &COUNT IS &SUBSTR(&COUNT,&ALPHABET)
END
```

Figure 5-29 A repetitive DO loop

loop in figure 5-29, the value of &COUNT is initialized to 1 and incremented by 1 each time the loop is executed, until it reaches a value of 26.

Note that the BY clause is optional in the repetitive DO loop. If you omit it, the variable is incremented by 1 each time through the loop. So, in figure 5-29, the result would have been the same if I had omitted the BY clause.

HOW TO TERMINATE A PROCEDURE: THE EXIT STATEMENT

You use the EXIT statement to terminate your command procedure. If you code just the word EXIT, your CLIST returns to TSO. If you also include a CODE operand, like this:

```
EXIT CODE(12)
```

your CLIST returns the *condition code* you specify when it ends. In this case, the condition code is 12. This value goes into the control variable &LASTCC, where it can be examined by another procedure. Usually, a condition code greater than zero indicates that an error occurred during the execution of a statement or command.

In general, there are two places where you'll issue an EXIT statement. The first is at the end of your CLIST. Although you don't have to code an EXIT statement there, it's often a good idea. The second is where you detect an error condition and want to abort the CLIST immediately. I showed you an example of that in the SELECT statement in figure 5-23. In that case, you should issue an EXIT statement that sets an appropriate condition code.

```
 10 /*  &JOBCHAR HAS BEEN PREVIOUSLY SET TO THE LAST JOB CHARACTER */
 20 SET CHARS = ABCDEFGHIJKLMNOPQRSTUVWXYZ0123456789A
 30 SET COUNT = 1
 40 DO WHILE &JOBCHAR ¬= &SUBSTR(&COUNT,&CHARS)
 50     SET COUNT = &COUNT + 1
 60 END
 70 SET JOBCHAR = &SUBSTR(&COUNT + 1,&CHARS)
 80 IF &BG = BG THEN DO
 90     SUBMIT JCL(&MEMBER) JOBCHAR(&JOBCHA)
100     WRITE JOB &SYSUID&JOBCHAR SUBMITTED AT &SYSTIME ON &SYSDATE
110     END
```

Figure 5-30   A segment of a command procedure that submits a job for background processing

A SAMPLE COMMAND PROCEDURE

Figure 5-30 presents a short section of a command procedure that submits a job for background processing. Although this is an incomplete example, it illustrates many of the command procedure facilities I've described in this topic. Note that I included line numbers in this example so I can refer to specific lines. The procedure doesn't actually contain line numbers.

If a submitted data set doesn't contain a JOB statement, the JOBCHAR operand of the SUBMIT command supplies a character that's appended to your user-id to form an appropriate job name. The code in figure 5-30 assigns a new value to JOBCHAR each time you run the procedure so your job names are unique. You can assume that the variable &JOBCHAR has been previously set to the character used in the job name the last time you submitted a job.

Lines 20 through 70 change &JOBCHAR to the next character in sequence. In other words, if the procedure starts with &JOBCHAR equal to A, these lines change &JOBCHAR to B. If &JOBCHAR starts out as M, it's changed to N. And the digits follow the letters, so if &JOBCHAR is Z on entry, it's changed to 0.

Line 20 sets &CHARS to a string that contains all the possible characters &JOBCHAR can have. Notice the string ends with an A. That way, if &JOBCHAR is 9, it's changed to A, thus returning to the start of the list. Line 30 initializes a counter variable, &COUNT, to 1. Then, lines 40 through 60 set up a DO-WHILE loop that searches through &CHARS one character at a time until the character that matches &JOBCHAR is found. It does this by executing the loop repeatedly as long as this condition is met:

```
&JOBCHAR ¬= &SUBSTR(&COUNT,&CHARS)
```

In other words, the loop continues to execute as long as the value of &JOBCHAR is *not* equal to the character at position &COUNT in &CHARS. The first time through the loop, &COUNT is 1. So the condition compares &JOBCHAR with the letter A (the first character in &CHARS).

Assuming the condition is not true, &COUNT is incremented with this SET statement:

```
SET COUNT = &COUNT + 1
```

Then, the condition is tested again. This time, the next character in &CHARS in used in the test. This process continues until the character in &CHARS matches &JOBCHAR. At that point, the WHILE condition becomes false, and the loop ends with &COUNT indicating the position of the matching character within &CHARS.

Since I want to use the next character in the sequence as the job identifier, line 70 sets &JOBCHAR like this:

```
SET JOBCHAR = &SUBSTR(&COUNT + 1,&CHARS)
```

Thus, if the loop ends with &COUNT set to 10, this statement sets &JOBCHAR to the eleventh character in &CHARS. As a result, the proper job identifier is found.

It's lines 80 through 110 that actually submit the job for background processing. Here, I assume that a symbolic variable, &BG, will have a real value of BG if the background job is submitted. Although it's not apparent from the segment of code shown in figure 5-30, this variable is set as a keyword parameter when the procedure is invoked. For example, suppose the procedure starts with a PROC statement like this:

```
PROC 1 MEMBER BG
```

Then, if the procedure is invoked like this:

```
%TEST COMPRESS BG
```

&BG is set to BG. (For the sake of the illustration, assume here that TEST is the name of the procedure and &MEMBER is the name of the member you want to submit for background processing.)

Assuming that &BG equals BG, line 90 submits the background job. The SUBMIT command specifies &MEMBER as the member name; the library name is user-id.JCL.CNTL. The JOBCHAR operand supplies &JOBCHAR, which was set in line 70, to use in the job name. Finally, line 100 writes a message to the terminal saying that the job was submitted.

DISCUSSION

In this topic, I've presented command procedure elements that let you create complex expressions and control the flow of execution within your procedure. While these facilities raise CLIST to the status of a high-level programming language, I must again caution you to use them with discretion. Whenever possible, you should consider using a high-level programming language like PL/I or COBOL rather than using CLIST.

A COBOL or PL/I program has a couple of advantages over a command procedure. To begin with, both COBOL and PL/I are much easier to code than CLIST, because of their simpler syntax. And because they are compiled rather than interpreted, they execute faster–perhaps dramatically faster–than a CLIST. So save the complicated command procedures for applications that require facilities only a command procedure can offer, such as dynamic file allocation, background job processing, and so on.

Terms

comment	label
expression	comparative expression
null value	comparative operator
arithmetic expression	logical operator
arithmetic operator	logical expression
modulus arithmetic	DO group
built-in function	nested IF statement
control variable	condition code

Objective

Given a problem requiring any of the command procedure facilities described in this topic, code a command procedure for its solution.

Chapter 6

Advanced CLIST facilities

In this chapter, you'll build on the CLIST basics you learned in chapter 5. There are two topics in this chapter. The first presents advanced CLIST programming techniques that can be useful in all but the simplest CLIST procedures. In it, you'll learn how to control the CLIST environment, how to detect and trap errors, and other useful techniques. Then, in the second topic, you'll learn how to use CLIST facilities that let you process files and interact with the terminal user.

Topic 1 — Advanced CLIST techniques

In the last chapter, I presented a subset of the features of command procedures. Now, I'll build upon that subset by presenting additional command procedure facilities. Specifically, I'll show you how to use the CONTROL statement to control the command procedure environment, how to use DATA/ENDDATA statements to avoid a peculiar problem often encountered in a DO group, how to code exit routines to handle error conditions and attention interruptions, how to nest procedures (that is, how to invoke one procedure from another) and how to use subprocedures.

HOW TO CONTROL THE CLIST ENVIRONMENT

Figure 6-1 presents the format of the CONTROL statement. You use this statement to turn on or off various options that affect how a command procedure executes. Normally, you place the CONTROL statement near the beginning of your command procedure. That way, the control options are in effect for the entire procedure.

To activate one of the control options presented in figure 6-1, you code it on the CONTROL statement. For example, if you code

```
CONTROL MSG
```

you turn on the MSG option. To turn it off, you code

```
CONTROL NOMSG
```

To control more than one option, you list them on the CONTROL statement, like this:

```
CONTROL MSG NOFLUSH NOLIST
```

This statement turns the MSG option on, but turns the FLUSH and LIST options off.

Now, I'll explain how each of the control options affects the way your command procedures execute.

The CONTROL statement

```
CONTROL [{MSG   }]
         {NOMSG }

        [{FLUSH   }]
         {NOFLUSH }

        [ MAIN ]

        [{LIST   }]
         {NOLIST }

        [{CONLIST   }]
         {NOCONLIST }

        [{SYMLIST   }]
         {NOSYMLIST }

        [{PROMPT   }]
         {NOPROMPT }

        [{CAPS   }]
         {NOCAPS  }]
         {ASIS    }

        [ END(string) ]
```

Explanation

MSG NOMSG	If MSG is on, messages generated by commands are displayed at the terminal. Otherwise, they're suppressed. MSG is the default.
FLUSH NOFLUSH	If FLUSH is on, the procedure is removed from the system when an error occurs and error exits are ignored. FLUSH is the default. Note that the MAIN option overrides the FLUSH option.
MAIN	The MAIN option says that a procedure should not be deleted from the system because of an error or attention interruption. If you specify MAIN, NOFLUSH is assumed. MAIN is normally off.
LIST NOLIST	If LIST is on, TSO commands are listed before they're executed but after symbolic substitution has taken place. Otherwise, they're not listed. NOLIST is the default.
CONLIST NOCONLIST	If CONLIST is on, command procedure statements are listed before they're executed but after symbolic substitution has taken place. Otherwise, they're not listed. NOCONLIST is the default.

Figure 6-1   The CONTROL statement (part 1 of 2)

Explanation (continued)

SYMLIST NOSYMLIST	If SYMLIST is on, TSO commands and command procedures are listed *before* symbolic substitution. Otherwise, they're not listed. NOSYMLIST is the default.
PROMPT NOPROMPT	If PROMPT is on, the terminal user is prompted for missing information on TSO commands in the procedure. NOPROMPT is the default.
CAPS NOCAPS ASIS	If CAPS is on, all character strings are converted to uppercase letters before they're processed. Otherwise, they're not converted. CAPS is the default.
END	Specifies an alternate string that's used to end a DO group.

Figure 6-1   The CONTROL statement (part 2 of 2)

The MSG/NOMSG option

The MSG/NOMSG option controls whether messages created by TSO commands are displayed. If you say MSG, the messages are displayed. If you say NOMSG, they're suppressed.

How you set this option depends on the function of your procedure. If the user needs to see the TSO command output, you want the MSG option on. Since it's activated by default when a command procedure starts, you don't need to code CONTROL MSG unless you previously coded CONTROL NOMSG. If your procedure invokes TSO commands that create output the user doesn't need to see, code CONTROL NOMSG.

The FLUSH/NOFLUSH and MAIN options

Normally, when an error condition occurs, the system flushes your procedure–that is, it removes it from the system–even if you provide an error exit. (An error exit is a routine that handles error processing. I'll present error exits in detail later in this topic.) But if you code the CONTROL statement

```
CONTROL NOFLUSH
```

at the start of the procedure, the system won't flush your procedure when an error occurs, so your error exits are processed.

```
PROC 0 TEST
CONTROL NOFLUSH NOMSG
IF &TEST = TEST THEN DO
    WRITE PROCEDURE EXECUTING IN TEST MODE
    CONTROL MSG LIST CONLIST
    END
```

Figure 6-2   Setting control options for test and production runs of a CLIST

Alternatively, you can code this CONTROL statement:

CONTROL MAIN

The MAIN option is similar to the NOFLUSH option. But in addition to preventing the system from flushing your procedure in the event of an error, it inhibits the Attention key. As a result, the terminal user can't interrupt your procedure by pressing the PA1 key if you say CONTROL MAIN. Normally, you use CONTROL NOFLUSH, especially during testing. That way, you can interrupt your procedure whenever necessary. Note that there is no option for turning MAIN off.

The LIST/NOLIST, CONLIST/NOCONLIST, and SYMLIST/NOSYMLIST options

You use the LIST/NOLIST, CONLIST/NOCONLIST, and SYMLIST/NOSYMLIST options when you test a CLIST. The LIST option causes CLIST to display all TSO commands before they're executed. They're displayed in their final form, after symbolic substitution. The CONLIST option causes CLIST to display all command procedure statements, again before execution but after symbolic substitution. And the SYMLIST option simply lists all TSO commands and procedure statements before any symbolic substitution. The default settings for these three options are NOLIST, NOCONLIST, and NOSYMLIST.

I often provide a keyword parameter, TEST, on my PROC statements so I can establish a testing environment when I invoke a procedure for a test run. To do this, I include the statements shown in figure 6-2 at the start of the procedure. The first CONTROL statement establishes the production environment for my procedure: It turns the MSG option off and turns the MAIN option on. Then, if the TEST keyword is specified, I issue another CONTROL statement so that the MSG, LIST, and CONLIST options are in effect. As a result, during a test run, I get the extra output I need to help me debug the procedure.

The PROMPT/NOPROMPT option

The PROMPT/NOPROMPT option determines whether TSO prompts a user when required information is omitted from a TSO command in the procedure. The PROMPT option is off by default, so TSO terminates your procedure if it includes an incomplete command. If you say PROMPT, TSO prompts the terminal user to supply the missing information.

The CAPS/NOCAPS/ASIS option

The CAPS/NOCAPS/ASIS option determines how character strings are handled. If you say CAPS or let it default, all character strings are converted to uppercase letters before they're processed. If you say NOCAPS or ASIS, the character strings are not converted.

The END option

The last option you can control with the CONTROL statement is the string used to delimit a DO group. Normally, this string is the word END. But END has other meanings under TSO, such as indicating the end of an EDIT session. If you need to include END as a TSO command or subcommand in a DO group, you must change the end string, like this:

```
CONTROL END(ENDDO)
```

Then, you code a DO group like this:

```
DO
    20 //SYSUT1 DD   DSN=&DATASET,DISP=OLD
    END SAVE
ENDDO
```

Here, the ENDDO statement marks the end of the DO group, and END SAVE is recognized as a TSO command. An alternative to this technique is to code the END SAVE command in a DATA/ENDDATA group, which I'll describe in a moment.

How to specify control options on the EXEC command

You can set two of the CONTROL options, LIST and PROMPT, on the explicit form of the EXEC command. For example, you might invoke a procedure like this:

```
EXEC COBTEST 'MKTG1200,LIBRARY(MASTER)',LIST,PROMPT
```

Here, the procedure begins with the LIST and PROMPT options set. Since LIST and PROMPT aren't part of the parameters sent to the procedure, they're coded outside the apostrophes that contain the parameters.

HOW TO USE A DATA/ENDDATA GROUP

As I mentioned before, you can use the CONTROL statement to change the END statement to another character string. That way, you can code END as a TSO command or subcommand without having it confused as a procedure statement. An alternative is to use the DATA and ENDDATA statements. Basically, the DATA statement tells TSO that it is to treat each line that follows as a TSO command or subcommand until the word ENDDATA is encountered. TSO still performs symbolic substitution, but doesn't interpret any procedure statements.

To illustrate, consider figure 6-3. In this example, I coded a DATA/ENDDATA group that includes an END subcommand to end an editing session. If it weren't for the DATA/ENDDATA statements, TSO would have interpreted the END subcommand as the end of the DO group that contains the entire editing session. As a result, it would not have executed the procedure properly.

HOW TO CODE EXIT ROUTINES

An *exit routine* is a single statement, or, more commonly, a series of statements contained in a DO group, that's executed whenever an exit condition occurs. There are two types of exits you can

```
DO
    EDIT JCL(TEST) CNTL
    40 //SYSUT1       DD   DSN=&&TEMPSET,
    50 //                  UNIT=SYSDA,
    60 //                  SPACE=(TRK,(10,1),
    70 //                  DISP=,PASS
    80 //SYSIN        DD   *
    90  COPY OUTDD=DD1,INDD=DD2
    95 /*
    DATA
    END SAVE
    ENDDATA
END
```

Figure 6-3   A DATA/ENDDATA group

provide in a command procedure: *error exits* and *attention exits*. You use an error exit to process error conditions your procedure encounters as it executes. And you use an attention exit to invoke special processing when the terminal user presses the Attention key, PA1.

To establish an error exit, you use an ERROR statement; to establish an attention exit, you use an ATTN statement. Since both statements have the same format, they're shown together in figure 6-4.

Error exits

Normally, when a TSO command or procedure statement issues a return code greater than zero, TSO generates an error message and terminates your procedure. An error exit lets you anticipate possible errors and provide a more meaningful error message or perhaps provide special processing for the error so that your procedure doesn't terminate.

To establish an error exit, you issue an ERROR statement *before* an error occurs. Then, any error causes control to transfer to your error exit (that is, your ERROR statement). It's important to realize that TSO doesn't execute the statements in an error exit when it first encounters the ERROR statement; it doesn't execute them until an error occurs.

When an error occurs and an error exit is in effect, you want to do one of two things following the special processing in the error

---

The ERROR statement

ERROR $\begin{Bmatrix} \text{statement} \\ \text{OFF} \end{Bmatrix}$

The ATTN statement

ATTN [$\begin{Bmatrix} \text{statement} \\ \underline{\text{OFF}} \end{Bmatrix}$]

Explanation

statement	A single statement or several statements contained in a DO group that's executed whenever an error or attention interruption occurs.
OFF	Says that any previous error or attention exit should be deleted. OFF is the default for ATTN.

Figure 6-4   The ERROR and ATTN statements

routine: terminate the procedure or continue processing. To terminate a procedure, code an EXIT statement as the last statement in the error routine. To return control to the statement following the one that caused the error, code a RETURN statement without any operands as the last statement in the error routine.

One common use of an error exit is to trap errors that may occur as a result of an ALLOCATE command. To illustrate, consider figure 6-5. Here, an ERROR statement establishes an error exit that consists of two statements. The first writes an error message to the terminal; the second terminates the procedure with a condition code of 12. Then, an ALLOCATE command attempts to allocate a data set. If the allocation fails, TSO executes the statements in the error exit. If the allocation is successful, control falls through to the next statement in sequence, in this case, ERROR OFF. The ERROR OFF statement simply deactivates an error exit. So after an ERROR OFF statement, no error exit is in effect.

At any given point during the execution of a command procedure, only one error exit is in effect. So if you code several ERROR statements in a row, only the most recent one is in effect. As a result, it's not necessary to issue ERROR OFF statements if you're replacing one error exit with another. But if you don't provide a

```
ERROR DO
    WRITE UNABLE TO ALLOCATE &DATASET--COMPLETION CODE &LASTCC
    EXIT CODE(12)
    END
ALLOCATE DSNAME(&DATASET) DDNAME(SYSUT1)
ERROR OFF
```

Figure 6-5   An error exit

```
ERROR DO
    WRITE AN ERROR HAS OCCURRED DURING &SYSPCMD
    WRITE LAST CONDITION CODE WAS &LASTCC
    EXIT CODE(&MAXCC)
END
```

Figure 6-6   A generalized error exit

replacement error exit, you should use an ERROR OFF statement
to clear the previous error exit.

A generalized error exit   If you want, you can provide a generalized error exit like the one in figure 6-6. This simple routine
displays the command that was executing and the condition code
that resulted from the error, then exits with the highest condition
code encountered. For example, if an error occurs during an ALLO-
CATE command, the terminal user might see this:

```
AN ERROR HAS OCCURRED DURING ALLOCATE
LAST CONDITION CODE WAS 12
```

Of course, a generalized exit routine can easily become very complicated, testing for specific error conditions and even trying to
correct common ones.

An error exit with multiple exit points   In complicated error
exits, it's often necessary to leave the error exit at several points. To
do this, code a RETURN or EXIT statement at each point you want
to exit. For example, consider the error exit in figure 6-7, used to
trap errors from a COBOL command. When the condition code is
four or less, the error exit writes an error message, and then issues

```
ERROR DO
    IF &LASTCC <= 4 THEN DO
        WRITE YOUR PROGRAM CONTAINS MINOR ERRORS
        RETURN
        END
    IF &LASTCC > 4 THEN DO
        WRITE YOUR PROGRAM CONTAINS SERIOUS ERRORS
        EXIT CODE(&LASTCC)
        END
END
```

Figure 6-7   An error exit that uses both RETURN and EXIT statements

a RETURN statement to return control to the statement following the command that caused the error. But if the condition code is greater than four, the error exit writes a different error message and terminates the procedure with an EXIT statement.

Attention exits

When a terminal user presses the Attention key, PA1, any processing currently active is terminated, whether it's a TSO command, a foreground program, or a command procedure. In many cases, you need to disable the Attention key so the user can't interrupt a procedure in the middle of an important series of steps. To do this, you use the ATTN statement to establish an attention exit. An attention exit works just like an error exit except that it's invoked by the Attention key, not by an error condition.

Here's a simple attention exit:

```
ATTN WRITE YOU CANNOT INTERRUPT THIS PROCEDURE
```

If you issue this statement at the start of a procedure, the Attention key won't interrupt the procedure. To restore the function of the Attention key, issue the statement

```
ATTN OFF
```

or just

```
ATTN
```

since OFF is the default. Then, the user can once again use the Attention key to interrupt the procedure.

Of course, you can make an attention exit as complex as you want. You can allow the user to terminate the procedure under certain conditions. You can use the terminal I/O facilities I'll present in the next topic to verify that the user wants to terminate the procedure. Or you can perform any other type of special processing. The only restriction is that you can code only one TSO command, TSO subcommand, or null line in an attention exit. If you code a null line, control returns to the statement or command that was executing when the attention interrupt occurred. If the attention exit doesn't include a TSO command or subcommand or a null line, it must include a RETURN or EXIT statement. EXIT ends the CLIST, and RETURN returns control to the statement following the one that was executing when the interrupt occurred.

One word of warning: If you use an attention exit that doesn't terminate the CLIST, make sure it's not in effect when the procedure executes a loop. If it is, you'll be in trouble if the loop repeats indefinitely.

HOW TO USE NESTED PROCEDURES

When one procedure calls a second procedure, the procedures are said to be *nested*. The first procedure, that is, the one that does the calling, is an *outer procedure*. The procedure that is called is an *inner procedure*. Once the inner procedure has finished executing– either because all its statements have completed or because it issues an EXIT statement–control returns to the outer procedure. Execution then continues with the statement following the one that invoked the inner procedure.

You can nest many levels of procedures. In other words, one procedure can invoke a second procedure, which can in turn invoke a third procedure, and so on. As a result, a procedure can be both an inner and an outer procedure. Any given procedure is an inner procedure with respect to the procedure that invoked it, and an outer procedure with respect to the procedures it invokes.

Like many advanced command procedure facilities, you should limit your use of nested procedures. Two or three levels of nesting is acceptable, but if you need much more than that, your CLIST is getting too complex. You should consider using a high-level language like COBOL or PL/I instead.

How control options are passed among nested procedures

When you invoke a nested procedure, the environment set by any CONTROL statements in the outer procedure is passed to the inner procedure. Note, however, that the effect of any CONTROL statements in the inner procedure is *not* passed back to the outer procedure. When control returns to an outer procedure, the control options are restored to their status just before the inner procedure was invoked.

How to pass data between nested procedures

Unless you specify otherwise, the symbolic variables you use in a nested procedure are unique to that procedure. In other words, they can't be accessed by other procedures in the nest. This is true even if the variables have the same name. For example, if I code the statement

```
SET COUNT = 1
```

in both an inner and an outer procedure, two separate variables are established. So, if you change the value of &COUNT in one procedure, it doesn't effect the value of &COUNT in the other procedure. In many cases, however, an inner procedure needs to access data from its outer procedure. It can do that in one of two ways: by receiving values coded as parameters on the EXEC command that invokes it or by using global variables.

How to pass data as EXEC parameters   One way to pass data between procedures is to use parameters on the EXEC command that invokes the inner procedure and provide a PROC statement within the inner procedure. Figure 6-8 shows how to do this. Here, PROC1 invokes PROC2, passing it two parameters: &MEMBER and BG. PROC2 receives these parameters via its PROC statement.

Notice that the first parameter I passed is a symbolic variable. When you code a parameter as a symbolic variable, its value is substituted before it's passed to the inner procedure. So, in figure 6-8 for example, if the value of &MEMBER in PROC1 is MKTG1200, that value is passed to PROC2. Notice also that, although in this case the variable has the same name in both the outer and inner procedures, it doesn't have to.

```
Procedure PROC1

.
.
.
%PROC2 &MEMBER BG
.
.
.


Procedure PROC2

PROC 1 MEMBER BG
IF &BG = BG THEN DO
        .
        .
        .
```

Figure 6-8   Passing data among nested procedures as parameters

How to pass data as global variables   Another way to pass data
between nested procedures is to use *global variables.* When you use
global variables, they are available to any procedure in a group of
nested procedures that defines them. For example, figure 6-9
shows how a procedure named PROC1 defines two global variables, &MEMBER and &BG, using the GLOBAL statement

```
GLOBAL MEMBER BG
```

PROC2 contains an identical GLOBAL statement. Then, both
PROC1 and PROC2 can refer to &MEMBER and &BG.

There are a few rules that govern how you use the GLOBAL
statement. To begin with, you must list all global variables on a
GLOBAL statement before you refer to them in your procedure.
That causes a special problem when you want a variable received
as a parameter to be global. In short, you can't do it. For example,
this sequence of statements is invalid:

```
PROC 1 MEMBER
GLOBAL MEMBER
```

To get around this problem, create another variable for global use,
like this:

```
PROC 1 MEMBER
GLOBAL GMEMBER
SET GMEMBER = &MEMBER
```

```
Procedure PROC1

GLOBAL MEMBER BG
  .
  .
  .
%PROC2
  .
  .
  .


Procedure PROC2

GLOBAL MEMBER BG
IF &BG = BG THEN DO
      .
      .
      .
```

Figure 6-9   Passing data among nested procedures as global variables

Then, you can use &GMEMBER in your nested procedures.

It's important to realize that the global variables listed in a GLOBAL statement are positional. The actual names you use in the procedures that access the global variables don't matter. To illustrate, suppose an outer procedure uses the GLOBAL statement

```
GLOBAL VAR1 VAR2 VAR3 VAR4
```

while its inner procedure uses the GLOBAL statement

```
GLOBAL FIELD1 FIELD2 FIELD3 FIELD4
```

In this case, VAR1 in the outer procedure and FIELD1 in the inner procedure refer to the same global variable even though their names are different. That's because they appear in the same position in the GLOBAL statements. Similarly, VAR2 in the outer procedure and FIELD2 in the inner procedure refer to the same global variable. As you can imagine, nested procedures can become quite confusing if you refer to the same global variable using two or more names.

To further complicate matters, an inner procedure doesn't have to list all its outer procedure's global variables in its GLOBAL statement. For example, suppose a second inner procedure needs to access only the first two global variables defined above. You could code its GLOBAL statement like this:

```
GLOBAL PARM1 PARM2
```

Now, VAR1, FIELD1, and PARM1 all refer to the same global variable in three different procedures.

How to restrict the use of a nested procedure

Sometimes, you need to restrict a procedure so it can be executed only as a nested procedure. In other words, you need to make sure a TSO user doesn't invoke the procedure directly. To do that, include lines like these near the beginning of your procedure:

```
IF &SYSNEST = NO THEN DO
    WRITE YOU CANNOT INVOKE THIS PROCEDURE BY ITSELF
    EXIT
    END
```

&SYSNEST is a system control variable that contains YES if the current procedure was invoked from another procedure and NO if it was invoked directly by a TSO user. So, if &SYSNEST contains NO, this routine writes a message to the user and exits.

HOW TO USE SUBPROCEDURES

In general, you'll use nested procedures to perform generalized functions. That way, you can invoke them from many different procedures that require their function. In contrast, you'll generally use subprocedures to perform functions that are unique to a particular procedure. You code subprocedures in the same CLIST as the procedure that calls them rather than in a separate CLIST like nested procedures.

How to code a subprocedure

You code a subprocedure just like you do any other procedure except for two things: a subprocedure must begin with a labeled PROC statement, and it must end with an END statement. Figure 6-10 presents the general format of a subprocedure. The label on the PROC statement identifies the subprocedure. As you'll see in a

```
label: PROC ...
         .
         .
         .
       END
```

Figure 6-10   The general format of a subprocedure

minute, you use this label when you execute the subprocedure. The END statement passes control back to the statement following the one that executed the subprocedure.

If you use subprocedures, I recommend you include them at the end of your CLISTs. That way, they're easy to find and they don't get in the way of the control logic of the procedure.

How to invoke a subprocedure

You invoke a subprocedure using the SYSCALL statement. Figure 6-11 presents its format. On the SYSCALL statement, you specify the name of the subprocedure you want to execute and any data you want to pass to the subprocedure. I'll show you how to pass data in just a minute.

The name you code on the SYSCALL statement is the label on the PROC statement in the subprocedure. For example, in figure 6-12, I coded this SYSCALL statement:

```
SYSCALL ALLOCATE &MEMBER
```

Then, the CLIST gives control to the subprocedure labeled ALLOCATE.

How to pass data between a procedure and a subprocedure

Like nested procedures, the data you use in a procedure is independent of the data you use in its subprocedures, unless you specify otherwise. If you want to share data between a procedure and a subprocedure, you can do so in one of two ways: by passing the data as SYSCALL parameters or by using named global variables.

The SYSCALL statement

```
SYSCALL subprocedure-name [parameters]
```

Explanation

subprocedure-name	The name of the subprocedure to be invoked. A subprocedure name is the label on its PROC statement.
parameters	A list of valid CLIST expressions separated by blanks or commas.

Figure 6-11   The SYSCALL statement

How to pass data as parameters   The easiest way to pass data to a subprocedure is to code parameters on the SYSCALL statement that invokes the subprocedure. Although the parameters can be any valid CLIST expression, you usually use constants or symbolic variables. For example, in figure 6-12, I passed the variable named &MEMBER. Before it's passed, however, its real value is substituted for the symbolic variable. Then, the subprocedure receives this value via its PROC statement.

If you code the name of a variable without the ampersand on a SYSCALL statement, the name is treated as a constant. In figure 6-12, for example, if I had coded the statement

```
SYSCALL ALLOCATE MEMBER
```

the value MEMBER would have been passed to the subprocedure.

You can let the subprocedure know that the parameter is the name of a symbolic variable, however, by coding the name on a SYSREF statement following the PROC statement. To illustrate, consider figure 6-13. Here, the SYSCALL statement passes two parameters to the ALLOCATE subprocedure: &MEMBER and VOLUME. Even though VOLUME is the name of a symbolic variable, it's treated as a constant because it's specified without a leading ampersand. Following the PROC statement in the subprocedure, I coded a SYSREF statement that specifies &VOLUME. Then, any subsequent references to &VOLUME in the subprocedure refer to the &VOLUME variable in the calling procedure.

The calling procedure

.
.
.

```
SYSCALL ALLOCATE &MEMBER
```

.
.
.

The subprocedure

```
ALLOCATE: PROC 1 MEMBER
          .
          .
          .
          END
```

Figure 6-12   How to invoke a subprocedure

You should be aware that when you pass a symbolic variable this way, the variable name in the calling procedure and the variable name in the subprocedure identify the same variable. In other words, if you change the value of the variable in the subprocedure, the value of the variable in the calling procedure is changed too. As a result, when I set the value of &VOLUME to the value of the variable named &VOL1 in the subprocedure in figure 6-13, the value of &VOLUME in both the subprocedure and the calling procedure is changed.

How to pass data as global variables   You can also pass variables between a procedure and a subprocedure by defining them as *named global variables*. Named global variables are similar to the global variables you use with nested procedures. However, there are three differences. First, you use an NGLOBAL statement to identify them. On the NGLOBAL statement, you code the names of all the variables you want to define as global. If you code this statement in the calling procedure, you can reference the global variables in any subprocedure it calls. Second, you do not have to define the named global variables in each subprocedure that references them. That's because they're identified by name instead of by position like global variables. Third, you can't share them with

```
The calling procedure

.
.
.
SYSCALL ALLOCATE &MEMBER VOLUME
.
.
.


The subprocedure

ALLOCATE:  PROC 2 MEMBER VOLUME
           SYSREF &VOLUME
           .
           .
           .
           SET VOLUME = &VOL1
           .
           .
           .
           END
```

Figure 6-13   How to pass a variable name to a subprocedure

other CLISTs. You can only share them with the subprocedures within a single CLIST.

To illustrate, consider the procedure in figure 6-14. This procedure defines two named global variables with this statement:

```
NGLOBAL MEMBER VOLUME
```

Then, the procedure and any subprocedures it calls can refer to &MEMBER and &VOLUME. Note that you must list all named global variables on an NGLOBAL statement before you refer to them in a procedure. And, just like global variables, if you want a variable received as a parameter to be global, you have to create another variable for global use, then assign the value of that parameter to the named global variable.

How to pass a return code back to the calling procedure

You can pass a return code from a subprocedure to the calling procedure using the RETURN statement. To do that, include a

```
Calling procedure
   .
   .
   .
NGLOBAL MEMBER VOLUME
   .
   .
   .
SYSCALL ALLOCATE
   .
   .
   .


Subprocedure

ALLOCATE: PROC 0
          .
          .
          .
          SET VOLUME = &VOL1
          .
          .
          .
          END
```

Figure 6-14   How to pass data between a procedure and subprocedure using named global variables

CODE operand on the statement. For example, to return a code of 4, code this statement:

```
RETURN CODE(4)
```

Then, when control returns to the calling procedure, the value you specify is stored in the variable named &LASTCC.

Other considerations for using subprocedures

The control environment established in a calling procedure is passed to a subprocedure just like it is in a nested procedure. The effect of any CONTROL statements you code in a subprocedure, however, is not passed back to the calling procedure. When control returns to the calling procedure, the control options are restored to their status just before the subprocedure was invoked.

Subprocedures can also have their own error and attention exits. Then, when an error occurs or the user presses the Attention key during the execution of a subprocedure, control passes to the exit routine coded in the subprocedure. If there is no exit in the subprocedure, control passes to the exit routine coded in the calling procedure, if there is one. Otherwise, TSO terminates the procedure.

Finally, you should know that if a subprocedure contains a GOTO statement, it must branch to a label in the same sub-procedure. In other words, it can't branch outside of the proce-dure. In addition, it can't branch to the label on the PROC state-ment in the subprocedure.

Terms

exit routine
error exit
attention exit
nested procedure
outer procedure
inner procedure
global variable
named global variable

Objective

Given a problem requiring the use of the command procedure facil-ities described in this topic, create a command procedure for its solution.

Topic 2

CLIST facilities for terminal and file processing

In this topic, you'll learn how to use a variety of CLIST facilities that let you do simple input and output involving the terminal user and sequential files. First, you'll learn the basic elements for terminal and file I/O. Then, you'll learn two advanced I/O features: the READDVAL statement and the TERMIN statement.

BASIC CLIST ELEMENTS FOR TERMINAL AND FILE I/O

CLIST provides three basic statements for terminal I/O (WRITE, WRITENR, and READ) and four basic statements for file I/O (OPEN, GETFILE, PUTFILE, and CLOSFILE). After I explain how you code these statements, I'll present a complete command procedure that illustrates how the statements work together.

Terminal I/O features

Figure 6-15 summarizes the command procedure statements for terminal I/O. Since displaying messages to the terminal user is a critical function of just about any command procedure, I presented the WRITE statement in chapter 5. So here, I'll show you how to use just the WRITENR and READ statements.

The WRITENR statement The WRITENR statement works much the same as the WRITE statement. The only difference is that the WRITENR statement doesn't generate a carriage return at the end of the line (the NR stands for No Return). As a result, the cursor stays on the same line as the displayed text instead of returning to the start of the next line.

Statement	Function
`WRITE text`	Writes text to the terminal. Used to display error or informational messages.
`WRITENR text`	Writes text to the terminal but doesn't issue a carriage return. Used to prompt the user for input data.
`READ variables`	Reads values from the terminal into the variables listed. Used to accept data from a terminal user.

Figure 6-15   Command procedure statements used for terminal I/O

You use the WRITENR statement most often to prompt the user for input that will be processed later by a READ statement. For example, suppose you code this WRITENR statement:

```
WRITENR PLEASE ENTER YOUR SELECTION:
```

Here, the message

```
PLEASE ENTER YOUR SELECTION:
```

is displayed at the terminal, and the cursor is positioned right after the colon.

The READ statement   The READ statement accepts one or more values from the terminal user and stores them in the variables you specify. For example, suppose you code this sequence of statements:

```
WRITENR PLEASE ENTER YOUR SELECTION:
READ SELECTION
```

Here, the WRITENR statement displays a prompting message. Then, the READ statement accepts a response from the user. After the user enters a value and presses the Enter key, the READ statement stores the value in &SELECTION.

You can specify more than one variable in a READ statement, like this:

```
WRITE ENTER PRINCIPAL, TERM, AND INTEREST:
READ PRINCIPAL TERM INTEREST
```

Here, the WRITE statement prompts the user to enter three values. These values must be separated by spaces or commas. So if the user enters

    125000,30,10

the READ statement sets &PRINCIPAL to 125000, &TERM to 30, and &INTEREST to 10.

If the user enters more information than the READ statement requests, the extra information is ignored. For example, if you code the READ statement

    READ A B C D

and the user enters

    15,25,30,35,50

the last value, 50, is ignored because there's no corresponding variable specified on the READ statement.

Similarly, if the user omits a value from a READ statement, the corresponding variable is assigned a null value. So, for the previous READ statement, suppose the user enters

    15,20,25

Then, &D is given a null value since the user didn't supply a value for it.

To give a null value to a variable other than the last one in the sequence, the user enters two commas, like this:

    15,20,,25

Here, &A is set to 15, &B to 20, and &D to 25. &C is given a null value, since the double commas indicate that a value is omitted.

In general, you should always code one or more WRITE or WRITENR statements before a READ statement. And the WRITE statements should fully identify the data requested. That way, the terminal user always knows what type of response the procedure expects.

File I/O features

The CLIST facilities for file processing let you do simple input and output operations on sequential files. To process a sequential file in a CLIST, you must do four things: (1) use an ALLOCATE command to allocate the file; (2) use an OPENFILE statement to

Command/statement	Function
ALLOCATE DDNAME(ddname) DSNAME(data-set-name)	You use the standard TSO ALLOCATE command to prepare a data set for processing.
OPENFILE ddname [{ OUTPUT UPDATE INPUT }]	Opens the file. Mode is OUTPUT for output files, UPDATE for update files, or INPUT for input files. INPUT is the default. If an output file already exists and you want to add the new records on to the end of it, you must code MOD as the file's disposition in its ALLOCATE command.
GETFILE ddname	Reads a record from the file and places it in &ddname.
PUTFILE ddname	Writes the record contained in &ddname to the file.
CLOSFILE ddname	Closes the file.
FREE DDNAME(ddname)	Frees the file so it can be processed by other users.

Figure 6-16   Commands and procedure statements used for file I/O

open the file; (3) use one or more GETFILE or PUTFILE statements to read or write records in the file; and (4) use a CLOSFILE statement to close the file. In addition, you may use a FREE command to deallocate the file when you're done with it.

Figure 6-16 summarizes these elements. You already know how to use the ALLOCATE and FREE commands. So now I'll describe the four procedure statements.

The OPENFILE statement   Before you can read or write records in a file, you must open the file using an OPENFILE statement. On the OPENFILE statement, you specify the ddname allocated to the file and a processing mode (INPUT, OUTPUT, or UPDATE).

For example, the statement

```
OPENFILE SALESRPT OUTPUT
```

opens the file whose ddname is SALESRPT for output processing. Similarly, the statement

```
OPENFILE CUSTMST UPDATE
```

opens CUSTMST for both input and output processing. If you omit the processing mode or code INPUT, the file is opened for input processing. Thus,

```
OPENFILE ORDERS
```

opens ORDERS as an input file.

Normally, you code an ALLOCATE command just before an OPENFILE statement, like this:

```
ALLOCATE DDNAME(ORDERS) DSNAME(ORDERS.DATA)
OPENFILE ORDERS
```

Here, ORDERS is allocated and opened for input. If you're allocating an output file that already exists and you want to add records to the end of the file, be sure you code a file disposition of MOD on the ALLOCATE command. Otherwise, the existing records are overwritten by the new ones.

When you specify a ddname on an OPENFILE statement, that name becomes a symbolic variable whose real value represents the record area for the file. Thus, in the previous example, &ORDERS is used to store data written to or read from the file.

The GETFILE statement   The GETFILE statement reads a record from a file. On it, you specify the symbolic variable that corresponds to the ddname for the file. For example,

```
GETFILE ORDERS
```

performs a read operation for the ORDERS file, placing the input record in &ORDERS.

After you read a record, you can use the &SUBSTR built-in function to extract data from specific fields in the record. For example, if the first five positions of the input record contain an item number, you might code the SET statement

```
SET ITEMNO = &SUBSTR(1:5,&ORDERS)
```

to extract the item number from the record.

When an end-of-file condition occurs on a GETFILE statement, TSO returns a condition code of 400. Thus, to continue processing

after an end-of-file condition, you must supply an error exit, like
this:

```
ERROR DO
    IF &LASTCC = 400 THEN DO
        SET EOF = Y
        RETURN
        END
    ELSE
        EXIT
    END
```

Here, an IF statement tests to see whether the condition code is
400. If it is, a symbolic variable (&EOF) is given a value of Y. Then,
control returns to the statement following the GETFILE statement,
where you can test &EOF. If &LASTCC is not 400, a genuine error
has occurred, so the EXIT statement terminates the procedure.

The PUTFILE statement   The PUTFILE statement adds a record
to a file. For example, the statement

```
PUTFILE ORDERS
```

adds the record contained in &ORDERS to the ORDERS file.

Normally, you'll use one or more SET statements to build a
record before you issue a PUTFILE statement. For example, the
statements

```
SET ORDERS = &ITEMNO&DESCR&QUANTITY
PUTFILE ORDERS
```

concatenate &ITEMNO, &DESCR, and &QUANTITY to form the
record in &ORDERS before the PUTFILE statement transfers the
record to the file.

If you opened the file in UPDATE mode, a PUTFILE statement
overwrites the record read by the previous GETFILE statement. In
other words, the file is updated in place. Unfortunately, all updates
must be done sequentially. So to update the 50th record in a file,
you must first issue a GETFILE statement for each of the first 49
records.

The CLOSFILE statement   After you finish processing a file, you
should close it by issuing a CLOSFILE statement. For example,
here's a valid CLOSFILE statement for the ORDERS file:

```
CLOSFILE ORDERS
```

```
000100 ALLOCATE DDNAME(ORDER) DSNAME(ORDER.DATA) MOD
000200 OPENFILE ORDER OUTPUT
000300 WRITE PLEASE PLACE YOUR PUBLICATIONS ORDER
000400 WRITE
000500 WRITENR YOUR EMPLOYEE NUMBER:
000600 READ EMPNO
000700 WRITENR YOUR DEPARTMENT CODE:
000800 READ DEPTCODE
000900 WRITE
001000 SET NULL =
001100 DO UNTIL &STR(&DOCID) = &NULL
001200     WRITENR DOCUMENT-ID, QUANTITY (LEAVE BLANK TO END):
001300     READ DOCID QUANTITY
001400     IF &STR(&DOCID) ¬= &NULL THEN DO
001500         SET ORDER = &EMPNO &SYSUID &DEPTCODE &STR(&DOCID) &QUANTITY
001600         PUTFILE ORDER
001700         END
001800     END
001900 WRITE
002000 WRITE YOUR ORDER HAS BEEN PLACED
002100 CLOSFILE ORDER
002200 FREE DDNAME(ORDER)
```

Figure 6-17   The ORDER procedure

In addition, you may want to issue a FREE command to release the file.

A command procedure example

Figure 6-17 presents a simple command procedure that illustrates the statements for terminal and file I/O I've presented so far. This procedure is used to enter an order for one or more publications, such as IBM manuals or textbooks. First, it asks you to enter your employee number and department. Then, for each publication you want to order, it requests the document id and quantity. Finally, when you finish your order, it writes a record to a file named ORDER.

Figure 6-18 shows a sample execution of this procedure. Here, I invoke the procedure implicitly by entering %ORDER. Then, I provide my employee number (3822) and department code (D10) and order two manuals (1 copy each of GC26-3841 and GC28-0692).

```
READY
%ORDER
PLEASE PLACE YOUR PUBLICATIONS ORDER

YOUR EMPLOYEE NUMBER:  3822
YOUR DEPARTMENT CODE:  D10

DOCUMENT-ID, QUANTITY (LEAVE BLANK TO END):  GC26-3841,1
DOCUMENT-ID, QUANTITY (LEAVE BLANK TO END):  GC28-0692,1
DOCUMENT-ID, QUANTITY (LEAVE BLANK TO END):

YOUR ORDER HAS BEEN PLACED
READY
```

Figure 6-18   Executing the ORDER procedure

To be sure you understand how this procedure works, let's step through it line by line. Lines 100 and 200 allocate and open the ORDER file. The file is opened for OUTPUT, so records will be added to the file. And since I say MOD on the ALLOCATE command, existing records won't be overwritten; instead, the file is positioned after the last record when it's opened.

Lines 300 and 400 display the heading

PLEASE PLACE YOUR PUBLICATIONS ORDER

followed by a blank line. Then, line 500 prompts the user to enter an employee number that is read into &EMPNO by line 600. Similarly, line 700 prompts the user for a department code that is read into &DEPTCODE by line 800. And line 900 displays a blank line.

Line 1100 sets up a loop that accepts orders until the user enters a null value for the document id. Lines 1200 and 1300 prompt the user and read two values: &DOCID and &QUANTITY. If &DOCID isn't a null value, line 1500 builds the record containing &EMPNO, &SYSUID, &DEPTCODE, &DOCID, and &QUANTITY, leaving a space between each of the fields. Then, line 1600 writes the record to the file.

After the loop finishes, line 2000 writes the message

`YOUR ORDER HAS BEEN PLACED`

and lines 2100 and 2200 close and free the file.

I also want to point out the use of the &STR function in this procedure. I used this function with the &DOCID variable so the &DOCID variable wouldn't be evaluated. For example, the first document id entered is GC26-3841. If I had coded &DOCID without the &STR function, CLIST would try to subtract 3841 from GC26, causing an error. However, since I used the &STR function, that error doesn't occur.

HOW TO USE THE READDVAL STATEMENT

As I mentioned before, when you read a record from a file, the entire record is stored in the symbolic variable associated with the file. Then, you must use SET statements and the &SUBSTR function to extract individual fields from the record.

The READDVAL statement makes this process easier. Quite simply, the READDVAL statement reads one or more values from a system variable named &SYSDVAL. In &SYSDVAL, the values are separated by standard TSO delimiters (spaces or commas) just as if they had been entered by an operator. To illustrate, suppose &SYSDVAL contains this:

`JONES 103`

If you issue a READDVAL statement like this one:

`READDVAL NAME EMPNO`

&NAME is set to JONES and &EMPNO is set to 103. I'll show you how to get these values into &SYSDVAL in just a moment.

If one of the values in &SYSDVAL contains spaces, commas, or other special characters, it must be enclosed in apostrophes, or the READDVAL statement treats it as two values. For example, suppose &SYSDVAL contains this:

`'WILLIAM JONES, MD' 103`

Then, the previous READDVAL statement sets &NAME to WILLIAM JONES, MD and &EMPNO to 103. Notice that the apostrophes in &SYSDVAL aren't part of the value assigned by READDVAL.

If there are more variables in the READDVAL statement than values in &SYSDVAL, the extra variables are assigned null values. If there are fewer variables than values, the extra values are ignored. For example, suppose you code the READDVAL statement

`READDVAL NAME EMPNO TITLE`

and &SYSDVAL contains this:

`JONES 103`

Then, &NAME is set to JONES, &EMPNO is set to 103, and &TITLE is set to a null value. On the other hand, if &SYSDVAL contains

`TAYLOR 1750 SUPERVISOR 'APRIL 18, 1990'`

&NAME is set to TAYLOR, &EMPNO is set to 1750, &TITLE is set to SUPERVISOR, and the last value, April 18, 1990, is ignored. Note here that the READDVAL statement can extract values of varying lengths with the same variable.

How to assign and use the values in &SYSDVAL

In general, there are two ways you can assign values to &SYSDVAL so you can use the READDVAL statement. First, you can assign terminal input by coding a READ statement without any symbolic variables. Then, the entire text entered by the user is copied to &SYSDVAL.

A second, perhaps more useful, way to use &SYSDVAL is for file processing. For example, you might create a file whose records contain values separated by spaces or commas. When you process the file in your CLIST, you assign it a ddname of SYSDVAL. That way, any GETFILE statements for the file transfer records to &SYSDVAL, so you can use the READDVAL statement to extract the individual fields from the record.

To illustrate this technique, consider the LSTORDER procedure in figure 6-19. It reads the file created by the CLIST in figure 6-17, formatting and listing each record at the terminal. Figure 6-19 also shows the terminal output from the procedure using the ORDER file given.

The key to understanding this CLIST is understanding the DO loop in lines 1500 through 2200. In line 1600, a GETFILE statement reads a record from the file. Since the ddname for the file is SYSDVAL, the record is placed in &SYSDVAL. Then, line 1900 extracts five values from &SYSDVAL. Line 2000 writes those five

The LSTORDER procedure

```
000100 CONTROL NOFLUSH NOMSG
000200 ALLOCATE DDNAME(SYSDVAL) DSNAME(ORDER.DATA)
000300 OPENFILE SYSDVAL
000400 WRITE
000500 WRITE              PUBLICATIONS CURRENTLY REQUESTED
000600 WRITE
000700 WRITE EMP NO    USER ID    DEPT    DOCUMENT ID    QUANTITY
000800 WRITE
000900 SET EOF = N
001000 SET COUNT = 0
001100 ERROR DO
001200      SET EOF = Y
001300      RETURN
001400      END
001500 DO WHILE &EOF = N
001600      GETFILE SYSDVAL
001700      IF &EOF = N THEN DO
001800          SET COUNT = &COUNT + 1
001900          READDVAL EMPNO USER DEPTCODE DOCID QUANTITY
002000          WRITE &EMPNO    &USER    &DEPTCODE    &DOCID    &QUANTITY
002100          END
002200      END
002300 WRITE
002400 WRITE &COUNT RECORDS IN ORDER FILE
002500 CLOSFILE SYSDVAL
002600 FREE DDNAME(&SYSDVAL)
```

Figure 6-19   Executing a procedure that uses &SYSDVAL for file processing (part 1 of 2)

values with appropriate spacing so the report is formatted correctly.

The end-of-file logic is handled by the error exit in lines 1100 through 1400. Here, a symbolic variable (&EOF) is used to indicate the end-of-file condition. The error exit simply sets &EOF to Y and returns to statement 1700, the statement following the GETFILE that caused the error. &EOF is tested both by the DO-WHILE statement in line 1500 and the IF statement in line 1700.

HOW TO USE THE TERMIN STATEMENT

The TERMIN statement is an I/O statement unlike the ones found in other high-level programming languages. Basically, the TERMIN

The contents of the ORDER file

```
4939  MURAC  D10  GC28-4826  1
4939  MURAC  D10  SC28-6652  2
4939  MURAC  D10  GC30-5757  1
5037  STEVE  A33  GC22-7746  1
5037  STEVE  A33  SC22-7490  1
3822  DLOWE  D10  GC26-3841  1
3822  DLOWE  D10  GC28-0692  1
```

Resulting output

```
%LSTORDER


        PUBLICATIONS CURRENTLY REQUESTED

EMP NO   USER ID   DEPT    DOCUMENT ID   QUANTITY

4939     MURAC     D10     GC28-4826        1
4939     MURAC     D10     SC28-6652        2
4939     MURAC     D10     GC30-5757        1
5037     STEVE     A33     GC22-7746        1
5037     STEVE     A33     SC22-7490        1
3822     DLOWE     D10     GC26-3841        1
3822     DLOWE     D10     GC28-0692        1

7 RECORDS IN ORDER FILE
READY
```

Figure 6-19   Executing a procedure that uses &SYSDVAL for file processing (part 2 of 2)

statement returns control to the terminal user but provides a way for the user to return control to the command procedure. For example, suppose you code this statement:

```
TERMIN GO
```

When it's executed, control returns to the terminal user, who can enter any TSO commands or subcommands. But once the terminal

Command procedure statements

```
WRITE ENTER ALLOCATE COMMANDS FOR REQUIRED DATA SETS
WRITE ENTER 'GO' WHEN FINISHED
TERMIN GO
WRITE COMMAND PROCEDURE CONTINUING
```

Sample terminal session

```
  ENTER ALLOCATE COMMANDS FOR REQUIRED DATA SETS
  ENTER 'GO' WHEN FINISHED
  READY
ALLOCATE DDNAME(CUSTMST) DSNAME(CUSTMAST.DATA)
  READY
ALLOCATE DDNAME(SALESMN) DSNAME(SALESMAN.DATA)
  READY
ALLOCATE DDNAME(SALESRPT) DSNAME(*)
  READY
GO
  COMMAND PROCEDURE CONTINUING
  READY
```

Figure 6-20   Using the TERMIN statement

user enters the delimiter GO, control returns to the command
procedure.

Figure 6-20 shows a portion of a CLIST that uses TERMIN along
with a sample terminal session. If you follow the sample terminal
session, comparing it with the command procedure statements,
you can see that control returns to the terminal user when the
TERMIN statement is executed. The terminal user enters three
ALLOCATE commands that are processed by TSO. Then, the user
enters GO, which returns control to the command procedure.

If you want, you can specify more than one delimiter on a TERMIN statement, like this:

```
TERMIN GO CANCEL
```

Here, control is returned to the CLIST when the user enters GO or CANCEL. You can find out what delimiter the user entered by testing a system variable named &SYSDLM. After a TERMIN statement, &SYSDLM contains a number that corresponds to the delimiter entered by the user. So in this example, &SYSDLM contains 1 if the user enters GO; if the user enters CANCEL, &SYSDLM contains 2.

Since the TERMIN statement gives the terminal user complete control under TSO, you should use it only with experienced TSO users. And since you can code anything you want as a delimiter, you should always use a WRITE statement before a TERMIN statement to tell the user how to return to the procedure.

DISCUSSION

I presented just a brief introduction to the terminal and file I/O capabilities of CLIST in this topic. In general, I don't think you'll use these capabilities often. Interactive applications that involve extensive terminal and file I/O are usually best implemented under CICS or some other advanced communications monitor. But for short, uncomplicated applications that must be implemented in a CLIST, the terminal and file I/O features I presented here are sufficient.

Objective

Given a programming problem involving simple terminal and file handling, code a command procedure for its solution using the terminal and file handling features presented in this topic.

Section 3

REXX

The two chapters in this section show you how to create and use procedures using the REXX programming language. REXX is one of two procedure languages provided under TSO/E; the other, CLIST, was covered in section 2. Because CLIST is the older procedure language, it is more familiar and more widely used. The REXX language has been available under the VM operating system since the early 1980's, but didn't become available under TSO until TSO/E Version 2 was announced.

If you are experienced with CLIST programming, you might wonder why you should bother learning a new procedure language. There are two reasons. First, REXX is significantly more powerful than CLIST in many areas. And second, REXX is the "official procedure language" of IBM's SAA (System Applications Architecture), which means that it is available under several operating system environments, including VM and OS/2 on microcomputers.

Chapter 7

A basic subset of REXX facilities

As you gain experience with TSO, you'll often find yourself entering the same series of TSO commands repeatedly. In chapter 3, for example, I described the commands you must issue to invoke COBTEST, the VS COBOL II interactive debugger. In the simplest case, you must issue two commands to invoke COBTEST: an ALLOCATE command and the COBTEST command. If you're testing a program extensively, entering these commands for each test run can be a genuine inconvenience.

Under TSO, however, you can store a sequence of commands in a *procedure*. Then, you can invoke the procedure by name to cause MVS to execute each of its commands. As you can imagine, procedures can be real time-savers.

TSO provides two separate command procedure facilities that let you include high-level programming features in your command procedures. In section 2 of this book, I presented CLIST, which is the standard procedure language for TSO. Now, in this section, I'll present another procedure language: *REXX*. REXX, the standard procedure language for the VM/CMS operating system, is available under Version 2 of TSO and under the OS/2 operating system for microcomputers.

In the two topics of this chapter, I present a basic subset of REXX. In topic 1, you'll learn how to create and execute simple REXX procedures. Then, in topic 2, you'll learn the basic features of the REXX procedure language, such as variables, expressions, and logic control statements like IF, SELECT, and DO.

When you complete this chapter, you should be able to create REXX procedures of considerable complexity. And you'll be ready to learn how to use the more advanced REXX features presented in the next chapter.

Topic 1   An introduction to REXX procedures

Suppose you're in the process of testing and debugging a COBOL program named MKTG1200. As you proceed, you find yourself repeatedly issuing the commands to invoke the VS COBOL II debugger. To avoid entering these commands each time you test and debug the program, you can store them in a *REXX procedure*, sometimes called an *exec*. Then, you can issue the commands at any time by simply typing the name of the exec.

Figure 7-1 shows a procedure that contains the commands necessary to allocate a VS COBOL II program, invoke the debugger, and free the allocated file. I'll use this procedure as an example as I show you how to create and invoke a REXX procedure.

How to create a REXX procedure

You create a REXX procedure using a text editor, such as the ISPF edit option or the TSO EDIT command. Every line of a REXX exec should be either a REXX instruction or a TSO command. In fact, any line that isn't a valid REXX instruction is assumed to be a TSO command. Note in figure 7-1 that all the TSO commands are in quotes. In topic 2 of this chapter, I'll explain why. For now, though, just realize that you should enclose every TSO command you code in a REXX exec in quotes.

Notice the first line in figure 7-1:

```
/* REXX */
```

This is a comment that identifies the procedure as a REXX exec. Comments begin with the characters /* and end with the characters */. The first line of every REXX exec should be a comment that includes the word REXX. That's how TSO distinguishes REXX execs from CLISTs. The word REXX can appear anywhere in the comment, in upper- or lowercase letters.

REXX execs are usually stored as members of a partitioned data set whose type qualifier is EXEC. When you create the EXEC

```
/* REXX */
"ALLOCATE DSNAME(TEST.LOAD) DDNAME(LOADLIB)"
"COBTEST LOAD(MKTG1200:LOADLIB)"
"FREE DDNAME(LOADLIB)"
```

Figure 7-1   A simple REXX procedure

library, you should pattern it after the existing system-wide CLIST
procedure library, which should have a name like SYS1.CLIST. To
find out the name of the system CLIST procedure library, use the
TSO LISTALC STATUS command and note the name of the data set
assigned to SYSPROC. Then, to create a private exec library using
the system procedure library's characteristics, use the LIKE
operand on an ALLOCATE command, like this:

```
ALLOCATE DSNAME(EXEC) LIKE('SYS1.CLIST')
```

Here, a library named DLOWE.EXEC is created (assuming DLOWE
is the user-id) with the same characteristics as SYS1.CLIST.

Most EXEC libraries have either fixed-length records of 80 bytes
each or variable-length records of up to 255 bytes. If you need to
include a line that's longer than the maximum, you can continue it
to the next line by using a comma as a continuation character. For
example, consider this ALLOCATE command:

```
"ALLOCATE DSNAME(TEST.COBOL) DDNAME(SYSUT2) NEW CATALOG",
         "SPACE(100 10) CYLINDERS DIR(20)"
```

Here, the comma tells REXX that the command is continued on the
next line.

Although it isn't apparent in figure 7-1, it's common to mix
upper- and lowercase characters in a REXX procedure. As a result,
you should make sure that CAPS mode in your ISPF edit profile is
off. If the ISPF editor automatically converts any lowercase text
you enter to uppercase, simply enter the command CAPS OFF.

How to execute a REXX procedure

To execute a REXX procedure, you use the EXEC command. The
format of this command is shown in figure 7-2. As you can see, you
can code the EXEC command in two forms: explicit and implicit.

Explicit form of the EXEC command for REXX procedures

```
EXEC library-name(member-name) 'parameters' EXEC
```

Implicit form of the EXEC command for REXX procedures

```
[%] member-name parameters
```

Explanation

library-name	The name of the library containing the REXX procedure (a type qualifier of EXEC is assumed). May be omitted if the library is named user-id.EXEC.
member-name	The member name of the procedure to be invoked.
parameters	A parameter string to be passed to the procedure. The procedure may use an ARG instruction to parse this string into variables.
EXEC	Tells TSO that member-name is a REXX procedure rather than a CLIST.
%	Tells TSO to bypass the search of its command libraries and instead search SYSEXEC and SYSPROC directly.

Figure 7-2　The EXEC command

The explicit form of the EXEC command　On the *explicit form* of the EXEC command, you specify the word EXEC followed by the name of the exec library and member you want to execute. Assuming the name of the exec in figure 7-1 is MKTGTEST in DLOWE.TEST.EXEC, you can invoke it with this command:

```
EXEC TEST(MKTGTEST) EXEC
```

The EXEC keyword tells TSO that the procedure is a REXX exec rather than a CLIST procedure. TSO assumes that the type quali-fier for the library is EXEC, so you don't have to specify that in the command. And it assumes that the data set's high-level qualifier is your user-id, so usually you don't have to specify that either. In fact, for a library named user-id.EXEC, you can omit the library name entirely and just specify the member name, like this:

```
EXEC (MKTGTEST) EXEC
```

The implicit form of the EXEC command　On the *implicit form* of the EXEC command, you don't specify the word EXEC or the name of the library that contains the procedure. Instead, you specify just the procedure name, like this:

```
MKTGTEST
```

This command invokes the procedure named MKTGTEST. In a minute, I'll show you how to specify the library where the member is stored when you use the implicit form.

Notice that the implicit form of the EXEC command makes your exec look like another TSO command. In fact, it looks so similar that TSO has to search its own command libraries first to be sure it isn't a TSO command. Since you know it's not a TSO command when you enter it, type a percent sign in front of the procedure name, like this:

```
%MKTGTEST
```

The percent sign tells TSO that MKTGTEST is a procedure, not a command, so TSO doesn't search its command libraries. Using a percent sign in this way can result in better execution time, since TSO will find your procedure quicker.

As you can see in figure 7-2, both forms of the EXEC command let you pass parameters to the exec you're invoking. Don't worry about that for now, though. I'll explain how and when to code parameters on the EXEC command in topic 2 of this chapter.

Library allocation for the implicit form   When you use the implicit form of the EXEC command, TSO looks in the library allocated to the ddname SYSEXEC to find your procedure. As a result, before you issue an implicit EXEC command, you must allocate your command procedure library to SYSEXEC with an ALLOCATE command, like this:

```
ALLOCATE DDNAME(SYSEXEC) DSNAME(TEST.EXEC) SHR REUSE
```

SHR means that other TSO users can allocate this exec library as well. If you omit SHR, you have exclusive control of the exec library. REUSE means that SYSEXEC is freed and reallocated if it is currently allocated. If you don't code REUSE and SYSEXEC is already allocated, an error occurs.

You can also allocate REXX procedure libraries to SYSPROC, but that's usually used for CLIST procedure libraries. When both SYSPROC and SYSEXEC are allocated, TSO searches SYSEXEC first. That way, if both a REXX procedure and a CLIST have the same name, TSO executes the REXX procedure.

Command	Explanation
ALTLIB ACTIVATE USER(EXEC)	Activates a user exec library. Before you issue this command, use an ALLOCATE command to allocate your exec library to the ddname SYSEXEC.
ALTLIB DEACTIVATE USER(EXEC)	Deactivates the user exec library.
ALTLIB DISPLAY	Displays the current search order for procedure libraries.

Figure 7-3   The ALTLIB command

At some installations, if your REXX library is named according to shop standards, it's automatically allocated when you log on. Check with your supervisor to see if that's the case at your shop. If so, you won't have to allocate your exec library since your logon procedure allocates it for you.

If your shop uses MVS/ESA, you can also allocate your procedure library using the ALTLIB command. To do that, you must first allocate the library to the ddname SYSUEXEC, like this:

```
ALLOCATE DDNAME(SYSUEXEC) DSN(TEST.EXEC) SHR REUSE
```

Then, use an ALTLIB command to activate the user library:

```
ALTLIB ACTIVATE USER(EXEC)
```

The advantage of allocating your procedure library this way is that you don't have to worry about overriding the system-wide procedure library. That's because the system procedure library remains allocated under the ddname SYSEXEC or SYSPROC. When you use ALTLIB, TSO searches the SYSUEXEC library *before* it searches the system procedure library.

Figure 7-3 shows the most common forms of the ALTLIB command. As you can see, it also includes options to deactivate a user library and to display the order libraries are searched. You probably won't use these forms often, though.

How to invoke a procedure from ISPF   Keep in mind that the examples I've shown so far assume you're invoking the REXX procedure from the TSO READY prompt. To allocate the procedure library and invoke a procedure from ISPF, you have to make sure

ISPF knows you're issuing a TSO command rather than an ISPF command. You can do that from any ISPF panel by prefixing the command with the word TSO. Thus, to allocate a user exec library, you would enter these two commands in the ISPF primary command area:

```
TSO ALLOCATE DDNAME(SYSUEXEC) DSN(TEST.EXEC) SHR REUSE
TSO ALTLIB ACTIVATE USER(EXEC)
```

Then, to invoke a procedure from the user library, you would enter a command like this:

```
TSO %MKTGTEST
```

You can also use ISPF's primary option 6 to enter the TSO commands. When you do, you don't have to prefix the command with the word TSO.

There are two other ways to invoke a REXX procedure from ISPF. The first is from a member list displayed by the data set list utility, option 3.4. To do that, just type the name of the procedure you want to execute next to the member name. The second is as an *edit macro* from the ISPF editor. I'll show you how to do that in chapter 9.

Discussion

In this topic, I showed you how to create and execute a simple REXX procedure. Frankly, though, the REXX procedure in figure 7-1 isn't very useful because it's restricted to a single use: It invokes the COBOL debugger for the program named MKTG1200. In the next topic, you'll learn how to create more sophisticated REXX procedures that use symbolic variables and logic control statements to provide general-purpose functions.

Terms

procedure	explicit form
REXX	implicit form
REXX procedure	edit macro
exec	

Objectives

1. Allocate a REXX procedure library so you can invoke REXX procedures using the implicit form of the EXEC command.

2. Create and execute a simple REXX procedure that does nothing but execute TSO commands.

Topic 2   Completing the basic subset

REXX is more than just a facility that lets you put TSO commands into a procedure; it's a full-fledged programming language. Like all modern programming languages, it lets you create variables and use them in expressions to perform calculations or test for specific conditions. It provides a full set of control instructions, including IF-THEN-ELSE and a powerful DO instruction that gives you better control over looping than most compiled languages. And it lets you communicate with the terminal user by displaying messages and accepting data entered at the keyboard.

Unfortunately, REXX can be a difficult programming language to learn, especially for COBOL programmers. REXX has a syntax that, though simple, is very different from COBOL's syntax. Once you work with REXX a while, though, I think you'll come to appreciate it. But it can be a struggle at first.

In this topic, I'll present the basic features of the REXX programming language. First, I'll show you how to create REXX procedures that use instructions, variables, and expressions. Then, I'll show you how to receive command-line parameters and how to obtain input from the terminal user. Next, I'll present the four REXX logic control instructions: IF-THEN-ELSE, SELECT, DO, and EXIT. Finally, I'll show you how to debug a procedure using the interactive trace feature.

One important point to keep in mind as you read this topic is that REXX is an *interpreted* language rather than a *compiled* language. As a result, you don't have to compile and link-edit a REXX exec before you can use it. Instead, the REXX *interpreter* reads and interprets the instructions in your exec one at a time.

```
/* REXX */
arg Member Library
"ALLOCATE DSNAME("Library".LOAD) DDNAME(LOADLIB)"
"COBTEST LOAD("Member":LOADLIB)"
"FREE DDNAME(LOADLIB)"
```

Figure 7-4   A generalized REXX procedure that uses variables

HOW TO USE INSTRUCTIONS, VARIABLES, AND EXPRESSIONS IN A REXX PROCEDURE

Instructions, variables, and expressions are among the most basic features of any programming language. All programming languages have rules that govern how you use these features. For example, in COBOL, all statements must end with a period and all variables must be defined in the Data Division. In this section, you'll learn the rules you must follow when you use these features in REXX.

Figure 7-4 presents a sample procedure named COBTEST. I'll use this procedure as an illustration throughout this section. It's a generalized version of the MKTGTEST procedure I presented in figure 7-1. The procedure in figure 7-4 uses instructions, variables, and expressions to let you debug any COBOL program.

To invoke the COBTEST procedure, you list the name of the member you want to debug and the library that contains it as parameters on the command line, like this:

```
%COBTEST MKTG1200 MASTER
```

This command invokes COBTEST for a program named MKTG1200 in a library named DLOWE.MASTER.EXEC (assuming DLOWE is the user-id).

Instructions

Since REXX was not originally developed to run under TSO, the rules you must follow when you code its instructions are not the same as the coding rules for TSO commands. Before you begin creating REXX procedures that include even simple REXX instructions, you need to have a thorough understanding of these rules.

REXX uses a unique terminology to describe its syntax. A REXX procedure consists of one or more *clauses*. A clause is what most other programming languages call a statement or command. There are five types of REXX clauses: labels, keyword instructions, assignments (like x=5), host commands, and null clauses. The REXX procedure in figure 7-4 consists of five clauses: a null clause that contains only a comment, a keyword instruction (arg), and three host commands.

Before I go on, you should know about another type of null clause used in REXX procedures: blank lines. Blank lines are used frequently to separate sections of code. You'll see procedures that use blank lines for this purpose in the next chapter.

Each clause consists of one or more *tokens*, which also come in several types. The most common types of tokens are comments marked by /* and */, literal strings enclosed in quotation marks, numbers, operators (like + and -), and symbols, such as variable names, instruction keywords, and labels. Tokens are usually separated from one another by one or more spaces, but in some cases (such as comments, string literals, and operators), spaces aren't required. When REXX evaluates tokens, it converts lowercase letters to uppercase, unless the token is a string literal.

In general, you should code one REXX clause per line. If you want to code two or more REXX clauses on a single line, you should separate them with a semicolon, like this:

```
say; say; say
```

Here, the keyword instruction *say* is coded three times on the same line.

If a REXX clause is too long to fit on one line, you can continue it on the following lines. To do that, code a comma at the end of each continued line, like this:

```
"ALLOCATE DSNAME(TEST.COBOL) SPACE(100 50) TRACKS",
"DIR(10) DSORG(PS) RECFM(F,B) LRECL(80) BLKSIZE (6160)",
"RETPD(60)"
```

Notice here that the commas appear outside the quotation marks. That's because you cannot split a line in the middle of a token. Instead, you must split lines *between* tokens. If the commas had appeared inside the quotation marks, they would have been considered part of the string literals rather than continuation characters.

Frankly, terms like clause, token, and symbol are important only to people who write REXX interpreters, so I avoid them in this book. Whenever I use the word *instruction*, I'm referring to a keyword instruction or an assignment clause. I use the word *command* to refer to a clause that contains a TSO command. And I refer to tokens as what they are: comments, string literals, numbers, operators, variables, keywords, and labels.

Variables

A REXX variable is a symbol that takes on a value as a procedure executes. Since a variable's value can change from one execution of an exec to the next, the exec can perform differently with each execution.

Unlike other programming languages, REXX treats all variables as strings of characters. When necessary, REXX converts the contents of a string into numeric data so it can be operated on. But that conversion is strictly internal, so you don't have to worry about it.

Variable names can be up to 250 characters long and may include upper- and lowercase letters, numbers, and the special characters _@#$!?. A variable name should begin with a letter or special character. Thus, the variable names

```
a
MEMBER
Member1
```

are valid, while

```
1member
MEMBER*
a(37)
```

are not. For the sake of readability, it's best to keep your variable names meaningful, but short.

As I've already mentioned, REXX converts all lowercase letters to uppercase when you use them in a variable name. As a result, these three names represent the same variable:

```
FIRSTNAME
firstname
FirstName
```

It's common practice to mix upper- and lowercase letters within variable names to make them more readable.

In figure 7-4, I used two variables in the ALLOCATE and COBTEST commands: Library and Member. Before these commands are passed to TSO for processing, the values of the

variables are substituted for the variable names. For example, if
the value of Library is MASTER and the value of Member is
MKTG1200, the commands will be passed to TSO in this form:

```
ALLOCATE DSNAME(MASTER.LOAD) DDNAME(LOADLIB)
COBTEST LOAD(MKTG1200:LOADLIB)
```

That way, the MKTG1200 program will be debugged.

Notice that in figure 7-4, the variable names are placed outside
of the quotation marks. That's because REXX does not interpret
anything within quotation marks. As a result, if the variable names
were included in the quotation marks along with the rest of the
TSO commands, their values would not have been substituted.
Instead, they would have been treated as a part of the literal string.

REXX handles uninitialized variables in an unusual manner.
You might expect REXX to assign them null values, or leave their
values undefined like most other languages do. Instead, the value
of an uninitialized REXX variable is the name of the variable. So, if
you use a variable named Test before you initialize it, the variable's value is the string "TEST". (Remember, lowercase letters are
converted to uppercase.)

This is why it's a good idea to place the fixed portion of all TSO
commands inside quotation marks. If you code them outside the
quotation marks, REXX assumes each word in the command is a
REXX variable. In figure 7-4, that evaluation wouldn't cause any
problems. But in some cases, REXX might mistake a TSO command
keyword for a REXX variable with the same name. So to avoid
confusion, you should always place the fixed portion of any TSO
commands contained in an exec in quotation marks.

How to assign a value to a variable

The easiest way to assign a value to a variable in REXX is by using
an *assignment*. For example, the assignment

```
Count=0
```

sets the value of the variable Count to zero. And the assignment

```
Name="John Smith"
```

assigns the literal string *John Smith* to the variable Name.

The value you code on the right side of the equals sign can be a
simple number or literal string, as I've shown. Or, it can be a

Arithmetic operators

+	Addition
-	Subtraction
*	Multiplication
/	Division
%	Integer division
//	Remainder
**	Exponentiation

String operators

(blank)	Concatenate with intervening space.
||	Concatenate without intervening space.
(abuttal)	Concatenate without intervening space (only when syntactically discernable).

Figure 7-5   REXX arithmetic and string operators

complex REXX expression. You'll learn how to code expressions next.

How to use expressions

Although variables can be used individually, they are most useful when used in combinations with literals and other variables to form *expressions*. The two types of expressions you'll use most often are *arithmetic expressions* and *string expressions*. REXX also supports *conditional expressions* and *logical expressions*, but since they're used most often with conditional instructions (like IF), I'll explain them together a little later in this topic. Figure 7-5 lists the *operators* you use to construct arithmetic and string expressions.

REXX treats arithmetic expressions like most programming languages do. For example, it evaluates multiplication and division before addition and subtraction, but you can change that order by using parentheses. Thus, the expression 2+3*4 yields 14, but (2+3)*4 yields 20.

Example	As coded in exec	As interpreted by REXX
1	"DSN=" Var1	DSN= TEST
2	"DSN="||Var1	DSN=TEST
3	"DSN="Var1	DSN=TEST
4	"DSN="Var1"."Var2	DSN=TEST.LIST
5	"PARM=' "Var1","Var2"'"	PARM='TEST,LIST'
6	"DSN="Var1||Var2	DSN=TESTLIST

Note: In each example, the value of Var1 is TEST and the value of Var2 is LIST.

Figure 7-6   Examples of concatenation in string expressions

Two operators you may not be familiar with are % and //. The % operator returns the integer result of a division. For example, the expression 7/2 yields 3.5, but 7%2 yields 3. The // operator returns the remainder of a division. Thus, the result of 7//2 is 1.

String expressions are a little more complicated, because they involve two different types of *concatenation* and syntax that can be confusing. The examples in figure 7-6 should help clarify the rules.

In example 1, I used the most basic form of REXX concatenation. Here, two elements, a literal and a variable, are separated by a space. When this expression is evaluated, REXX substitutes the variable value and separates the concatenated elements with a single space. As a result, a space appears between the literal DSN= and the variable value TEST.

Example 2 shows the double-bar concatenation operator (||) that concatenates a literal and a variable without an intervening space. As you can see, the result of this expression is DSN=TEST. Example 3 shows that the concatenation operator in example 2 was not necessary, since the closing quotation mark lets REXX distinguish between the end of the literal and the beginning of the variable name. The REXX documentation refers to this type of concatenation as an *abuttal*.

Example 4 shows how a sequence of literals and variables can be concatenated together to form a more complex expression. Unfortunately, the two pairs of quotation marks in the expression can be confusing. So be sure you pair your quotation marks properly when you use this type of concatenation.

Example 5 shows how to include apostrophes in quoted literals. As you can see, mixing quotes and apostrophes together makes the expression even more difficult to decipher. So you have to be extra careful when you use both.

Example 6 shows how to concatenate two variables without an intervening space. Here, you have to use the double-bar concatenation operator (||). If you simply abut the two variable names, REXX can't distinguish them. Instead, it looks for a variable named Var1Var2.

How to use built-in functions in REXX expressions

You can also use *built-in functions* in a REXX expression to perform certain pre-defined calculations. To use a built-in function, simply code the name of the function followed by one or more arguments in parentheses, like this:

```
x=length(FirstName)
```

This assignment sets the variable x to the length of the FirstName variable.

REXX provides about 75 built-in functions that perform arithmetic calculations, convert data between different formats, manipulate strings, and return system information, such as the userid and the current time and date. Because many REXX procedures manipulate strings, I'll present those functions in the next chapter. And appendix C lists many of the REXX functions along with the arguments each requires.

How to use the RC built-in variable

Whenever REXX passes a command to TSO for execution, it stores the return code issued by that command in a special variable named *rc*. As a result, you can use the rc variable to determine whether or not a command executed properly. Usually, a return code greater than zero means the command encountered some sort of error condition. A return code of zero, however, always means the command executed successfully.

The ARG instruction

```
ARG variable [variable...]
```

Explanation

variable   Specifies one or more variables the data from the parameter string is parsed
                  into.

Figure 7-7   The ARG instruction

You'll see an example of the rc variable when I explain how to use conditional instructions like IF and SELECT.

HOW TO RECEIVE COMMAND-LINE PARAMETERS

When you invoke a REXX procedure, you can pass a parameter string to it by specifying the PARM operand on an explicit EXEC command, or by typing the parameter string after the procedure name on an implicit EXEC command. To receive the parameter string into one or more variables that can be processed in the exec, you use the ARG instruction.

Figure 7-7 shows the format of the ARG instruction. Like most REXX instructions, ARG has a simple format: It consists of the word ARG followed by one or more variable names. When the ARG instruction is executed, the parameter string specified for the procedure is *parsed*, and each word is placed in a variable. (A *word* is any sequence of characters delimited by one or more spaces. The spaces are discarded.) If there are more words in the parameter string than variables, the last variable specified in the ARG instruction receives the rest of the parameter string. If there are more variables in the ARG instruction than words in the parameter string, the extra variables are assigned null values.

Looking back at figure 7-4, you can see that it contains this ARG instruction:

```
arg Member Library
```

ARG instruction

```
arg Member Library
```

Example	Command used to invoke exec	Resulting value of Member	Library
1	%COBTEST MKTG1200 TEST	MKTG1200	TEST
2	%COBTEST MKTG1200	MKTG1200	(null)
3	%COBTEST MKTG1200 TEST LIST	MKTG1200	TEST LIST

Figure 7-8 How a parameter string is parsed into variables specified in an ARG instruction

Notice that this instruction is the first line of the exec. While it isn't necessary to code the ARG instruction near the beginning of the exec, it's a good idea.

Figure 7-8 gives three examples of how parameters specified on the command line are parsed into the variables specified by this ARG instruction. The first example shows a two-word parameter string parsed into two variables. The second example shows what happens when only one word is specified in the parameter string, and the third example shows what happens when three or more words are specified.

If you're familiar with CLIST, you're probably comparing the ARG instruction with the CLIST PROC statement. Because CLIST was designed specifically as TSO's procedure language, its PROC statement lets you receive parameters according to TSO's command syntax. As a result, it lets you receive keyword as well as positional parameters, and it lets you specify default parameter values. Unfortunately, the REXX ARG instruction doesn't provide this flexibility. Providing for keyword parameters and default parameter values in REXX requires additional programming. As a result, most REXX execs rely on positional parameters that can be easily parsed using the ARG instruction.

The SAY instruction

```
SAY  expression
```

The PULL instruction

```
PULL  variable  [variable...]
```

Explanation

expression	An expression to be displayed at the terminal. Usually a combination of string literals and variables.
variable	Specifies one or more variables the data entered by the terminal user is parsed into.

Figure 7-9   The SAY and PULL instructions

HOW TO OBTAIN INPUT
FROM THE TERMINAL USER

Rather than rely on command line parameters to set the value of REXX variables, you can also ask the terminal user to enter the values as the procedure executes. To do that, you have to use two REXX instructions: SAY, which displays a message on the terminal screen, and PULL, which receives a value entered from the keyboard. Figure 7-9 shows the format of these two instructions, and figure 7-10 shows a version of the COBTEST exec that uses these instructions to set the values of the Member and Library variables.

The operation of the exec in figure 7-10 is straightforward. The first SAY instruction asks the user to enter the name of the member to be debugged, and the first PULL instruction assigns the value entered into the variable Member. Then, the second SAY instruction asks for the name of the library and the second PULL instruction assigns the entered value into the variable Library. Notice I enclose the entire message displayed by the two SAY commands in quotation marks. If I don't, REXX treats the word *member* in the second SAY instruction as the variable Member, and displays the value of the variable rather than the literal as intended.

The PULL instruction works much like the ARG instruction, in that it treats the data entered by the user as a single character

```
/* REXX */
say "Enter the name of the member you want to debug"
pull Member
say "Enter the name of the library that contains the member"
pull Library
"ALLOCATE DSNAME("Library".LOAD) DDNAME(LOADLIB)"
"COBTEST LOAD("Member":LOADLIB)"
"FREE DDNAME(LOADLIB)"
```

Figure 7-10   A REXX procedure that obtains values from the terminal user

string, then parses it into one or more variables listed on the instruction. As a result, I can combine the entry of the member and library name into a single PULL instruction, like this:

```
pull Member Library
```

Then, the user has to type the name of the member and the library on the same line, separated by one or more spaces. Of course, the SAY instruction also has to be altered so it prompts the user for both values.

HOW TO CONTROL A PROCEDURE'S EXECUTION

Like other high-level languages, REXX provides extensive facilities to control the flow of execution through the procedure. These facilities include the IF-THEN-ELSE instruction, the SELECT instruction, the DO instruction, and the EXIT instruction. REXX does *not* include a GOTO instruction.

The IF instruction

You use the IF instruction when you want to perform one of two actions based on a condition that is either true or false. Figure 7-11 presents the format of the IF instruction. As you can see, you code the condition you want to test as an expression. If the expression is true, REXX executes the instruction associated with the THEN action. If the expression is false, REXX executes the instruction associated with the ELSE action, if one is coded.

The IF instruction

```
IF expression THEN
    instruction-1
[ELSE
    instruction-2]
```

Explanation

expression	A relational or logical expression that is either true or false.
instruction-1	A single TSO command or procedure instruction or a DO group that's executed if *expression* is true.
instruction-2	A single TSO command or procedure instruction or a DO group that's executed if *expression* is false.

Figure 7-11   The IF instruction

To illustrate, consider this simple IF instruction:

```
if Average > 1000 then
    say "The average is greater than 1000"
else
    say "The average is not greater than 1000"
```

This instruction displays one of two messages, depending on the value of the variable named Average.

REXX uses the values 1 and 0 to represent true and false conditions. Thus, any expression that yields a value of 1 is true, and any expression that yields a value of 0 is false. In most cases, you'll use one of two types of expressions with the IF instruction: relational expressions and logical expressions. Keep in mind, however, that you can also use any other expression that evaluates to 0 or 1.

Relational expressions   A *relational expression* compares two variables or expressions in a format similar to that found in most high-level languages. For example, in the previous IF instruction, the relational expression was this:

```
Average > 1000
```

This relational expression compares the value of the variable Average with the literal value 1000. And the relational expression

```
Count+1 < Total*Units
```

compares the value Count+1 with the value Total*Units.

Operator	Function
=	Equal
==	Strictly equal
>	Greater than
<	Less than
>>	Strictly greater than
<<	Strictly less than
<> or ><	Not equal
>=	Greater than or equal to
<=	Less than or equal to
>>=	Strictly greater than or equal to
<<=	Strictly less than or equal to
\ or ¬	Not; used before operator to reverse meaning

Figure 7-12   Relational operators

Figure 7-12 lists the *relational operators* you can use in a relational expression. Notice that you can use the normal algebraic forms familiar to BASIC, PL/I, and COBOL, or you can use a unique set of relational operators that test for *strict relations*. For example, these two expressions are not the same:

```
A = B
A == B
```

In the first, REXX ignores leading and trailing blanks and the mixture of upper- and lowercase letters when it compares the values. Thus, the strings "YES" and " Yes" are considered equal. In contrast, when you use the strictly-equal-to operator, REXX checks to see if the strings are identical. So "YES" and " Yes" are not strictly equal.

Logical expressions   Using the *logical operators* shown in figure 7-13, you can combine two or more relational expressions to form a

Operator	Function
&	And; true if both conditions are true.
|	Or; true if either or both conditions are true.
&&	Exclusive Or; true if either but not both conditions are true.

Figure 7-13   Logical operators

logical expression. If you use the AND operator (&), all the relational expressions involved must be true for the entire expression to be true. For example, the expression

    50 < 75 & 100 > 75

is true, and the expression

    A < X & B < X & C < X

is true if A, B, and C are all less than X; otherwise, it's false.

If you use the OR operator (|), only one of the relational expressions must be true for the entire expression to be true. For example, the expression

    50 < 75 | 80 < 75

is true because 50 is less than 75, even though 80 is not. However, the expression

    100 < 75 | 80 < 75

is false since neither 100 nor 80 is less than 75.

When you use the exclusive OR operator (&&), the entire expression is true if either expression is true, but not if both expressions are true. Thus,

    50 < 75 && 80 < 75

is true, since 50 is less than 75 but 80 is not. But the expression

    50 < 75 && 60 < 75

is false, because both 50 and 60 are less than 75.

If an expression contains both AND and OR conditions, REXX evaluates all the ANDs from left to right, then combines them with the ORs from left to right. I recommend you avoid mixing AND with OR, however, because the resulting expressions are often very confusing. For example, try to determine what's meant by this expression:

```
A < X & B < X | C < X && D < X & E < X
```

Even knowing the order of evaluation REXX uses doesn't make this expression any easier to follow.

DO groups   One limitation of the IF instruction is that you can code only one instruction for the THEN and ELSE actions. Fortunately, there's a facility called a *DO group* that lets you code a series of instructions that REXX treats as a single instruction.

To code a DO group in an IF instruction, enter the word DO, followed by one or more instructions, followed by the word END, like this:

```
if Average > 1000 then do
    say "The average is greater than 1000"
    Over1000=Over1000+1
    end
```

Here, REXX treats the two instructions in the DO group as if they were a single instruction.

Nested IF instructions   Within an IF instruction, or within a DO group under the control of an IF instruction, you can code another IF instruction. If you do, the IF instruction is said to be *nested*. Within a nested IF instruction, each ELSE clause is paired with the previous unpaired IF.

Since ELSE clauses are optional, you can code nested IF instructions in a variety of different forms. In each case, however, you should use indentation to show the levels of nesting. In particular, you should align each ELSE clause with its corresponding IF instruction so you can easily see how IF and ELSE instructions are paired. But be careful. Your indentation doesn't affect how REXX interprets your exec. In other words, REXX always pairs each ELSE with the previous IF instruction, regardless of what your indentation shows.

To illustrate, figure 7-14 shows some common variations for three levels of nesting. Note that in each case, the indentation corresponds to the way TSO interprets these instructions.

REXX provides a special instruction, NOP, that is sometimes useful when you use nested IF instructions. It lets you code a THEN or ELSE that doesn't do anything. To illustrate, figure 7-15 shows the structure of a nested IF instruction that specifies ELSE

Example 1

```
IF expression THEN DO
    instructions
    IF expression THEN DO
        instructions
        IF expression THEN DO
            instructions
            END
        END
    END
```

Example 2

```
IF expression THEN DO
    instructions
    IF expression THEN DO
        instructions
        IF expression THEN DO
            instructions
            END
        ELSE DO
            instructions
        END
    ELSE DO
        instructions
        END
ELSE DO
    instructions
    END
```

Example 3

```
IF expression THEN DO
    instructions
    END
ELSE IF expression THEN DO
    instructions
    END
ELSE IF expression THEN DO
    instructions
    END
```

Figure 7-14   Some common examples of nested IF statements

```
IF expression THEN
     IF expression THEN
          instruction
     ELSE
          NOP
ELSE
     instruction
```

Figure 7-15   Using NOP in an IF instruction

NOP. If I had omitted ELSE NOP, the last ELSE would have been paired with the second IF, not the first IF.

The SELECT instruction

One of the limitations of the IF instruction is that it lets you specify only two actions: one to take if the condition is true, the other if the condition is false. The SELECT instruction lets you specify more than two possible actions to take depending on the results of a condition test. For example, suppose you want to display an error message that explains the meaning of a return code whose value can be 0, 4, 8, 12, or 16. To do this with IF instructions, you have to nest a series of them, each testing the value of the return code. With the SELECT instruction, however, you can perform this processing with a single test.

Figure 7-16 presents the format of the SELECT instruction. To use it, you code the word SELECT followed by a series of WHEN clauses. Each WHEN clause resembles an IF instruction: It includes a condition test and a single instruction that's executed if the condition is true. You can code multiple instructions on a WHEN clause by coding them as a DO group, just like on an IF instruction. Following the WHEN clauses, you can code an OTHERWISE clause. The instruction in the OTHERWISE clause is executed if none of the WHEN conditions are true. After the WHEN clauses and the optional OTHERWISE clause, you must code END to end the SELECT structure.

To illustrate how the SELECT structure works, consider figure 7-17. Here, the SELECT instruction tests for the value of a return code from a DELETE command. If the return code is 4, 8, or 12, a SAY instruction displays a message on the terminal that indicates

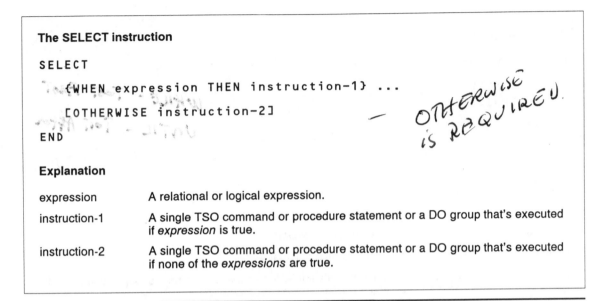

Figure 7-16   The SELECT instruction

```
select
      when  rc=4  then  say  "Warning message issued"
      when  rc=8  then  say  "Processing incomplete"
      when  rc=12 then  say  "Processing unsuccessful"
      when  rc=16 then  do
            say "Severe error"
            exit 16
            end
end
```

Figure 7-17   A SELECT instruction that tests a return code

the severity of the error. If the return code is 16, a SAY instruction displays a message and the procedure is terminated with an EXIT instruction. (I'll present the EXIT instruction later in this topic.) On this SELECT instruction, I don't code an OTHERWISE clause because the WHEN clauses account for all the possible return codes from a DELETE command, except zero, for which no action is required.

The DO instruction

```
DO   [ variable=from-exp [to-exp] [by-exp] ]

     [ {UNTIL}   expression ]
       {WHILE}

     instructions...

END
```

WHILE - Test First

UNTIL - Test After

Explanation

variable	A symbolic variable that controls the execution of the DO loop.
from-exp	Specifies the initial value of *variable*.
to-exp	Specifies the terminal value of *variable*.
by-exp	Specifies the amount that's addes to *variable* each time the loop is executed. If omitted, the default is one.
expression	A relational or logical expression that controls the execution of the DO loop.
instructions	A sequence of TSO commands or procedure statements. If coded on the DO-WHILE instruction, they're executed as long as *expression* is true. If coded on the DO-UNTIL instruction, they're executed as long as the condition is false. And if coded on a DO instruction with the repeat option, they're executed until *variable* reaches the value of *to-expression*.

Figure 7-18   The DO instruction

The DO instruction for looping

Earlier in this topic, I mentioned that REXX does not provide a GOTO instruction. Instead, it provides comprehensive looping control with the DO instruction. Figure 7-18 shows the format of the DO instruction when used to control a loop. As you can see, it can include a repeat option, a condition option, or both.

The DO repeat option   The DO repeat option lets you vary the value of a variable for each execution of the instructions in the DO group. This is similar to the PERFORM VARYING statement in COBOL or the FOR statement in BASIC. For example, the DO instruction

```
do Count=1 to 100 by 1
```

The Procedure

```
/* REXX */
do Power=0 to 16
     say Power  2**Power
     end
```

The resulting output

```
0   1
1   2
2   4
3   8
4   16
5   32
6   64
7   128
8   256
9   512
10  1024
11  2048
12  4096
13  8192
14  16384
15  32768
16  65536
```

Figure 7-19   A program that calculates powers of 2 from 0 to 16

varies the value of the Count variable from 1 to 100. If you omit the BY phrase, the assumed increment is 1. So the instruction

```
do Count=1 to 100
```

has the same effect.

You can also omit the TO phrase. But if you do, you should be sure to provide some other way to terminate the loop, such as a condition option (UNTIL or WHILE). Otherwise, the loop will execute indefinitely.

Figure 7-19 shows an example of a REXX procedure that uses a DO loop with a repeat option. This exec simply displays the powers of 2 from 0 to 16. Each iteration of the DO loop executes a SAY instruction that calculates a power of 2 based on the Power variable and displays the result.

The Procedure

```
/* REXX */
say "What power of two do you wish to calculate?"
say "Enter a null line to end"
do until Power=""
    pull Power
    if Power<>"" then
        say "2**"Power "is" 2**Power
    end
say "Goodbye"
```

The resulting output

```
 What power of two do you wish to calculate?"
 Enter a null line to end"
5
 2**5 is 32
12
 2**12 is 4096

 Goodbye
```

Figure 7-20   A procedure that displays the powers of two for values entered by the operator

The DO condition option   The DO instruction's condition option lets you specify a condition that's evaluated to determine when the loop should stop executing. If you specify WHILE, the loop continues to execute as long as the condition is true. If you specify UNTIL, the loop executes as long as the condition is false.

There is one significant difference between WHILE and UNTIL you should know about. If you specify WHILE, REXX evaluates the condition before each execution of the loop. Thus, if the condition is false to begin with, the instructions in the loop are never executed when you specify WHILE. In contrast, if you specify UNTIL, REXX evaluates the condition after each execution of the loop. As a result, the instructions in the loop are always executed at least once when you specify UNTIL.

Figure 7-20 shows a REXX procedure that displays powers of two for values entered by the operator. In each pass through the DO loop, a PULL instruction obtains a value from the user, and a SAY instruction calculates and displays the corresponding power of two. The loop continues until the user enters a null line.

The DO count instruction

```
DO count
    instructions...
END
```

The DO FOREVER instruction

```
DO FOREVER
    instructions...
END
```

Explanation

count   Specifies the number of times *instructions* are executed.

instructions   A sequence of TSO commands or procedure statements.

Figure 7-21   Two other forms of the DO instruction

By the way, you can combine the repeat and condition options in a single DO group. For example, consider this DO group:

```
do Count=1 by 1 until Name=""
    instructions...
    end
```

Here, the variable Count is incremented by 1 each time through the loop, and the loop continues until the variable Name is null.

Two other DO loop forms   Figure 7-21 illustrates two other forms of the DO instruction you may use on occasion. The first, DO count, simply repeats the instructions in the DO group the specified number of times. When you use this form of the DO instruction, no variable is incremented during the loop execution.

The second, DO FOREVER, repeats the loop indefinitely. When you use DO FOREVER, you should be sure to provide some other way for the loop to terminate. Otherwise, the loop will do just what it says: execute forever. To exit a DO FOREVER loop, use a LEAVE instruction, like this:

```
do forever
    instructions...
    IF condition THEN LEAVE
    instructions...
end
```

Frankly, there aren't many situations where a DO FOREVER loop with a LEAVE instruction couldn't be better coded with a DO WHILE or DO UNTIL loop. So I recommend that you avoid the DO FOREVER loop altogether.

The EXIT instruction

You use the EXIT instruction to terminate your REXX procedure. If you code just the word EXIT, REXX returns you to TSO. If you also include a return code, like this:

```
exit 12
```

your exec returns the *condition code* you specify (in this case, 12) when it ends.

In general, there are two places where you issue an EXIT instruction. The first is at the end of your exec. Although you don't have to code an EXIT instruction there, it's often a good idea. The second is where you detect an error condition and want to abort the exec immediately. I showed you an example of that in the SELECT instruction in figure 7-17. In that case, you should issue an EXIT instruction that sets an appropriate condition code.

HOW TO DEBUG A REXX PROCEDURE INTERACTIVELY

With the features I've presented so far in this topic, you can create REXX procedures of considerable complexity. Of course, the more complex your procedure is, the more error prone it is. Fortunately, REXX provides a feature called *interactive tracing* that makes it easy to locate errors in a REXX procedure. When you use interactive tracing, REXX displays each instruction before it executes it, displays the results of any expressions that were evaluated, and lets you enter commands that can alter how your procedure executes.

There are several ways you can start an interactive tracing session. The easiest is to include the command TS at the beginning of your procedure, as figure 7-22 shows. When the TS command is executed, REXX enters trace mode. Then, you can debug the procedure interactively.

```
/* REXX */
"ts"
say "Enter the name of the member you want to debug"
pull Member
say "Enter the name of the library that contains the member"
pull Library
"ALLOCATE DSNAME("Library".LOAD) DDNAME(LOADLIB)"
"COBTEST LOAD("Member":LOADLIB)"
"FREE DDNAME(LOADLIB)"
```

Figure 7-22   A REXX procedure that starts an interactive trace

The TS command is classified as a *TSO/REXX command*, which means it's a TSO command that can be used only in a REXX procedure. Because it's a TSO command, you should enclose it in quotation marks when you use it.

Another way to start an interactive trace is to press the PA1 key while a REXX procedure is executing. Then, you can enter the TS command to start the interactive trace. Yet another alternative is to issue the TSO command EXECUTIL TS before you invoke the REXX procedure. Then, TSO automatically places you in interactive trace mode when the procedure begins.

For each instruction in the procedure, interactive trace follows this sequence: (1) it displays the instruction exactly as it appears in the procedure, prefixing the instruction with the line number and the characters *-*; (2) it evaluates any expressions in the instruction and displays the results of the evaluation, prefixed with >>>; (3) it executes the instruction (in the case of a PULL instruction, this requires you to enter data); (4) it evaluates any expressions that result from the instruction's execution and displays them; and (5) it pauses for input.

Whenever interactive trace pauses for input, you can do one of two things. You can simply press the Enter key, which tells REXX to continue with the next procedure instruction. Or, you can enter a REXX instruction for immediate execution. For example, you could enter a SAY instruction to display the contents of a variable, or you could enter an assignment to set the value of a variable.

Figure 7-23 shows a portion of a trace session for the procedure that was presented in figure 7-22. Here, you can see the execution of three lines from the procedure: a SAY instruction that displays a

```
      5 *-* say "Enter the name of the library that contains the member"
        >>>    "Enter the name of the library that contains the member"
Enter the name of the library that contains the member

      6 *-* pull Library
test
        >>>    "TEST"

      7 *-* "ALLOCATE DSNAME("Library".LOAD) DDNAME(LOADLIB)"
        >>>    "ALLOCATE DSNAME(TEST.LOAD) DDNAME(LOADLIB)"
```

Figure 7-23   A portion of a REXX interactive debugging session

message on the terminal, a PULL instruction that obtains data from the user, and an ALLOCATE command that's passed to TSO.

To help you understand how interactive tracing works, follow along with this figure as I explain it line-by-line. The first line shows the SAY instruction as it appears in line 5 of the procedure. Since the SAY instruction includes an expression, the next line (prefixed by >>>) displays the results of the expression. In this case, since the expression is a simple literal string, it appears the same in both lines. The third line is the result of the SAY instruction: the literal string that displays at the terminal.

After the say instruction executes, the procedure pauses so you can enter a debugging command or continue. At this point, the procedure is not ready to accept a value for the Library variable, since it hasn't yet executed the PULL instruction. So, I just press the Enter key to tell REXX to continue. Next, REXX displays the PULL instruction in line 6 of the procedure and waits for me to enter the data. After I type the word *test* and press the Enter key, REXX evaluates the expression and displays the results of the evaluation. Notice here that REXX converted the lowercase letters I entered to uppercase.

Having completed the PULL instruction in line 6, REXX once again pauses so I can enter a command or continue. When I press the Enter key to continue, REXX displays line 7, the ALLOCATE command, first as it appears in the procedure, and then after it has been evaluated. Here, you can see how the Library variable has been replaced by its value.

DISCUSSION

As I said at the start of this topic, REXX can be a difficult language to learn, especially if most of your programming experience is in COBOL. The best way to learn REXX is to spend some time writing simple procedures, finding out what works and what doesn't. If you're a little confused about some of the REXX elements I've presented in this topic, a little experience will help clear things up.

Terms

interpreted language
compiled language
interpreter
clause
token
assignment
expression
arithmetic expression
string expression
conditional expression
logical expression
operator
concatenation

abuttal
built-in function
parse
word
relational expression
relational operator
strict relation
logical operator
DO group
nested IF instruction
condition code
interactive tracing
TSO/REXX command

Objectives

1. Use variables to create a generalized command procedure.

2. Use the ARG instruction to receive values entered as command line parameters.

3. Use the SAY and PULL instructions to display messages on the terminal screen and receive data entered at the keyboard.

4. Use the IF-THEN-ELSE, SELECT, DO, and EXIT instructions to control the flow of execution in a REXX procedure.

5. Use the interactive trace feature to debug a REXX procedure.

Chapter 8

Advanced REXX facilities

In this chapter, I present a variety of advanced REXX programming facilities. Although you won't need these features for simple execs that just execute a few TSO commands, you'll find that these features let you create REXX execs that do much more. In short, these features make REXX as powerful as most high-level programming languages.

This chapter is divided into four topics. Topic 1 presents the REXX facilities that let you manipulate strings. In it, you'll learn how to use advanced forms of parsing and how to use REXX's built-in string handling functions. Topic 2 presents two advanced methods of managing data: compound variables and the stack. You'll use these features whenever you create an exec that needs to deal with large amounts of data. Topic 3 shows you how to create and use functions, subroutines, and error exits. Finally, topic 4 shows you how to read and write data from a file.

Topic 1   REXX facilities for string manipulation

As a procedure language, one of REXX's strengths is its ability to deal with strings. You've already seen some of its string-handling capabilities, such as the way it parses data obtained with an ARG or PULL instruction into variables. I don't know of any other widely-used programming language that can perform this kind of operation as easily as REXX.

In this topic, you'll learn more about REXX's string-handling features. First, you'll learn more about how parsing works. Then, you'll learn how to use REXX's built-in functions for string manipulation.

HOW TO PARSE STRINGS

As you already know, both the ARG and PULL instructions parse data from a string into one or more variables. Each variable contains one word from the string, unless the number of words in the string doesn't match the number of variables provided. If you provide too many variables, the extra variables are set to nulls. If you don't provide enough variables, the last variable you specify contains the extra words from the string. The only difference between the ARG and PULL instructions is the source of the string that's parsed. For the ARG instruction, the string that's parsed is passed to the procedure as a parameter. For PULL, the string is read from the terminal.

The ARG and PULL instructions are actually abbreviated versions of a more comprehensive instruction for parsing strings: PARSE. The PARSE instruction lets you parse strings from several sources and gives you additional control over how the data is parsed. After I show you how to use the PARSE instruction, I'll show you how to code advanced parsing options on a PARSE, ARG, or PULL instruction.

The PARSE instruction

Figure 8-1 shows the format of the PARSE instruction. You can use this instruction to parse data from one of five sources. The first source, ARG, works just like the ARG instruction: It parses data from a string passed to the procedure as a parameter. The only difference between the ARG and PARSE ARG instructions is that ARG converts all lowercase letters to uppercase, but PARSE ARG doesn't. If you specify UPPER on a PARSE ARG command, however, data *is* converted to uppercase. So the PARSE UPPER ARG instruction performs exactly the same function as the ARG instruction.

The next two sources, EXTERNAL and PULL, might seem a little confusing at first. If you specify EXTERNAL, data is parsed from a string read from the terminal. If you specify PULL, data is usually read from the terminal, but REXX checks a data storage area called the *stack* first. You'll learn about the stack in topic 2 of this chapter, but for now, just realize that if you don't use the stack, EXTERNAL and PULL have the same effect. (If you want to be certain that data is read from the terminal rather than the stack, use the PARSE EXTERNAL rather than the PULL or PARSE PULL commands.)

The last two sources let you parse data from an expression or a single variable. The PARSE VALUE instruction evaluates an expression, then parses the result. The PARSE VAR instruction parses a single variable. The difference between these two instructions is the WITH keyword. It's required on the PARSE VALUE instruction so REXX can tell when the expression ends and the list of variables to parse data into begins. Because the PARSE VAR instruction parses data from a single variable, the WITH keyword isn't necessary.

For all forms of the PARSE instruction, the list of variables you specify to receive the parsed data is called the *template*. A template can contain other information besides a simple list of variables. Depending on how you specify the template, it can result in any of three types of parsing techniques: word parsing, literal parsing, or column parsing. Here, I'll describe each of these techniques. (One other form of parsing, called multiple string parsing, can be used only in an ARG or PARSE ARG instruction. I'll explain how it works in topic 3 of this chapter, when I show you how to create subroutines and functions.)

The PARSE instruction

PARSE [UPPER] $\left\{ \begin{array}{l} \text{ARG} \\ \text{EXTERNAL} \\ \text{PULL} \\ \text{VALUE expression WITH} \\ \text{VAR} \end{array} \right\}$ template

Explanation

UPPER	Specifies that all lowercase letters are to be translated to uppercase as they are parsed.
ARG	Specifies that the argument string passed to the program, function, or subroutine is to be parsed.
EXTERNAL	Specifies that data read from the terminal is to be parsed.
PULL	Specifies that the string at the top of the data stack is to be parsed. If the stack is empty, data is read from the terminal and parsed.
VALUE	Specifies that an expression is to be evaluated and its result parsed.
VAR	Specifies that the value of a single variable is to be parsed.
template	Specifies one or more variable names, string literals to indicate delimiters, or numeric literals to indicate column positions.

Figure 8-1   The PARSE instruction

Word parsing

Word parsing is the form of parsing you're already familiar with. When you specify a simple list of variables in a template, REXX places one word in each, discarding any spaces that occur between words. If there are more variables in the template than there are words in the string, the extra variables are set to nulls. If there are more words in the string than variables in the template, the last variable is assigned the remainder of the string, blanks and all.

Figure 8-2 shows three examples of word parsing. In each example, I assigned a literal value to a variable named String, used a PARSE VAR instruction to parse the string, and used SAY instructions to display the contents of the template variables. By comparing the resulting output for each example with the value of the String variable and the form of the PARSE instruction, you should have no trouble understanding how word parsing works. (Keep in mind that the results would be the same for any form of the PARSE instruction. The only difference would be the source of the string that's parsed.)

Example 1 shows how two words in the String variable are parsed into variables named Member and Library. Here, Member receives the string *mktg1200* and Library receives the string *test*. Example 2 shows the same parse operation, but with UPPER specified on the PARSE instruction. As you can see, the lowercase letters in the string are converted to uppercase as the string is parsed.

Example 3 shows what happens when the String variable contains more words than the variables in the template can accommodate. Here, the Options variable is assigned the string *list xref lib*.

In some cases, the fact that the last variable might contain more than one word can create problems. To avoid that situation, you can code a period to serve as a *placeholder* for a variable in the template. Any data that would have been parsed into a variable at the location of the period is discarded. If you place the period at the end of the template, any extra words in the string won't be parsed into the last variable you specify.

To illustrate, figure 8-3 shows two parsing examples, one without and the other with a period placeholder at the end of the template. In example 1, the Library variable is assigned the excess data from the String variable. In example 2, the period placeholder prevents that. Here, the string *list xref lib* is simply discarded, and the word *test* is assigned to the Library variable.

You can also use a period placeholder in the middle of a template, as shown in example 3 in figure 8-3. In this example, the word *mktg1200* is assigned to Member, the string *list xref lib* is assigned to Options, and the word *test* is discarded.

Literal parsing

Although REXX's standard word parsing is useful for most situations, it only recognizes words delimited by spaces. To parse words separated by anything else, you have to use *literal parsing*.

To use literal parsing, you code the delimiter character as a string literal between the variables in the template on the PARSE instruction. Figure 8-4 shows three examples of how this works. In example 1, the words in the string are separated with a comma, and a comma is specified as a literal string between the Library

Example 1

```
String="mktg1200 test"
parse var String Member Library
say Member
say Library
```

Result:

```
mktg1200
test
```

Example 2

```
String="mktg1200 test"
parse upper var String Member Library
say Member
say Library
```

Result:

```
MKTG1200
TEST
```

Example 3

```
String="mktg1200 test list xref lib"
parse var String Member Library Options
say Member
say Library
say Options
```

Result:

```
mktg1200
test
list xref lib
```

Figure 8-2 Three examples of word parsing

Example 1

```
String="mktg1200 test list xref lib"
parse var String Member Library
say Member
say Library
```

Result:

```
mktg1200
test list xref lib
```

Example 2

```
String="mktg1200 test list xref lib"
parse var String Member Library .
say Member
say Library
```

Result:

```
mktg1200
test
```

Example 3

```
String="mktg1200 test list xref lib"
parse var String Member . Options
say Member
say Options
```

Result:

```
mktg1200
list xref lib
```

Figure 8-3   Using a period as a place holder

and Member variables in the template. To parse this string, REXX assigns everything before the comma to the Member variable and everything after the comma to the Library variable.

Example 2 shows one of the pitfalls of literal parsing. Here, the words in String are *not* separated with commas as the template expects them to be. Since REXX can't find a comma delimiter, it assigns the entire string to the Member variable, and a null value

Example 1

```
String="mktg1200,test"
parse var String Member "," Library
say Member
say Library
```

Result:

```
mktg1200
test
```

Example 2

```
String="mktg1200 test"
parse var String Member "," Library
say Member
say Library
```

Result:

```
mktg1200 test
```

Example 3

```
String="mktg1200 test data /list xref lib"
parse var String Member  Library . "/" Options
say Member
say Library
say Options
```

Result:

```
mktg1200
test
list xref lib
```

Figure 8-4   Three examples of literal parsing

to the Library variable. Unfortunately, REXX does not provide a
way to parse words separated by any one of several delimiters.

Example 3 in figure 8-4 shows how you can use a period
placeholder to discard data that appears before a delimiter. In this
case, the first two variables are parsed using standard word

The procedure

```
/* REXX */
say "Enter a series of commands separated by semicolons"
parse pull Commands
say
do while Commands<>""
    parse var Commands SubCommand ";" Rest
    say SubCommand
    Commands=Rest
    end
```

A sample execution

```
 Enter a series of commands separated by semicolons
up;right 5;down;down;left;stop

 up
 right 5
 down
 down
 left
 stop
```

Figure 8-5   A REXX procedure that extracts data from a string

parsing. Then, everything else up to the first slash is discarded, and the data after the slash is assigned to the Options variable.

Figure 8-5 illustrates a technique that is sometimes useful when multiple options or commands separated by a delimiter are specified in a single string. Here, I use a DO instruction to parse the string one command at a time. Each time the Commands string is parsed, it is broken into two variables: SubCommand, which contains the first command in the string, and Rest, which contains everything after the first semicolon. Then, the assignment

```
Commands=Rest
```

replaces the previous Commands string with the portion of the string that hasn't yet been processed. This continues until the Commands string is null, indicating that each command in the string has been processed.

Example 1

```
String="10358152Belt Sander"
parse var String ItemNo 6 Vendor 9 Description
say ItemNo
say Vendor
say Description
```

Result:

```
10358
152
Belt Sander
```

Example 2

```
String=10358152Belt Sander"
parse var String ItemNo 6 9 Description
say ItemNo
say Description
```

Result:

```
10358
Belt Sander
```

Figure 8-6   Four examples of numeric templates (part 1 of 2)

Numeric templates

Numeric parsing lets you parse data from specific character locations in a string. For example, you could parse the data in character positions 1 through 5 into one variable, the data in character positions 6 through 8 into a second variable, and the rest of the string into a third. Figure 8-6 shows four examples of numeric parsing.

To use numeric parsing, you code one or two numbers for each variable in the template. The first number, which you code before the variable, represents the starting position of the data to be parsed. The second number, which you code after the variable, represents the character immediately to the right of the last character to be parsed. If you omit either number, REXX uses the current character position based on the parsing it's done to that point. If you omit the starting position for the first variable, 1 is

Example 3

```
String=10358152Belt Sander"
parse var String ItemNo +5 Vendor +3 Description
say ItemNo
say Vendor
say Description
```

Result:

```
10358
152
Belt Sander
```

Example 4

```
String=10358152Belt Sander"
parse var String ItemNo +5 Vendor +3 1 ItemSpec +8 Descrip-
tion
say ItemNo
say Vendor
say ItemSpec
say Description
```

Result:

```
10358
152
10358152
Belt Sander
```

Figure 8-6   Four examples of numeric templates (part 2 of 2)

assumed, and if you omit the ending postion for the last variable, the end of the string is assumed.

To illustrate, example 1 in figure 8-6 shows how to parse a string into three variables based on character positions. Here, the first variable, ItemNo, will be parsed from character positions 1 through 5. The second variable, Vendor, will be parsed from character positions 6 through 8. And the third variable, Description, will contain the characters from position 9 to the end of the string. Note that I omit the ending positions for each variable. When you're parsing data from adjacent positions in the string, there's no reason to specify ending positions.

Example 2 shows how to parse data from non-adjacent string positions. In this example, I need only two fields from the input string: ItemNo and Description. Thus, I specified 6 as the ending position for ItemNo and 9 as the starting position for Description. (Remember that the ending position specifies the character to the right of the last character you want parsed.)

Example 3 shows how you can specify *relative positions* in a template. When you precede a number with a plus sign, REXX adds it to the previous character position to determine the new *absolute position*. Since the template in example 3 starts at position 1 by default, coding +5 for the ending position is the same as coding 6. And the +3 moves the character position from 6 to 9. Using relative positions can sometimes make your numeric templates easier to follow, especially if you're parsing data from fields that aren't adjacent.

There's no rule that says you have to parse the string from left to right, or that you can parse data only once. For instance, consider example 4 in figure 8-6. Here, I use relative positions to parse the ItemNo and Vendor variables from positions 1-5 and 6-8. Next, I reset the starting position for the ItemSpec field to position 1 and specify its length as 9 characters. Then, I parse the Description variable as before. As you can see, the result of this parse is that the data for the ItemNo and Vendor variables is also used to create the ItemSpec variable.

HOW TO USE BUILT-IN FUNCTIONS FOR STRING HANDLING

In addition to its powerful parsing feature, REXX provides 25 built-in functions for manipulating strings. Figure 8-7 presents the format and a brief description of each of these functions. Most of the functions in figure 8-7 fall into one of three broad categories: character-oriented functions, word-oriented functions, and formatting functions.

How to use character-oriented functions

Character-oriented string functions let you manipulate strings on a character-by-character basis. The character-oriented functions

ωstRing = translate (string)

Function	Description
ABBREV(string1,string2,n)	Returns 1 (true) if *string2* is an abbreviation of *string1*; otherwise returns 0 (false). *String2* must contain at least *n* characters. The default value for *n* is 1.
CENTER(string1,len)	Returns a string of length *len* where *string1* is centered. The returned string is padded with spaces on the left and right if necessary.
COMPARE(string1,string2)	Returns 0 (false) if *string1* and *string2* are the same; otherwise, returns the position of the first character that differs.
DELSTR(string,n,len)	Deletes *len* characters from *string* beginning at position *n*. If *len* is omitted, the rest of the string is deleted.
DELWORD(string,n,len)	Deletes *len* words from *string* beginning with the *n*th word. If *len* is omitted, the rest of the string is deleted.
FIND(string,phrase)	Returns the word number of the first occurrence of *phrase* in *string*. Returns 0 (false) if *phrase* is not found.
FORMAT(number,before,after)	Returns a string that contains a formatted number with *before* characters on the left of the decimal point and *after* characters on the right. The returned string is padded on the left with spaces and on the right with zeros if necessary.
INSERT(string1,string2,n,len)	Inserts *string1* into *string2* at the character location *n*. If *len* is specified, *string1* is padded to the specified length.
LASTPOS(string1,string2,start)	Returns the character position of the last occurrence of *string1* in *string2*. If specified, the search begins at location *start*.
LEFT(string1,len)	Returns a string of length *len* where *string1* is left-aligned. The returned string is padded with spaces on the right if necessary.
LENGTH(string)	Returns the length of *string*.

Figure 8-7   REXX string-handling functions (part 1 of 2)

result = Datatype (string, type)
  ↳ A = Alpha Num   ε / IF TRUE
    N = Numeric

Function	Description
OVERLAY(string1,string2,n,len)	Replaces *len* characters in *string2* starting at position *n* with the characters in *string1*. The default for *len* is the length of *string1*.
POS(string1,string2,start)	Returns the character position of the first occurrence of *string1* in *string2*. If specified, the search begins at location *start*.
REVERSE(string)	Reverses the characters in *string*.
RIGHT(string,len)	Returns a string of length *len* where *string* is right-aligned. The returned string is padded with spaces on the left if necessary.
STRIP(string,option,char)	Deletes spaces (or character *char*) from *string* based on the value specified for *option*: L deletes leading characters, T deletes trailing characters, and B deletes both leading and trailing characters.
SUBSTR(string,n,len)	Returns a substring of length *len* extracted from *string* beginning at position *n*.
SUBWORD(string,n,len)	Returns a substring of length *len* words extracted at the *n*th word of *string*.
TRANSLATE(string,table1,table2)	Translates the characters in *string* found in *table2* to the corresponding characters in *table1*. If both tables are omitted, translates *string* to uppercase.
VERIFY(string,ref)	Returns 0 (false) if all characters in *string* also appear in the string *ref*. Otherwise returns the position of the first character in *string* that doesn't appear in *ref*.
WORD(string,n)	Returns the *n*th word in *string*.
WORDINDEX(string,n)	Returns the character position of the *n*th word in *string*.
WORDLENGTH(string,n)	Returns the length of the *n*th word in *string*.
WORDPOS(string1,string2,start)	Returns the word number of the first occurrence of *string1* in *string2*. If specified, the search begins at word *start*.
WORDS(string)	Returns the number of words in *string*.

Figure 8-7   REXX string-handling functions (part 2 of 2)

```
/* REXX */

/*  JobChar has been assigned to previous job character */

ValidJobChars="ABCDEFGHIJKLMNOPQRSTUVWXYZ0123456789A"

JobCharPos=pos(JobChar,ValidJobChars)+1
JobChar=substr(ValidJobChars,JobCharPos,1)

say "Now submitting job" userid||JobChar
```

Figure 8-8   A REXX procedure that uses character oriented functions

you'll use most are LENGTH, SUBSTR, and POS. The LENGTH function determines the number of characters in a string. The SUBSTR function extracts a portion of a character string based on the starting character position and length you specify for the substring. And the POS function determines whether or not one character string occurs within another string, and returns the starting position if it does.

Figure 8-8 shows a portion of a REXX procedure that uses the POS and SUBSTR functions to determine which letter to append to a user-id to form a job name. For this routine to work, the JobChar variable must first be set to the character that was used for the user's last job. Then, this routine determines the character to use for the next job. For example, if the previous job character was K, this routine sets JobChar to L.

Figure 8-8 begins by assigning a string containing all of the valid job characters to a variable named ValidJobChars. The characters appear in the string in the order they will be selected. Notice that the string ends with an A. That way, if JobChar is 9, it's changed to A, thus returning to the start of the list.

The next line determines the position of the current job character (JobChar) within the ValidJobChars string, and adds one to it to set the position of the next character. For example, if JobChar is C, the POS function returns 3, and the JobCharPos variable is assigned a value of 4. Keep in mind that the POS function always finds the first occurrence of the string it looks for. So if JobChar is A, JobCharPos will be set to 2 because the POS function returns the position of the first A in the string, not the position of the A at the end of the string.

The next instruction uses the SUBSTR function to assign a new value for the JobChar variable:

```
JobChar=substr(ValidJobChars,JobCharPos,1)
```

This function extracts a 1-character string from the ValidJobChars variable, starting at the position indicated by the JobCharPos variable. So if JobCharPos is 4, JobChar is assigned the letter D.

Finally, the last line in figure 8-8 simply displays a message indicating the job name that will be used for the job. The job name is formed by concatenating the user's user-id (obtained with the USERID function) with the JobChar variable. So if the user-id is DLOWE and JobChar is D, the line

```
Now submitting job DLOWED
```

is displayed.

Although POS, SUBSTR, and LENGTH are the character-oriented string functions you'll use most, some of the others are also useful. For example, the VERIFY function lets you make sure that each character in one string occurs in a second string. If so, the VERIFY function returns a value of 0 (false). So, if you want to make sure that a user enters only the letters A, B, or C, you could code an IF instruction like this:

```
if verify(String,"ABC") then
    say "Invalid entry"
```

Then, if any characters other than A, B, or C appear in the variable String, the "Invalid entry" message is displayed.

Another useful function is TRANSLATE, which lets you change all occurrences of one character to another character. Earlier in this chapter, I mentioned that one of the PARSE instruction's weaknesses is that it can recognize only one delimiter at a time. One way around that limitation is to use a TRANSLATE function to convert all delimiters to spaces; then, the PARSE instruction will recognize them. For example, the instruction

```
NormString=translate(String,"  ",",;")
```

converts every comma or semicolon in String to a space and assigns the translated string to NormString.

```
 100   /* REXX */
 200   parse upper arg Language Options
 300
 400   ValidLanguages="COBOL ASM EXEC CLIST C PLI FORT"
 500   if wordpos(Language,ValidLanguages)=0 then
 600       say "Unrecognized language:" Language
 700   else
 800       say "Language:" Language
 900
1000   List=1; Xref=0; Load=0
1100   do Count=1 to words(Options)
1200       String=word(Options,Count)
1300       select
1400           when abbrev("LIST",String,2)    then List=1
1500           when abbrev("NOLIST",String,4)  then List=0
1600           when abbrev("XREF",String)      then Xref=1
1700           when abbrev("NOXREF",String,3)  then Xref=0
1800           when abbrev("LOAD",String,2)    then Load=1
1900           when abbrev("NOLOAD",String,4)  then Load=0
2000           otherwise say "Unrecognized option:" String
2100           end
2200       end
2300   say
2400   say "Options in effect:"
2500   if List then say "     LIST"
2600           else say "     NOLIST"
2700   if Xref then say "     XREF"
2800           else say "     NOXREF"
2900   if Load then say "     LOAD"
3000           else say "     NOLOAD"
```

Figure 8-9   A REXX procedure that uses word-oriented functions

How to use word-oriented functions

Many of the functions listed in figure 8-7 are *word-oriented*. In other words, they recognize the words within a string, and discard the spaces surrounding them. Three of these word-oriented functions, WORDS, WORDPOS, and WORD, are equivalent to the LENGTH, POS, and SUBSTR character-oriented functions. The WORDS function returns the number of words in a string, the WORDPOS function returns the position of a word in a string, and the WORD function extracts a single word from a string.

Figure 8-9 shows a REXX procedure that uses several of the word-oriented functions. Here, the user enters a Language, such as COBOL, and one of several options. (For the sake of simplicity, this procedure implements only three options: LIST, XREF, and LOAD.) It lets the user abbreviate the options, using only as many characters as necessary to distinguish the options from one another. Thus, X, XR, and XRE are valid abbreviations for XREF. LI and LIS are valid abbreviations for LIST, but L is not, since that might be confused with the LOAD option. In addition, the user can enter the negative forms of the options (NOLIST, NOXREF, and NOLOAD) to turn them off. The negative forms can be abbreviated too.

In line 200, the command line argument is parsed into two variables: Language and Options. Line 400 sets up a variable named ValidLanguages that contains each acceptable language as a separate word. Then, line 500 uses a WORDPOS function to find out if the Language variable is one of the words listed in ValidLanguages. If it isn't, the WORDPOS function returns a value of zero (false), and an error message is displayed.

Line 1000 initializes three variables that will be used to keep track of options that have been set. A value of 1 means the option is on, and a value of 0 means the option is off. Notice that List is initialized to 1, but Xref and Load are initialized to 0. That way, the default condition for the LIST option is on, and the default condition for both XREF and LOAD is off.

Line 1100 sets up a DO loop that executes once for each word in the Options variable, incrementing a variable named Count on each pass through the loop. Notice how it uses the WORDS function to determine how many words are in Options. Then, line 1200 uses the WORD function to extract the word indicated by the Count variable from the Options string.

The SELECT instruction in line 1300 evaluates the word extracted in line 1200 and determines if it represents a valid option. Each WHEN clause uses an ABBREV function to determine if the word is an abbreviation of one of the valid options (LIST, NOLIST, XREF, NOXREF, LOAD, or NOLOAD). If so, the WHEN clause sets the appropriate variable to 1 or 0. If the word isn't recognized by any of the WHEN clauses, an error message is displayed.

Finally, the IF instructions beginning at line 2500 display the current option settings based on the values of the List, Xref, and Load variables.

Format function	---- Num values ----		
	20796	3175.337	91.6
format(Num,,2)	"20796.00"	"3175.34"	"91.60"
format(Num,,0)	"20796"	"3175"	"92"
format(Num,5,2)	"20796.00"	" 3175.34"	" 91.60"

Figure 8-10   Formatting numeric data with the FORMAT function

How to use the formatting functions

Four of the string-handling functions listed in figure 8-7 are designed to manipulate strings so they can be displayed in a suitable format. Three of these *formatting functions*, LEFT, RIGHT, and CENTER, take two arguments each: a string and a number representing a length. All three return a string of the specified length, with the input string aligned at the left, right, or center of the output string. These functions are especially useful when you want to line up columns of information displayed with SAY instructions.

The fourth of these functions, the FORMAT function, lets you control the size of numeric output by specifying how many digits you want to appear before and after the decimal point. Figure 8-10 shows how three different FORMAT functions format three numeric values. In the first two examples, I omit the number of digits that should appear before the decimal point. As a result, REXX used as many digits as necessary, and each number resulted in a different length string. The third example specifies five digits before the decimal point and two after. Notice how REXX inserted leading spaces when necessary so that each string would have the same length.

Figure 8-11 shows a simple procedure that uses the FORMAT function to align numeric output. This procedure simply displays the powers of 2 from 0 to 16. It uses two FORMAT function calls: the first specifies 2 digits before the decimal point, the other 8. As you can see, the resulting output is properly aligned.

The procedure

```
/* REXX */
do Power=0 to 16
    say format(Power,2) "     " format(2**Power,8)
    end
```

The resulting output

```
 0           1
 1           2
 2           4
 3           8
 4          16
 5          32
 6          64
 7         128
 8         256
 9         512
10        1024
11        2048
12        4096
13        8192
14       16384
15       32768
16       65536
```

Figure 8-11   A REXX procedure that uses the FORMAT function

Terms

stack
template
word parsing
placeholder
literal parsing
numeric parsing
relative position
absolute position
character-oriented string function
word-oriented string function
formatting function

Objectives

1. Use the PARSE instruction to properly parse a text string using word, literal, or numeric templates.

2. Given a programming problem involving string manipulation, code an appropriate solution using the string-handling functions presented in this topic.

Topic 2

Advanced REXX
data management features

Although REXX variables are adequate for most of the data your procedures will require, they are not designed to store large amounts of data. In this topic, you'll learn about two advanced REXX features that are: compound variables and the REXX data stack.

HOW TO USE COMPOUND VARIABLES

A *compound variable* in REXX is similar to an array or table in other languages. It lets you create a set of variables that can be accessed together as a group or individually using subscripts. The syntax you use for compound variables may be confusing at first, but you'll have no trouble with it once you get used to it.

To illustrate how compound variables work, figure 8-12 presents an exec that calculates batting averages for the members of a baseball team. This exec begins by asking the terminal user to enter the name, times at bat, and number of hits for each player on the team. Then, it displays a formatted listing of the players' batting averages. To keep track of the data for each player, this exec uses compound variables.

To format a compound variable name, you specify a *stem* (a variable name followed by a period) and the subscript variable. As REXX evaluates the compound variable name, it uses the subscript variable's value to determine what occurrence of the compound variable to access. For example, the batting average exec uses four compound variables:

```
First.Count
Last.Count
AtBats.Count
Hits.Count
```

The procedure

```
100   /* REXX */
200   say "Enter each player's first and last name, times at bat, and hits"
300   say "Enter a null line to end"
400   say
500   do Count=1 by 1 until First.Count=""
600       pull First.Count Last.Count AtBats.Count Hits.Count
700       end
800   Max=Count-1
900   say
1000  say "PLAYER                AVG"
1100  say "==================== ====="
1200  do Count=1 to Max
1300      Name=First.Count Last.Count
1400      Average=Hits.Count/AtBats.Count
1500      say left(Name,20) format(Average,1,3)
1600      end
```

A sample execution

```
 Enter each player's first and last name, times at bat, and hits
 Enter a null line to end

Billy Biggs 41 18
Johnny Anderson 35 19
Mary Johnson 37 21
Cici Anderson 30 14
Marty Smith 28 16


 PLAYER               AVG
 ==================== =====
 BILLY BIGGS          0.439
 JOHNNY ANDERSON      0.543
 MARY JOHNSON         0.568
 CICI ANDERSON        0.467
 MARTY SMITH          0.571
```

Figure 8-12   A batting average procedure that uses compound variables

If the value of Count is 3, these compound variables reference variables named First.3, Last.3, AtBats.3, and Hits.3. When the value of Count is 5, a different set of variables is referenced: First.5, Last.5, AtBats.5, and Hits.5.

You can create tables with two or more dimensions simply by using two or more subscripts. For example, the compound variable

Rate.Zone.Class has two subscripts: Zone and Class. If Zone is 5 and Class is 3, the compound variable references the variable Rate.5.3.

To use compound variables effectively, you'll usually use them in conjunction with DO-loops. For example, the batting average exec in figure 8-12 includes two DO-loops: one to store the information entered by the terminal user, the other to display the stored information. The DO instructions increment the value of Count so that each pass through the DO loop processes a different compound variable.

Unlike tables and arrays supported by most programming languages, the subscripts in a REXX compound variable do not have to be consecutive integers. In fact, they don't even have to be numbers. For example, you could create a state sales tax table using the compound variable Tax.State. Then, if the subscript State had values like CA, AL, and TX, the compound variable Tax.State references variables named Tax.CA, Tax.AL, and Tax.TX.

Another feature unique to REXX compound variables is that you can initialize all of the variables that make up an array at once by using just the variables' stem in an assignment. For example, you can initialize all of the state tax variables described above with this assignment:

```
Tax.=0
```

Then, all of the variables whose stem is Tax. are initialized to zero.

HOW TO USE THE REXX DATA STACK

The REXX *data stack* is an area of storage where you store large amounts of data without creating a variable name for each data item. To place data on the stack, you use one of two REXX instructions: PUSH or QUEUE. To retrieve data from the stack you use an instruction you're already familiar with: PULL. The formats of these three instructions are presented in figure 8-13.

Each item stored in the stack with a PUSH or QUEUE instruction is an expression that is evaluated and stored as a string value. If you list more than one variable or expression in a PUSH or QUEUE instruction, REXX concatenates them and stores the result on the stack as a single string. When you retrieve an item

---

The PUSH instruction

`PUSH expression`

The QUEUE instruction

`QUEUE expression`

The PULL instruction

`PULL template`

Explanation

expression	An expression that is evaluated. The resulting string is either pushed or queued onto the stack.
template	A series of variable names and/or template patterns used to parse the string retrieved from the top of the stack.

Figure 8-13   Basic REXX stack management commands

with the PULL instruction, you can parse it into several variables if necessary.

Figure 8-14 should help you understand how the PUSH, QUEUE, and PULL instructions work. As you can see, the PUSH and QUEUE instructions both add a data item to the stack. As its name suggests, the PUSH instruction pushes an item onto the top of the stack; that forces all other stack items down one position. In contrast, the QUEUE instruction adds a data item to the bottom of the stack. So it doesn't affect the position of other items in the stack.

The PULL instruction always retrieves data from the top of the stack. As it retrieves a data item, it deletes it from the stack. Then, the next item in the stack becomes the top item, ready to be retrieved by another PULL instruction. For example, suppose the stack contains three strings: MARY, JOHN, and LEE. When you issue a PULL instruction, it will retrieve the string MARY from the top of the stack, leaving the other two strings in the stack. Then, the next PULL instruction will retrieve JOHN, leaving just one string in the stack. The next PULL instruction will retrieve LEE, leaving the stack empty.

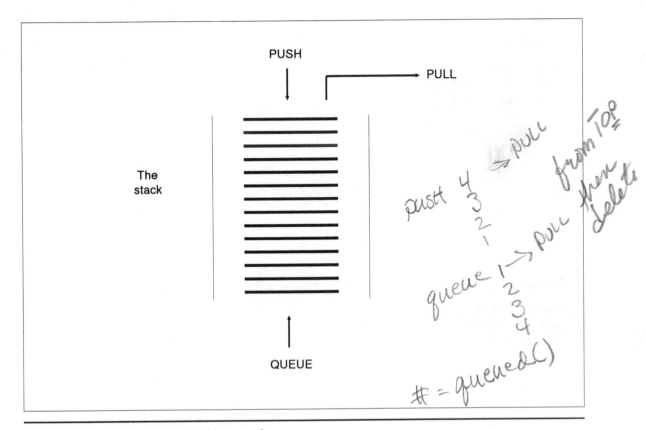

Figure 8-14   The REXX data stack

Figure 8-15 presents three examples that illustrate the difference between pushing and queueing data on the stack. Each of
these three examples ends with this DO loop:

```
do queued()
    pull String
    say String
end
```

Here, the DO instruction uses the QUEUED built-in function,
which returns the number of data items currently in the stack. So,
if there are three items in the stack, the DO loop will execute three
times. The instructions in the loop pull the top item off the stack,
store it in the String variable, and display it with a SAY instruction.
As a result, this loop displays each item in the stack on a separate
line.

Example 1

```
push "string 1"
push "string 2"
push "string 3"
do queued()
    pull String
    say String
    end
```

Result:

```
string 3
string 2
string 1
```

Example 2

```
queue "string 1"
queue "string 2"
queue "string 3"
do queued()
    pull String
    say String
    end
```

Result:

```
string 1
string 2
string 3
```

Figure 8-15   Three examples of storing and retrieving data on the stack (part 1 of 2)

Example 1 shows the result of pushing data onto the stack. Here, three PUSH instructions push three string literals on the stack. The resulting output for this example shows that when you push items on the stack, they are retrieved in reverse order. That's because as each item is pushed onto the stack, it becomes the top item, and the existing items are pushed down one position.

Example 2 shows the result of queueing data onto the stack. Here, the same three string literals are added to the stack, this time using the QUEUE instruction rather than the PUSH instruction. As

Example 3

```
push "string 1"
queue "string 2"
push "string 3"
do queued()
    pull String
    say String
    end
```

Result:

```
string 3
string 1
string 2
```

Figure 8-15   Three examples of storing and retrieving data on the stack (part 2 of 2)

you can see, the items are retrieved in the same order they were added. That's because as each item is added to the stack, it is added to the bottom of the stack rather than to the top.

Example 3 shows what happens if you mix PUSH and QUEUE instructions when adding data to the stack. Here, I pushed the value *string 1* to the stack, then queued the value *string 2* and pushed the value *string 3*. The result is that *string 3* is at the top of the stack, followed by *string 1* and *string 2*. As you can imagine, mixing PUSH and QUEUE instructions in the same procedure can render the stack almost useless. So I recommend that you don't do it unless you have a good reason.

A sample stack program

Figure 8-16 shows a version of the batting average procedure that uses the stack rather than compound variables to store data for each member of the team. Since this procedure is similar to the procedure in 8-12, I'll just highlight the differences. The two procedures appear the same to the user, so I didn't include a sample execution in figure 8-16.

The first thing to notice in figure 8-16 is that I used a PARSE EXTERNAL instruction to obtain input from the terminal. When you use the stack, you should use PARSE EXTERNAL rather than

```
100    /* REXX */
200    say "Enter each player's first and last name, times at bat, and hits"
300    say "Enter a null line to end"
400    say
500    do until First=""
600        parse external First Last AtBats Hits
700        if First<>"" then
800            queue First Last AtBats Hits
900        end
1000   say
1100   say "PLAYER                    AVG"
1200   say "==================== ====="
1300   do queued()
1400       pull First Last AtBats Hits
1500       Name=First Last
1600       Average=Hits/AtBats
1700       say left(Name,20) format(Average,1,3)
1800       end
```

Figure 8-16   A batting average procedure that uses the data stack

PULL for terminal input. Otherwise, the PULL instruction will retrieve data from the stack instead of from the terminal user.

After the PARSE EXTERNAL instruction, an IF instruction checks to make sure the user didn't enter a null line. Then, a QUEUE instruction queues the First, Last, AtBats, and Hits variables to the stack. These four variables are concatenated and added to the end of the stack as a single string.

In the DO loop at line 1400, the PULL instruction retrieves each item from the stack and parses it into the variables First, Last, AtBats, and Hits. Then, the batting averages are calculated and displayed.

How to use the stack with TSO commands

In addition to providing a convenient way to store and retrieve large amounts of data, the stack can also be used to pass subcommands to TSO commands like EDIT and COBTEST. That's because, like the PULL instruction, these commands obtain their input from the stack. They read data from the terminal only when the stack is empty.

```
queue "30 //SYSUT1       DD   DSN=&&TEMPSET,"
queue "40 //                  UNIT=SYSDA,"
queue "50 //                  SPACE=(TRK,(10,1)),"
queue "60 //                  DISP=,PASS"
queue "70 //SYSIN        DD   *"
queue "80   COPY OUTDD=DD1,INDD=DD2
queue "90 /*"
queue "END SAVE"
"EDIT JCL(TEST) CNTL"
```

Figure 8-17   A segment of a REXX procedure that uses the stack to pass subcommands to a TSO command

To illustrate how this works, figure 8-17 shows a portion of a REXX procedure that invokes the TSO EDIT command after queuing a series of EDIT subcommands to the stack. When EDIT executes, it retrieves the subcommands from the stack and processes them one at a time. Notice that the last EDIT subcommand I queued to the stack is END SAVE. If EDIT reaches the end of the stack without encountering an END command, it prompts the terminal user for input. Then, the terminal user has to enter an END command before control returns to the REXX procedure.

In some cases, you don't want a TSO command to read its subcommands from the stack. For example, suppose a procedure that uses the stack also invokes COBTEST, the interactive COBOL debugger, to allow the terminal user to debug a program. In this case, you don't want COBTEST to read commands from the stack. Instead, you want to protect the stack so that any data on it will be intact when COBTEST ends.

To do that, you use the NEWSTACK and DELSTACK commands, shown in figure 8-18. The NEWSTACK command creates an entirely new data stack. The previous data stack still exists, but can't be accessed until the new stack is deleted with a DELSTACK command. The DELSTACK command removes the current stack and reinstates the previous stack. Any data items in the stack when you issue a DELSTACK command are discarded. Note that these commands are TSO commands, not REXX instructions. As a result, you should enclose them in quotation marks when you use them.

Figure 8-19 shows a portion of a procedure that uses these commands to prevent COBTEST from retrieving data from the

---

The NEWSTACK command

```
"NEWSTACK"
```

The DELSTACK command

```
"DELSTACK"
```

Note: Since these are TSO commands, they should be enclosed in quotes so REXX won't evaluate them before passing them to TSO for execution.

Figure 8-18   The NEWSTACK and DELSTACK commands

```
"NEWSTACK"
"ALLOCATE DSNAME("Library".LOAD) DDNAME(LOADLIB)"
"COBTEST ("Member":LOADLIB)"
"DELSTACK"
```

Figure 8-19   A segment of a REXX procedure that protects its stack using the NEWSTACK and DELSTACK commands

stack. First, a NEWSTACK command sets up a new stack, protecting any data in the current stack. Next, the COBTEST command is issued. Since the new stack is empty, it reads its input from the terminal. Finally, a DELSTACK command deletes the current stack and restores the previous stack.

There's one more thing you should know about the data stack. When a REXX procedure returns control to TSO, each item remaining in the stack is processed by TSO as if it were a TSO command. This happens even when you invoke the procedure from ISPF. As a result, you should always empty the stack before your procedure ends, either by pulling all of its data or by using a DELSTACK command.

Terms

compound variable
stem
data stack

Objectives

1. Given a programming problem involving the use of a table,
    code a REXX procedure for its solution, implementing the table
    using compound variables.

2. Code REXX procedures that use the data stack to store large
    amounts of data or to store subcommands to be processed by
    an interactive TSO command such as EDIT or COBTEST.

Topic 3 User-defined functions and subroutines

Most REXX procedures are short enough and simple enough that they can be easily understood. However, when a REXX procedure becomes so complicated that you can't easily follow its logic, you should consider breaking it up into smaller pieces. You can do this by creating user-defined functions and subroutines.

User-defined functions are useful when you need to perform a complicated calculation that returns a single value. For example, you can create a user-defined function that calculates monthly loan payments based on the amount of the loan, the interest rate, and the loan's duration. Once you define a function, you can use it as if it were a built-in function.

Subroutines are similar to COBOL paragraphs called by PERFORM statements. You use them when the processing requirements of a procedure are so extensive that you want to break it into several modules. Then, the main routine of your REXX procedure can focus on the overall logic required for the procedure, leaving the details for the subroutines.

The coding requirements for functions and subroutines are similar. In fact, any user-defined function can be invoked as a function or as a subroutine, and many subroutines can be invoked as functions. Since user-defined functions are a little easier to understand, I'll present them first. Then, I'll show you how to create subroutines.

How to create and use a user-defined function

Figure 8-20 shows a REXX procedure that calculates monthly loan payments after the user enters the loan amount, number of years, and interest rate. To calculate the loan amount, the procedure uses a *user-defined function* called PAYMENT. In line 400, the procedure invokes the user-defined function like this:

```
payment(Principal, Years, Rate)
```

The procedure

```
100   /* REXX */
200   say "Enter principal amount, number of years, and interest rate"
300   pull Principal Years Rate
400   say "The monthly payment is " payment(Principal,Years,Rate)
500   exit
600
700   payment: procedure
800      arg Amount, Years, Rate
900      Months=Years*12
1000     MonthlyRate=Rate/12
1100     MonthlyPayment=Amount/(((1-(1/(1+MonthlyRate)**Months))/MonthlyRate)
1200     return MonthlyPayment
```

A sample execution

```
Enter principal amount, number of years, and interest rate
12000 3 .12
The monthly payment is 398.571692
```

Figure 8-20   A procedure that uses a function to calculate loan payments

As you can see, you invoke the PAYMENT function the same way you invoke a built-in function. When the SAY instruction is evaluated, the PAYMENT function is invoked and the value it returns is displayed.

If you want to use a user-defined function, you must define it somewhere in the procedure. The definition for the PAYMENT function begins in line 700:

```
payment: procedure
```

Here, the colon following the word PAYMENT indicates that PAYMENT is a *label*. When a reference to a user-defined function is found in an expression, REXX immediately transfers control to the label that corresponds to the function name. Thus, control is transferred to the PAYMENT label when the PAYMENT function is invoked.

PROCEDURE is an optional REXX instruction that causes any variables created outside of the function to be temporarily hidden. Then, when the function ends, any variables it created are deleted and the variables that were hidden are made available once again. Because the PROCEDURE instruction insures that the function

---

The PROCEDURE instruction

```
PROCEDURE [EXPOSE variable...]
```

Explanation

variable   One or more variables that are shared with the calling procedure.

Figure 8-21   The PROCEDURE instruction

won't change variables that are used elsewhere in the procedure, I recommend you use it whenever you create a user-defined function.

Figure 8-21 presents the full format of the PROCEDURE instruction. As you can see, you can use the EXPOSE option of this instruction to specify one or more variables that aren't hidden from the function. For example, if you code a PROCEDURE instruction like this:

```
procedure expose Flight, Time
```

the function can access the Flight and Time variables from the main procedure. But since you shouldn't need to access any variables that are used in the main procedure, I recommend that you avoid the EXPOSE option of the PROCEDURE instruction.

Of course, the function must be able to access the data passed to it as arguments in the function call. To do that, you use an ARG instruction. The ARG instruction in figure 8-20 is this:

```
arg Amount, Years, Rate
```

This ARG instruction specifies that the three argument strings passed to the function should be received in the variables Amount, Years, and Rate.

I want to be sure you realize that when a function is invoked, the arguments it uses are first evaluated, and the resulting *values* are passed to the function. The variables used in the function call are not themselves passed to the function. In figure 8-20, I used the name Principal in the main procedure and the name Amount in the function to emphasize this point. When the function is called, REXX passes the value of the Principal variable to the Amount variable in the function.

Notice that I used the same variable names for the number of years and the interest rate in both the main routine and the function definition. However, because I used the PROCEDURE instruction, the Years and Rate variables in the function are not the same as the Years and Rate variables in the main routine. Thus, if the function changes either of these variables, the corresponding variables in the main routine will remain unchanged.

Incidentally, you may have noticed that the PAYMENT function call and the ARG instruction use commas to separate the arguments from one another. Although it looks straightforward enough in this example, this is actually an advanced form of parsing called *multiple string parsing*. Because it can be used only with the ARG instruction, I didn't explain how it works in topic 1 of this chapter. Instead, I explain it later in this topic. Until then, you can assume that the values of the main routine's Payment, Years, and Rate variables are passed to the function's Amount, Years, and Rate variables.

After the function receives the variable values, it continues processing. In figure 8-20, for example, the three instructions after the ARG instruction calculate the monthly payment based on the Amount, Years, and Rate variables. As you can see, the formula for calculating loan payments is quite complex. Fortunately, it doesn't have anything to do with the purpose of the example, which is simply to show you how to create and use a user-defined function. So if you don't understand how the expression that calculates the monthly payment works, don't worry. All you really need to see here is that the MonthlyPayment variable is set to the correct value.

You use the RETURN instruction to mark the end of a user-defined function. The complete format of this instruction is presented in figure 8-22. All user-defined functions must end with a RETURN instruction, and that RETURN instruction must specify a value that's passed back to the calling routine. In this example, the RETURN instruction returns the value of the MonthlyPayment variable to the calling routine.

When you create user-defined functions, you should always place them at the end of the procedure. Then, you should use an EXIT instruction, as shown in figure 8-20, to terminate the procedure before it reaches the functions. Otherwise, at the end of the procedure, REXX will pass control to the user-defined functions instead of completing the procedure normally.

The RETURN instruction

```
RETURN [expression]
```

Explanation

expression	A value that is returned to the caller. If the routine is called as a function, the value is substituted for the function call in the expression. If the routine is called as a subroutine, the value is returned in the special variable RESULT.

Figure 8-22   The RETURN instruction

How to create and use a subroutine

Now that you know how to create and use a user-defined function, you should have no trouble learning how to create and use *subroutines*. Figure 8-23 shows a version of the loan calculation procedure that uses a subroutine rather than a function to calculate the monthly loan payment.

There are two things I want you to notice about this procedure. First, the PAYMENT subroutine is invoked by a CALL instruction rather than a function call. Figure 8-24 gives the format of the CALL instruction. On this instruction, you specify the name of the subroutine you want to call and the arguments you want to pass to it.

Second, notice that the PAYMENT subroutine in figure 8-23 is identical to the PAYMENT function in figure 8-20. In this case, you can tell it's a subroutine because a CALL instruction invokes it. Any value a subroutine returns to the main procedure via the RETURN instruction is placed in a special variable named Result. So, when control returns from the PAYMENT subroutine in figure 8-23, the monthly payment is stored in the Result variable. That's why the variable Result is listed on the SAY instruction in line 500.

Although you can code a subroutine exactly the same as a function, you usually won't. Typically, subroutines don't return a value via the RETURN instruction. If the sole purpose of a subroutine is to calculate a single value, you should use a user-defined function instead. Then, you can use subroutines for more general purposes.

```
100   /* REXX */
200   say "Enter principal amount, number of years, and interest rate"
300   pull Principal Years Rate
400   call payment Principal,Years,Rate
500   say "The monthly payment is " Result
600   exit
700
800   payment: procedure
900       arg Amount, Years, Rate
1000      Months=Years*12
1100      MonthlyRate=Rate/12
1200      MonthlyPayment=Amount/((1-(1/(1+MonthlyRate)**Months))/MonthlyRate
1300      return MonthlyPayment
```

Figure 8-23   A procedure that uses a subroutine to calculate loan payments

The CALL instruction

```
CALL name [expression] [,expression...]
```

Explanation

name   The name of the subroutine to be invoked.

expression   An expression to be evaluated and passed as an argument to the subroutine.

Figure 8-24   The CALL instruction

The REXX procedure in figure 8-25 shows a more likely use of a subroutine. The main procedure in this example calls a subroutine to get the Principal, Years, and Rate values from the terminal user. Then, the procedure displays the loan payment calculated by the PAYMENT function. Notice that the INPUT subroutine doesn't use a PROCEDURE or ARG instruction, and that the CALL instruction doesn't list any arguments. As a result, the INPUT subroutine shares variables with the main procedure, and the values parsed into the Principal, Year, and Rate variables are used in the main procedure when it invokes the PAYMENT function.

```
100   /* REXX */
200   call input
300   say "The monthly payment is " payment(Principal,Years,Rate)
400   exit
500
600   input: say "Enter principal amount"
700       pull Principal
800       say "Enter number of years"
900       pull Years
1000      say "Enter interest rate"
1100      pull Rate
1200      return
1300
1400  payment: procedure
1500      arg Amount, Years, Rate
1600      Months=Years*12
1700      MonthlyRate=Rate/12
1800      MonthlyPayment=Amount/((1-(1/(1+MonthlyRate)**Months))/MonthlyRate
1900      return MonthlyPayment
```

Figure 8-25   A procedure that uses a subroutine without arguments

As you probably know, modern structured programming techniques discourage the sharing of data between subroutines and the routines that call them. Frankly, the procedure in figure 8-25 isn't complicated enough to worry about unnecessary data sharing. If you're coding a more complicated procedure that involves many variables and many subroutines, however, don't give the subroutines access to all of the procedure's variables. Instead, use a PROCEDURE instruction to give each subroutine access to only the variables it needs. For example, you can use this PROCEDURE instruction for the INPUT subroutine in figure 8-25:

```
Input: procedure expose Principal, Years, Rate
```

Then, the INPUT subroutine can access the Principal, Years, and Rate variables. Any other variables the subroutine uses are unique to it.

How to use multiple string parsing

I mentioned earlier that the ARG instruction in figure 8-20 used an advanced type of parsing called multiple string parsing. In contrast to simple parsing, which parses the words in a single string, multiple string parsing parses the strings in a list of strings. Using multiple string parsing, you can also parse the words in each of the strings in the list.

In the simplest form of multiple string parsing, you parse each string into a single variable. To do that, you separate each string to be passed to the function or subroutine with a comma. Then, in the ARG instruction, you code a comma between each variable. As a result, each variable will contain an entire string.

To illustrate multiple string parsing, consider the two examples in figure 8-26. In each example, I invoke a function called Display that displays two strings passed to it. In the first example, both strings consist of a single word. So after the ARG instruction

```
arg String1, String2
```

is executed, String1 contains the string DOUG and String2 contains the string 100. In the second example, the first string still consists of a single word, but the second string consists of two words: 100 and 200. So when the same ARG instruction is executed, String 1 contains the string DOUG and String2 contains the string 100 200.

Note that you could have performed the parse operation in example 1 with simple parsing by omitting the commas in the function call and the ARG instruction. Although many of the functions you write won't require you to use multiple string parsing, I recommend you use this form anyway. That way, your user-defined functions will be consistent with the REXX built-in functions, which always use multiple string parsing for their arguments.

Both the examples in figure 8-26 parse each string into a single variable. But one of the biggest advantages of using multiple string parsing is that you can also parse the words within each string. To illustrate, suppose you invoke a function called Display1 using this function call:

```
display1(DOUG ANNE,100 200)
```

Then, in the function definition, you code this ARG instruction:

```
arg Name1 Name2, Dept1 Dept2
```

The result is that Name1 contains the first word of the first string, DOUG, Name2 contains the second word of the first string, ANNE, Dept1 contains the first word of the second string, 100, and Dept2 contains the second word of the second string, 200. Note that the parsing within each string works the same as parsing for a single string. So if you specify more variables than there are words in the string, the extra variables are assigned null values. And if you

The function definition

```
display: procedure
         arg String1, String2
         say String1
         say String2
         return 0
```

Example 1

The function call

```
display(DOUG,100)
```

The resulting output

```
Doug
100
```

Example 2

The function call

```
display(DOUG,100 200)
```

The resulting output

```
DOUG
100 200
```

Figure 8-26   How multiple string arguments are parsed

specify fewer variables than there are words in the string, the remaining words are all parsed into the last variable specified.

How to create and use external routines

In all of the examples I've presented so far, the functions and subroutines have appeared at the end of the REXX procedure that calls them. Functions and subroutines coded in this way are called *internal routines*. REXX also lets you create and use *external routines*. An external routine is simply a function or subroutine

The main procedure

```
100   /* REXX */
200   say "Enter principal amount, number of years, and interest rate"
300   pull Principal Years Rate
400   say "The monthly payment is " payment(Principal,Years,Rate)
```

The PAYMENT routine

```
100   arg Amount, Years, Rate
200   Months=Years*12
300   MonthlyRate=Rate/12
400   MonthlyPayment=Amount/(((1-(1/(1+MonthlyRate)**Months))/MonthlyRate
500   return MonthlyPayment
```

Figure 8-27   A procedure that uses an external routine

that is stored separately from the REXX procedure that calls it. That way, the routine can be used by more than one procedure.

An external routine must be stored in a member whose name is the same as the name of the function or subroutine. In other words, if the name of the function or subroutine is PAYMENT, the external routine must be stored in a member named PAYMENT. As a result, external routine names are limited to eight characters. In addition, if the external routine isn't contained in the same library as the procedure that invokes it, the library that contains the external routine must be properly allocated so that REXX can locate the routine. So, if your external routines are stored in another library, make sure that library is allocated in the same manner as implicit procedure libraries, as I explained in topic 1 of chapter 7. On the other hand, if the external routine is in the same library as the procedure that invokes it, you don't have to allocate it.

Figure 8-27 shows the PAYMENT function implemented as an external routine. Here, the function is stored in its own member: PAYMENT. Since the member name identifies the function name, a label isn't required at the beginning of the function. Also, there isn't a PROCEDURE instruction because an external routine can't share variables with the routine that invokes it.

Terms

user-defined function
label
subroutine
multiple string parsing
internal routine
external routine

Objectives

1. Given specifications for a calculation that returns a single value, code a user-defined function that performs the calculation and a function call that properly invokes it.

2. Code a REXX procedure that uses subroutines to simplify the logic of the main processing routine.

Topic 4   REXX facilities for file processing

Many REXX procedures process files. The easiest and usually the best way to process files in a REXX procedure is by invoking TSO commands to process the files for you. For example, you can use the ALLOCATE, DELETE or RENAME commands to create, delete or rename a file. You can even use the EDIT command to change the contents of a file. Although these commands are often useful, they don't let your REXX procedure process a file directly. To do that, you have to use REXX's built-in file-handling features.

In this chapter, you'll learn how to use those features for simple file handling. Before you begin, though, I want you to realize that to process a file in REXX, you have to know how to use the data stack and compound variables. If you don't know how to use those features, read topic 2 of this chapter before you read this topic.

The EXECIO command

Strictly speaking, the REXX language, as it was originally designed, doesn't have any file-handling features. Under VM/CMS, REXX file handling is done using the CMS EXECIO command, which lets you read, write, and update file records. The TSO implementation of REXX includes an EXECIO command that's compatible with the CMS EXECIO command. The EXECIO command is another TSO/REXX command, which means that it can be used only in a REXX procedure. Like other TSO commands, you should enclose it in quotation marks when you use it in a REXX procedure.

Figure 8-28 gives the format of the EXECIO command. Because it is designed to be compatible with the VM/CMS EXECIO command, its syntax may be a little strange to TSO users. In particular, notice that the left parenthesis that precedes the FINIS or STEM operand has no balancing right parenthesis. The EXECIO command is the only TSO command that uses this peculiar CMS convention.

The EXECIO command to read records

$$
\text{EXECIO} \begin{Bmatrix} \text{count} \\ * \end{Bmatrix} \begin{Bmatrix} \text{DISKR} \\ \text{DISKRU} \end{Bmatrix} \text{ddname} \quad [\text{start}] \begin{Bmatrix} (\ [\text{FINIS}]\ [\ \begin{Bmatrix} \text{LIFO} \\ \text{FIFO} \\ \text{SKIP} \end{Bmatrix} \ ] \\ (\ [\text{STEM var}]\ [\text{FINIS}] \end{Bmatrix}
$$

The EXECIO command to write records

$$
\text{EXECIO} \begin{Bmatrix} \text{count} \\ * \end{Bmatrix} \quad \text{DISKW} \quad \text{ddname} \quad (\ [\text{STEM var}]\ [\text{FINIS}]
$$

Explanation

count	Specifies the number of records to be read or written.
*	Specifies that all of the records in the data set are to be read, or all of the items in the stack up to the first null item are to be written.
DISKR	Reads records from a file.
DISKRU	Reads records from a file and allows the last record read to be updated by an EXECIO DISKW command.
DISKW	Writes records to a file or updates the record most recently read by EXECIO DISKRU.
ddname	The ddname associated with the file.
start	The number of the first record to be read by DISKR or DISKRU.
FINIS	Closes the data set when EXECIO completes.
LIFO FIFO SKIP	Specifies how records are added to the stack as they are read. LIFO means PUSH records onto the stack. FIFO means QUEUE records onto the stack. SKIP means don't add records to the stack at all. FIFO is the default.
STEM var	Use the compound variable whose stem is *var* instead of the stack. EXECIO numbers the subscript beginning with 1.

Figure 8-28   The EXECIO command

The first three EXECIO operands are the ones you'll use most often. The count operand tells EXECIO how many records you want it to process. To process one record at a time, specify 1. To process an entire file in one EXECIO command, use an asterisk. After the count operand, you specify DISKR, DISKRU, or DISKW to tell EXECIO whether you want to read or write records. Then, you specify the ddname for the file you want to process.

If a file isn't open, EXECIO opens it for you, so you don't have to code a separate instruction to open your file. You do, however, have to use a TSO ALLOCATE command before you can use EXECIO. The ALLOCATE command should specify the name of the data set you want to process and the ddname you'll use in the EXECIO command to refer to the file.

EXECIO does *not* automatically close files. As a result, you can use successive EXECIO commands to read records from a file in sequential order. If you want EXECIO to close the file, you can specify the FINIS operand. Otherwise, the file will be closed automatically when the REXX procedure ends.

By default, EXECIO uses the REXX data stack to store input records or to obtain records for output. So after you use EXECIO to read records, you can use PULL instructions to retrieve the records from the data stack. And before you use an EXECIO command to write records, you should PUSH or QUEUE them to the stack, or read them into the stack using an EXECIO command. If you'd rather process the records using compound variables, you can use the STEM operand to specify the compound variable's stem name. It's usually more convenient to process records from the stack, though.

How to use the EXECIO command to read file records

Figure 8-29 gives five examples of the EXECIO command as it's used to read records from a file. In example 1, all of the records from the file allocated to the INFILE ddname are read into the data stack. EXECIO queues records into the stack, so you can retrieve them in order by using PULL instructions. The FINIS operand tells EXECIO to close the data set after all the records have been read.

Example 2 shows how to read a single record. Here, I specify 1 for the count, so only one record is read. I leave off the FINIS operand so the data set isn't closed.

Example 3 shows how to read a record so it can be updated. When you specify DISKRU instead of DISKR, the next record written to the file replaces the record just read. If the count operand specifies that more than one record is to be read, only the last record read is held for update.

Example 4 shows how to read records into compound variables instead of the stack. Here, I specify RECORD. as the stem for the compound variables. As a result, EXECIO reads the file's first

---

Example 1

```
"EXECIO * DISKR INFILE (FINIS"
```

Example 2

```
"EXECIO 1 DISKR INFILE"
```

Example 3

```
"EXECIO 1 DISKRU INFILE"
```

Example 4

```
"EXECIO 1 DISKR INFILE (STEM RECORD."
```

Example 5

```
"EXECIO * DISKR INFILE (LIFO FINIS"
```

Figure 8-29   Five examples of the EXECIO command as it's used to read file data

record into RECORD.1, the second record into RECORD.2, and so on.

Example 5 shows how to read records into the stack in reverse order. When you specify LIFO on an EXECIO command, EXECIO pushes records onto the stack rather than queueing them. That way, when you pull the records off the stack, the first record retrieved will be the last record in the file.

How to use the EXECIO command to write file records

Figure 8-30 shows five examples of the EXECIO command as it's used to write records to a file. Example 1 writes records from the stack until it encounters a null record. Note that this command does not necessarily write all of the records in the stack; if it encounters a null record before the end of the stack, it stops. Nor does it stop automatically when it reaches the end of the stack. If it reaches the end of the stack without encountering a null record, it

---

Example 1

```
"EXECIO * DISKW OUTFILE (FINIS"
```

Example 2

```
Count=Queued()
"EXECIO" Count "DISKW OUTFILE (FINIS"
```

Example 3

```
"EXECIO 1 DISKW OUTFILE"
```

Example 4

```
"EXECIO * DISKW OUTFILE (STEM RECORD."
```

Example 5

```
"ALLOCATE DSNAME(ORDERS.DATA) DDNAME(ORDERS) MOD"
"EXECIO * DISKW ORDERS (FINIS"
```

Figure 8-30   Five examples of the EXECIO command as it's used to write file data

does just what the PULL instruction does: prompts the terminal user for input.

There are two techniques to prevent the EXECIO command from reaching past the end of the stack. The first is to queue a null record to the stack before you issue the EXECIO command. To do that, use this instruction:

```
queue ""
```

The second technique is shown in example 2 in figure 8-30. Here, you use the QUEUED function to determine how many entries are in the queue. Then, you use that value to tell EXECIO how many records to write.

Example 3 in figure 8-30 shows how to write a single record from the top of the stack. And example 4 shows how to write records contained in compound variables. Here, I coded an asterisk so the command is executed until it encounters a null value. Note that since it isn't possible to run out of compound variables, you

Return code	Meaning
0	Successful completion.
1	Data was truncated as it was written.
2	The end of the file was reached before the specified number of records could be read.
20	A severe error occurred.

Figure 8-31 EXECIO return codes

don't have to worry about EXECIO prompting the user for input like you do when you use the stack.

Example 5 shows how to write records to the end of an existing file. Here, I used the MOD operand on the ALLOCATE command. This tells TSO to establish position at the end of the file, so the subsequent EXECIO command writes records at the end of the file.

How to test for file errors with the EXECIO command

Whenever you issue an EXECIO command, you should test the rc variable to see if the I/O operation was successfully completed. Figure 8-31 lists the return code values that the EXECIO command returns in the rc variable. As you can see, a return code of zero indicates that the I/O operation was successful. Other return codes indicate that some sort of error occurred.

Return code 1 occurs while you are updating a record read with the DISKRU option if the record you're writing is longer than the record you read. It indicates that the record was updated, but the data was truncated to the length of the original record.

Return code 2 indicates an end-of-file condition. If you're reading records one at a time, you should test rc for end-of-file after each read. If you're reading more than one record by specifying a count, return code 2 indicates that the end of the file was reached before the specified number of records were read. The only way to determine how many records were actually read is to examine the stack or the compound variables the records were read into. Return code 2 never occurs when you specify an asterisk

```
100   /* REXX */
200   say "Please place your publication order"
300   say
400   say "Enter your employee number"
500   parse external EmpNo
600   say "Enter your department code"
700   parse external DeptCode
800   say
900   do until Document=""
1000      say "Enter document-id and quantity"
1100      parse external Document Quantity
1200      if Document<>"" then
1300          queue EmpNo DeptCode Document Quantity
1400      end
1500  queue ""
1600  "ALLOCATE DDNAME(ORDER) DSNAME(ORDER.DATA) MOD"
1700  "EXECIO * DISKW ORDER (FINIS)"
1800  if rc=0 then
1900      say "Your order has been placed"
2000  else do
2100      say "Your order could not be placed"
2200      say "EXECIO error code " rc
2300      end
2400  "FREE DDNAME(ORDER)"
```

Figure 8-32   The ORDER procedure

as the count, since that always causes EXECIO to read to the end of the file.

Return code 20 means that a serious error has occurred and processing cannot continue. When EXECIO returns this code, you should terminate the exec with an EXIT instruction.

A sample file-processing procedure

To help you understand how file processing works in REXX, figure 8-32 presents a simple procedure that writes records to a file. This procedure lets a user enter an order for one or more publications, such as IBM manuals or textbooks. First, it asks the user to enter an employee number and department code. Then, for each publication ordered, it asks the user to enter the document id and quantity, and queues the employee number, department code, document id, and quantity onto the stack. When the user is finished entering orders, the procedure writes all of the queued records to a file.

Although this procedure is easy enough to understand, there are several details I want to be sure you notice. First, notice in lines 500, 700, and 1100 that I use the PARSE EXTERNAL instruction rather than the PULL instruction to obtain input from the terminal user. That's because this procedure uses the stack to store the records that will be written.

Second, notice that line 1500 queues a null line to the stack after the user enters all of his or her orders. That way, the EXECIO command will end when it reaches this record. Third, notice that I specify MOD on the ALLOCATE command in line 1600 so that any records written by this procedure will be added to the file after any existing records. Fourth, notice that I use an IF instruction in line 1800 to test the return code issued by the EXECIO command.

Finally, notice that I use a FREE command in line 2400 to free the ORDER data set. If I omit the FREE command, other terminal users can't access the data set.

Term

TSO/REXX command

Objective

Given a programming problem involving file I/O, code an appropriate REXX procedure that uses the EXECIO command to process the file.

Section 4

Advanced CLIST and REXX applications

The two chapters in this section present two common applications for CLIST and REXX procedures. In chapter 9, you'll learn how to create edit macros that you can invoke from within the ISPF/PDF editor. These edit macros can issue edit primary commands, directly manipulate the data in the source member being edited, and perform many other useful functions. Since you probably spend most of your computing time using the ISPF/PDF editor, it pays to learn how to use this valuable feature to customize the editor to your needs.

In chapter 10, you'll learn how to use ISPF dialog management services in your CLIST and REXX procedures so that your procedures can display full-screen panels similar to ISPF/PDF's panels rather than use the clumsy CLIST and

REXX terminal I/O features you learned in chapters 6 and 8. The effort required to do this probably isn't worth it for simple procedures that you'll seldom use. But if you're developing procedures that will be used frequently by you and others, it makes sense to use the facilities chapter 10 presents.

Since both of these applications can be implemented using either CLIST or REXX procedures, I'll use both languages to illustrate them. Whenever I present a procedure, I'll present both a CLIST and a REXX version.

Chapter 9

How to create and use edit macros

An *edit macro* is a CLIST or REXX procedure that you invoke from the ISPF editor as if it were an ISPF primary command. Edit macros provide a flexible method for tailoring the ISPF editor to your working style. For example, if there is a sequence of ISPF editor commands that you frequently use, you can store them in an edit macro. Then, when you type the name of the macro in the primary command area, ISPF executes each of the commands in the macro.

Within an edit macro, you can use any of the CLIST or REXX programming elements I presented in sections 2 and 3 of this book. As a result, edit macros can include variables, expressions, looping and branching instructions, and so on. They can also include the TSO commands I presented in section 1. So you can create edit macros that allocate data sets or perform other TSO functions. In addition to these elements, edit macros can include any ISPF primary edit command, and a few ISPF edit features that can be used only in a macro. And they can include any of the dialog features I'll present in the next chapter.

As you can imagine, edit macros can become overwhelmingly complicated. In this chapter, I'll focus on the techniques you need to know to create relatively simple edit macros that can simplify common edit operations. If you master these techniques, you should have no trouble creating more complicated macros if you should ever need to. For the most part, though, I think you'll find that the most useful edit macros are rarely more complicated than the ones I'll present in this chapter.

Edit macros can be created using CLIST or REXX as the underlying procedure language, so I'll present all of the sample edit macros in both of those languages. But because of its superior text handling capabilities, I recommend you code your macros in REXX if it is available at your installation.

MACRO BASICS

Figure 9-1 shows the CLIST and REXX versions of a simple edit macro called SHOWONLY. This macro invokes two edit primary commands. First, an EXCLUDE ALL command excludes every line in the source file. Then, a FIND command reveals all of the lines that contain a specified search string. The effect of this macro is to exclude all of the lines in a source member except those that contain a particular string.

The two parts of figure 9-2 show the SHOWONLY macro in use. In part 1, I entered this command in the primary command area:

```
SHOWONLY CUSTMST
```

Part 2 shows the edit display after SHOWONLY has finished. Here, only the lines that contain the string CUSTMST are displayed.

How to create and execute a macro

Like any CLIST or REXX procedure, an edit macro is a member of a partitioned data set. You can include edit macros in the same library with other procedures, or you can place them in a separate library. Before you can use an edit macro, you must either allocate its library to the SYSPROC or SYSEXEC ddname or use the ALTLIB command. I explained how to do this in topic 1 of chapters 5 and 7, so I won't repeat it here. If you aren't sure how to properly allocate your macro library, refer back to those chapters.

As I already mentioned, an edit macro consists of a mixture of CLIST or REXX statements, TSO commands, and ISPF edit commands. Every ISPF edit command in an edit macro must begin with the word ISREDIT. This tells ISPF that the command is to be interpreted as an edit command, not as one of the dialog manage-

---

The SHOWONLY macro (CLIST version)

```
ISREDIT MACRO (STRING)
ISREDIT EXCLUDE ALL
ISREDIT FIND &STRING ALL
```

The SHOWONLY macro (REXX version)

```
/* REXX */
address ispexec
"ISREDIT MACRO (STRING)"
"ISREDIT EXCLUDE ALL"
"ISREDIT FIND" String "ALL"
```

Figure 9-1　　The SHOWONLY macro

---

ment commands you'll learn about in the next chapter. With just a few exceptions, which I explain in a moment, you can code any edit primary command following the word ISREDIT. In addition, you can code special edit macro commands as well.

The first ISREDIT command in an edit macro must be an ISREDIT MACRO command. This command identifies the procedure as an edit macro and lists any command-line parameters the macro can accept. When you invoke an edit macro, you separate the parameters from one another with spaces or commas. If a parameter value includes a space or comma, you must enclose it in quotes or apostrophes. As you can see, the SHOWONLY macro in figure 9-1 uses one parameter named STRING. So in figure 9-2, when I invoked the macro, I included one parameter: CUSTMST.

The two commands after the ISREDIT MACRO command in figure 9-1 are edit primary commands. First, an EXCLUDE ALL command excludes the entire source file. Then, a FIND command finds all occurrences of the parameter passed to the variable STRING. Notice in the CLIST version that an ampersand is required to identify the STRING variable. In the REXX version, the variable name String is coded outside of the quotes that enclose the rest of the command.

The REXX version of the SHOWONLY macro begins with two lines that aren't included in the CLIST version. The first is a comment containing the word REXX, which identifies the procedure as a REXX procedure rather than a CLIST procedure. This line is required only if the macro is stored in a CLIST library (a library

Part 1:

To invoke the
SHOWONLY macro,
enter its name in the
command area
followed by a search
string

```
EDIT ---- DLOWE.TEST.COBOL(MKTG1200) - 01.06 ------------------ COLUMNS 007 072
COMMAND ===> SHOWONLY CUSTMST                                   SCROLL ===> DATA
****** *********************************** TOP OF DATA ************************************
000100  IDENTIFICATION DIVISION.
000200 *
000300  PROGRAM-ID.     MKTG1200.
000400 *
000500  ENVIRONMENT DIVISION.
000600 *
000700  CONFIGURATION SECTION.
000800 *
000900  INPUT-OUTPUT SECTION.
001000 *
001100  FILE-CONTROL.
001200      SELECT CUSTMST  ASSIGN TO AS-CUSTMST.
001300      SELECT SALESMN  ASSIGN TO SALESMN
001400                      ORGANIZATION IS INDEXED
001500                      ACCESS IS RANDOM
001600                      RECORD KEY IS SM-SALESMAN-KEY.
001700      SELECT SALESRPT ASSIGN TO SALESRPT.
001800 *
001900  DATA DIVISION.
002000 *
002100  FILE SECTION.
```

Part 2:

When you press the
Enter key, all lines
except those that
contain the search
string are excluded

```
EDIT ---- DLOWE.TEST.COBOL(MKTG1200) - 01.06 ------------------ COLUMNS 007 072
COMMAND ===>                                                    SCROLL ===> DATA
****** *********************************** TOP OF DATA ************************************
- - - - - - - - - - - - - - - - - 11 LINE(S) NOT DISPLAYED
001200      SELECT CUSTMST  ASSIGN TO AS-CUSTMST.
- - - - - - - - - - - - - - - - - 10 LINE(S) NOT DISPLAYED
002201 FD  CUSTMST
- - - - - - - - - - - - - - - - 163 LINE(S) NOT DISPLAYED
016100      OPEN INPUT  CUSTMST
- - - - - - - - - - - - - - - - - - 6 LINE(S) NOT DISPLAYED
016800      CLOSE CUSTMST
- - - - - - - - - - - - - - - - 45 LINE(S) NOT DISPLAYED
021500      READ CUSTMST
- - - - - - - - - - - - - - - 170 LINE(S) NOT DISPLAYED
****** *********************************** BOTTOM OF DATA ************************************
```

Figure 9-2   Using the SHOWONLY macro

allocated to SYSPROC or SYSUPROC). If you store your macros in a library allocated to SYSEXEC or SYSUEXEC, this line isn't required, but I recommend that you include it anyway.

The next line in the REXX version, ADDRESS ISPEXEC, tells REXX that any host commands that follow are to be processed by ISPF rather than by TSO. The rest of the REXX procedure is the same as the CLIST procedure, except for the syntactical differences required by the REXX language.

How to use edit primary commands in a macro

As I've already mentioned, you can include edit primary commands in an edit macro by simply preceding the command with the word ISREDIT. The only edit primary command you can *not* use in an edit macro is UNDO. Although UNDO is extremely useful as a primary command, it would have little purpose as an edit macro command.

In figure 9-1, the EXCLUDE and FIND commands are coded the same as they would be if you entered them in the editor's primary command area. In fact, the syntax for every edit command except one is the same whether you use it as a primary command or in a macro. As a result, I won't cover the syntax of these commands here. You'll find a description of these commands in *Part 1: Concepts and ISPF*.

The only ISPF edit command that has a different syntax when you use it in a macro is DELETE. Figure 9-3 shows the format of the DELETE command you use in a macro. There are a few minor syntactical differences between this format and the DELETE primary command's format. The most significant difference is that as a macro command, DELETE lets you specify a single line pointer, so you can delete a single line. Normally, you use the D line command to do this, but you can't use line commands in an edit macro. As a result, you must use this alternate form of the DELETE command.

ISPF provides an alternative to the FIND command that can be used only in an edit macro: SEEK. Figure 9-4 shows the syntax of the SEEK command. Its parameters are identical to the parameters you can code for a FIND command. In fact, the FIND and SEEK commands function identically, with one difference. When a FIND command finds the search string in an excluded line, it resets the line so it is no longer excluded. As a result, the user can see the

---

The DELETE macro command

Format 1:

```
ISREDIT DELETE   [ALL] [range]   [ {  X  } ]
                                   {  NX }
```

Format 2:

```
ISREDIT DELETE  line-pointer
```

Explanation

ALL	Specifies that all lines falling within the specified range are to be deleted. You cannot specify ALL by itself.
range	Specifies two relative line numbers or labels that mark the beginning and ending of the range of lines to be deleted.
X	Specifies that only excluded lines should be deleted.
NX	Specifies that only non-excluded lines should be deleted.
line-pointer	Specifies a relative line number or label that indicates a single line to be deleted.

Note: The format 1 DELETE command must specify ALL or a range, and you cannot specify ALL by itself.

Figure 9-3   The DELETE macro command

line. When a SEEK command finds the search string in an excluded line, the line is not reset, so the user cannot see it.

As I mentioned earlier, you cannot use line commands, such as I, D, and X, in an edit macro. But since most of the line commands have primary command equivalents, this isn't a problem. For example, I've already described how you can use the DELETE primary command rather than the D line command to delete a single source line.

Unfortunately, not all line commands have primary command equivalents. To perform the functions provided by these line commands, you use the macro commands shown in figure 9-5. As you can see, you use the INSERT command to insert one or more blank lines at a specified location, and the SHIFT command to shift data.

The SEEK macro command

```
                                    ( NEXT )   ( CHARS  )
                                    | PREV |   | PREFIX |
ISREDIT SEEK string [range]         { FIRST}   { SUFFIX }
                                    | LAST |   ( WORD   )
                                    ( ALL  )

        [{ X  }]  [col-1 [col-2]]
         { NX }
```

Explanation

string	The text string to be found. Must be in apostrophes or quotes if it contains spaces or commas. May be a hex string in the form X'hex-digits', a text string in the form T'text-string', or a picture string in the form P'picture-string'.
range	A range of lines identified by two labels. The default range is the first and last lines of the file.
NEXT	Start search at current line and locate the next occurrence of *string*. This is the default.
PREV	Start search at current line and locate the previous occurrence of *string* (search backwards).
FIRST	Start search at top of data and locate the first occurrence of *string*.
LAST	Start search at bottom of data and locate the last occurrence of *string* (search backwards).
ALL	Same as FIRST, but also indicate a count of the occurrences of *string* in the file.
CHARS	Any occurrence of *string* satisfies the search. This is the default.
PREFIX	*String* must be at the beginning of a word to satisfy the search.
SUFFIX	*String* must be at the end of a word to satisfy the search.
WORD	*String* must be surrounded by spaces or special characters to satisfy the search.
X NX	Controls the search of excluded lines. X says to search only excluded lines; NX says to search only lines that are not excluded. If neither X nor NX is coded, all lines, excluded or not, are searched.
col-1	Starting column number. If *col-2* is *not* specified, *string* must begin in this column to satisfy the search. Default value is the current left boundary.
col-2	Ending column number. If specified, *string* must be found between *col-1* and *col-2* to satisfy the search. Default value is the current right boundary.

Figure 9-4   The SEEK macro command

The INSERT macro command

```
ISREDIT INSERT line-pointer [count]
```

The SHIFT command

$$
\texttt{ISREDIT SHIFT} \begin{Bmatrix}) \\ (\\ < \\ > \end{Bmatrix} \texttt{line-pointer} \quad \texttt{[cols]}
$$

Explanation

line-pointer	The line new lines are to be inserted after, or the line where data is to be shifted.
count	The number of lines to insert. The default is 1.
)	Shift characters right.
(	Shift characters left.
>	Shift data right.
<	Shift data left.
cols	The number of columns to shift. The default is 2.

Figure 9-5 Macro commands that perform edit line command functions

How to use relative line numbers and labels in a macro

There are two features you can use to refer to specific lines in an edit macro command: relative line numbers and labels. *Relative line numbers* identify each line in a source member using sequential numbers. Don't confuse relative line numbers with line numbers that are stored as a part of the file. The line numbers stored with the source member are always maintained in ascending sequence, but they usually aren't consecutive. For example, stored line numbers may be in increments of 100. And, as lines are inserted and deleted, these line numbers may become irregular. In contrast, relative line numbers are always consecutive. The first line is always line 1, the second line is always line 2, and so on.

To use a relative line number, you simply include the line number wherever a command's syntax calls for a line pointer. For example, to delete relative line 100, you could use this DELETE command:

```
ISREDIT DELETE 100
```

Or, you could put the relative line number in a variable, as in this CLIST example:

```
SET &LINE = 100
ISREDIT DELETE &LINE
```

Here, the relative line number is assigned to the variable &LINE. Then, the DELETE command uses the variable's value to determine what line to delete.

There are several problems with using relative line numbers in a macro. The most obvious is that relative line numbers refer to lines by their position in the file rather than by their contents. For most of the files you work with, the position of each individual line in the file isn't important; the line's content is. So a macro that finds a particular text string and deletes the line that contains it is much more useful than a macro that deletes relative line 100, no matter what it contains.

A more subtle problem with relative line numbers is that they can change after the execution of any edit command. For example, if you delete relative line 100, the data that was in relative line 250 is no longer in relative line 250; it's moved to relative line 249. That's because the lines following the deleted line are renumbered. Similarly, relative line numbers change whenever you insert a line.

Because of these limitations, you'll use a label more often than a relative line number to refer to an individual line in a source member. A *label* is an alphabetic name that begins with a period and marks a particular line in a file. Labels don't move when lines are inserted or deleted. As a result, once a label has been assigned to a line, it stays with that line even when the line numbers are resequenced.

ISPF maintains the three predefined labels shown in figure 9-6 automatically, and you'll use them extensively in edit macros. The most useful is .ZCSR, which represents the *current line*. When an edit macro is invoked, .ZCSR is assigned to the line that contains the last cursor position. But remember that many edit commands invoked from a macro, such as FIND, SEEK, and LOCATE, alter this current line.

Label	Assigned to
.ZCSR	The current line.
.ZFIRST	The first line in the file.
.ZLAST	The last line in the file.

Figure 9-6   Predefined labels

To illustrate how you might use .ZCSR, suppose you want to delete the next occurrence of a line that contains a search string stored in the CLIST variable &STRING. You can do that with two edit commands:

```
ISREDIT FIND &STRING
ISREDIT DELETE .ZCSR
```

First, the FIND command positions the current line to the line that contains &STRING. Then, the DELETE command deletes the current line.

To assign your own label to a line, you use the LABEL command, shown in figure 9-7. On the left side of the equals sign, you identify the line you want the label assigned to. Usually, you'll specify .ZCSR here so the label is assigned to the current line. On the right of the equals sign, you specify the label you want to assign. You can use any combination of one to eight alphabetic characters, but you can't start the label with the letter Z; labels that start with .Z are reserved for ISPF's use.

The *level* parameter lets you control whether your label exists only during the execution of your macro or whether it persists after your macro completes. If you are creating a label you want to use in your macro, but want deleted when the macro finishes, omit this parameter. Then, ISPF creates the label at the *current level*, which means it exists only within the current macro. If you want the user to be able to use the label after the macro finishes, specify 0 for the level. Level 0 is the *user level*. (Labels at the user level are restricted to 5 characters.)

To illustrate the LABEL command, figure 9-8 shows a macro that assigns labels to the lines in a COBOL program that contain the File Section, Working-Storage Section, and Procedure Division headers. As you can see in both the CLIST and REXX versions, this

---

The LABEL macro command

```
ISREDIT LABEL line-pointer = .label [level]
```

Explanation

line-pointer	A relative line number or label identifying the line where a label is to be assigned.
.label	A one- to eight-character alphabetic name assigned to the line. The name can start with any letter other than Z. If the label is assigned at level 0, it must be five characters or less. It must be preceded by a period.
level	Specifies the nesting level where the label is visible. Labels defined at level 0 can be used by the terminal user. Labels defined at the current level (by omitting the level option) can be referenced in the macro, but can't be seen by the user.

Figure 9-7 The LABEL macro command

The SETLABEL macro (CLIST version)

```
ISREDIT MACRO
ISREDIT LABEL .ZCSR = .HERE
ISREDIT FIND "FILE SECTION" FIRST
ISREDIT LABEL .ZCSR = .FILE 0
ISREDIT FIND "WORKING-STORAGE SECTION" NEXT
ISREDIT LABEL .ZCSR = .WS 0
ISREDIT FIND "PROCEDURE DIVISION" NEXT
ISREDIT LABEL .ZCSR = .PROC 0
ISREDIT LOCATE .HERE
```

The SETLABEL macro (REXX version)

```
/* REXX */
address ispexec
"ISREDIT MACRO"
"ISREDIT LABEL .ZCSR = .HERE"
"ISREDIT FIND 'FILE SECTION' FIRST"
"ISREDIT LABEL .ZCSR = .FILE 0"
"ISREDIT FIND 'WORKING-STORAGE SECTION' NEXT"
"ISREDIT LABEL .ZCSR = .WS 0"
"ISREDIT FIND 'PROCEDURE DIVISION' NEXT"
"ISREDIT LABEL .ZCSR = .PROC 0"
"ISREDIT LOCATE .HERE"
```

Figure 9-8 The SETLABEL macro

The LINENUM macro command

```
ISREDIT (variable) = LINENUM label
```

Explanation

variable   A CLIST or REXX variable name that will receieve the line number.

label   A label that identifies the line whose line number is to be returned. To return
            the line number of the current line, specify .ZCSR.

Figure 9-9   The LINENUM macro command

macro consists of a series of FIND and LABEL commands. Each FIND command locates a particular line in the COBOL program. Then, the corresponding LABEL command assigns a meaningful label to the line. You invoke this macro by typing SETLABEL in the primary command area. Then, you can scroll directly to the File Section, Working-Storage Section, or Procedure Division by entering LOCATE .FILE, LOCATE .WS, or LOCATE .PROC.

Notice here that before the first FIND command, a LABEL command assigns the label .HERE to the current line, indicated by .ZCSR. That way, after the level-0 labels have been assigned, a LOCATE command returns the cursor to its original position. Because the .HERE label is assigned at the current level rather than at the user level, it is deleted when the macro finishes.

In some cases, you might want to know the relative line number of a label. For example, you can determine the number of lines in a source file by extracting the relative line number of the .ZLAST label, which marks the last line in the file. To do that, you use the LINENUM command, shown in figure 9-9. The LINENUM command shows the special format you must use to set the value of a variable in an edit macro command. As you can see, you must enclose the variable in parentheses, like this:

```
ISREDIT (COUNT) = LINENUM .ZLAST
```

Here, the relative line number of the last line is assigned to the variable COUNT. Note that you don't use an ampersand in the variable name, even when you use this command in a CLIST. To refer to the value of this variable later in the CLIST, however, you must use the ampersand.

MACRO PROGRAMMING TECHNIQUES

Now that you know the basics of creating and using macros, you're ready to learn the programming techniques that let you create more complex macros. So here, you'll learn those techniques. ·

How to handle errors in a macro

The macros I've shown you so far haven't included error checking. However, any but the most trivial macros should test for error conditions that are likely to occur. For example, what if a FIND command cannot find a specified search string? Or what if a LOCATE command directs the editor to scroll to a label that doesn't exist?

The basic technique for error checking is to test the *return code* issued by each edit macro command. In a CLIST procedure, you check the return code by testing the &LASTCC variable. In a REXX procedure, you test the RC variable. Depending on the return code issued for each command, your procedure can display an error message, terminate the macro by issuing an EXIT command, or simply ignore the error condition.

All ISPF edit commands issue a return code of zero to indicate that the command completed successfully. Any non-zero return code means that the command encountered some type of error. Many commands issue a non-zero return code below 12 to indicate that a minor error occurred, and a return code of 12 or more to indicate that a serious error occurred. Figure 9-10 lists the return codes most often encountered when using edit commands. The action you take when one of these return codes is detected depends, of course, on your procedure's requirements. (All of the commands in figure 9-10 except LINE, LINE_AFTER, LINE_BEFORE, and PROCESS should be familiar. I'll explain these commands later in this chapter.)

To properly handle errors, you must know how to display a message to the edit user. To do that, you use an ISPF SETMSG command, whose format is shown in figure 9-11. Note that this

Command	Return code	Meaning
CHANGE	4	String not found
	8	Unable to make change
CREATE	8	Member already exists
DELETE	4	No lines deleted
	8	No records in file
	12	Invalid line number
EXCLUDE	4	String not found
	8	Lines not excluded
FIND	4	String not found
INSERT	12	Invalid line number
LABEL	8	Duplicate label replaced
	12	Invalid line number
LINE	4	Source data truncated
	8	Variable not found
	12	Invalid line number
	16	Variable data truncated
LINE_AFTER	4	Data truncated
LINE_BEFORE	12	Invalid line number
LINENUM	8	Label not found
LOCATE	4	Line not found
	8	Empty file
PROCESS	4	Default range used
	8	Default destination used
	12	Default range and destination used
	16	Invalid line commands
SAVE	4	New member created
	12	Not enough space
SEEK	4	String not found
SHIFT	12	Invalid line number

Figure 9-10   Some commonly encountered return codes from edit commands

---

The SETMSG command

```
ISPEXEC SETMSG MSG(message-id)
```

Explanation

message-id   Specify ISRZ000 to display a message without sounding the terminal's audible alarm or ISRZ001 to display a message and sound the alarm.

Note: Before issuing the SETMSG command, set the variable ZEDSMSG to the short message text and set the variable ZEDLMSG to the long message text.

Figure 9-11   The SETMSG command

command is *not* an edit macro command. As a result, it does not begin with the word ISREDIT. Instead, when you use CLIST, you must precede it with the word ISPEXEC. That way, it will be processed by ISPF. In a REXX procedure, the ADDRESS ISPEXEC command causes all host commands to be automatically processed by ISPF. So when you use REXX, you shouldn't specify ISPEXEC in a SETMSG command.

The SETMSG command doesn't actually display a message at the terminal. Instead, it sets up the messages that will be displayed when the macro ends. SETMSG can set two messages: a short message, which is displayed at the top right of the screen, and a longer message, which is displayed only if the user presses the Help key, PF1/13. Before you invoke SETMSG, you must set two system variables to the messages you wish to display. For the short message, the variable name is ZEDSMSG; for the long message, the variable name is ZEDLMSG.

You use the MSG parameter to specify whether or not you want the terminal's audible alarm to sound when the message is displayed. If you want the alarm to sound, specify ISRZ001 in the MSG parameter. Otherwise, specify ISRZ000. Usually, you'll specify ISRZ000.

To illustrate the techniques for detecting errors and displaying messages, figure 9-12 shows an expanded version of the SETLABEL macro. This procedure is similar to the one shown in figure 9-8, but displays a message if any of the FIND commands fail. As you

The SETLABEL macro (CLIST version)

```
ISREDIT MACRO
ISREDIT LABEL .ZCSR = .HERE
ISREDIT FIND "FILE SECTION" FIRST
IF &LASTCC = 0 THEN -
    ISREDIT LABEL .ZCSR = .FILE 0
ELSE DO
    SET &ZEDSMSG = NO FILE SECTION
    SET &ZEDLMSG = FILE SECTION HEADER NOT FOUND
    ISPEXEC SETMSG MSG(ISRZ001)
    END
ISREDIT FIND "WORKING-STORAGE SECTION" NEXT
IF &LASTCC = 0 THEN -
    ISREDIT LABEL .ZCSR = .WS 0
ELSE DO
    SET &ZEDSMSG = NO WORKING STORAGE
    SET &ZEDLMSG = WORKING-STORAGE SECTION HEADER NOT FOUND
    ISPEXEC SETMSG MSG(ISRZ001)
    END
ISREDIT FIND "PROCEDURE DIVISION" NEXT
IF &LASTCC = 0 THEN -
    ISREDIT LABEL .ZCSR = .PROC 0
ELSE DO
    SET &ZEDSMSG = NO PROCEDURE DIVISION
    SET &ZEDLMSG = PROCEDURE DIVISION HEADER NOT FOUND
    ISPEXEC SETMSG MSG(ISRZ001)
    END
ISREDIT LOCATE .HERE
```

Figure 9-12   A SETLABEL macro with error checking (part 1 of 2)

can see, I followed each FIND command with an IF statement to test the return code. If the return code is 0, the ISREDIT LABEL command assigns the label. If the return code is not zero, the ZEDSMSG and ZEDLMSG variables are set to appropriate error messages and the SETMSG command is used to establish the error messages.

One thing to note about this procedure is that although any or all of the FIND commands can fail, only one error message, the last one formatted, is displayed. As a result, if the SETLABEL macro cannot find either a Working-Storage Section or a Procedure Division header, only the message for the Procedure Division is displayed.

The SETLABEL macro (REXX version)

```
/* REXX */
address ispexec
"ISREDIT MACRO"
"ISREDIT LABEL .ZCSR = .HERE"
"ISREDIT FIND 'FILE SECTION' FIRST"
if rc = 0 then
    "ISREDIT LABEL .ZCSR = .FILE 0"
else do
    zedsmsg="NO FILE SECTION"
    zedlmsg="FILE SECTION HEADER NOT FOUND"
    "SETMSG MSG(ISRZ001)"
    end
"ISREDIT FIND 'WORKING-STORAGE SECTION' NEXT"
if rc = 0 then
    "ISREDIT LABEL .ZCSR = .WS 0"
else do
    zedsmsg="NO WORKING STORAGE"
    zedlmsg="WORKING STORAGE SECTION HEADER NOT FOUND"
    "SETMSG MSG(ISRZ001)"
    end
"ISREDIT FIND 'PROCEDURE DIVISION' NEXT"
if rc = 0 then
    "ISREDIT LABEL .ZCSR = .WS 0"
else do
    zedsmsg="NO PROCEDURE DIVISION"
    zedlmsg="PROCEDURE DIVISION HEADER NOT FOUND"
    "SETMSG MSG(ISRZ001)"
    end
"ISREDIT LOCATE .HERE"
```

Figure 9-12   A SETLABEL macro with error checking (part 2 of 2)

How to insert lines in a source member

As you already know, ISPF lets you use the INSERT command in a
macro to insert blank lines the user can enter data into. You can't,
however, insert data into those blank lines directly from your
macro. To do that, you must use one of the two macro commands
ISPF provides for inserting lines: LINE_AFTER and LINE_BEFORE.
Both commands have the same syntax, as shown in figure 9-13.
The only difference is that the LINE_AFTER command inserts a
line after the specified location, and LINE_BEFORE inserts a line

The LINE_AFTER and LINE_BEFORE commands

$$\text{ISREDIT} \begin{Bmatrix} \text{LINE\_AFTER} \\ \text{LINE\_BEFORE} \end{Bmatrix} \text{line-pointer} = \begin{Bmatrix} \text{DATALINE} \\ \text{INFOLINE} \\ \text{MSGLINE} \\ \text{NOTELINE} \end{Bmatrix} \begin{Bmatrix} \text{value} \\ \text{LINE} \\ \text{LINE pointer} \\ \text{MASKLINE} \\ \text{TABSLINE} \end{Bmatrix}$$

Explanation

LINE_AFTER	Insert a line after the line indicated by *line-pointer*.
LINE_BEFORE	Insert a line before the line indicated by *line-pointer*.
line-pointer	A line number or label that specifies the position where a line is inserted.
DATALINE	Insert a line of normal text data.
INFOLINE	Insert an information line using ====== in the line command area. The line is not saved as part of the file.
MSGLINE	Insert a message line using ==MSG> in the line command area. The line is not saved as part of the file.
NOTELINE	Insert a note line using =NOTE= in the line command area. The line is not saved as part of the data.
value	A variable or literal string.
LINE	Specifies that data from the preceding line is used for the inserted line.
LINE pointer	Specifies that data from the specified line is used for the inserted line.
MASKLINE	Specifies that data from the mask line is used for the inserted line.
TABSLINE	Specifies that data from the tabs line is used for the inserted line.

Figure 9-13   The LINE_AFTER and LINE_BEFORE commands

before it. Otherwise, the operation of these two commands is the same.

On the left of the equals sign, you indicate the location of the line you want to insert. In most cases, you'll want the line inserted immediately before or after the current location, so you'll specify .ZCSR. On the right of the equals sign, you code two parameters. The first indicates what type of line you want to insert, the second provides the data to be inserted.

To specify the type of line to be inserted, you code one of four options: DATALINE, INFOLINE, MSGLINE, and NOTELINE. If you specify DATALINE, the line is inserted as a standard data line that can be edited just like any other line in the member. If you specify one of the other three options, INFOLINE, MSGLINE, and NOTE-LINE, a special line is inserted that is not actually a part of the source member and cannot be edited. Since the line is not part of the source member, ISPF displays it only for the current editing session. When the editing session ends, the line is deleted. (During the editing session, you can delete the line by entering the RESET edit primary command.)

The only real difference between INFOLINE, MSGLINE, and NOTELINE is how the data is displayed. An INFOLINE is identified by the characters ====== in the line command area and is displayed in high intensity. A MSGLINE is identified by the characters ==MSG> in the line command area and is also displayed in high intensity. A NOTELINE is indicated by the characters =NOTE= in the line command area and is displayed in low intensity.

After you specify what type of line you want to insert, you must indicate what data you want to insert. The most common way to do this is to simply code the value as a string literal or specify a variable that contains the value. Alternatively, you can code LINE to use data from the preceding line, or LINE pointer to use data from a specified line. These options are most useful if you want to duplicate data, or if you want to copy a line from one type to another, such as from a DATALINE to a NOTELINE or vice-versa. The other two options, MASKLINE and TABSLINE, let you use the current mask line or tabs line for the data source.

To illustrate how the LINE_AFTER and LINE_BEFORE commands might be used, figure 9-14 shows a macro named BMS. This macro enters the COBOL statements needed to define a mapset for CICS programming. (If you're not familiar with CICS programming, don't be distracted with the details of setting up the BMS map fields. Instead, concentrate on how the macro works.) When you invoke the BMS macro, you specify three parameters: a prefix, a name, and a picture. The BMS macro uses the values you supply to generate the required data definitions.

If you study the BMS macro for a moment, you'll see that its operation is straightforward. It uses a series of LINE_AFTER commands to insert data lines into the source member, using the contents of the TEXT variable to obtain the data. Before each LINE_AFTER command, the TEXT variable is formatted with the

```
The BMS macro (CLIST version)

ISREDIT MACRO (PREFIX, NAME, PIC)
ISREDIT (LINE) = LINENUM .ZCSR
SET &TEXT = &STR(    05   &PREFIX-L-&NAME PIC S9(4) COMP.)
ISREDIT LINE_AFTER &LINE DATALINE '&TEXT'
SET &TEXT = &STR(    05   &PREFIX-A-&NAME PIC X.)
ISREDIT LINE_AFTER &EVAL(&LINE+1) = DATALINE '&TEXT'
SET &TEXT = &STR(    05   &PREFIX-D-&NAME PIC &PIC.)
ISREDIT LINE_AFTER &EVAL(&LINE+2) = DATALINE '&TEXT'
ISREDIT LINE_AFTER &EVAL(&LINE+3) DATALINE '*'


The BMS macro (REXX version)

/* REXX */
address ispexec
"ISREDIT MACRO (PREFIX, NAME, PIC)"
"ISREDIT (LINE) = LINENUM .ZCSR
Text = "    05   "Prefix"-L-"Name"    PIC S9(4) COMP."
"ISREDIT LINE_AFTER" Line "= DATALINE '"Text"'"
Text = "    05   "Prefix"-A-"Name"    PIC X."
"ISREDIT LINE_AFTER" Line+1 "= DATALINE '"Text"'"
Text = "    05   "Prefix"-D-"Name"    PIC "Pic"."
"ISREDIT LINE_AFTER" Line+2 "= DATALINE '"Text"'"
"ISREDIT LINE_AFTER" Line+3 "= DATALINE '*'"
```

Figure 9-14   The BMS macro

data for the line to be inserted. The last LINE_AFTER command uses a literal string rather than the TEXT variable.

Figure 9-15 shows the BMS macro in operation. In part 1, I typed this command in the command area:

```
BMS CM,CUSTOMER-ADDRESS,X(30)
```

Then, I positioned the cursor to the line where I want the lines inserted and pressed the Enter key. Part 2 shows the result. As you can see, the BMS macro inserts these lines into the program:

```
05   CM-L-CUSTOMER-ADDRESS   PIC S9(4) COMP.
05   CM-A-CUSTOMER-ADDRESS   PIC X.
05   CM-D-CUSTOMER-ADDRESS   PIC X(30).
*
```

The lines are inserted as regular data lines after the current cursor position.

Part 1:

Enter the BMS
command in the
command area and
position the cursor
where you want the
lines inserted

```
EDIT ---- DLOWE.TEST.COBOL(CUSTMAP) - 01.00 ------------------- COLUMNS 007 072
COMMAND ===> BMS CM,CUSTOMER-ADDRESS,X(30)                       SCROLL ===> DATA
****** ************************************* TOP OF DATA ****************************************
000100       05  CM-L-CUSTOMER-NUMBER    PIC S9(4) COMP.
000200       05  CM-A-CUSTOMER-NUMBER    PIC X.
000300       05  CM-D-CUSTOMER-NUMBER    PIC X(5).
000400 *
000500       05  CM-L-CUSTOMER-NAME      PIC S9(4) COMP.
000600       05  CM-A-CUSTOMER-NAME      PIC X.
000700       05  CM-D-CUSTOMER-NAME      PIC X(30).
000800 *




.  .  .  .  .  .  .  .  .  .  .  .  .  .  .  .  .  .  .  .  .  .  .  .  .  .
EDIT ---- DLOWE.TEST.EXEC(BMS) - 01.00 -------------------- MEMBER BMS SAVED
```

Part 2:

The BMS macro adds
four lines to the source
member

```
EDIT ---- DLOWE.TEST.COBOL(CUSTMAP) - 01.00 ------------------- COLUMNS 007 072
COMMAND ===>                                                    SCROLL ===> DATA
****** ************************************* TOP OF DATA ****************************************
000100       05  CM-L-CUSTOMER-NUMBER    PIC S9(4) COMP.
000200       05  CM-A-CUSTOMER-NUMBER    PIC X.
000300       05  CM-D-CUSTOMER-NUMBER    PIC X(5).
000400 *
000500       05  CM-L-CUSTOMER-NAME      PIC S9(4) COMP.
000600       05  CM-A-CUSTOMER-NAME      PIC X.
000700       05  CM-D-CUSTOMER-NAME      PIC X(30).
000800 *
000900       05  CM-L-CUSTOMER-ADDRESS   PIC S9(4) COMP.
001000       05  CM-A-CUSTOMER-ADDRESS   PIC X.
001100       05  CM-D-CUSTOMER-ADDRESS   PIC X(30).
001200 *
****** ************************************* BOTTOM OF DATA ****************************************



.  .  .  .  .  .  .  .  .  .  .  .  .  .  .  .  .  .  .  .  .  .  .  .  .  .
EDIT ---- DLOWE.TEST.EXEC(BMS) - 01.00 -------------------- MEMBER BMS SAVED
```

Figure 9-15   Using the BMS macro

The LINE command

Format 1:

```
ISREDIT (variable) = LINE line-pointer
```

Format 2:

```
ISREDIT LINE line-pointer = value
```

Explanation

variable	The variable that receives the line data.
line-pointer	A line number or label that identifies the line to be retrieved or replaced.
value	A variable or literal value that replaces the line specified by *line-pointer*.

Figure 9-16   The LINE command

How to retrieve and replace source data in a macro

In addition to adding data, a macro should also be able to retrieve and replace data in the source member. To do that, you use the LINE command, shown in figure 9-16. You can use this command to copy the contents of a specified line into a variable, or to copy the contents of a variable into a specified line.

Figure 9-17 shows a macro that uses the LINE command. This macro, named GOTO, uses a LINE command to retrieve the current line, scans it to see if it contains a PERFORM or GO TO statement, then uses a FIND command to scroll to the paragraph or section specified in the PERFORM or GO TO statement. The only confusing part of the macro is the code that evaluates the line to determine if it contains a PERFORM or GO TO statement and, if so, to extract the paragraph or section name. It allows for any number of spaces before and after the paragraph or section name, and removes a period that may or may not be present.

I hope this macro helps you see the value of using REXX rather than CLIST for edit macros. In the REXX version of the macro, the code required to determine whether the line contains a PERFORM or GO TO statement and to extract the paragraph or section label

The GOTO macro (CLIST version)

```
ISREDIT MACRO
ISREDIT (TEXT) = LINE .ZCSR                          /* Extract line      */
SET TEXT = &SYSCAPS(&TEXT)
SET VERBPOS = &SYSINDEX(PERFORM,&TEXT)               /* Locate PERFORM    */
SET LABELPOS = &VERBPOS+7
IF &VERBPOS = 0 THEN DO
    SET VERBPOS = &SYSINDEX(&STR(GO TO),&TEXT)       /* or GO TO          */
    SET LABELPOS = &VERBPOS+5
    END
IF VERBPOS = 0 THEN DO                               /* No label          */
    SET ZEDSMSG = &STR(NO LABEL)
    SET ZEDLMSG = &STR(THE CURRENT LINE DOES NOT CONTAIN A LABEL)
    ISPEXEC SETMSG MSG(ISRZ001)
    EXIT
    END
DO LABELPOS = &LABELPOS TO 80 +                      /* Find start of     */
    UNTIL &SUBSTR(&LABELPOS,&TEXT) ¬= &STR( )        /* label             */
END
DO LABELEND = &LABELPOS TO 80 +                      /* Find end of       */
    UNTIL &SUBSTR(&LABELEND,&TEXT) ¬= &STR( )        /* label             */
        OR &SUBSTR(&LABELEND,&TEXT) ¬= .
END
SET LABEL = &SUBSTR(&LABELPOS:&LABELEND-1,&TEXT)     /* Extract label     */
ISREDIT SEEK LABEL FIRST 2                           /* SEEK label        */
IF &LASTCC = 4 THEN DO                               /* Not found         */
    SET ZEDSMSG = &STR(NOT FOUND)
    SET ZEDLMSG = &STR(THE PARAGRAPH OR SECTION COULD NOT BE FOUND)
    ISPEXEC SETMSG MSG(ISRZ001)
    END
```

Figure 9-17   The GOTO macro (Part 1 of 2)

from the line is simple: two PARSE instructions do the job. Then, a STRIP function removes any leading and trailing blanks and the trailing period that is likely to occur. In contrast, the code required to accomplish this same function in the CLIST is confusing. CLIST doesn't provide text parsing functions that are as powerful as the REXX PARSE instruction, so I had to use a combination of &SYSINDEX functions and DO loops that contain &SUBSTR functions. In short, any time you need to code a macro that extracts text from the file and processes it in any but the most trivial ways, you're better off if you implement the macro in REXX rather than CLIST.

The GOTO macro (REXX version)

```
/* REXX */
address ispexec
"ISREDIT MACRO"
"ISREDIT (TEXT) = LINE .ZCSR"                        /* Extract line    */
parse upper value Text with "PERFORM" Label .        /* Find PERFORM or */
if Label = "" then                                   /* GO TO and       */
    parse upper value Text with "GO TO" Label .      /* extract label   */
if Label = "" then do                                /* No label        */
    zedsmsg = "NO LABEL"
    zedlmsg = "THE CURRENT LINE DOES NOT CONTAIN A LABEL"
    "SETMSG MSG(ISRZ001)"
    exit
    end
Label = strip(strip(Label,"L"),"T",".")              /* Strip label     */
"ISREDIT SEEK" Label "FIRST 2"                        /* Seek label      */
if rc = 4 then do                                    /* Not found       */
    zedsmsg = "NOT FOUND"
    zedlmsg = "THE PARAGRAPH OR SECTION COULD NOT BE FOUND"
    "SETMSG MSG(ISRZ001)"
    end
```

Figure 9-17 The GOTO macro (Part 2 of 2)

How to use edit assignment statements

Edit assignment statements let you manipulate information maintained by the editor. Edit assignment statements are similar to TSO or REXX system variables; they contain information about the current editing environment, such as the name of the data set being edited and the current cursor position. Some of them, such as the name of the data set, can be queried but not changed. Others, such as the cursor position, can be both queried and changed.

Any of the ISPF edit modes can be queried in an edit assignment statement. For example, the following assignment determines the current status of the STATS mode:

```
ISREDIT (STATSMODE) = STATS
```

If STATS is on, the variable STATSMODE will be set to ON; if it is off, STATSMODE will be set to OFF. You can also set an edit mode in an assignment statement, like this:

```
ISREDIT STATS = ON
```

Assignment statement	Description
CHANGE_COUNTS	Returns two values: the number of strings that were changed and the number of strings that could not be changed.
CURSOR	Returns two values representing the line and column position of the cursor.
DATA_CHANGED	Returns YES if the data has been changed since it was last saved, and NO if it hasn't.
DATASET	Returns the name of the current data set.
EXCLUDE_COUNTS	Returns two values: the number of strings that were found, and the number of lines that were excluded.
FIND_COUNTS	Returns two values: the number of strings that were found, and the number of lines where strings were found.
MEMBER	Returns the name of the current member.
RANGE_CMD	The line command that was used to mark a range.
SEEK_COUNTS	Returns two values: the number of strings that were found, and the number of lines where strings were found.
USER_STATE	Returns the current edit profile in an internal form that can be later restored.

Figure 9-18 Useful edit macro assignments that can be queried

This is equivalent to issuing a STATS ON command.

In addition to assignment statements for edit modes, ISPF provides many other edit assignments. Figure 9-18 lists the most useful ones. All of these assignments can be queried, but only CURSOR and USER_STATE can be set. For example, you can determine the name of the data set being edited with this statement:

```
ISREDIT (DSN) = DATASET
```

However, you can't change the name of the data set by using the DATASET assignment statement.

As you can see in figure 9-18, some of the edit assignment statements return two values. For example, the FIND_COUNTS assignment statement returns the number of strings found, and the number of lines where strings were found. To use this assignment, you must provide two variables in parentheses, separated by a space or comma, like this:

```
ISREDIT (STRINGS,LINES) = FIND_COUNTS
```

Here, STRINGS will be set to the number of strings found, and LINES will be set to the number of lines where strings were found.

One edit assignment statement that's particularly useful is USER_STATE. It lets you save and restore the current user profile, cursor position, and other aspects of the user's editing environment. To save the user's state, add this statement near the beginning of your macro:

```
ISREDIT (STATE) = USER_STATE
```

Then, to restore the user state, add this statement at the end of your macro:

```
ISREDIT USER_STATE = (STATE)
```

Unlike other assignment statements, USER_STATE requires that you code the variable on the right side of the equals sign in parentheses. That's because USER_STATE stores the user's edit environment in an internal form that shouldn't be parsed by the REXX or CLIST command processor.

How to process line commands

All of the macros I've shown so far operate as if they were primary commands. Although you can't invoke a macro as a line command, you can create macros that work with line commands in much the same way that the CREATE and REPLACE primary commands use the C and M line commands to mark the text you want copied to a file, and that the COPY and MOVE commands use the A and B line commands to mark the location where you want data copied into a file. To do this, you have to use the ISREDIT PROCESS command, shown in figure 9-19.

The ISREDIT PROCESS command actually has two functions. First, it tells ISPF when to process the line commands and text changes the user made on the screen before invoking the macro. Usually, any line commands and text changes are processed before the macro begins to execute. But if you code the keyword NO-PROCESS on the ISREDIT MACRO command, like this:

```
ISREDIT MACRO NOPROCESS
```

The PROCESS macro command

```
ISREDIT PROCESS [DEST] [RANGE line-command]
```

Explanation

DEST	Causes ISPF to assign the label .ZDEST to the destination line indicated by a B or A line command.
RANGE	Causes ISPF to assign the labels .ZFRANGE and .ZLRANGE to the first and last lines indicated by *line-command*.

Figure 9-19   The PROCESS macro command

the line commands and text changes aren't processed until the ISREDIT PROCESS command is encountered. As a result, the macro can perform operations on source data in its original form, before line commands and text changes are applied.

In most cases, you should avoid using the ISREDIT PROCESS command for this purpose. ISPF users are accustomed to line commands being processed before primary commands, and a change in this processing sequence can be confusing. So if you use an ISREDIT PROCESS command, you should normally place it immediately after the ISREDIT MACRO command.

The second function of the ISREDIT PROCESS command is to let the macro define its own line commands. ISPF macros can process two types of line commands. The first marks a destination line; the second marks a range of lines. Although you can use these line commands in any way you wish, you'll probably use them as they are used in the CREATE/REPLACE and COPY/MOVE commands. In other words, you'll use the range line commands to mark a range of lines that will be processed by your macro, and you'll use the destination line commands to mark the location of data that your macro inserts into the source file.

To use destination line commands, you simply code the word DEST on the ISREDIT PROCESS command, like this:

```
ISREDIT PROCESS DEST
```

When you issue this command, ISPF looks for an A or B line command and assigns the label .ZDEST to the line immediately before the destination. Thus, if the user uses an A line command,

.ZDEST will be assigned to the line where the A line command was entered. But if the user uses a B line command, .ZDEST will be assigned to the line before the line where the B line command was entered. Because A and B are standard destination commands for other edit line commands, most users should have no trouble using them.

To use range line commands, you code the word RANGE on the ISREDIT PROCESS command, followed by one or two line commands each one to six characters long. For example, the command

```
ISREDIT PROCESS RANGE N
```

locates the lines the user marked with N line commands before invoking the macro. The user can use the same range marking techniques that are available for standard line commands. Thus, N alone marks a single line, N5 marks a range of five lines, and a pair of NN line commands marks a range that includes the lines with the NN commands and all the lines between them.

So you can use the range in your macro, ISPF assigns the label .ZFRANGE to the first line in the range and .ZLRANGE to the last line in the range. If there is only one line in the range, both .ZFRANGE and .ZLRANGE are assigned to the same line.

If you specify two line commands, the PROCESS RANGE command will locate a range of lines marked by either of the commands. Then, the macro can determine what processing to perform based on the line command entered. For example, suppose you code the ISREDIT PROCESS command like this:

```
ISREDIT PROCESS RANGE Y Z
```

Here, the user can mark a range using either Y or Z line commands. To determine what command was used, use a RANGE_CMD assignment statement, like this:

```
ISREDIT (COMMAND) = RANGE_CMD
```

This statement will assign either Y or Z to the variable COMMAND, depending on what range command the user entered.

If you want to provide for both range and destination line commands in a macro, you can specify both RANGE and DEST options on the ISREDIT PROCESS command, like this:

```
ISREDIT PROCESS DEST RANGE Q
```

A macro that includes this command can process A and B destination line commands as well as a range of lines marked by Q commands.

If the user incorrectly enters the line commands, the ISREDIT PROCESS command will issue a non-zero return code. A return code of 4 means the ISREDIT PROCESS command specified a range but none was marked by the user. A return code of 8 means the ISREDIT PROCESS command specified a destination but none was marked. A return code of 12 means both a destination and a range were expected, but neither was provided. In all three cases, default settings are used: for the range, the default is the entire file; for the destination, the default is the last line in the file. A return code of 16 means that line commands were used but entered improperly. For this return code, no defaults are set, so the macro probably cannot continue.

To illustrate how line commands can be used in an edit macro, figure 9-20 shows a CLIST and REXX version of a macro named MAKENOTE. This macro converts lines marked by N commands to note lines. To do this, it first locates the lines to be converted using an ISREDIT PROCESS RANGE command. Then, it assigns the line numbers of the first and last lines in the range to the variables FIRST and LAST. Next, it issues ISREDIT LINE_BEFORE commands to copy data lines to note lines. Finally, it issues ISREDIT DELETE commands to delete the data lines.

Figure 9-21 shows the MAKENOTE macro in action. In part 1, I marked a range of lines with NN line commands and entered MAKENOTE in the primary command area. Part 2 shows the result: The marked lines have been converted to note lines.

I want you to notice two things in this macro. First, notice the error checking that follows the ISREDIT PROCESS command. If a non-zero return code is encountered, the macro displays an error message and terminates. Although the macro could continue if a return code of 4 is encountered, the default settings for the range labels would cause the macro to convert the entire source file to notes. Since that's probably not the user's intention, it's better to terminate the macro in this case.

Second, notice the technique I used to process each line in the range. After I obtained the line numbers for the first and last lines in the range, I processed the range *backwards* in a DO loop that varies a line-pointer from the last line to the first line, subtracting one for each iteration of the loop. I did this for a simple reason. Since each pass through the loop deletes a line from the file, lines

The MAKENOTE macro (CLIST version)

```
ISREDIT MACRO NOPROCESS
ISREDIT PROCESS RANGE N
IF &LASTCC > 0 THEN DO
    SET &ZEDSMSG = MISSING LINE COMMAND
    SET &ZEDLMSG = &STR(ISREDIT PROCESS RETURN CODE =) &LASTCC
    ISPEXEC SETMSG MSG(ISRZ001)
    EXIT
    END
ISREDIT (FIRST) = LINENUM .ZFRANGE
ISREDIT (LAST) = LINENUM .ZLRANGE
DO &RLINE = &LAST TO &FIRST BY -1
    ISREDIT LINE_BEFORE &RLINE = NOTELINE LINE
    ISREDIT DELETE &RLINE
END
```

The MAKENOTE macro (REXX version)

```
/* REXX */
address ispexec
"ISREDIT MACRO NOPROCESS"
"ISREDIT PROCESS RANGE N"
if rc > 0 then do
    zedsmsg="MISSING LINE COMMAND"
    zedlmsg="ISREDIT PROCESS RETURN CODE =" rc
    "SETMSG MSG(ISRZ001)"
    exit
    end
"ISREDIT (FIRST) = LINENUM .ZFRANGE"
"ISREDIT (LAST) = LINENUM .ZLRANGE"
do Rline = Last to First by -1
    "ISREDIT LINE_BEFORE" Rline "= NOTELINE LINE"
    "ISREDIT DELETE" Rline
end
```

Figure 9-20   The MAKENOTE macro

that follow the deleted line are renumbered. If I processed the range from the first line, I would have to adjust the line numbers on each pass. But because I processed the range backwards, the line number of the current line for each iteration of the loop isn't affected. Processing the range backwards, whenever possible, is considerably easier.

Part 1:

Mark the lines to be converted to notes with NN line commands and invoke the MAKENOTE macro

```
EDIT ---- DLOWE.TEST.COBOL(MKTG1200) - 01.07 --------------- COLUMNS 007 072
COMMAND ===> MAKENOTE                                        SCROLL ===> DATA
****** ********************************** TOP OF DATA ***********************************
000100  IDENTIFICATION DIVISION.
000200 *
000300  PROGRAM-ID.       MKTG1200.
000400 *
000500  ENVIRONMENT DIVISION.
000600 *
000700  CONFIGURATION SECTION.
000800 *
000900  INPUT-OUTPUT SECTION.
001000 *
001100  FILE-CONTROL.
001200      SELECT CUSTMST  ASSIGN TO AS-CUSTMST.
NN          SELECT SALESMN  ASSIGN TO SALESMN
001400                      ORGANIZATION IS INDEXED
001500                      ACCESS IS RANDOM
NN                          RECORD KEY IS SM-SALESMAN-KEY.
001700      SELECT SALESRPT ASSIGN TO SALESRPT.
001800 *
001900  DATA DIVISION.
002000 *
002100  FILE SECTION.
```

Part 2:

The MAKENOTE macro converts the marked lines to notes

```
EDIT ---- DLOWE.TEST.COBOL(MKTG1200) - 01.08 --------------- COLUMNS 007 072
COMMAND ===>                                                 SCROLL ===> DATA
****** ********************************** TOP OF DATA ***********************************
000100  IDENTIFICATION DIVISION.
000200 *
000300  PROGRAM-ID.       MKTG1200.
000400 *
000500  ENVIRONMENT DIVISION.
000600 *
000700  CONFIGURATION SECTION.
000800 *
000900  INPUT-OUTPUT SECTION.
001000 *
001100  FILE-CONTROL.
001200      SELECT CUSTMST  ASSIGN TO AS-CUSTMST.
=NOTE=      SELECT SALESMN  ASSIGN TO SALESMN
=NOTE=                      ORGANIZATION IS INDEXED
=NOTE=                      ACCESS IS RANDOM
=NOTE=                      RECORD KEY IS SM-SALESMAN-KEY.
001700      SELECT SALESRPT ASSIGN TO SALESRPT.
001800 *
001900  DATA DIVISION.
002000 *
002100  FILE SECTION.
```

Figure 9-21   Using the MAKENOTE macro

How to use an initial macro

Ordinarily, you invoke a macro by typing its name on the primary command line. However, if you have a macro that you want to invoke every time you edit a certain type of file, you can specify that macro as the *initial macro* in the profile for that file type. For example, you might want to use the SETLABEL macro that was presented in figure 9-8 as an initial macro for COBOL files. That way, labels are automatically set up whenever you edit a COBOL program.

To use an initial macro for an edit profile, you use the edit IMACRO command. For example, to specify SETLABEL as the initial macro for COBOL files, enter this command while you are editing a COBOL file:

    IMACRO SETLABEL

Then, when you save the file, the IMACRO specification will be recorded as a part of the COBOL profile, so the SETLABEL macro will be executed automatically whenever you edit a COBOL file. To disable an initial macro setting in a profile, enter this command:

    IMACRO NONE

Then, when you save the member, the profile will be updated again and the IMACRO setting will be disabled.

You can override the profile's initial macro setting by filling in the INITIAL MACRO field on the ISPF edit entry panel. For example, to use the macro COBINIT instead of the initial macro specified in the profile, enter this:

    INITIAL MACRO ===> COBINIT

If you want to bypass the initial macro altogether, enter the word NONE in the INITIAL MACRO field:

    INITIAL MACRO ===> NONE

Then, no initial macro is executed at all. Note that using the INITIAL MACRO field changes the initial macro only for the current editing session; it doesn't change the initial macro setting in the profile.

DISCUSSION

Edit macros are one of the most powerful features of the ISPF editor. As a result, if you use the ISPF editor on a regular basis, you should learn how to use the edit macro features I've presented here. As I said at the outset, I've presented only a small subset of what you can do with edit macros in this chapter. But I've presented all of the edit macro facilities you need for most macros.

Terms

edit macro
relative line number
label
current line
level
current level
user level
return code
edit assignment statements
initial macro

Objective

Use the facilities presented in this chapter to create simple edit macros that make routine editing tasks easier.

Chapter 10

How to create and use ISPF dialogs

ISPF is more than just a text editor and some utilities; it's a complete application development system that can support any type of terminal-based application. *PDF*, which stands for *Program Development Facility*, is one example of the applications ISPF can support.

All ISPF applications are based on dialogs between the user and the computer using panels similar to the panels you use with PDF. As a result, ISPF is often called the *dialog manager* and ISPF applications are often called *dialogs*. In this chapter, you'll learn how to create your own dialogs by incorporating dialog manager features into your CLIST or REXX procedures. Although you can use ISPF to create dialogs that function as stand-alone applications, the details required to do that are beyond the scope of this book. Instead, I'll show you how to use dialog manager features to create simple dialogs that you can invoke from within ISPF/PDF.

Because dialog manager is a complex subject, I've divided this chapter into two topics. In topic 1, you'll learn how to create dialogs that use simple display panels. In topic 2, you'll learn how to create dialogs that utilize a more advanced dialog manager feature called table services.

Topic 1

How to create dialogs that use full-screen entry panels

One of the most common reasons for using dialog manager is to create CLIST and REXX procedures that communicate with the terminal user via full-screen panels instead of line-by-line terminal I/O. In chapter 6, for example, I presented a CLIST that lets a terminal user order manuals or other documents on-line. That CLIST used WRITE commands to prompt the user for input and READ commands to read the input values the user entered. In chapter 8, I presented a REXX version of the same procedure. It used SAY and PARSE instructions for terminal I/O. In this topic, you'll learn how to use ISPF to perform these and other terminal I/O functions using full-screen panels.

ISPF DIALOG BASICS

Before you can start coding ISPF dialogs, you have to learn some basic concepts. In particular, you must understand how the various components that make up a dialog work together, how a simple dialog works, how to allocate the ISPF libraries required for a dialog, and how to use the ISPF/PDF dialog test option.

How dialog components work together

In the simplest sense, an ISPF dialog is a REXX or CLIST procedure that includes commands that invoke ISPF dialog services. As you learn how to invoke those services, however, you'll see that a dialog actually consists of several *components*. Figure 10-1 shows how these components work together.

The primary component of an ISPF dialog is the CLIST or REXX procedure that controls the dialog's execution. In ISPF terminology, this procedure is called a *function*. A function can also be a

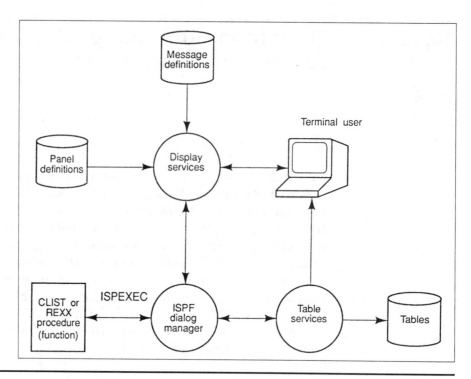

Figure 10-1   Dialog components

compiled program written in the COBOL, PL/I, or C language. However, developing a compiled program function is more complicated than developing a CLIST or REXX procedure function, so I don't show you how to do it here.

The function invokes dialog manager services by issuing ISPEXEC commands, which are processed by the ISPF dialog manager. The dialog manager, in turn, passes these commands on to one of the ISPF dialog services. I've included two of these services in figure 10-1: display services and table services. There are other services available besides these, but I don't cover them in this book.

Display services, used to process full-screen panels, use two additional types of components: panel definitions and message definitions. In a *panel definition*, you describe the format of a panel by supplying the location of each field on the screen and by identifying the variables that are used to provide values for output fields and that receive values from input fields. In addition, you can specify certain processing options to be performed before and after the panel is displayed.

ISPF *message definitions* let you store messages in a library so you can refer to them by number in any procedure. You can either create your own message definitions, or use generic message definitions provided with ISPF/PDF. I'll show you how to use display services and how to define panels and messages later in this topic.

Table services let you maintain simple databases in the form of tables. Each row in the table represents a record and each column represents a field. With table services, you can create a new table by specifying the characteristics of each column. And you can insert, update, retrieve, and delete rows in an existing table. In addition, table services can display the contents of a table, automatically handling scrolling functions so the user can scroll forward and backward through the table using standard ISPF scrolling keys. I'll show you how to use table services in the next topic.

A simple ISPF dialog

Figures 10-2, 10-3, and 10-4 present a simple ISPF dialog that should help you see how these components work together. This dialog is similar to the ORDERS CLIST I presented in chapter 6, and to the ORDERS exec I presented in chapter 8. It lets a user order up to five technical manuals by entering an employee and department number and the document id and quantity for each manual ordered. The CLIST and REXX versions I presented in chapters 6 and 8 prompted the user for this information line-by-line. The dialog version obtains the required information from the user using the full-screen panel shown in figure 10-2.

Figure 10-3 is the panel definition for the ORDER panel. I'll explain the details of this panel definition later in this chapter, so don't worry if you don't understand all of it now. What I want you to notice here is how the lines following the)BODY line specify the format of the panel when it's displayed. The special characters in these lines (%, +, _, and #) are attribute characters that mark the beginning and end of fields on the screen. And the names following the underscores (ZCMD, EMPNO, DEPT, DOCID1 through DOCID5, and QT1 through QT5) identify the variables that will contain the data entered into these fields.

Figure 10-4 shows the CLIST and REXX versions of the procedure that controls this dialog. Again, I'll explain the details of these

```
------------------------ DOCUMENT ORDER - ENTRY PANEL ------------------------

EMPLOYEE NUMBER ===> 37
DEPARTMENT       ===> 100


DOCUMENT ID ===> SC34-4213    QUANTITY ===> 1
            ===> SC34-4215             ===> 1
            ===>                       ===>
            ===>                       ===>
            ===>                       ===>
```

Figure 10-2   The ORDER dialog panel

```
)ATTR
# TYPE(TEXT) INTENS(LOW) SKIP(ON)
)BODY
%-------------------- DOCUMENT ORDER -- ENTRY PANEL ----------------------
%COMMAND ===>_ZCMD
%
+EMPLOYEE NUMBER ===>_EMPNO    #
+DEPARTMENT      ===>_DEPT#
%
%
+DOCUMENT ID ===>_DOCID1    #    QUANTITY ===>_QT1#
+DOCUMENT ID ===>_DOCID2    #    QUANTITY ===>_QT2#
+DOCUMENT ID ===>_DOCID3    #    QUANTITY ===>_QT3#
+DOCUMENT ID ===>_DOCID4    #    QUANTITY ===>_QT4#
+DOCUMENT ID ===>_DOCID5    #    QUANTITY ===>_QT5#
)END
```

Figure 10-3   The ORDER panel definition

The ORDER procedure (CLIST version)

```
ISPEXEC LIBDEF ISPPLIB DATASET ID(USER.PANELS)
ALLOCATE DDNAME(ORDER) DSNAME(ORDER.DATA) MOD
OPENFILE ORDER OUTPUT
ISPEXEC DISPLAY PANEL(ORDER)
IF &STR(&DOCID1) ¬= &STR() THEN DO
    SET ORDER = &EMPNO &SYSUID &DEPT &STR(&DOCID1) &QT1
    PUTFILE ORDER
    END
IF &STR(&DOCID2) ¬= &STR() THEN DO
    SET ORDER = &EMPNO &SYSUID &DEPT &STR(&DOCID2) &QT2
    PUTFILE ORDER
    END
IF &STR(&DOCID3) ¬= &STR() THEN DO
    SET ORDER = &EMPNO &SYSUID &DEPT &STR(&DOCID3) &QT3
    PUTFILE ORDER
    END
IF &STR(&DOCID4) ¬= &STR() THEN DO
    SET ORDER = &EMPNO &SYSUID &DEPT &STR(&DOCID4) &QT4
    PUTFILE ORDER
    END
IF &STR(&DOCID5) ¬= &STR() THEN DO
    SET ORDER = &EMPNO &SYSUID &DEPT &STR(&DOCID5) &QT5
    PUTFILE ORDER
    END
WRITE YOUR ORDER HAS BEEN PLACED
CLOSFILE ORDER
FREE DDNAME(ORDER)
ISPEXEC LIBDEF ISPPLIB
```

The ORDER procedure (REXX version)

```
/* REXX */
"ALLOCATE DDNAME(ORDER) DSNAME(ORDER.DATA) MOD"
address ispexec
"LIBDEF ISPPLIB DATASET ID(USER.PANELS)"
"DISPLAY PANEL(ORDER)"
if Docid1 ¬= "" then
    queue Empno Sysuid Dept Docid1 Qt1
if Docid2 ¬= "" then
    queue Empno Sysuid Dept Docid2 Qt2
if Docid3 ¬= "" then
    queue Empno Sysuid Dept Docid3 Qt3
if Docid4 ¬= "" then
    queue Empno Sysuid Dept Docid4 Qt4
if Docid5 ¬= "" then
    queue Empno Sysuid Dept Docid5 Qt5
queue
address tso
"EXECIO * DISKW ORDER (FINIS"
say YOUR ORDER HAS BEEN PLACED
"FREE DDNAME(ORDER)"
address ispexec
"LIBDEF ISPPLIB"
```

Figure 10-4   The ORDER procedure

Library type	Contents
ISPPLIB	Panel definitions
ISPMLIB	Message definitions
ISPTLIB	Table input library
ISPTABL	Table output library

Figure 10-5   ISPF libraries

procedures later. For now, notice the two ISPEXEC commands that are highlighted in each procedure. (In a REXX procedure, you don't have to code the word ISPEXEC in these commands. I'll explain why in a moment.) The first ISPEXEC command is a LIBDEF command; it allocates the ISPF panel library that contains the ORDER panel definition. I'll show you how to code it next. The second is a DISPLAY command; it displays the ORDER panel and waits for the user to enter data. I'll present this command later in this topic.

How to allocate ISPF libraries for dialogs

Dialog components, such as panel definitions and tables, are stored in ISPF libraries. For example, panel definitions are stored in an ISPF panel library. Before a dialog can use a particular panel, you must allocate the library that contains it. Likewise, you must allocate other component libraries before you can use the components they contain.

Figure 10-5 lists the ddnames ISPF uses to refer to its libraries. Usually, one or more libraries are allocated to each of these ddnames in your TSO logon procedure. For example, your logon procedure probably allocates the ISPF panel library, named ISP.V3R1M0.ISPPLIB and the ISPF/PDF panel library, named ISR.V3R1M0.ISPPLIB, to ISPPLIB. (The names of these data sets might be different at your installation; these are IBM's standard names for ISPF Version 3.1.) In addition, other panel libraries might be allocated to ISPPLIB. Whenever a dialog requests a panel,

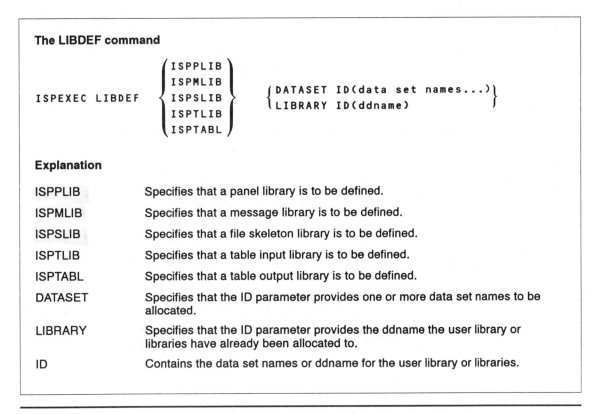

Figure 10-6   The LIBDEF command

the libraries allocated to ISPPLIB are searched in the order specified when they were allocated.

Before you can use your own panel definitions and other ISPF components, you have to make sure the libraries that contain them are properly allocated. In some cases, user libraries may already be allocated for you in your TSO logon procedure. Then, all you have to do is put your components in the correct library. Most installations, however, do not automatically allocate user ISPF libraries. So you must add your libraries to the existing library concatenations.

To do that, you use the ISPF LIBDEF command, shown in figure 10-6. After the words ISPEXEC LIBDEF, you specify the type of library you are allocating, such as ISPPLIB or ISPMLIB. Then, you code the word DATASET followed by an ID parameter containing one or more data set names. Alternatively, you can code the word LIBRARY followed by an ID parameter containing a

---

Example 1

```
ISPEXEC LIBDEF ISPPLIB DATASET ID(USER.PANELS)
```

Example 2

```
ALLOCATE DDNAME(UPANEL) DSNAME(USER.PANELS) SHR REUSE
ISPEXEC LIBDEF ISPPLIB LIBRARY ID(UPANEL)
```

Example 3

```
ALLOCATE LIBDEF ISPPLIB       Cancel prev. LIBDef
```

Figure 10-7   Three examples of the LIBDEF command

---

ddname. If you do, you must first issue an ALLOCATE command to allocate your libraries to the ddname you specify. Because it's easier to use, I recommend the DATASET form of the LIBDEF command.

Figure 10-7 shows three examples of the LIBDEF command. Example 1 uses the DATASET parameter to allocate a user panel library by name; example 2 uses the LIBRARY parameter to specify the ddname of a previously allocated user panel library.

In example 3, I omitted the DATASET, LIBRARY, and ID parameters altogether. That cancels the previous LIBDEF for the specified library type, so ISPF no longer searches the user library. You should do this at the end of your CLIST or REXX procedure so ISPF doesn't continue searching your user library after your dialog has finished.

By the way, if you're coding your procedure in REXX, you can omit the word ISPEXEC if you first issue this instruction:

```
address ispexec
```

That's because this ADDRESS instruction automatically addresses all host commands to the ISPEXEC command processor rather than the TSO command processor.

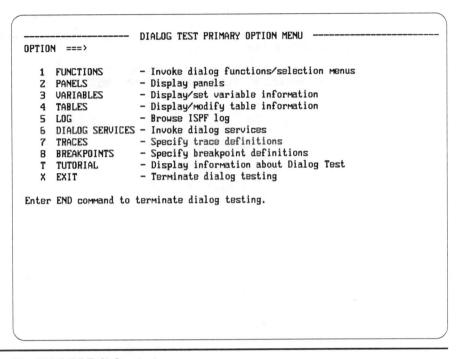

```
----------------------  DIALOG TEST PRIMARY OPTION MENU  -------------------------
OPTION  ===>

     1  FUNCTIONS       - Invoke dialog functions/selection menus
     2  PANELS          - Display panels
     3  VARIABLES       - Display/set variable information
     4  TABLES          - Display/modify table information
     5  LOG             - Browse ISPF log
     6  DIALOG SERVICES - Invoke dialog services
     7  TRACES          - Specify trace definitions
     8  BREAKPOINTS     - Specify breakpoint definitions
     T  TUTORIAL        - Display information about Dialog Test
     X  EXIT            - Terminate dialog testing

Enter END command to terminate dialog testing.
```

Figure 10-8   The ISPF/PDF dialog test menu

How to use the ISPF/PDF dialog test option

When you develop a procedure that invokes dialog services, you should use the ISPF/PDF dialog test option. To invoke it, select option 7 from the ISPF/PDF primary option menu. Then, ISPF displays the dialog test primary option menu, shown in figure 10-8. Although the dialog test menu lists 9 options (including the tutorial), I'm going to describe only three of them here: 7.1, FUNCTIONS, which lets you invoke a CLIST or REXX procedure that issues dialog commands; 7.2, PANELS, which lets you test a panel definition before you code a procedure to display it; and 7.6, DIALOG SERVICES, which lets you issue any ISPEXEC command. The other functions are useful only when you're coding dialogs that are considerably more complicated than the ones you'll learn to create here.

Incidentally, the fact that the dialog test menu is a *primary option menu* means that it is itself running as a separate dialog,

```
------------------------------  INVOKE DIALOG SERVICE  -----------------------------
COMMAND ===>

ENTER DIALOG SERVICE AND ITS PARAMETERS:
===> LIBDEF ISPPLIB DATASET ID(TEST.PANELS)
```

Figure 10-9   Using the dialog services option to issue a LIBDEF command

isolated from ISPF/PDF. As a result, if your dialog fails (and during testing, it probably will), it won't corrupt your ISPF/PDF session. Once you get the bugs worked out, you can safely run your procedure using the TSO command from any ISPF/PDF panel. But until then, it's safest to invoke it from the dialog test option.

Figure 10-9 shows how to invoke an ISPEXEC command using the dialog services option, option 7.6. Here, after selecting the dialog services option, I entered a LIBDEF command to allocate the library that contains my panel definitions. The keyword ISPEXEC isn't required, since any command you enter here is assumed to be an ISPEXEC command. When the command completes, ISPF displays a message indicating the return code in the short message area (the right-hand portion of the top line).

Figure 10-10 shows the entry panel that's displayed when you select the panels option, option 7.2. Here, I entered ORDER, the name of the panel I want to display. When I press the Enter key, the ORDER panel is displayed just as it was shown in figure 10-2. To return to the entry panel, press the Enter key again.

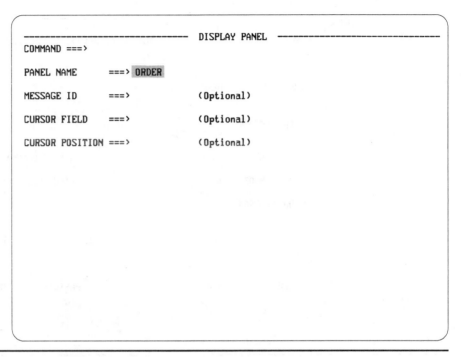

```
--------------------------------  DISPLAY PANEL  --------------------------------
COMMAND ===>

PANEL NAME       ===> ORDER

MESSAGE ID       ===>              (Optional)

CURSOR FIELD     ===>              (Optional)

CURSOR POSITION ===>               (Optional)
```

Figure 10-10   Using the panels option to display a panel

Figure 10-11 shows the functions panel, option 7.1. Using this panel, you can invoke a CLIST or REXX procedure by entering the name of the procedure in the CMD field. Alternatively, you can invoke a compiled program by entering its name in the PGM field, or you can use the PANEL field to invoke a menu by specifying its panel definition. In figure 10-11, I entered ORDER, the name of the procedure, in the CMD field.

If ISPF detects an error while you are testing a dialog, it displays a panel similar to the one in figure 10-12. In this case, I tried to display a panel that couldn't be located. Notice the question at the bottom of the screen. If you press the Enter key leaving the default answer NO, the dialog test option is terminated, and you are returned to the ISPF primary option menu. If you change the response to YES, you'll be returned to the dialog test menu. Since the error may have corrupted ISPF data, there's no guarantee that you'll be able to continue safely. However, for the types of errors you'll encounter while testing simple dialogs, you can usually continue without any problems.

```
--------------------- INVOKE DIALOG FUNCTION/SELECTION MENU ---------------------
COMMAND ===>


INVOKE SELECTION MENU:
         PANEL  ===>                              OPT    ===>

INVOKE COMMAND:
         CMD    ===> ORDER

         LANG   ===>                              (APL OR BLANK)

         MODE   ===>                              (LINE, FSCR, OR BLANK)

INVOKE PROGRAM:
         PGM    ===>                              PARM   ===>

         MODE   ===>                              (LINE, FSCR, OR BLANK)

NEWAPPL         ===> NO                           ID     ===>

NEWPOOL         ===> NO                           PASSLIB ===> NO
```

Figure 10-11   Using the functions option to invoke a dialog

```
---------------------------- ISPF DIALOG ERROR ----------------------------
COMMAND ===>


**********************************************************************************
*                                                                              *
*    PANEL 'ORDER' ERROR                                                        *
*    PANEL NOT FOUND.                                                           *
*                                                                              *
*                                                                              *
*                                                                              *
*                                                                              *
*                                                                              *
*                                                                              *
*    Enter HELP command for further information regarding this error.          *
*    Press ENTER key to terminate the dialog.                                  *
*                                                                              *
*    OVERRIDE TERMINATION AND ATTEMPT TO CONTINUE                              *
*                     ===> NO  (YES or NO)                                      *
*                                                                              *
**********************************************************************************
```

Figure 10-12   An ISPF dialog error panel

```
)ATTR
# TYPE(TEXT) INTENS(LOW) SKIP(ON)
)BODY
%---------------------- DOCUMENT ORDER - ENTRY PANEL --------------------
%COMMAND ===>_ZCMD
%
+EMPLOYEE NUMBER ===>_EMPNO      #
+DEPARTMENT      ===>_DEPT#
%
%
+DOCUMENT ID ===>_DOCID1    #    QUANTITY ===>_QT1#
+DOCUMENT ID ===>_DOCID2    #    QUANTITY ===>_QT2#
+DOCUMENT ID ===>_DOCID3    #    QUANTITY ===>_QT3#
+DOCUMENT ID ===>_DOCID4    #    QUANTITY ===>_QT4#
+DOCUMENT ID ===>_DOCID5    #    QUANTITY ===>_QT5#
)END
```

Figure 10-13   The ORDER panel definition

HOW TO CREATE A PANEL DEFINITION

As I've already mentioned, you must create a panel definition
before you can use ISPF to display a panel. The panel definition
contains formatting information that specifies the location of each
field on the screen. In addition, it identifies CLIST or REXX variables that provide values for output fields and receive values from
input fields. The easiest way to create a panel definition is using
the ISPF/PDF editor. Just make sure you turn NUMBERS mode
OFF so ISPF/PDF doesn't add line numbers to the member.

I first presented the panel definition for the ORDER dialog in
figure 10-3. For your convenience, I've duplicated it in figure 10-13.
The first thing I want you to notice about it is that it is divided into
two sections. The first section is marked by an)ATTR statement
and the second is marked by a)BODY statement. The last line
contains an)END statement, which marks the end of the panel
definition. Although there are other sections you can include in a
panel definition, these two are all you need to define most panels.

How to specify attributes: The)ATTR section

To define each field in a panel, you use *attribute characters*. Each
attribute character identifies the characteristics of a field, such as

Attribute character	Description
%	High-intensity output field
+	Low-intensity output field
_	High-intensity input field

Figure 10-14   ISPF's default attributes

whether the field is used for input or output, whether it is displayed in high or low intensity, and so on. You use these attribute characters in the)BODY section of the panel definition, where you specify the placement of each field in the panel.

Figure 10-14 shows ISPF's three default attribute characters: %, +, and _. The % character specifies a high-intensity output-only field. The + character specifies a low-intensity output-only field. You use these attributes to mark fields that contain headings and other constant data. The _ character specifies a high-intensity input field. You use this attribute to mark fields that accept information from the user.

You use the attribute section of a panel definition to specify additional attribute characters you would like to use in the body section. Each attribute character definition consists of the character you want to use, followed by one or more of the attribute settings listed in figure 10-15. Although you can define any character except an ampersand (&) or a blank as an attribute character, you should limit yourself to special characters that you don't want to appear as text in your panel, like !, @, #, and $.

The attribute section in figure 10-13 defines just one attribute character, #, which is used to indicate an output-only field displayed in low intensity with the SKIP attribute on. When the cursor reaches a field with this attribute, it automatically skips to the beginning of the next input field. As a result, skip attributes are often used to mark the end of input fields, so that the cursor automatically advances to the next input field. Since ISPF doesn't provide a default attribute character with this setting, you need to define one yourself.

The first attribute in figure 10-15, TYPE, specifies one of three field types: INPUT, OUTPUT, or TEXT. In the)BODY section, INPUT

Attribute value	Description
TYPE($\left\{\begin{array}{l}\text{TEXT}\\\text{INPUT}\\\text{OUTPUT}\end{array}\right\}$)	Specifies the type of a field. TEXT indicates a protected field that contains a mixture of literal text and symbolic variables. INPUT indicates an unprotected field that's defined by a symbolic variable. OUPUT indicates a protected field that's defined by a symbolic variable.
INTENS($\left\{\begin{array}{l}\text{HIGH}\\\text{LOW}\end{array}\right\}$)	Specifies the intensity of a field. HIGH indicates high-intensity and LOW indicates low-intensity.
CAPS($\left\{\begin{array}{l}\text{ON}\\\text{OFF}\end{array}\right\}$)	Specifies whether data is translated to uppercase. ON indicates that data is translated to uppercase before it's displayed and input fields are translated to uppercase before they're stored. OFF indicates that data is displayed as stored and input fields are stored as entered. This attribute doesn't apply to text fields.
JUST($\left\{\begin{array}{l}\text{LEFT}\\\text{RIGHT}\\\text{ASIS}\end{array}\right\}$)	Specifies how the data in a field is justified when it's displayed. LEFT indicates that the field is left justified. RIGHT indicates that the field is right justified. And ASIS indicates that no justification is done. This attribute doesn't apply to text fields.
SKIP($\left\{\begin{array}{l}\text{ON}\\\text{OFF}\end{array}\right\}$)	Specifies whether protected fields are skipped during data entry. ON indicates that the field is skipped. OFF indicates that it's not skipped. This attribute doesn't apply to input fields.
NUMERIC($\left\{\begin{array}{l}\text{ON}\\\text{OFF}\end{array}\right\}$)	Specifies whether the numeric lock feature is activated for a field. ON indicates that the feature is activated and only a numeric value can be entered into the field. OFF indicates that the feature is not activated and any characters can be entered into the field. This attribute applies only to input fields.
COLOR(color)	Specifies the field's color when displayed on a seven-color terminal. Color may be WHITE, RED, BLUE, GREEN, PINK, YELLOW, or TURQ (for turquoise).
HILITE($\left\{\begin{array}{l}\text{USCORE}\\\text{BLINK}\\\text{REVERSE}\end{array}\right\}$)	Specifies an extended highlighting option used when the field is displayed on a terminal that supports extended highlighting. Hilite may be USCORE (underscore), BLINK, or REVERSE (dark characters on a light background).

Figure 10-15   Attribute settings you can use in the)ATTR section

and OUTPUT fields are associated with CLIST or REXX variables that supply the field's contents. The only difference between an INPUT and an OUTPUT field is that an INPUT field is unprotected, so the terminal user can modify its contents. In contrast, an OUTPUT field is protected, so its contents cannot be changed. A TEXT field is similar to an OUTPUT field, but it can contain literal data as well as CLIST or REXX variables.

Most of the other attribute settings listed in figure 10-15 control the appearance of data displayed in the field. For example, the INTENS attribute controls whether a field is displayed with low or high intensity. And the COLOR attribute controls the field's color. If you've done any on-line programming (for example, with CICS), these attributes should already be familiar to you. Even if you haven't, the descriptions in figure 10-15 should be adequate.

How to specify a panel's format: The)BODY section

The)BODY section of an ISPF panel defines what the panel looks like when it's displayed. Each line in the)BODY section corresponds to a line on the display. On each line, you can define one or more fields by coding an attribute character followed by a text string or CLIST or REXX variable.

The first three lines in the body section in figure 10-13 set up the top three lines of the panel so they'll appear similar to other ISPF panels. Thus, the first line contains a single text field (marked by the % attribute character in column 1) that contains the panel's title. The second line contains two fields. The first, marked by the % attribute character, contains the literal value COMMAND ===>. The second, marked by the _ attribute character, is an input field that uses the variable ZCMD. ZCMD is a reserved ISPF variable that processes the command line. By including it, you enable the user to enter ISPF primary commands. The third line is a blank line, defined with a % attribute character.

The rest of the)BODY section lines define the remaining input fields. Each begins with a low-intensity text field that serves as a caption for the input field that follows. Each input field begins with the _ attribute character, which is immediately followed by the name of the CLIST or REXX variable that is used to store the contents of the field. The end of the field is indicated by a # attribute character, which specifies that the cursor should automatically skip to the next input field. The size of the field on the screen

---

The DISPLAY command

```
ISPEXEC DISPLAY PANEL(panel-name)
```

Explanation

panel-name   The name of the panel you want to display. The panel must be in a library
              allocated to ISPPLIB or specified in a LIBDEF command.

Figure 10-16   The DISPLAY command

is determined by the number of column positions between the
starting _ attribute character and the ending # attribute character.
(Incidentally, ISPF lets you use a special technique to create variable
names that are longer than the names of the panel fields that
contain them. I'll show you how to use this technique later in this
topic.)

Once you've created your panel definition, you can display it
under ISPF/PDF using the panels option on the dialog test menu.
First, allocate your panel library by entering a LIBDEF command
from the dialog services panel, as shown in figure 10-9. Then, use
the panels option to display the panel, as shown in figure 10-10.
The resulting display will help you determine whether or not
you've entered your panel definition correctly.

HOW TO DISPLAY A PANEL FROM A PROCEDURE

To display a panel from a CLIST or REXX procedure, you use the
DISPLAY command, shown in figure 10-16. Just as for the LIBDEF
command, you can omit the word ISPEXEC if you're coding the
command in a REXX procedure that first issues an ADDRESS
ISPEXEC instruction.

To use this command, you specify the name of the panel you
want to display on the PANEL operand. For example, to display the
ORDER panel, code this command:

```
ISPEXEC DISPLAY PANEL(ORDER)
```

Then, the DISPLAY command searches its panel libraries to find the member named ORDER, and displays the panel according to the format ORDER specifies.

It's important to realize that the DISPLAY command provides for both panel output and input. First, the DISPLAY command formats and displays the output panel. Then, the user can type data into any of the panel's input fields. When the user presses the Enter key or a PF key, the DISPLAY command places the data entered by the user into the symbolic variables specified as the input fields. That way, the CLIST or REXX procedure can process the data entered by the user. If the user presses the End key, PF3/15, the DISPLAY command issues a return code of 8, which can be detected by testing the &LASTCC variable in a CLIST or the RC variable in a REXX procedure.

I first presented the CLIST and REXX versions of the procedure that displays and processes the ORDER panel in figure 10-4. For your convenience, I've duplicated it in figure 10-17. This procedure should be easy enough to understand. First, a LIBDEF command establishes USER.PANELS as the panel library. Next, a TSO ALLOCATE command allocates the output data set. Then, a DISPLAY command displays the panel. The CLIST version also includes an OPENFILE command to open the ORDER file for output. This command isn't required in the REXX version.

After the panel is displayed, a series of IF statements tests each DOCID variable to see if a record should be written to the ORDER file. Depending on how many document ids the user enters, as many as five records are written. In the CLIST version, a SET command formats the &ORDER variable and a PUTFILE command writes it to the file. In the REXX version, the output data is queued to the stack; then, the entire stack is written to the file in a single EXECIO command. Notice that a final queue instruction places a null entry at the bottom of the queue. If I had omitted this instruction, REXX would have waited for terminal input before completing the EXECIO command.

After the data is written, a message displays indicating the order has been placed. Then, the ORDER file is freed, and the user panel library is deactivated. The CLIST version also includes a CLOSFILE command to close the ORDER file.

The ORDER procedure (CLIST version)

```
ISPEXEC LIBDEF ISPPLIB DATASET ID(USER.PANELS)
ALLOCATE DDNAME(ORDER) DSNAME(ORDER.DATA) MOD
OPENFILE ORDER OUTPUT
ISPEXEC DISPLAY PANEL(ORDER)
IF &STR(&DOCID1) ¬= &STR() THEN DO
    SET ORDER = &EMPNO &SYSUID &DEPT &STR(&DOCID1) &QT1
    PUTFILE ORDER
    END
IF &STR(&DOCID2) ¬= &STR() THEN DO
    SET ORDER = &EMPNO &SYSUID &DEPT &STR(&DOCID2) &QT2
    PUTFILE ORDER
    END
IF &STR(&DOCID3) ¬= &STR() THEN DO
    SET ORDER = &EMPNO &SYSUID &DEPT &STR(&DOCID3) &QT3
    PUTFILE ORDER
    END
IF &STR(&DOCID4) ¬= &STR() THEN DO
    SET ORDER = &EMPNO &SYSUID &DEPT &STR(&DOCID4) &QT4
    PUTFILE ORDER
    END
IF &STR(&DOCID5) ¬= &STR() THEN DO
    SET ORDER = &EMPNO &SYSUID &DEPT &STR(&DOCID5) &QT5
    PUTFILE ORDER
    END
WRITE YOUR ORDER HAS BEEN PLACED
CLOSFILE ORDER
FREE DDNAME(ORDER)
ISPEXEC LIBDEF ISPPLIB
```

The ORDER procedure (REXX version)

```
/* REXX */
"ALLOCATE DDNAME(ORDER) DSNAME(ORDER.DATA) MOD"
address ispexec
"LIBDEF ISPPLIB DATASET ID(USER.PANELS)"
"DISPLAY PANEL(ORDER)"
if Docid1 ¬= "" then
    queue Empno Sysuid Dept Docid1 Qt1
if Docid2 ¬= "" then
    queue Empno Sysuid Dept Docid2 Qt2
if Docid3 ¬= "" then
    queue Empno Sysuid Dept Docid3 Qt3
if Docid4 ¬= "" then
    queue Empno Sysuid Dept Docid4 Qt4
if Docid5 ¬= "" then
    queue Empno Sysuid Dept Docid5 Qt5
queue
address tso
"EXECIO * DISKW ORDER (FINIS"
say YOUR ORDER HAS BEEN PLACED
"FREE DDNAME(ORDER)"
address ispexec
"LIBDEF ISPPLIB"
```

Figure 10-17   The ORDER procedure

HOW TO USE EXECUTABLE PANEL SECTIONS

As I mentioned earlier, ISPF panel definitions can contain other sections besides the)ATTR and)BODY sections. The three other sections you can include are)INIT,)REINIT, and)PROC. These sections are called *executable sections* because they contain executable statements like assignment statements and IF statements. Although you can code many ISPF dialogs without these sections, using them can often simplify your dialogs.

The)INIT section includes statements that are processed before a panel is displayed, and the)PROC section contains statements that are executed after a panel is displayed. If the)PROC section detects a user input error, the panel will be displayed again. But first, the statements in the)REINIT section are processed. Then, after the panel is displayed, the)PROC section is executed again.

Figure 10-18 summarizes this processing. Notice how most of the panel display processing occurs in a loop that ends when the user enters an END or RETURN command, or when a special ISPF variable named .MSG is blank. If you don't include a)PROC section, the .MSG variable will always be blank, so the loop will execute only once. But in the)PROC section, you can include statements that test the data entered by the user. Then, if invalid data is detected, you can set the .MSG variable to a non-blank value to force the procedure to display the panel again. However, if the user enters an END or RETURN command, the loop ends regardless of the contents of the .MSG variable.

How to validate input data in the)PROC section

One of the most useful features of the)PROC section is that it lets you include statements that validate the input data entered by the user and force the procedure to display the panel again if an error is detected. Because you can include the validation processing in a panel definition, you don't have to code any special CLIST or REXX statements to validate data and redisplay the panel.

ISPF provides several statements you can include in a)PROC section to validate input data. The most versatile is the VER statement, shown in figure 10-19. The VER statement tests a variable to determine if it meets the validation test you specify. If the variable fails the validation test, ISPF sets the .MSG variable to a default

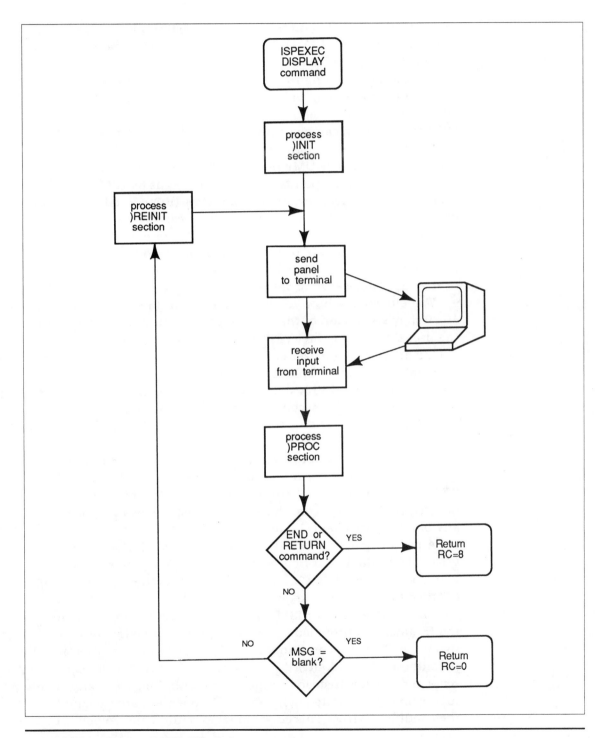

Figure 10-18 DISPLAY service processing

message-id, depending on the type of validation test you specified. This causes the DISPLAY command to redisplay the panel with an appropriate short message.

As you can see in figure 10-19, the VER statement provides for many different types of validation tests. The most basic is NONBLANK, which means that the variable must contain a value. Other tests, which can be combined with NONBLANK, let you test whether a variable contains: alphabetic characters (ALPHA); numeric characters (NUM); numeric characters and numeric symbols like decimal points, commas, and signs (ENUM); hexadecimal characters (HEX); or binary characters (BIN). In addition, you can make sure that the variable contains a certain number of characters (LEN), matches a picture string (PICT), or contains a member or data set name (NAME or DSNAME). Finally, you can test a variable to make sure its value falls within a particular range (RANGE) or matches one of several values in a list (LIST).

To help you see how you can use the VER statement, figure 10-20 shows a version of the ORDER panel definition that validates the user's input. The first VER statement tests the &EMPNO variable to make sure the user enters an employee number. Any entry is acceptable for the employee number, as long as some data is entered. The second VER statement makes sure the user enters one of the company's five acceptable department numbers: 100, 200, 300, 400, or 500.

The next five VER statements test the DOCID fields to make sure that the document ids follow IBM's document numbering system. They accept document ids in the form AANN-NNNN. Thus, SC34-4213 and SC28-1876 are acceptable document ids. Because I omitted NONBLANK from these statements, the user may leave any or all of these fields blank.

After verifying the DOCID fields, the)PROC section verifies the QT fields. To do that, it first tests each DOCID field to see if it is blank. If it contains data, a VER statement tests the corresponding QT field to make sure the quantity is nonblank and numeric.

The IF statement for ISPF panel definitions is different from the IF statement provided by most programming languages in two ways. First, the conditional expression must be enclosed in parentheses. Second, the IF statement doesn't provide an explicit scope terminator. Instead, it relies on indentation. Thus, any statements that are indented beneath the IF statement are executed if the condition is true. This conditional execution ends when ISPF

The VER statement

```
VER (variable [,NONBLANK] [validation-test] [,MSG=value])
```

Explanation

variable	The name of the variable to be tested.
NONBLANK	Specifies that the variable must contain a non-blank value.
validation-test	One of the following keyword tests:

	ALPHA	The variable must contain only alphabetic characters (A-Z, a-z, #, $, or @).
	NUM	The variable must contain only numeric characters (leading blanks are allowed, but trailing blanks are not).
	ENUM	The variable must contain only numeric characters or symbols commonly used to format numeric values, such as signs, commas, decimals, and so on.
	HEX	The variable must contain only hexadecimal characters (0-9, A-F).
	BIN	The variable must contain only zeros and ones.
	LEN,operator,length	The variable's length must match the specified condition. Any operator valid for an IF statement can be used.
	PICT,string	The variable's data must match the picture string. The picture string can include the following characters:

	C	any character
	A	any alphabetic character
	N	any numeric character
	9	same as N
	X	any hexadecimal character

Any other special characters represent themselves.

	NAME	The variable must contain a valid member name.
	DSNAME	The variable must contain a valid data set name.
	RANGE,lower,upper	The variable must be a number that falls within the given range.
	LIST,value-1,value-2...	The variable must match one of the values listed. Up to 100 values may be listed.
MSG		Specifies the message-id of the message to be issued if the variable fails the validation. If omitted, ISPF supplies a default message.

Figure 10-19 The VER statement

```
)ATTR
# TYPE(TEXT) INTENS(LOW) SKIP(ON)
)BODY
%---------------------- DOCUMENT ORDER - ENTRY PANEL --------------------
%COMMAND ===>_ZCMD
%
+EMPLOYEE NUMBER ===>_EMPNO    #
+DEPARTMENT       ===>_DEPT#
%
%
+DOCUMENT ID ===>_DOCID1   #    QUANTITY ===>_QT1#
+DOCUMENT ID ===>_DOCID2   #    QUANTITY ===>_QT2#
+DOCUMENT ID ===>_DOCID3   #    QUANTITY ===>_QT3#
+DOCUMENT ID ===>_DOCID4   #    QUANTITY ===>_QT4#
+DOCUMENT ID ===>_DOCID5   #    QUANTITY ===>_QT5#
)PROC
VER(&EMPNO,NONBLANK)
VER(&DEPT,NONBLANK,LIST,100,200,300,400,500)
VER(&DOCID1,PICT,AANN-NNNN)
VER(&DOCID2,PICT,AANN-NNNN)
VER(&DOCID3,PICT,AANN-NNNN)
VER(&DOCID4,PICT,AANN-NNNN)
VER(&DOCID5,PICT,AANN-NNNN)
IF (&DOCID1 ¬= ' ')
    VER(&QT1,NONBLANK,NUM)
IF (&DOCID2 ¬= ' ')
    VER(&QT2,NONBLANK,NUM)
IF (&DOCID3 ¬= ' ')
    VER(&QT3,NONBLANK,NUM)
IF (&DOCID4 ¬= ' ')
    VER(&QT4,NONBLANK,NUM)
IF (&DOCID5 ¬= ' ')
    VER(&QT5,NONBLANK,NUM)
)END
```

Figure 10-20   A version of the ORDER panel definition that validates input

encounters a statement that is aligned with the IF clause. You can include an ELSE structure by aligning the word ELSE with the word IF, then indenting the statements to be executed if the original condition is false. The examples in figure 10-21 should make this convention clear.

Example 1	Explanation
| ```
IF (condition)
    statement-1
    statement-2
statement-3
``` | Statement-1 and statement-2 are executed if condition is true. Statement-3 is executed regardless of whether condition is true or false. |

Example 2	
| ```
IF (condition)
    statement-1
    statement-2
ELSE
    statement-3
    statement-4
statement-5
``` | Statement-1 and statement-2 are executed if condition is true. Statement-3 and statement-4 are executed if condition is false. Statement-5 is executed regardless of whether condition is true or false. |

Example 3	
| ```
IF (condition-1)
    statement-1
    statement-2
    IF (condition-2)
        statement-3
        statement-4
    statement-5
    statement-6
statement-7
``` | Statement-1 and statement-2 are executed if condition-1 is true. Statement-3 and statement-4 are executed if both condition-1 and condition-2 are true. Statement-5 and statement-6 are executed if condition-1 is true, regardless of whether condition-2 is true or false. And statement-7 is executed regardless of whether condition-1 and condition-2 are true or false. |

Figure 10-21   Examples of using indentation in an IF statement

How to use Z variable placeholders in the)INIT section

One of the most common uses of the)INIT section involves a technique called *Z variable placeholders*. This technique lets you create panel fields whose names are longer than the fields they define. For example, you can use a Z variable placeholder to create a one-character input field assigned to a variable named JCLASS.

Figure 10-22 shows how the placeholder technique works. In the)BODY section of the panel, you use the variable name Z whenever you want to assign a placeholder variable. In this example, I
```

```
)ATTR
#  TYPE(TEXT) INTENS(LOW) SKIP(ON)
)BODY
  .
  .
  .
+JOB CLASS       ===>_Z#
+MESSAGE CLASS ===>_Z#
+STMT LEVEL     ===>_Z#
+MESSAGE LEVEL ===>_Z#
  .
  .
  .
)INIT
.ZVARS='(JCLASS MCLASS SLEVEL MLEVEL)'
)PROC
  .
  .
  .
```

Figure 10-22   Using the Z variable as a placeholder for short fields

created four Z variable placeholders. Then, in the)INIT section, I coded this statement:

```
.ZVARS='(JCLASS MCLASS SLEVEL MLEVEL)'
```

This causes ISPF to substitute the variable names within the parentheses for the Z placeholder variables specified in the)BODY section. As a result, JCLASS is used for the first input field, MCLASS for the second, SLEVEL for the third, and MLEVEL for the fourth.

If you use only one Z placeholder, you can omit the parentheses and the apostrophes. For example, you could include this statement in the)INIT section:

```
.ZVARS=JCLASS
```

Here, the variable JCLASS will be used for the field marked by the Z placeholder in the)BODY section.

HOW TO CONTROL THE POSITION OF THE CURSOR

When ISPF displays a panel, it determines the default cursor position as follows:

- If a VER statement detects an error, the cursor will be placed in the last panel field that was referenced. Usually, this means the cursor will be placed in the field that is in error.

- If there hasn't been an error, the cursor is placed in the first input field that: (1) does not have an initial value; (2) is the first or only input field on a line; and (3) is not named ZCMD.

- If no input field meets the above conditions, the cursor is placed in the first input field on the panel.

- If the panel contains no input fields, the cursor is placed in column 1 of line 1.

For most panels, ISPF's default cursor position is just what you want. So you'll seldom have a need to control cursor position yourself.

Sometimes, however, you do. For example, you might want the cursor positioned in an input field that contains an initial value. Or you might want to position the cursor in an empty input field, but not the first empty input field on the screen. To do that, you must include a statement like this one in the)INIT section of the panel definition:

`.CURSOR=DEPT`

This instruction tells ISPF to place the cursor in the field named DEPT. You can use this technique to place the cursor in any field that has a symbolic variable associated with it.

ISPF provides many other techniques for positioning the cursor. For example, you can position the cursor to a specific line and column position. Or you can determine the last line and column position of the cursor in the)PROC section. For most applications, though, placing the cursor in a specific field as I've just described is the only cursor control you need.

HOW TO DISPLAY MESSAGES

Although the CLIST and REXX versions of the ORDERS dialog I've presented in this topic use full-screen panels to obtain user input, they both use line-mode terminal I/O to display a confirmation message after the order is placed. The CLIST procedure does this using a WRITE command; the REXX procedure uses a SAY command. Either way, the WRITE or SAY command clears the terminal screen, displays the message, and requires the user to press the Enter key to display the next ISPF panel. But, using the SETMSG command, you can display this message in the message area of the first panel ISPF displays after the dialog has finished.

Figure 10-23 presents the format of the SETMSG command. As you can see, it has two parameters. The first specifies the *message-id* of the message you want to display. Notice that you don't specify the actual text of the message in the SETMSG command. Under ISPF, all messages have to be predefined and stored in a *message library*. Fortunately, ISPF/PDF provides a set of generic messages so you probably won't have to define your own. I'll show you how to use them in a moment.

The second parameter, COND, tells ISPF whether you want the message to replace the message specified by a previous SETMSG command. If you want a message to take precedence over any previously specified message, omit COND. If you include COND, the message is displayed only if there is no pending message.

As I mentioned, all messages must be predefined to ISPF and stored in a message library. The message library can be concatenated to the ISPMLIB ddname, or it can be allocated using a LIBDEF command, like this:

```
ISPEXEC LIBDEF ISPMLIB DATASET ID(USER.MESSAGE)
```

If you create your own message definitions, you'll have to make sure the message library is available. If you use the generic messages supplied by ISPF/PDF, you don't have to worry about allocating the message library.

Message definitions are grouped in sets; each set of message definitions is stored in a member of a message library. The message-id identifies not only the message to be displayed, but the member that contains the message definition as well. To determine the name of the member that contains a message definition, ISPF truncates the message-id after the second numeric digit. Thus, the definition for message MMA001 is stored in the member

---

The SETMSG command

```
ISPEXEC SETMSG MSG(message-id) [COND]
```

Explanation

message-id   The message-id of the message to be displayed on the next panel. The name
              of the member that contains the message is derived by truncating the
              message-id after the second numeric digit; therefore, ISRZ001 refers to a
              message in the member ISRZ00.

COND   Specifies that the message is to be displayed only if there is not a pending
              message. If COND is not specified, any previously specified message will be
              ignored.

Figure 10-23   The SETMSG command

MMA00. And the definition for message B172 is stored in member
B17.

Each message definition consists of two lines and follows the
format given in figure 10-24. The first line specifies the message-id,
the text of the short message, and optional keyword parameters
that specify an optional help panel, whether or not the alarm
sounds when the message is displayed, and a message type of
either NOTIFY, WARNING, or CRITICAL. The second line specifies
the text of the long message that's displayed on line 2 of the panel
if the user presses the Help key.

Figure 10-25 shows the message definitions for the three
ISPF/PDF generic messages you're likely to use. As you can see, the
message ids for these messages are ISRZ000, ISRZ001, and
ISRZ002. That means they are stored in a member named ISRZ00.
Because this member is in the ISPF/PDF message library, which is
automatically allocated when you start ISPF/PDF, you don't have
to allocate a message library when you use one of these generic
messages.

Notice that the text for each message consists simply of a
symbolic variable. For ISRZ000 and ISRZ001, the short message
variable is &ZEDSMSG and the long message variable is
&ZEDLMSG; for ISRZ002, the short message variable is &ZEERSM
and the long message variable is &ZEERLM. Because the values of
these variables are substituted before the message is displayed, you
can use these messages to display any text you want. All you have

Line 1

```
msgid 'short message' [.HELP=panel] [.ALARM= {YES} ] [.TYPE= {NOTIFY }
                                              {NO }           {WARNING }]
                                                              {CRITICAL}
```

Line 2

`'long message'`

Explanation

msgid	The message-id for this message. It can be four to eight characters long, consisting of three parts: (1) a one to five character alphabetic prefix; (2) a three character numeric message number; and (3) an optional one-character alphabetic suffix. The prefix and first two characters of the number identify the member that contains the message.
'short message'	The message text displayed in the short message area (the rightmost characters of the first display line).
.HELP	Specifies the name of a panel that's displayed if the user presses the Help key twice.
.ALARM	Specifies whether or not the terminal's audible alarm is sounded when the message is displayed.
.TYPE	Specifies the type of message. A NOTIFY message is displayed in high-intensity white with no alarm. A WARNING message is displayed in high-intensity yellow with an alarm. And a CRITICAL message sounds the alarm and is displayed in a pop-up window that requires the user to press the Enter key before continuing.
'long message'	The message text displayed on line 2 of the panel if the user presses the Help key.

Note: Each message definition requires two lines. Message definitions may be separated from each another by one or more blank lines.

Figure 10-24   The syntax of a message definition

to do is set the appropriate variables before you issue the SETMSG command. The difference between the three messages is that ISRZ001 sounds the alarm but ISRZ000 does not, and ISRZ002 lets you control both the alarm and help panel settings using symbolic variables.

To illustrate how you can use these generic messages, figure 10-26 shows a version of the ORDERS procedure that displays the

```
ISRZ000 '&ZEDSMSG' .ALARM=NO .HELP=ISR2MACR
'&ZEDLMSG'

ISRZ001 '&ZEDSMSG' .ALARM=YES .HELP=ISR2MACR
'&ZEDLMSG'

ISRZ002 '&ZERRSM' .ALARM=&ZERRALRM .HELP=&ZERRHM
'&ZERRLM'
```

Figure 10-25   Generic error messages supplied in the member ISRZ00

message "ORDER PLACED" on the panel that's displayed when the dialog finishes. To do this, I added the three highlighted lines to each procedure. The first two set the &ZEDSMSG and &ZEDLMSG variables, and the third invokes the SETMSG service to set up the messages. From this example, I hope you can see that adding messages to your own dialogs is relatively easy.

DISCUSSION

I've presented only a small subset of ISPF display services in this topic. In addition to the features you've learned here, ISPF lets you code statements in the)INIT,)REINIT, and)PROC sections of your panel definitions to manipulate the cursor position, change attribute settings for individual fields, and perform many other advanced functions. However, these are skills that are more useful when you're creating complete applications that run under ISPF. For simple, single-panel dialogs, the ISPF facilities in this topic are more than adequate.

In the next topic, you'll learn about another useful ISPF dialog service: table services. Table services not only let you create and maintain table data bases, but also let you display tables using panel formats that take advantage of ISPF's standard scrolling capabilities.

The ORDER procedure (CLIST version)

```
ISPEXEC LIBDEF ISPPLIB DATASET ID(USER.PANELS)
ALLOCATE DDNAME(ORDER) DSNAME(ORDER.DATA) MOD
OPENFILE ORDER OUTPUT
ISPEXEC DISPLAY PANEL(ORDER)
IF &STR(&DOCID1) ¬= &STR() THEN DO
    SET ORDER = &EMPNO &SYSUID &DEPT &STR(&DOCID1) &QT1
    PUTFILE ORDER
    END
IF &STR(&DOCID2) ¬= &STR() THEN DO
    SET ORDER = &EMPNO &SYSUID &DEPT &STR(&DOCID2) &QT2
    PUTFILE ORDER
    END
IF &STR(&DOCID3) ¬= &STR() THEN DO
    SET ORDER = &EMPNO &SYSUID &DEPT &STR(&DOCID3) &QT3
    PUTFILE ORDER
    END
IF &STR(&DOCID4) ¬= &STR() THEN DO
    SET ORDER = &EMPNO &SYSUID &DEPT &STR(&DOCID4) &QT4
    PUTFILE ORDER
    END
IF &STR(&DOCID5) ¬= &STR() THEN DO
    SET ORDER = &EMPNO &SYSUID &DEPT &STR(&DOCID5) &QT5
    PUTFILE ORDER
    END
SET ZEDSMSG = ORDER PLACED
SET ZEDLMSG = YOUR ORDER WAS WRITTEN TO THE ORDER FILE
ISPEXEC SETMSG MSG(ISRZ000)
CLOSFILE ORDER
FREE DDNAME(ORDER)
ISPEXEC LIBDEF ISPPLIB
```

Figure 10-26   The ORDER procedure with a SETMSG command (part 1 of 2)

Terms

PDF

Program Development Facility

dialog manager

dialog

dialog components

function

display services

panel definition

message definition

table services

attribute character

primary option menu

executable section

Z variable placeholder

message-id

message library

The ORDER procedure (REXX version)

```
/* REXX */
"ALLOCATE DDNAME(ORDER) DSNAME(ORDER.DATA) MOD"
address ispexec
"LIBDEF ISPPLIB DATASET ID(USER.PANELS)"
"DISPLAY PANEL(ORDER)"
if Docid1 ¬= "" then
    queue Empno Sysuid Dept Docid1 Qt1
if Docid2 ¬= "" then
    queue Empno Sysuid Dept Docid2 Qt2
if Docid3 ¬= "" then
    queue Empno Sysuid Dept Docid3 Qt3
if Docid4 ¬= "" then
    queue Empno Sysuid Dept Docid4 Qt4
if Docid5 ¬= "" then
    queue Empno Sysuid Dept Docid5 Qt5
queue
address tso
"EXECIO * DISKW ORDER (FINIS"
Zedsmsg = "ORDER PLACED"
Zedlmsg = "YOUR ORDER WAS WRITTEN TO THE ORDER FILE"
"SETMSG MSG(ISRZ000)"
"FREE DDNAME(ORDER)"
address ispexec
"LIBDEF ISPPLIB"
```

Figure 10-26   The ORDER procedure with a SETMSG command (Part 2 of 2)

Objectives

1. Given the layout of a full-screen panel, code a panel definition for it.

2. Code a CLIST or REXX procedure that displays a panel and processes the data entered by the user.

Topic 2 How to use table services

An ISPF *table* is a simple database. Each row in the table is like a record in a standard file, and each column is like a field. You use ISPF *table services* to create and manipulate tables in many ways. You can add, delete, or change individual rows, search for specific rows based on their contents, and display rows so that the terminal user can use standard ISPF scrolling functions to scroll through the table. In short, tables services provide one of the ISPF dialog manager's most powerful and useful features.

In this topic, you'll learn how to create dialogs that use tables. But keep in mind that this topic is just an introduction to ISPF tables. There are many advanced table handling features I'm not going to cover here. The table features I do cover here, however, are adequate for many applications.

TABLE BASICS

A table is a collection of data arranged into rows and columns. Strictly speaking, a table is a set of dialog variables. Each row in the table represents one combination of values for each of the variables stored in the table. To illustrate, figure 10-27 shows a simple table that consists of just two variables: DOCID and TITLE. This particular table has 10 rows. While tables can contain many more rows and columns, this table is sufficient to illustrate how you can use tables.

Note that although I included the column labeled *Row* in this illustration, it isn't actually stored as part of the table. Instead, it illustrates that each row in a table can be uniquely identified by its row number. At any given time, one of the rows is the *current row*. In figure 10-27, I highlighted row 4 to show that when it is the current row, the value of the dialog variable DOCID is SC34-4213, and the value of the variable TITLE is ISPF Dialog Management Guide. ISPF keeps track of the current row for a table by maintaining a *current row pointer*, or *CRP*.

	Row	Doc id	Title
	1	GC34-4133	ISPF and ISPF/PDF General Information
	2	SC34-4134	ISPF and ISPF/PDF Planning and Customization
Current	3	SC34-4139	ISPF and ISPF/PDF Primer
Row ⟶	4	SC34-4213	ISPF Dialog Management Guide
	5	SC34-4215	ISPF Dialog Management Services and Examples
	6	SC34-4216	ISPF Conversion Utility User's Guide and Reference
	7	SC34-4135	ISPF/PDF Guide
	8	SC34-4136	ISPF/PDF Services
	9	SC34-4137	ISPF/PDF Library Management Facility
	10	SC34-4138	ISPF/PDF Edit and Edit Macros

Figure 10-27   An ISPF table with 10 rows

To process a table, you use one of the ISPEXEC commands listed in figure 10-28. I'll present the details of using these commands later in this topic. For now, I just want you to get an overview of the functions provided by these commands.

Two types of table variables

When you create an ISPF table, you specify what variables each row contains. ISPF lets you include two types of variables in a table: *keys* and *names*. If you specify a key, you can use that variable to directly access rows in the table, much like a key lets you directly access records in a VSAM key-sequenced file.

Although ISPF lets you specify more than one key variable, that doesn't mean it lets you maintain alternate keys. Instead, the key variables are combined to form a complete key value for each row. For example, if you create a table with two key fields named LNAME (last name) and FNAME (first name), ISPF combines the LNAME and FNAME variables to form a unique key for each row. This scheme allows duplicate values for the LNAME variable, but only if each has a unique FNAME value.

Name variables are simply non-key variables that are included in each row as data. You cannot retrieve a row directly based on a value in one of its name variables. However, ISPF does provide commands that let you search a table to find a row or rows based on the values in one or more name variables.

Command	Function
TBADD	Adds a row to a table.
TBBOTTOM	Moves to the bottom of the table.
TBCLOSE	Saves and closes a table.
TBCREATE	Creates and opens a new table.
TBDELETE	Deletes an existing row.
TBDISPLY	Displays table rows using a model panel.
TBGET	Retrieves a row from a table.
TBMOD	Updates an existing row or adds a new row.
TBOPEN	Opens an existing permanent table.
TBPUT	Updates an existing row.
TBSARG	Sets up a search argument for TBSCAN or TBDISPLY.
TBSCAN	Locates a row based on its contents.
TBSKIP	Moves forward or backwards a specified number of rows.
TBSORT	Sorts the rows of an existing table and causes all new rows to be placed according to the specified sequence.
TBTOP	Moves to the top of the table.

Figure 10-28   ISPEXEC commands for processing a table

Two types of tables

ISPF lets you create and use two distinct types of tables: *permanent* and *temporary*. The difference between the two is that a permanent table is stored on disk, so its data remains from one ISPF session to the next. In contrast, a temporary table is built entirely in virtual storage and never stored on disk. Thus, when you are finished processing a temporary table, it's removed from virtual storage and its contents are lost. Although there are many uses of temporary tables, all the illustrations in this topic involve permanent tables.

Other than this difference, temporary and permanent tables are the same. Data in both kinds of tables is stored in rows and columns, both tables can have key or name variables, and both are processed with the same ISPEXEC commands. However, there are

```
ISPEXEC LIBDEF ISPTLIB DATASET ID(USER.TABLES)
ISPEXEC LIBDEF ISPTABL DATASET ID(USER.TABLES)
```

Figure 10-29   LIBDEF commands used to allocate user table libraries

a number of practical differences in the way you use temporary and permanent tables. For example, a procedure that processes a temporary table must use the appropriate ISPEXEC command to create the table and define the variables it contains. In contrast, a procedure that processes a permanent table does not have to define it; instead, it simply opens the existing table.

How to allocate table libraries

Permanent tables are stored in ISPF libraries allocated to the ddname ISPTLIB. Thus, to access your own tables, you have to add your private table library to the ISPF table libraries concatenated to ISPTLIB. The easiest way to do that is with a LIBDEF command, in much the same way you allocate a private panel library.

Whenever you create or update an existing permanent table, you must also allocate the library that will contain the table to the ddname ISPTABL. ISPF uses this ddname whenever it writes data to a table library. Unlike ISPTLIB, ISPTABL can *not* have more than one library concatenated to it. You can use LIBDEF to allocate ISPTABL as well.

Figure 10-29 shows LIBDEF commands that allocate ISPTLIB and ISPTABL. As you can see, both commands allocate the same library. So USER.TABLES is added to the concatenation sequence for ISPTLIB, and will be used as the sole table output library (ISPTABL). Usually, you'll allocate the same table library to ISPTLIB and ISPTABL.

If you need to create your own table library, you should create it as a partitioned data set with 80-byte records and 3120-byte blocks. Because ISPF maintains the data for each table in an internal format, the record and block size of the table library doesn't limit the amount of data that can be stored in each table row. Once you create the table library, you don't have to be concerned with the details of how the data is stored in it.

HOW TO SET UP A TABLE

Now that you understand the basic characteristics of ISPF tables, you're ready to learn how to set up your own tables. To do that, you use two commands: TBCREATE and TBSORT. It's the TBCREATE command that actually creates the table; the TBSORT command specifies the sorting order for the table and is required only if you want ISPF to maintain the table in a particular sequence.

The easiest way to create a ISPF permanent table is to use the dialog services option of ISPF/PDF from the dialog test menu, option 7.6. Alternatively, you can write a short CLIST or REXX procedure that contains the appropriate commands. On the other hand, since a temporary table is available only while the procedure that creates it is running, you must create a temporary table in the procedure that uses it.

How to create a table: The TBCREATE command

Figure 10-30 gives the format of the TBCREATE command, which creates a new table. Immediately after the word TBCREATE, you specify a one- to eight-character *table name* that uniquely identifies the table. The table name can include letters, numbers, and special characters, but it must start with a letter. After the table name, you list the key and name variables you want to use in the KEYS and NAMES parameters.

The WRITE/NOWRITE option specifies whether the table is permanent or temporary. To create a permanent table, specify WRITE or allow it to default. To create a temporary table, specify NOWRITE.

The REPLACE option tells ISPF what to do if you create a permanent table using the name of an existing table in the ISPTABL library. If you specify REPLACE, the new table will replace the existing table. If you omit REPLACE, an error results.

Figure 10-31 shows three examples of the TBCREATE command. Examples 1 and 2 create the table that I presented in figure 10-27, using the name TDOCS. The difference between the two examples is that in example 1, I specified DOCID as a key variable and TITLE as a name variable. In example 2, I specified both as name variables. Example 3 shows how to create a temporary table. Here, each row contains five variables: DEPT, EMPNO,

The TBCREATE command

```
ISPEXEC TBCREATE table-name   [ KEYS(key-name-list) ]

                              [ NAMES(name-list) ]

                              [ {WRITE  } ]
                                {NOWRITE}

                              [ REPLACE ]
```

Explanation

table-name	The one- to eight-character name of the table to be created. The name must start with a letter.
key-name-list	A list of names that will be used to identify key variables.
name-list	A list of names that will be used to identify non-key variables.
WRITE NOWRITE	Specifies whether you are creating a permanent or temporary table. WRITE creates a permanent table that's stored on disk. NOWRITE creates a temporary table that is not stored on disk. WRITE is the default.
REPLACE	Specifies that if a table with the same name already exists, the new table should replace it.

Figure 10-30   The TBCREATE command

Example 1

```
ISPEXEC TBCREATE TDOCS KEYS(DOCID) NAMES(TITLE)
```

Example 2

```
ISPEXEC TBCREATE TDOCS NAMES(DOCID TITLE)
```

Example 3

```
ISPEXEC TBCREATE TORDER NAMES(DEPT EMPNO USERID DOCID QTY) NOWRITE
```

Figure 10-31   Three examples of the TBCREATE command

The TBSORT command

```
ISPEXEC TBSORT table-name FIELDS(variable-1, {C}, {A} [variable-2...])
                                             {N}   {D}
```

Explanation

table-name	The table to be sorted.
variable	A sort field; one of the variables specified in the KEYS or NAMES option on the TBCREATE command.
C/ N	Specifies whether the variable should be treated as character (C) or numeric (N) data.
A/ D	Specifies whether the variable should be sorted in ascending (A) or descending (D) sequence.

Note: TBSORT needs to be specified only once for each table. The sort specification is maintained along with the table, and any additions to the table are made in the correct sequence.

Figure 10-32   The TBSORT command

USERID, DOCID, and QTY. NOWRITE specifies that the table is temporary.

How to specify a table's sort sequence: The TBSORT command

The TBSORT command, shown in figure 10-32, performs two functions. First, it sorts existing table rows into a specified sequence. Second, and perhaps more important, it stores a record of the sort sequence along with the table so ISPF can maintain that sequence as new rows are added or existing rows are changed.

To specify the sort sequence, you include one or more sort specifications in the FIELDS parameter. For each sort specification, you list a table variable followed by C or N to indicate whether you want the data treated as character or numeric data, and A or D to indicate whether you want the data sorted in ascending or descending sequence.

To illustrate how this works, figure 10-33 shows three examples of the TBSORT command. Examples 1 and 2 show how to sort the

Example 1

```
ISPEXEC TBSORT TDOCS FIELDS(DOCID,C,A)
```

Example 2

```
ISPEXEC TBSORT TDOCS FIELDS(TITLE,C,A)
```

Example 3

```
ISPEXEC TBSORT TUSERS FIELDS(LNAME,C,A,FNAME,C,A)
```

Figure 10-33   Three examples of the TBSORT command

TDOCS table in ascending sequence by the DOCID variable or the TITLE variable. Example 3 shows how you might sort a table that contains first and last names. Here, the table is sorted into last name sequence. Then, any rows with the same last name are sorted into first name sequence.

How to use the ISPF dialog test tables option

As I mentioned, the easiest way to enter the TBCREATE and TBSORT commands for a permanent table is by using the dialog services option of ISPF/PDF dialog test, option 7.6. To perform other types of processing for permanent or temporary tables, you can use the dialog test tables option, option 4 from the dialog test primary option menu. The option is particularly useful for entering initial data into a table, displaying individual table rows to make sure the dialogs that process the table work properly, and checking the table's status to see how many rows it contains, when it was last modified, and so on.

Figure 10-34 shows the panel ISPF displays when you select the dialog test tables option. As you can see, it lets you perform six table functions: display a row, delete a row, modify a row, add a row, display the table's structure, and display the table's status. You select one of these processing options by entering the corresponding number in the OPTION field. In the TABLE NAME field, you enter the name of the table you want to process.

```
------------------------------------------------ TABLES ------------------------------------------
OPTION  ===>  4

      1  Display row                          4  Add row
      2  Delete row                           5  Display structure
      3  Modify row                           6  Display status

   TABLE NAME      ===>  TDOCS              CURRENT ROW:

   ROW IDENTIFICATION:
     BY ROW NUMBER ===> *                   (* = current row)

     BY VARIABLE     VALUE                  (Search for row if row number blank)
     _____       _____
     _____       _____
     _____       _____
     _____       _____
     _____       _____


   DBCS COLUMN SPECIFICATION:

     _____    _____    _____    _____    _____    _____
     _____    _____    _____    _____    _____    _____
```

Figure 10-34   The ISPF dialog test tables panel, option 7.4

The dialog test tables option doesn't let you create or open a table. As a result, you must first create the table by issuing a TBCREATE command from the dialog services option. Alternatively, if the table already exists on disk, you must issue a TBOPEN command. Either way, when you are finished processing a table, you must close it by issuing a TBCLOSE command from the dialog services option. I'll explain the format of the TBOPEN and TBCLOSE commands in a few moments.

The fields indented under the heading ROW IDENTIFICATION let you specify the table row you want to process. You can do this in one of three ways. First, you can leave the default asterisk in the BY ROW NUMBER field. This tells ISPF to process the current row. For a newly created or opened table, the first row is current. Second, you can type a row number in the BY ROW NUMBER field. For example, to display row 3, enter the number 3 in the BY ROW NUMBER field. And third, you can specify one or more search arguments by entering a variable name in one of the BY VARIABLE fields and a value in the corresponding VALUE field. For example, if you entered DOCID in the BY VARIABLE field and GC34-4213 in

Part 1:

Display the add row
entry panel

```
/  ADD ROW    TABLE TDOCS    AFTER ROW 3 ----------------------------- ROW 1 OF 15
   COMMAND ===>                                                  SCROLL ===> PAGE

   ADD VARIABLE VALUES AND SAVENAMES.   UNDERSCORES NEED NOT BE BLANKED.
   ENTER END COMMAND TO FINALIZE CHANGES.

           VARIABLE   T A VALUE

   ''''    DOCID___   K
   ''''    TITLE___   N
   ''''    _____    S
   ''''    _____    S
   ''''    _____    S
   ''''    _____    S
   ''''    _____    S
   ''''    _____    S
   ''''    _____    S
   ''''    _____    S
   ''''    _____    S
   ''''    _____    S
   ''''    _____    S
   ''''    _____    S
   ''''    _____    S
   ************************************* BOTTOM OF DATA *************************************
```

Figure 10-35   Adding a row to a table

the VALUE field, ISPF would select the row whose DOCID variable is GC34-4213.

The three parts of figure 10-35 show how you can use the dialog test tables option to add a row to a table. Part 1 shows the panel ISPF displays when you select option 4 from the dialog test tables panel. As you can see, ISPF fills in the name of each variable in the table in the VARIABLE column. To add a row to the table, you simply type in the correct value for each variable in the VALUE column. In part 2 of figure 10-35, I entered SC34-4213 for the DOCID variable and ISPF Dialog Management Guide for the TITLE variable. When I pressed the End key, PF3/15, ISPF returned to the dialog test tables panel, and displayed a message in the short message area to indicate that the row was added as illustrated in part 3 of figure 10-35.

The other table functions that operate on individual rows, display, delete, and modify, work in much the same way. The other two options, display structure and display status, display information about the entire table. Figure 10-36 shows the display structure panel for the TDOCS table. As you can see, this panel

Part 2:

Enter the values for
each variable in the
table

```
ADD ROW    TABLE TDOCS    AFTER ROW 3 ------------------------------ ROW 1 OF 15
COMMAND ===>                                               SCROLL ===> PAGE

ADD VARIABLE VALUES AND SAVENAMES.   UNDERSCORES NEED NOT BE BLANKED.
ENTER END COMMAND TO FINALIZE CHANGES.

        VARIABLE  T A VALUE

''''    DOCID___  K   SC34-4213
''''    TITLE___  N   ISPF Dialog Management Guide
''''    _____   S
''''    _____   S
''''    _____   S
''''    _____   S
''''    _____   S
''''    _____   S
''''    _____   S
''''    _____   S
''''    _____   S
''''    _____   S
''''    _____   S
''''    _____   S
''''    _____   S
*******************************  BOTTOM OF DATA  *******************************
```

Part 3:

When you press the
Enter key, ISPF
returns to the tables
panel and confirms
that the row was added

```
----------------------------------- TABLES ------------------------ ROW ADDED
OPTION ===> 4

   1  Display row                      4  Add row
   2  Delete row                       5  Display structure
   3  Modify row                       6  Display status

TABLE NAME     ===> TDOCS              CURRENT ROW:   4

ROW IDENTIFICATION:
  BY ROW NUMBER ===> *                 (* = current row)

  BY VARIABLE    VALUE                 (Search for row if row number blank)
      _____
      _____
      _____
      _____
      _____

DBCS COLUMN SPECIFICATION:

   _____  _____  _____  _____  _____  _____
   _____  _____  _____  _____  _____  _____
```

Figure 10-35   Adding a row to a table (continued)

```
-------------------------- STRUCTURE OF TABLE  TDOCS  --------------- ROW 1 OF 3
COMMAND ===>                                                     SCROLL ===> PAGE

NUMBER OF KEYS:  1            NUMBER OF ROWS:       22
NUMBER OF NAMES: 1           CURRENT ROW POINTER: 0


KEYS:     DOCID



NAMES:    TITLE
xxxxxxxxxxxxxxxxxxxxxxxxxxxxxxxxx BOTTOM OF DATA xxxxxxxxxxxxxxxxxxxxxxxxxxxxxxxxx
```

Figure 10-36 Displaying a table's structure

displays the number of key and name variables, the number of rows in the table, and the current row pointer. In addition, it lists the name of each key and name variable. This panel can be very useful if you need to process a table that someone else created, or if you forget the names of the variables you used when you created the table.

Figure 10-37 shows a display status panel for the TDOCS table. As you can see, this panel displays information about the current status of the table: whether or not it is open, what open option is in effect, whether or not the table is permanent on disk, and so on. In addition, it displays historical information such as the creation date, last modification date, original number of rows, and so on.

HOW TO USE ISPEXEC COMMANDS

Now that you know how to set up an ISPF table, you're ready to learn how to use the ISPEXEC commands that actually process the table. In this section, I describe twelve table processing commands

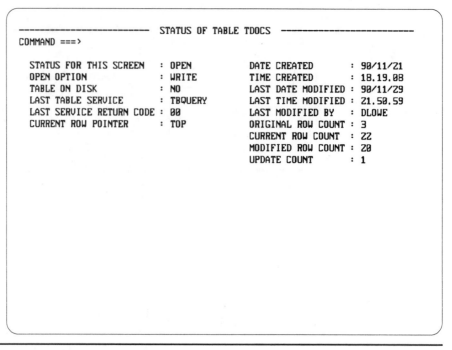

```
------------------------  STATUS OF TABLE TDOCS  ------------------------
COMMAND ===>

   STATUS FOR THIS SCREEN    : OPEN        DATE CREATED       : 90/11/21
   OPEN OPTION               : WRITE       TIME CREATED       : 18.19.08
   TABLE ON DISK             : NO          LAST DATE MODIFIED : 90/11/29
   LAST TABLE SERVICE        : TBQUERY     LAST TIME MODIFIED : 21.50.59
   LAST SERVICE RETURN CODE  : 00          LAST MODIFIED BY   : DLOWE
   CURRENT ROW POINTER       : TOP         ORIGINAL ROW COUNT : 3
                                           CURRENT ROW COUNT  : 22
                                           MODIFIED ROW COUNT : 20
                                           UPDATE COUNT       : 1
```

Figure 10-37   Displaying a table's status

you're likely to use. Figure 10-38 shows the format of these commands. Although you'll probably use the TBCREATE and TBSORT commands frequently too, I didn't include them in figure 10-38 because you already know how they work. And I left out one of the most important table processing commands, TBDISPL, because I cover it in more detail later.

How to open a table: The TBOPEN command

Before you can process a permanent table, you must open it using the TBOPEN command. The only exception is when you process a table immediately after creating it, because the TBCREATE command first creates and then opens the table automatically. As a result, the TBOPEN command isn't used for temporary tables since they must be created each time they are processed.

The syntax of the TBOPEN command is simple: just specify the name of the table you want to open and an optional WRITE or NOWRITE parameter. If you specify WRITE, or allow it to default,

The TBOPEN command

```
ISPEXEC TBOPEN table-name [ { WRITE
                              NOWRITE } ]
```

The TBADD command

```
ISPEXEC TBADD table-name [ORDER]
```

The TBGET command

```
ISPEXEC TBGET table-name
```

The TBPUT command

```
ISPEXEC TBPUT table-name
```

The TBMOD command

```
ISPEXEC TBMOD table-name
```

The TBDELETE command

```
ISPEXEC TBDELETE table-name
```

The TBSKIP command

```
ISPEXEC TBSKIP table-name [NUMBER(number)]
```

The TBTOP command

```
ISPEXEC TBTOP table-name
```

The TBBOTTOM command

```
ISPEXEC TBBOTTOM table-name
```

Figure 10-38   Format of commonly used table service commands (part 1 of 2)

The TBSCAN command

```
ISPEXEC TBSCAN table-name [ARGLIST(name-list)]

         [CONDLIST(cond-list)] [{NEXT    }]
                               {PREVIOUS}
```

The TBSARG command

```
ISPEXEC TBSARG table-name [NAMECOND(name-cond-list)]

         [{NEXT    }]
          {PREVIOUS}
```

The TBCLOSE command

```
ISPEXEC TBCLOSE table-name
```

Figure 10-38   Format of commonly used table service commands (part 2 of 2)

any changes you make to the table while it is open become permanent when you close the table by using a TBCLOSE command. In
addition, the WRITE option prevents other users from accessing
the table until you close it. If you specify NOWRITE, the table is
opened in read-only mode, so no changes are permanent and other
users can freely access the table.

Like all ISPEXEC commands, the TBOPEN command issues a
return code to indicate whether or not is was successful. Any
return code greater than zero indicates that the table was not
successfully opened and cannot be processed. Return code 8 means
the table doesn't exist, which in practice means either you haven't
created it, you are using the wrong name, or the library that
contains the table isn't properly allocated to ISPTLIB. Return code
12 means the table exists but is being used by another user, return
code 16 means no ISPTLIB library is allocated, and return code 20
means a severe error occurred.

How to insert rows: The TBADD command

To insert a row into a table, you use the TBADD command. Notice
that you don't specify any variables or data values on this

command. When ISPF processes the TBADD command, it uses the current values of the dialog table variables to create the row. Thus, you should set the dialog variables to the appropriate values before you issue the TBADD command.

The ORDER option tells ISPF to maintain the order specified by any existing TBSORT specification. If you used a TBSORT command to set up a sort order, and you want to preserve that order, be sure to specify this option. If you do, the row is added in the appropriate location to maintain the specified order. If you omit the ORDER option, the row is added following the current row. Then, any TBSORT specification is lost and you have to issue another TBSORT command to restore it.

TBADD issues a variety of return codes, but the only non-zero return code that doesn't indicate a serious error is 8. Return code 8 means that a duplicate row exists, so the new row wasn't added. A duplicate row condition can occur only if the table has one or more key variables.

How to retrieve rows: The TBGET command

The TBGET command retrieves a row from the table and copies its data into the corresponding variables in a dialog. The operation of the TBGET command depends on whether or not the table has key variables. If it does, the values of the key variables are used to determine what row to read. Therefore, you must move the key values of the row you want to retrieve to the key variables before you issue the TBGET command. If the table does not have keys, the TBGET command returns the current row. I'll show you how to change the current row pointer in a few moments.

Like TBADD, the only non-zero return code of interest for TBGET is 8. For a table with key variables, a return code of 8 means there isn't a row with the key value you specified. For a table without keys, it means the pointer was positioned before the first row in the table. Any other non-zero return code indicates a serious error.

How to update rows: The TBPUT and TBMOD commands

You use the TBPUT and TBMOD commands to update rows in a table. The only difference between the two commands is with

TBPUT, the row to be updated must already exist in the table. With TBMOD, if the row already exists, it will be updated; otherwise, a new row will be created. For both commands, you must first set the appropriate dialog variables to supply the data values for the updated row. If the table has keys, you should move appropriate values to the key variables to identify the row you want to update. Otherwise, the current row will be updated.

TBPUT and TBMOD both issue a zero return code to indicate successful update. In addition, TBMOD issues return code 8 if the row to be updated didn't exist and a new row was created. Any other return code represents a serious error.

How to delete rows: The TBDELETE command

The TBDELETE command deletes one row from the specified table. If the table has key variables, you must first set them to the key value of the row you want to delete. For non-keyed tables, the current row is deleted. TBDELETE issues a zero return code to indicate that the row was successfully deleted. Return code 8 indicates that the row didn't exist, so it couldn't be deleted. Any other return code indicates a serious error.

How to change the current position: The TBSKIP, TBTOP, and TBBOTTOM commands

The TBSKIP, TBTOP, and TBBOTTOM commands let you change the current row pointer. TBSKIP lets you move forward or backward a specified number of rows. For example, to move forward one row, you use this command:

```
ISPEXEC TBSKIP TDOCS NUMBER(1)
```

To move backwards, specify a negative number, like this:

```
ISPEXEC TBSKIP TDOCS NUMBER(-1)
```

This command moves backwards one row. If you omit the NUMBER parameter, the default value of 1 is used. The TBSKIP command also retrieves the row it points to, so a separate TBGET command isn't necessary.

As their names suggest, the TBTOP and TBBOTTOM commands let you move directly to the top and bottom of the table. The TBTOP command positions the current row pointer before the first row in the table. That way, you can insert rows ahead of the first row. The TBBOTTOM command positions the current row pointer at the last row, and like the TBSKIP command, it retrieves that row.

TBSKIP issues return code zero to indicate successful completion, and return code 8 to indicate that the move would have taken the current row pointer past the end or before the beginning of the table. Any other return code indicates a serious error. Any non-zero return code from TBTOP or TBBOTTOM indicates a serious error.

How to search for specific rows: The TBSCAN and TBSARG commands

Like the TBSKIP command, the TBSCAN command lets you move forward or backward through a table. But instead of moving a specific number of rows, TBSCAN moves one row at a time, scanning the contents of each row's variables until it finds a row that matches a search condition you specify. The TBSCAN command also retrieves the row it locates, so a separate TBGET command isn't necessary.

You can specify the search condition directly on the TBSCAN command, or by first issuing a TBSARG command. To specify search conditions on the TBSCAN command, you use the ARGLIST and CONDLIST parameters. In the ARGLIST parameter, you list the table variables to be used in the search. For example, to search for a row with a matching TITLE variable, you would use this command:

```
ISPEXEC TBSCAN TDOCS ARGLIST(TITLE)
```

Then, TBSCAN would move the current row pointer forward to the row whose TITLE variable equals the current contents of the dialog's TITLE variable. Obviously, your procedure should first set the dialog's TITLE variable to the desired value.

The CONDLIST parameter lets you specify a condition other than an exact match for the variables listed in the ARGLIST parameter. The conditions you can include are:

EQ	Equal
NE	Not Equal
LE	Less than or Equal
LT	Less than
GE	Greater then or Equal
GT	Greater than

For example, to scan to the first row of a table named TORDER whose QTY variable is greater than or equal to 10, you would first set the dialog's QTY variable to 10, then issue this command:

```
ISPEXEC TBSCAN TORDER ARGLIST(QTY) CONDLIST(GE)
```

If you specify more than one variable in the ARGLIST parameter, you specify the conditions in the CONDLIST parameter in the same order. For example, to find an order of 10 or more units of a particular title, you would use this command:

```
ISPEXEC TBSCAN TORDER ARGLIST(QTY TITLE) CONDLIST(GE EQ)
```

Here, the GE condition applies to the first ARGLIST variable, QTY, and the EQ condition applies to the second ARGLIST variable, TITLE.

If you wish, you can specify the search condition in a TBSARG command rather than directly on the TBSCAN command. TBSARG has a simpler syntax than TBSCAN. It combines the ARGLIST and CONDLIST parameters into a single NAMECOND parameter, which lists pairs of conditions and parameters. Thus, to find an order of 10 or more units of a particular title, you could use these commands:

```
ISPEXEC TBSARG TDOCS NAMECOND(QTY,GE,TITLE,EQ)
ISPEXEC TBSCAN TDOCS
```

Notice that because the search condition is specified on the TBSARG command, no parameters other than the table name are required on the TBSCAN command.

Both the TBSARG and TBSCAN commands let you specify *generic search arguments* in the variables used in search conditions. A generic search argument is any value that ends with an asterisk. For example, if the value of the TITLE variable in the previous example was ISPF*, any TITLE value that begins with ISPF would satisfy the search. Note that the asterisk must appear at the end of the value. If an asterisk appears within the value, it is considered a part of the search value, and the value is not treated as a generic search argument.

Whether you specify the search condition on the TBSCAN or TBSARG commands, you can use the NEXT or PREVIOUS parameters to control the direction of the search. Whichever search direction you specify, the search always proceeds from the current row pointer. Thus, if you want to search forward from the beginning of the table, you should first issue a TBTOP command. To search backwards from the end of the table, you should first use a TBBOTTOM command.

The TBSCAN command issues a zero return code if it finds the row you requested. If not, it issues return code 8. Other return codes indicate serious errors. For TBSARG, any non-zero return code indicates a serious error.

How to close a table: The TBCLOSE command

When you're finished processing a table, you should close it by issuing a TBCLOSE command. If the table is permanent and you opened it in WRITE mode, any changes you made are written to disk and the lock established on the table when you opened it is released. Even if the table isn't permanent, however, you should issue a TBCLOSE command because it releases the in-storage copy of the table.

A dialog that adds records to the TDOCS table

To illustrate how you can use ISPEXEC table commands in a dialog, figures 10-39 through 10-41 present a simple dialog that lets a user add rows to the TDOCS table. Figure 10-39 shows a sample execution of the dialog. When the user starts the dialog, it displays the panel shown in part 1. On it, the user can enter a document id and a title. In this case, the document id is SC28-1875 and the title is TSO/E Version 2 Programming Services. When the user presses the Enter key, the dialog adds the row to the table, clears the dialog variables, and redisplays the panel with the message ROW ADDED in the short message area, as illustrated in part 2 of figure 10-39. If the TBADD command in the dialog issues a non-zero return code, the message says NOT ADDED instead.

Figure 10-40 shows the panel definition for the dialog. There's nothing particularly difficult to understand about this panel definition. Notice that the)INIT section contains the statements that clear the &DOCID and &TITLE variables before the screen is displayed. And the)PROC section includes statements to validate the document id and title. The document id can be blank, but if a value is entered, it must conform to the picture. If a document id is entered, a title must also be entered.

Part 1:

The user enters the
data for a new docu-
ment

```
------------------------------ ADD A NEW DOCUMENT -------------------------------
COMMAND ===>

DOCUMENT ID ===> SC28-1875
TITLE       ===> TSO/E Version 2 Programming Services



PRESS END KEY TO EXIT
```

Part 2:

When the user
presses the Enter key,
the dialog confirms
that the row was added

```
------------------------------ ADD A NEW DOCUMENT --------------------- ROW ADDED
COMMAND ===>

DOCUMENT ID ===>
TITLE       ===>



PRESS END KEY TO EXIT
```

Figure 10-39 The DOCADD dialog

```
)ATTR
# TYPE(TEXT) INTENS(LOW) SKIP(ON)
)BODY
%-------------------------------- ADD A NEW DOCUMENT ----------------------
%COMMAND ===>_ZCMD
%
+DOCUMENT ID ===>_DOCID      #
+TITLE        ===>_TITLE
%
%
%
%
%PRESS END KEY TO EXIT
)INIT
&DOCID=' '
&TITLE=' '
)PROC
VER(&DOCID,PICT,AANN-NNNN)
IF (&DOCID ¬= ' ')
    VER(&TITLE,NONBLANK)
)END
```

Figure 10-40   Panel definition for the DOCADD dialog

Figure 10-41 shows the CLIST and REXX versions of the dialog's procedure. I've highlighted the table processing commands so you can see how the dialog processes the table. First, two LIBDEF commands allocate the same table data set to ISPTLIB and ISPTABL. Then, a TBOPEN command opens the existing table. In the processing loop, a TBADD command adds a row to the table if the &DOCID variable is nonblank. At the end of the loop, a TBCLOSE command closes the table and LIBDEF commands remove TEST.TABLE from ISPTLIB and ISPTABL. You should remove your user table library from ISPTLIB and IPSTABL for the same reason you remove your user panel library from ISPPLIB: so ISPF doesn't continue searching your user library after your dialog is finished.

HOW TO USE THE TBDISPL COMMAND

So far, the table processing features I've presented let you create and use tables as if they were standard files. If that's all ISPF table

The DOCADD procedure (CLIST version)

```
ISPEXEC LIBDEF ISPPLIB DATASET ID(TEST.PANELS)
ISPEXEC LIBDEF ISPTLIB DATASET ID(TEST.TABLES)
ISPEXEC LIBDEF ISPTABL DATASET ID(TEST.TABLES)
ISPEXEC TBOPEN TDOCS
DO UNTIL &ENDKEY = YES
    ISPEXEC DISPLAY PANEL(DOCADD)
    IF &LASTCC = 8 THEN +
        SET ENDKEY = YES
    IF &STR(&DOCID) ¬= &STR( ) THEN DO
        ISPEXEC TBADD TDOCS
        IF &LASTCC = 0 THEN DO
            SET ZEDSMSG = ROW ADDED
            SET ZEDLMSG = DOCUMENT &STR(&DOCID) ADDED TO TDOCS TABLE
            END
        ELSE DO
            SET ZEDSMSG = NOT ADDED
            SET ZEDLMSG = AN ERROR HAS OCCURRED
            END
        ISPEXEC SETMSG MSG(ISRZ000)
        END
    END
ISPEXEC TBCLOSE TDOCS
ISPEXEC LIBDEF ISPPLIB
ISPEXEC LIBDEF ISPTLIB
ISPEXEC LIBDEF ISPTABL
```

Figure 10-41   The DOCADD procedure (part 1 of 2)

services did, they would be useful enough. But by far the most useful aspect of ISPF's table services is the way it interacts with ISPF's display services. In this section, I'll show you how to create panel definitions you can use in conjunction with the TBDISPL command to create dialogs that let the user browse through the rows of a table using standard ISPF scrolling commands.

Figure 10-42 shows the TBDISPL command. As you can see, its syntax is simple enough. It takes just two parameters: the name of the table to be displayed, and the name of the panel definition used to format the display. Don't let this command's simple syntax deceive you, however. TBDISPL is one of ISPF's most powerful commands.

To fully explain how you use this command, I'll present two dialog examples. The first dialog lets a user browse through the TDOCS table described throughout this topic. The second is more complicated: it lets a user order one or more documents by

The DOCADD procedure (REXX version)

```
/* REXX */
address ispexec
"LIBDEF ISPPLIB DATASET ID(TEST.PANELS)"
"LIBDEF ISPTLIB DATASET ID(TEST.TABLES)"
"LIBDEF ISPTABL DATASET ID(TEST.TABLES)"
"TBOPEN TDOCS"
do until Endkey = "YES"
    DISPLAY PANEL(DOCADD)"
    if rc = 8 then
        Endkey = "YES"
    if Docid ¬= "" then do
        "TBADD TDOCS"
        if rc = 0 then do
            Zedsmsg = "ROW ADDED"
            Zedlmsg = "DOCUMENT &STR(&DOCID) ADDED TO TDOCS TABLE"
            end
        else do
            Zedsmsg = "NOT ADDED"
            Zedlmsg = "AN ERROR HAS OCCURRED"
            end
        SETMSG MSG(ISRZ000)"
        end
    end
"TBCLOSE TDOCS"
"LIBDEF ISPPLIB"
"LIBDEF ISPTLIB"
"LIBDEF ISPTABL"
```

Figure 10-41   The DOCADD procedure (part 2 of 2)

browsing through the TDOCS table and entering a quantity value next to each document to be ordered.

A dialog that browses table rows

Figure 10-43 shows a sample dialog that lets a user view all or selected rows in the TDOCS table. Part 1 shows the panel that's displayed when the user starts the dialog. As you can see, it lists each row in the table, one line for each row. Part 2 shows the display after the user presses the PF8/20 key to scroll down. Here, you can see the BOTTOM OF DATA line that indicates that the user has reached the end of the table.

The TBDISPL command

```
ISPEXEC TBDISPL table-name   [PANEL(panel)]
```

Explanation

table-name	The table to be displayed.
panel	The panel definition used to display the table.

Note: Each invocation of the TBDISPL command returns variable data for one selected table row. A count of the unprocessed selected rows, including the one currently returned, is returned in &ZTDSELS. To retrieve the second and subsequent selected rows, invoke the TBDISPL command without the PANEL option.

Figure 10-42   The TBDISPL command

In addition to scrolling through the table, this dialog lets the user select what rows are displayed. In part 3 of figure 10-43, the user entered a generic search argument to limit the display to those titles beginning with the word ISPF. Part 4 shows the resulting display. Here, only the selected titles are displayed.

The browse dialog panel definition   Figure 10-44 shows the panel definition for the browse dialog. The main thing to notice about this panel definition is the)MODEL section, which is high-lighted. The)MODEL section immediately follows the)BODY section and specifies the format of the line or lines that ISPF will use to format table rows. Since this)MODEL section consists of just one line, each table row will be displayed using one line. On each line, the value of the DOCID and TITLE table variables for one row will be displayed. If you want each table row to occupy more than one line, just include more than one line in the)MODEL section. Up to eight lines are allowed.

The ROWS(SCAN) parameter on the)MODEL section header is required if you want to restrict the rows displayed to those that match a search condition specified by a TBSARG command. If you omit ROWS(SCAN), all the rows in the table will be displayed. If you include it, you must issue a TBSARG command before you display the table.

Part 1:

The DOCBRWS dialog displays the first 15 rows of the table

```
------------------------------- BROWSE DOCUMENTS -------------------- ROW 1 OF 24
COMMAND ===>                                              SCROLL ===> DATA

SEARCH CRITERIA:
DOCUMENT ID ===> *
TITLE       ===> *

  DOCID    TITLE
-----------------------------------------------------------------------------
SC28-1875 TSO/E Version 2 Programming Services
SC28-1874 TSO/E Version 2 Programming Guide
GC34-4133 ISPF and ISPF/PDF General Information
SC34-4134 ISPF and ISPF/PDF Planning and Customizing
SC34-4139 ISPF and ISPF/PDF Primer
SC34-4213 ISPF Dialog Management Guide
SC34-4215 ISPF Dialog Management Services and Examples
SC34-4216 ISPF Conversion Utility User's Guide and Reference
SC34-4135 ISPF/PDF Guide
SC34-4136 ISPF/PDF Services
SC34-4137 ISPF/PDF Library Management Facility
SC34-4138 ISPF/PDF Edit and Edit Macros
SC34-4235 SCLM Guide and Reference
SC28-1876 TSO/E Version 2 CLISTs
SC28-1882 TSO/E Version 2 REXX User's Guide
```

Part 2:

When the user presses PF8/20, the DOCBRWS dialog scrolls down in the table

```
------------------------------- BROWSE DOCUMENTS -------------------- ROW 14 OF 24
COMMAND ===>                                              SCROLL ===> DATA

SEARCH CRITERIA:
DOCUMENT ID ===> *
TITLE       ===> *

  DOCID    TITLE
-----------------------------------------------------------------------------
SC28-1882 TSO/E Version 2 REXX User's Guide
SC28-1883 TSO/E Version 2 REXX Reference
GC28-1879 TSO/E Version 2 Primer
SC28-1880 TSO/E Version 2 User's Guide
SC28-1881 TSO/E Version 2 Command Reference
GX23-0026 TSO/E Version 2 Quick Reference
SC28-1872 TSO/E Version 2 Customization
SC28-1873 TSO/E Version 2 Administration
GC28-1866 TSO/E Version 2 Library Guide
GC28-1867 TSO/E Version 2 Master Index
********************************** BOTTOM OF DATA **********************************
```

Figure 10-43   The DOCBRWS dialog

Part 3:

The user enters
search criteria

```
-------------------------------- BROWSE DOCUMENTS ------------------- ROW 14 OF 24
COMMAND ===>                                                 SCROLL ===> DATA

SEARCH CRITERIA:
DOCUMENT ID ===> *
TITLE       ===> ISPF*

 DOCID     TITLE
-------------------------------------------------------------------------------
SC28-1882 TSO/E Version 2 REXX User's Guide
SC28-1883 TSO/E Version 2 REXX Reference
GC28-1879 TSO/E Version 2 Primer
SC28-1880 TSO/E Version 2 User's Guide
SC28-1881 TSO/E Version 2 Command Reference
GX23-0026 TSO/E Version 2 Quick Reference
SC28-1872 TSO/E Version 2 Customization
SC28-1873 TSO/E Version 2 Administration
GC28-1866 TSO/E Version 2 Library Guide
GC28-1867 TSO/E Version 2 Master Index
****************************** BOTTOM OF DATA **********************************
```

Part 4:

When the user
presses the Enter key,
the DOCBRWS dialog
displays the rows that
match the search
criteria

```
-------------------------------- BROWSE DOCUMENTS ------------------- ROW 3 OF 24
COMMAND ===>                                                 SCROLL ===> DATA

SEARCH CRITERIA:
DOCUMENT ID ===> *
TITLE       ===> ISPF*

 DOCID     TITLE
-------------------------------------------------------------------------------
GC34-4133 ISPF and ISPF/PDF General Information
SC34-4134 ISPF and ISPF/PDF Planning and Customizing
SC34-4139 ISPF and ISPF/PDF Primer
SC34-4213 ISPF Dialog Management Guide
SC34-4215 ISPF Dialog Management Services and Examples
SC34-4216 ISPF Conversion Utility User's Guide and Reference
SC34-4135 ISPF/PDF Guide
SC34-4136 ISPF/PDF Services
SC34-4137 ISPF/PDF Library Management Facility
SC34-4138 ISPF/PDF Edit and Edit Macros
****************************** BOTTOM OF DATA **********************************
```

Figure 10-43   The DOCBRWS dialog (continued)

```
)ATTR
# TYPE(TEXT) INTENS(LOW) SKIP(ON)
a TYPE(OUTPUT) INTENS(LOW)
)BODY
%-------------------------------- BROWSE DOCUMENTS ----------------------------
%COMMAND ===>_ZCMD                                            #SCROLL ===>_SCRO#
%
+SEARCH CRITERIA:
+DOCUMENT ID ===>_SDOCID      #
+TITLE       ===>_STITLE
%
+ DOCID      TITLE
+------------------------------------------------------------------------------
)MODEL ROWS(SCAN)
aDOCID      aTITLE
)INIT
&SCRO = DATA
.CURSOR = SDOCID
)REINIT
.CURSOR = SDOCID
)END
```

Figure 10-44   The DOCBRWS panel defination

The only other thing I want you to notice in figure 10-43 is the scroll amount field that's displayed on the right side of the second line in the)BODY section. If the second input field on the display is exactly four characters long, ISPF treats it as a scroll amount field. If the user issues an ISPF scrolling command, the value in this field is used to determine how much data should be scrolled. In figure 10-44, I named the scroll amount field SCRO for clarity, but you can use any name you wish for this field. Notice in the)INIT section that I initialized the scroll variable to DATA.

The browse dialog procedures   Figure 10-45 presents the CLIST and REXX versions of the procedures required to display the browse panel. After setting up the libraries and opening the table in read-only mode, I set the initial values of the SDOCID and STITLE variables to a single asterisk. Then, I coded a DO loop that repeats until the user presses the End key, indicated by a return code of 8 from the TBDISPL command.

Inside the loop, I set the DOCID and TITLE variables to the contents of the SDOCID and STITLE variables. Then, I issue a

The DOCBRWS procedure (CLIST version)

```
ISPEXEC LIBDEF ISPPLIB DATASET ID(TEST.PANELS)
ISPEXEC LIBDEF ISPTLIB DATASET ID(TEST.TABLES)
ISPEXEC TBOPEN TDOCS NOWRITE
SET SDOCID = &STR(*)
SET STITLE = &STR(*)
DO UNTIL &ENDKEY = YES
    SET DOCID = &STR(&SDOCID)
    SET TITLE = &STR(&STITLE)
    ISPEXEC TBSARG TDOCS NAMECOND(DOCID,EQ,TITLE,EQ)
    ISPEXEC TBDISPL TDOCS PANEL(DOCBRWS)
    IF &LASTCC = 8 THEN +
        SET ENDKEY = YES
    END
ISPEXEC TBCLOSE TDOCS
ISPEXEC LIBDEF ISPPLIB
ISPEXEC LIBDEF ISPTLIB
```

The DOCBRWS procedure (REXX version)

```
/* REXX */
address ispexec
"LIBDEF ISPPLIB DATASET ID(TEST.PANELS)"
"LIBDEF ISPTLIB DATASET ID(TEST.TABLES)"
"TBOPEN TDOCS NOWRITE"
Sdocid = "*"
Stitle = "*"
do until Endkey = "YES"
    Docid = Sdocid
    Title = Stitle
    "TBSARG TDOCS NAMECOND(DOCID,EQ,TITLE,EQ)"
    "TBDISPL TDOCS PANEL(DOCBRWS)"
    if rc = 8 then
        Endkey = "YES"
    end
"TBCLOSE TDOCS"
"LIBDEF ISPPLIB"
"LIBDEF ISPTLIB"
```

Figure 10-45   The DOCBRWS procedure

TBSARG command. This uses the values in the DOCID and TITLE variables to set up a search argument for the subsequent TBDISPL command. Since the initial values of these fields are asterisks, the initial search argument will allow all rows in the table to be displayed. If the user changes the value of one of these variables and presses the Enter key, the loop repeats with a new search condition established by the TBSARG command. (In this example, both of the table's name fields are listed in the NAMECOND parameter. If your table has name fields that aren't listed in the NAMECOND parameter, you should set those fields' table variables to nulls before you issue the TBSARG command.)

The TBDISPL command handles the actual display of the table, using the DOCBRWS panel definition shown in figure 10-44. When the TBDISPL command is issued, rows are read from the table and formatted according to the model section. Only rows that match the search criteria are included. Then, the panel is displayed on the screen. The user can use scrolling functions to scroll forward or backward through the table, completely under the control of the TBDISPL command. Control does not return to the procedure until the user presses the Enter or End key.

If the user presses the Enter key, the loop repeats: The TBSARG command is invoked again and the table is displayed again using the new search condition. If the user presses the End key, the loop ends, the table is closed, and the three LIBDEF commands free the dialog libraries.

A dialog that processes selected rows in the TDOCS table

In addition to displaying table rows, the TBDISPL command also lets the user select one or more rows by entering data into an input field that's defined in the panel's)MODEL section along with the table variables. Then, the dialog procedure can process the selected rows one at a time. Using this feature, you can create dialogs that work similarly to ISPF/PDF member lists or the data set utility, option 3.4. The coding for this type of dialog, however, is considerably more complex than the coding for a dialog that simply displays table rows without allowing input.

Figure 10-46 shows a sample execution of a dialog that lets a user order documents simply by typing a quantity next to each document to be ordered. Part 1 shows the panel displayed when the user starts the dialog. As you can see, it's similar to the panel shown in figure 10-43, but it includes a column labeled QTY. In part 2, I scrolled to the next page by pressing the PF8/20 key, and entered a 1 next to two documents, SC28-1872 and SC28-1873. When I press the Enter key, the dialog writes an order for these two documents to the ORDERS file.

The key to understanding how this dialog works is realizing that although the TBDISPL command manages the display of many table rows, it can return data values for only one selected row at a time. As a result, if the user selects five rows, you have to

Part 1:

The DOCORDER
dialog displays the first
15 rows of the table

```
------------------------------- DOCUMENT ORDER - ENTRY SCREEN ------ ROW 1 OF 22
COMMAND ===>                                                    SCROLL ===> DATA

EMPLOYEE NUMBER ===>
DEPARTMENT      ===>

QTY   DOCID     TITLE
------------------------------------------------------------------------------
      GC34-4133 ISPF and ISPF/PDF General Information
      SC34-4134 ISPF and ISPF/PDF Planning and Customizing
      SC34-4139 ISPF and ISPF/PDF Primer
      SC34-4213 ISPF Dialog Management Guide
      SC34-4215 ISPF Dialog Management Services and Examples
      SC34-4216 ISPF Conversion Utility User's Guide and Reference
      SC34-4135 ISPF/PDF Guide
      SC34-4136 ISPF/PDF Services
      SC34-4137 ISPF/PDF Library Management Facility
      SC34-4138 ISPF/PDF Edit and Edit Macros
      SC34-4235 SCLM Guide and Reference
      SC28-1876 TSO/E Version 2 CLISTs
      SC28-1882 TSO/E Version 2 REXX User's Guide
      SC28-1883 TSO/E Version 2 REXX Reference
      GC28-1879 TSO/E Version 2 Primer
      SC28-1880 TSO/E Version 2 User's Guide
```

Part 2:

The user scrolls the
table by pressing the
PF8/20 , then selects
two rows by entering a
value in the QTY
column

```
------------------------------- DOCUMENT ORDER - ENTRY SCREEN ------ ROW 16 OF 22
COMMAND ===>                                                    SCROLL ===> DATA

EMPLOYEE NUMBER ===> 44
DEPARTMENT      ===> 100

QTY   DOCID     TITLE
------------------------------------------------------------------------------
      SC28-1880 TSO/E Version 2 User's Guide
      SC28-1881 TSO/E Version 2 Command Reference
      GX23-0026 TSO/E Version 2 Quick Reference
  1   SC28-1872 TSO/E Version 2 Customization
  1   SC28-1873 TSO/E Version 2 Administration
      GC28-1866 TSO/E Version 2 Library Guide
      GC28-1867 TSO/E Version 2 Master Index
*********************************** BOTTOM OF DATA **********************************
```

Figure 10-46   The DOCORDER dialog

```
)ATTR
# TYPE(TEXT) INTENS(LOW) SKIP(ON)
@ TYPE(OUTPUT) INTENS(LOW)
)BODY
%----------------------- DOCUMENT ORDER - ENTRY PANEL --------------------
%COMMAND ===>_ZCMD                                    #SCROLL ===>_SCRO#
%
+EMPLOYEE NUMBER ===>_EMPNO     #
+DEPARTMENT      ===>_DEPT#
%
+QTY    DOCID      TITLE
+-------------------------------------------------------------------------
)MODEL
_QTY#  @DOCID     @TITLE
)INIT
&SCRO = DATA
)PROC
IF (&ZTDSELS > 0000)
    VER(&QTY,NUM)
)END
```

Figure 10-47   The DOCORDER panel definition

issue the TBDISPL command five times: once to process each
selected row. The first time you issue TBDISPL, it displays the
table, lets the user scroll forward or backward, and stores any
input entered by the user. Then, when the user presses the Enter
key, TBDISPL positions the current row pointer at the first selected
row and returns the dialog variables for that row. TBDISPL also
sets a system variable named ZTDSELS to indicate the total
number of rows that were selected. You can use this variable in a
loop to determine how many times to invoke TBDISPL again to
retrieve data for the remaining selected rows. Each time you invoke
TBDISPL, it sets ZTDSELS to indicate how many rows, including
the current row, remain to be processed. The details of how this
works will become obvious when you see the panel definition and
the dialog procedures.

The document order dialog panel definition   Figure 10-47
shows the panel definition for the document order dialog. There are
two new elements introduced here. First, notice that I included an
input field, _QTY#, in the)MODEL section. This is the field the
user will use to select rows. Otherwise, the)MODEL section is

The DOCORDER procedure (CLIST version)

```
ISPEXEC LIBDEF ISPPLIB DATASET ID(USER.PANELS)
ISPEXEC LIBDEF ISPTLIB DATASET ID(USER.TABLES)
ISPEXEC TBOPEN TDOCS NOWRITE
ALLOCATE DDNAME(ORDER) DSNAME(ORDER.DATA) MOD
OPENFILE ORDER OUTPUT
ISPEXEC TBDISPL TDOCS PANEL(DOCORDER)
IF &ZTDSELS > 0 THEN DO
    SET ORDER = &EMPNO &SYSUID &DEPT &STR(&DOCID) &QTY
    PUTFILE ORDER
    END
DO WHILE &ZTDSELS > 1
    ISPEXEC TBDISPL TDOCS
    IF &ZTDSELS > 0 THEN DO
        SET ORDER = &EMPNO &SYSUID &DEPT &STR(&DOCID) &QTY
        PUTFILE ORDER
        END
    END
SET ZEDSMSG = ORDER PLACED
SET ZEDLMSG = YOUR ORDER WAS WRITTEN TO THE ORDER FILE
ISPEXEC SETMSG MSG(ISRZ000)
CLOSFILE ORDER
FREE DDNAME(ORDER)
ISPEXEC TBCLOSE TDOCS
ISPEXEC LIBDEF ISPPLIB
ISPEXEC LIBDEF ISPTLIB
```

Figure 10-48   The DOCORDER procedure using table services (part 1 of 2)

coded much as it is in figure 10-44, except that I omitted the ROWS(SCAN) parameter.

Second, notice the coding for the)PROC section:

```
)PROC
IF (&ZTDSELS > 0000)
    VER(&QTY,NUM)
```

This coding allows you to validate input data for selected rows. The IF statement tests the ZTDSELS variable; if it is greater than zero, at least one row was selected, and the &QTY variable contains a value that should be validated.

The document order dialog procedures   Figure 10-48 shows the CLIST and REXX versions of the procedure for the document ordering dialog. After setting up the libraries and opening the table, the procedure issues a TBDISPL command to display the

The DOCORDER procedure (REXX version)

```
/* REXX */
"ALLOCATE DDNAME(ORDER) DSNAME(ORDER.DATA) MOD"
address ispexec
"LIBDEF ISPPLIB DATASET ID(USER.PANELS)"
"LIBDEF ISPTLIB DATASET ID(USER.TABLES)"
"TBOPEN TDOCS NOWRITE"
"TBDISPL TDOCS PANEL(DOCORDER)"
if Ztdsels > 0 then
      queue Empno Sysvar(Sysuid) Dept Docid Qty
do while Ztdsels > 1
    "TBDISPL TDOCS"
    if Ztdsels > 0 then
        queue Empno Sysvar(Sysuid) Dept Docid Qty
    end
Zedsmsg = "ORDER PLACED"
Zedlmsg = "YOUR ORDER WAS WRITTEN TO THE ORDER FILE"
"SETMSG MSG(ISRZ000)"
queue
address tso
"EXECIO * DISKW ORDER (FINIS
"FREE DDNAME(ORDER)"
"TBCLOSE TDOCS"
address ispexec
"LIBDEF ISPPLIB"
"LIBDEF ISPTLIB"
```

Figure 10-48 The DOCORDER procedure using table services (part 2 of 2)

table. Then, if the ZTDSELS variable indicates that a row was selected, the CLIST procedure formats a record using the dialog variables for the current row, and writes the record to the ORDERS file. In the REXX version, the record is queued to the stack; it is written later by an EXECIO command.

Next, a DO loop controls the execution of TBDISPL commands to process any additional selected rows. The loop repeats as long as ZTDSELS is greater than 1, which indicates that at least one selected row remains unprocessed. (Remember that the first row indicated by the ZTDSELS value refers to the current row, which at this point has already been processed.) Inside the loop, a TBDISPL command without the PANEL option retrieves the next selected row. Then, the retrieved row is processed.

After the loop finishes, a message is formatted. Then, in the CLIST version, the file is closed, and in the REXX version, the file is written by an EXECIO command. Last, the table is closed, and the libraries are freed.

DISCUSSION

I hope you've seen from this topic how powerful the ISPF table services are. They can be used as the basis for sophisticated applications, or they can be used for simple applications like the document ordering system I've presented here.

Terms

table
table services
current row
current row pointer
CRP
key variable
name variable
permanent table
temporary table
table name
generic search argument

Objectives

1. Given specifications for a table, code an appropriate TBCREATE command to create the table and an appropriate TBSORT command to establish the table's sort sequence.

2. Use the ISPF/PDF dialog test tables functions described in this topic to set up tables for testing purposes.

3. Develop ISPF dialogs that process tables on a row-by-row basis using the ISPEXEC table commands discussed in this chapter.

4. Develop ISPF dialogs that use the TBDISPL command to process tables using scrollable panels.

Appendix A

TSO command
reference summary

This appendix summarizes the TSO commands presented in this book. For each command, you'll find a complete format as well as a chapter reference you can use to get more detailed information. You can use this summary as a quick refresher on how to code a particular command.

The ALLOCATE command   Chapter 2, Topic 3

For a new data set

```
ALLOCATE      {DSNAME(data-set-name)}
              {DDNAME(ddname)        }

           [ {KEEP                   } ]
             {CATALOG                }
             {DELETE                 }

           [ UNIT(device) ]

           [ VOLUME(volume-serial-number) ]

           [ SPACE(primary secondary) ]

             {BLOCK(block-length)    }
           [ {TRACKS                 } ]
             {CYLINDERS              }

           [ DIR(directory-space) ]

           [ {EXPDT(expiration-date)  } ]
             {RETPD(retention-period)}

           [ DSORG(organization) ]

           [ RECFM(record-format) ]

           [ LRECL(record-length) ]

           [ BLKSIZE(block-size) ]

           [ DATACLAS(data-class) ]

           [ STORCLAS(storage-class) ]

           [ MGMTCLAS(management-class) ]

           [ LIKE(model-data-set-name) ]
```

The ALLOCATE command (continued)

For an existing data set

```
ALLOCATE        {DSNAME(data-set-name) }
                {DATASET(data-set-name)}

           [ {DDNAME(ddname)} ]
             {FILE(ddname)   }

           [ {OLD} ]
             {SHR}
             {MOD}

           [ {KEEP     } ]
             {DELETE   }
             {CATALOG  }
             {UNCATALOG}

           [ UNIT(device) ]

           [ VOLUME(volume-serial-number) ]
```

For terminal I/O

```
ALLOCATE    DSNAME(*)

            DDNAME(ddname)
```

For a dummy file

```
ALLOCATE    DUMMY

            DDNAME(ddname)
```

For SYSOUT output

```
ALLOCATE    DDNAME(ddname)

            SYSOUT(class)

           [ {HOLD  } ]
             {NOHOLD}

           [ DEST(station-id) ]
```

The ALTLIB command

Chapter 5, Topic 1
Chapter 7, Topic 1

```
ALTLIB ACTIVATE USER(EXEC)
ALTLIB DEACTIVATE USER(EXEC)
ALTLIB DISPLAY
```

The CALL command

Chapter 3

```
CALL   data-set-name

       ['parameter-string']
```

The CANCEL command

Chapter 4

```
CANCEL    {job-name          }
          {job-name(job-id)  }

       [ {PURGE   } ]
         {NOPURGE }
```

The COBOL command

Chapter 3

```
COBOL     data-set-name

       [ {LOAD(object-module-name)} ]
         {NOLOAD                   }

         {PRINT(print-file-name)}
       [ {PRINT(*)              } ]
         {NOPRINT               }

       [ {LIB(library-names)} ]
         {NOLIB              }

       [ options ]
```

The COBTEST command

Chapter 3

```
COBTEST    LOAD(member:ddname)

           [PARM('parameter-string')]
```

The COPY command
Chapter 2, Topic 1

```
COPY   old-data-set-name    new-data-set-name
```

The DELETE command
Chapter 2, Topic 1

```
DELETE   (data-set-names)   [PURGE]
```

The EDIT command
Chapter 2, Topic 2

$$\text{EDIT   library(member)   type   } \left[\begin{matrix} \text{OLD} \\ \text{NEW} \end{matrix}\right] \text{]}$$

Edit subcommands

```
BOTTOM

CHANGE   start-line [end-line] old-string new-string [ALL]
```

$$\text{DELETE } \left\{\begin{matrix} \text{start-line   [end-line]} \\ \text{* [count]} \end{matrix}\right\}$$

```
DOWN [count]
```

$$\text{END } \left\{\begin{matrix} \text{SAVE} \\ \text{NOSAVE} \end{matrix}\right\}$$

```
FIND text-string

INPUT   line-number   [increment]
```

$$\text{LIST } \left\{\begin{matrix} \text{[start-line]   [end-line]} \\ \text{* [count]} \end{matrix}\right\}$$

```
RENUM   [new-first-line]   [increment]

TOP

UP [count]
```

The EXEC command for CLISTs   Chapter 5, Topic 1

Explicit form

```
EXEC library-name(procedure-name) 'parameters'
```

Implicit form

```
[%] procedure-name parameters
```

The EXEC command for REXX procedures   Chapter 7, Topic 1

Explicit form

```
EXEC library-name(procedure-name) 'parameters' EXEC
```

Implicit form

```
[%] procedure-name parameters
```

The FREE command   Chapter 2, Topic 3

```
FREE     ⎧ALL                      ⎫
         ⎨DSNAME(data-set-names)⎬
         ⎩DDNAME(ddnames)          ⎭

         ⎧KEEP      ⎫
      [  ⎨CATALOG   ⎬  ]
         ⎪UNCATALOG ⎪
         ⎩DELETE    ⎭

      [ SYSOUT(class) ]

      [ ⎧HOLD   ⎫ ]
        ⎩NOHOLD⎭

      [ DEST(station-id) ]
```

The HELP command   Chapter 1, Topic 1

```
HELP [command-name]
```

The LINK command   Chapter 3

```
LINK    data-set-name

     [ LOAD(load-module-name) ]

       (PRINT(print-file-name))
     [ {PRINT(*)              }  ]
       (NOPRINT               )

     [ LIB(library-name) ]

     [ COBLIB ]
```

The LIST command   Chapter 2, Topic 1

```
LIST data-set-name
```

The LISTALC command   Chapter 2, Topic 3

```
LISTALC   [STATUS]

          [HISTORY]

          [MEMBERS]

          [SYSNAMES]
```

The LISTCAT command   Chapter 2, Topic 1

```
LISTCAT   [ {ENTRIES(data-set-names)}  ]
            {LEVEL(level)            }

            (NAME   )
          [ {HISTORY}  ]
            {VOLUME }
            (ALL    )
```

The LISTDS command   Chapter 2, Topic 1

```
LISTDS    (data-set-names)

          [MEMBERS]

          [HISTORY]

          [STATUS]

          [LEVEL]
```

The LOADGO command   Chapter 3

```
LOADGO    data-set-name

          [ 'parameter-string' ]

            (PRINT(print-file-name))
          [ {PRINT(*)               } ]
            (NOPRINT                )

          [ LIB(library-name) ]

          [ COBLIB ]
```

The LOGOFF command   Chapter 1, Topic 1

```
LOGOFF
```

The LOGON command   Chapter 1, Topic 1

```
LOGON user-id/password ACCT(account-number) [NONOTICE]
```

The OUTPUT command   Chapter 4

```
OUTPUT    (job-name          )
          {job-name(job-id)}

          [ NEWCLASS(class-name) ]

          [ DEST(station-id) ]

            (HOLD  )
          [ {NOHOLD} ]

          [ CLASS(class-names) ]

          [ DELETE ]

          [ PAUSE ]
```

OUTPUT subcommands

```
CONTINUE   [ (BEGIN)
             {HERE }]
             (NEXT )

           [ (PAUSE  )
             {NOPAUSE} ]

END

SAVE data-set-name
```

The PRINTDS command   Chapter 2, Topic 1

```
PRINTDS     {DSNAME(data-set-name) }
            {DATASET(data-set-name)}

            {NUM(location,length) }
          [ {SNUM(location,length)} ]
            {NONUM                 }

          [ LINES(start[:end]) ]

          [ COLUMNS(start[:end]) ]

            {SINGLE}
            {DOUBLE}
          [ {TRIPLE} ]
            {CCHAR }

            {FOLD(width)     }
          [ {TRUNCATE(width)} ]

          [ PAGELEN(lines) ]

          [ TMARGIN(lines ]

          [ BMARGIN(lines) ]

          [ COPIES(nnn) ]

            {MEMBERS  }
          [ {DIRECTORY} ]
            {ALL      }

            {CLASS(output-class) }
          [ {SYSOUT(output-class)} ]

            {HOLD  }
          [ {NOHOLD} ]
```

The RENAME command   Chapter 2, Topic 1

```
RENAME    old-name      new-name
          [ALIAS]
```

The SEND command   Chapter 1, Topic 1

```
SEND 'message'   {USER(user-id)}  [LOGON]
                 {OPERATOR(n)  }
```

The SMCOPY command   Chapter 2, Topic 1

```
SMCOPY  FROMDATASET(data-set-name)  TODATASET(data-set-name)
        [NOTRANS]
```

The STATUS command   Chapter 4

```
STATUS   [ {job-name          } ]
           {job-name(job-id)}
```

The SUBMIT command   Chapter 4

```
SUBMIT   data-set-name [JOBCHAR(character)]
```

The TESTCOB command   Chapter 3

```
TESTCOB   (program-id:ddname1)
          LOAD(member:ddname2)
          [PRINT(ddname3)]
          [PARM('parameter-string')]
```

Appendix B

CLIST reference
summary

This appendix summarizes the CLIST statements, built-in functions, and control variables presented in this book. For each element, you'll find a complete format as well as a chapter reference you can use to get more detailed information. You can use this summary as a quick refresher on how to code a particular statement or function, or what control variable to use to obtain certain system information.

CLIST STATEMENTS

The ATTN statement   Chapter 6, Topic 1

```
ATTN   [ {statement} ]
         {OFF      }
```

The CLOSFILE statement   Chapter 6, Topic 2

```
CLOSFILE ddname
```

The comment format   Chapter 5, Topic 2

```
/* [text] */
```

The CONTROL statement   Chapter 6, Topic 1

```
CONTROL   [ {MSG    } ]
            {NOMSG  }

          [ {FLUSH  } ]
            {NOFLUSH}

          [ MAIN ]

          [ {LIST   } ]
            {NOLIST }

          [ {CONLIST  } ]
            {NOCONLIST}

          [ {SYMLIST  } ]
            {NOSYMLIST}

          [ {PROMPT  } ]
            {NOPROMPT}

          [ {CAPS  } ]
            {NOCAPS}
            {ASIS  }

          [ END(string) ]
```

The DATA/ENDDATA statements   Chapter 6, Topic 1

```
DATA
TSO commands
ENDDATA
```

The DO-UNTIL statement

```
DO UNTIL expression
    statements
END
```

The DO-WHILE statement

```
DO WHILE expression
    statements
END
```

The repetitive DO statement

```
DO variable = from-exp TO to-exp [BY by-exp]
    statements
END
```

The END statement

```
END
```

The ERROR statement

```
ERROR  {statement}
       {OFF      }
```

The EXIT statement

```
EXIT [CODE(condition-code)]
```

The GETFILE statement

```
GETFILE ddname
```

The GLOBAL statement

```
GLOBAL variable-names
```

The GOTO statement

```
GOTO label
```

The label format

```
label: statement
```

The IF statement

```
IF expression THEN [statement-1]
[ELSE [statement-2]]
```

The NGLOBAL statement

```
NGLOBAL variable-names
```

The OPENFILE statement

```
OPENFILE ddname [ {OUTPUT
                   UPDATE} ]
                   INPUT
```

The PROC statement

```
PROC count [positional-parms] [keyword-parm[(value)]]...
```

The PUTFILE statement

```
PUTFILE ddname
```

The READ statement

```
READ variables
```

The READDVAL statement

```
READDVAL variables
```

The RETURN statement

```
RETURN [CODE(return-code)]
```

The SELECT statement

The simple format

```
SELECT
    {WHEN (expression) [statement-1]}...
    [OTHERWISE statement-2]
END
```

The compound format

```
SELECT expression-1
    {WHEN (expression-2) [statement-1]}...
    [OTHERWISE statement-2]
END
```

The SET statement

Chapter 5, Topic 2

```
SET variable-name = expression
```

The SYSCALL statement

Chapter 6, Topic 1

```
SYSCALL subprocedure-name [parameters]
```

The TERMIN statement

Chapter 6, Topic 2

```
TERMIN delimiters
```

The WRITE statement

Chapter 6, Topic 2

```
WRITE text
```

The WRITENR statement

Chapter 6, Topic 2

```
WRITENR text
```

CLIST FUNCTIONS

Chapter 5, Topic 2

`&DATATYPE(expression)`	Returns the data type of the expression: NUM for numeric values, CHAR for character values.
`&EVAL(expression)`	Forces the expression to be evaluated when it normally wouldn't be.
`&LENGTH(expression)`	Returns the length of the expression.

&STR(expression)   Suppresses the evaluation of an
                                          expression when it would
                                          normally be evaluated.

&SUBSTR(start:end,string)   Extracts a substring from *string*
                                          starting at *start* and ending at
                                          end.

&SYSDSN(data-set-name)   Returns the value OK if the speci-
                                          fied data set exists and is avail-
                                          able for use. Otherwise, returns
                                          one of several messages.

&SYSINDEX(string-1,string-2,start)   Returns the position of *string-1*
                                          in *string-2* starting at *start.*

CLIST CONTROL VARIABLES   Chapter 5, Topic 2

&LASTCC   The condition code returned by the last TSO command or
                 CLIST statement.

&MAXCC   The highest condition code encountered during a command
                 procedure.

&SYSDATE   The current date in the form mm/dd/yy.

&SYSDVAL   A special register that contains information entered by a user.

&SYSDLM   Used for terminal I/O when the TERMIN statement is used.

&SYSICMD   The name of the member invoked, if the procedure was
                 invoked implicitly.

&SYSNEST   Contains YES if a procedure is nested, NO if it isn't.

&SYSPCMD   The name of the most recently executed TSO command.

&SYSPREF   The default prefix added to the start of data set names for the
                 current user.

&SYSPROC   The name of the logon procedure used to start the current
                 user's terminal session.

&SYSSCMD   The name of the most recently executed TSO subcommand.

&SYSTIME   The current time in the format hh:mm:ss.

&SYSUID   The user-id of the current user.

Appendix C

REXX reference summary

This appendix summarizes the REXX instructions presented in this book, and over 60 REXX built-in functions. I've included a complete format for each instruction and function. For each instruction, I've also included a chapter reference you can use if you need to refer to the text for more detailed information.

REXX INSTRUCTIONS

The ARG instruction

Chapter 7, Topic 2

```
ARG variable [variable...]
```

The CALL instruction

Chapter 8, Topic 3

```
CALL name [expression] [,expression...]
```

The DO instruction

Chapter 7, Topic 2

```
DO   [ variable=from-exp [to-exp] [by-exp] ]

     [ {UNTIL}   expression]
       {WHILE}

        instructions...

END
```

The DO count instruction

Chapter 7, Topic 2

```
DO count
     instructions...
END
```

The DO FOREVER instruction

Chapter 7, Topic 2

```
DO FOREVER
     instructions...
END
```

The IF instruction

Chapter 7, Topic 2

```
IF expression THEN
     instruction-1
[ELSE
     instruction-2]
```

The PARSE instruction   Chapter 8, Topic 1

```
                  (ARG                       )
                  |EXTERNAL                  |
PARSE [UPPER]     <PULL                       >      template
                  |VALUE expression WITH     |
                  (VAR                       )
```

The PROCEDURE instruction   Chapter 8, Topic 3

```
PROCEDURE [EXPOSE variable...]
```

The PULL instruction   Chapter 7, Topic 2
                                                        Chapter 8, Topic 2

```
        (template                  )
PULL    <variable [variable...]>
```

The PUSH instruction   Chapter 8, Topic 2

```
PUSH expression
```

The QUEUE instruction   Chapter 8, Topic 2

```
QUEUE expression
```

The RETURN instruction   Chapter 8, Topic 3

```
RETURN [expression]
```

The SAY instruction   Chapter 7, Topic 2

```
SAY expression
```

The SELECT instruction   Chapter 7, Topic 2

```
SELECT
    {WHEN expression THEN instruction-1} ...
    [OTHERWISE instruction-2]
END
```

TSO COMMANDS USED IN REXX PROCEDURES

The DELSTACK command   Chapter 8, Topic 2

```
DELSTACK
```

The EXECIO command to read records   Chapter 8, Topic 4

$$
\texttt{EXECIO}\ \begin{Bmatrix} \texttt{count} \\ \texttt{*} \end{Bmatrix}\ \begin{Bmatrix} \texttt{DISKR} \\ \texttt{DISKRU} \end{Bmatrix} \texttt{ddname}\ \texttt{[start]}\ \begin{Bmatrix} \texttt{([FINIS] [} \begin{Bmatrix} \texttt{LIFO} \\ \underline{\texttt{FIFO}} \\ \texttt{SKIP} \end{Bmatrix} \texttt{])} \\ \texttt{([STEM var] [FINIS])} \end{Bmatrix}
$$

The EXECIO command to write records   Chapter 8, Topic 4

$$
\texttt{EXECIO}\ \begin{Bmatrix} \texttt{count} \\ \texttt{*} \end{Bmatrix}\ \texttt{DISKW}\ \texttt{ddname}\ \texttt{([STEM var] [FINIS]}
$$

The NEWSTACK command   Chapter 8, Topic 2

```
NEWSTACK
```

REXX BUILT-IN FUNCTIONS

`ABBREV(string1,string2,n)`	Returns 1 if *string2* is an abbreviation of *string1*; otherwise returns 0. *String2* must contain at least *n* characters.
`ABS(number)`	Returns the absolute value of *number*.
`ADDRESS()`	Returns the name of the environment where host commands are submitted.
`ARG(n,option)`	Returns the *n*th argument passed to a REXX procedure or subroutine. If *option* is included, ARG returns a value indicating the presence or absence of the argument. Valid options are E (for Exists), which returns 1 if the argument exists and 0 if it doesn't, and O (for Omitted), which returns 1 if the argument does *not* exist and 0 if it does. If you omit both *n* and *option*, ARG returns the number of arguments that were passed.

`BITAND(string1,string2)`	Returns the result of a bit-by-bit logical AND operation performed on the two strings.
`BITOR(string1,string2)`	Returns the result of a bit-by-bit logical OR operation performed on the two strings.
`BITXOR(string1,string2)`	Returns the result of a bit-by-bit logical XOR operation performed on the two strings.
`CENTER(string1,len)`	Returns a string of length *len* where *string1* is centered.
`COMPARE(string1,string2)`	Returns 0 if *string1* and *string2* are the same; otherwise, returns the position of the first character that differs.

`CONDITION(option)`

Returns information about the condition trapped by a CALL ON or SIGNAL ON instruction. *Option* specifies the information to be returned:

C   the name of the condition

D   a string that describes the condition

I   the instruction keyword (CALL or SIGNAL)

S   the condition's status (ON, OFF, or DELAY)

`COPIES(string,n)`	Returns *string* concatenated *n* times.
`C2D(string,n)`	Returns the decimal equivalent of a character string. *n* specifies the length of the result, which is truncated or padded on the left with hex 00s.
`C2X(string)`	Returns the hexadecimal equivalent of a character string.

`DATATYPE(string,type)`	If *type* is omitted, returns NUM if *string* is a valid REXX number; otherwise, returns CHAR. If *type* is specified, returns a 1 if the string matches the specified type or 0 if it doesn't:

A   alphanumeric

B   binary (zeros and ones only)

L   lowercase

M   mixed case

N   number

S   valid REXX symbols

U   uppercase

W   whole number

X   hexadecimal number

`DATE(option)`	Returns the date in the form specified by *option*:

B   number of days since January 1, 0001

C   number of days since January 1, 1900

D   number of days since January 1 of the current year

E   dd/mm/yy (European format)

J   yyddd (Julian format)

M   full name of the month

N   dd mon yyyy (the default)

O   yy/mm/dd (ordered format that can be sorted)

S   yyyymmdd (another sortable format)

U   mm/dd/yy (USA format)

W   full name of the day of week

`DELSTR(string,n,len)`	Deletes *len* characters from *string* beginning at position *n*. If *len* is omitted, the rest of the string is deleted.
`DELWORD(string,n,len)`	Deletes *len* words from *string* beginning with the *n*th word. If *len* is omitted, the rest of the string is deleted.
`DIGITS()`	Returns the current setting of NUMERIC DIGITS.
`D2C(number,n)`	Returns the character equivalent of *number*. If *n* is specified, it determines the number of characters in the result.

`D2X(number,n)`	Returns the hexadecimal equivalent of *number*. If *n* is specified, it determines the number of characters in the result.
`ERRORTEXT(n)`	Returns the message text for error number *n*. *n* represents a syntax error issued by the REXX interpreter.
`EXTERNALS()`	Always returns a zero.
`FIND(string,phrase)`	Returns the word number of the first occurrence of *phrase* in *string*. Returns 0 if *phrase* is not found.
`FORM()`	Returns the current setting of NUMERIC FORM.
`FORMAT(number,before,after)`	Returns a string that contains a formatted number with *before* characters on the left of the decimal point and *after* characters on the right.
`FUZZ()`	Returns the current setting of NUMERIC FUZZ.
`INDEX(string1,string2,start)`	Returns the character position of the first occurrence of *string1* in *string2*. If specified, the search begins at location *start*.
`INSERT(string1,string2,n)`	Inserts *string1* into *string2* at the character location *n*.
`JUSTIFY(string,n,pad)`	Returns a string of length *n* where the original string has been right- and left-justified. The characters specified by *pad* are inserted between words to achieve this justification. The default pad character is a space.
`LASTPOS(string1,string2,start)`	Returns the character position of the last occurrence of *string1* in *string2*. If specified, the search begins at location *start*.
`LEFT(string1,len)`	Returns a string of length *len* where *string1* is left-aligned.
`LENGTH(string)`	Returns the length of *string*.
`LINESIZE()`	Returns the width of the terminal line minus one character.

`MAX(number-list)`

Returns the largest number in *number-list*. Up to 20 numbers can be listed.

`MIN(number-list)`

Returns the smallest number in *number-list*. Up to 20 numbers can be listed.

`OVERLAY(string1,string2,n,len)`

Replaces *len* characters in *string2*, starting at position *n*, with the characters in *string1*. The default for *len* is the length of *string1*.

`POS(string1,string2,start)`

Returns the character position of the first occurrence of *string1* in *string2*. If specified, the search begins at location *start*.

`QUEUED()`

Returns the number of lines remaining in the stack.

`RANDOM(min,max,seed)`

Returns a random number between *min* and *max*. The default value for *min* and *max* are 0 and 999. If you want the procedure to return the same set of random numbers each time it is run, specify *seed* the first time you use the RANDOM function.

`REVERSE(string)`

Reverses the characters in *string*.

`RIGHT(string,len)`

Returns a string of length *len* where *string* is right-aligned.

`SIGN(number)`

Returns -1 if *number* is less than zero, 0 if *number* equals zero, or 1 if *number* is greater than zero.

`SOURCELINE(n)`

Returns the contents of the *n*th line in the source file. If *n* isn't specified, returns the number of the last line in the source file.

`SPACE(string,n,pad)`

Returns a string where the words in the original string are spaced evenly with *n* pad characters. The default for *n* is 1, and the default for *pad* is a space.

`STRIP(string,option,char)`

Deletes spaces (or character *char*) from *string* based on the value specified for *option*: L deletes leading characters, T deletes trailing characters, and B deletes both leading and trailing characters.

`SUBSTR(string,n,len)`   Returns a substring of length *len* extracted from *string* beginning at position A.

`SUBWORD(string,n,len)`   Returns a substring of length *len* words extracted from *string* beginning with the *n*th word.

`SYMBOL(name)`   Returns BAD if *name* is not a valid REXX symbol and VAR if *name* is a REXX variable. Otherwise, returns LIT.

`TIME(option)`   Returns the (24-hour clock) time in the format specified by *option*:

C   hh:mmxx (xx is am or pm)

E   elapsed time in seconds since last reset

H   number of hours since midnight

L   hh:mm:ss.uuuuuu (uuuuuu represents milliseconds)

M   number of minutes since midnight

N   hh:mm:ss (the default)

R   elapsed time in seconds since the last reset; also resets the elapsed time clock

S   number of seconds since midnight

`TRANSLATE(string,table1,table2)`   Translates the characters in *string* found in *table2* to the corresponding characters in *table1*. If both tables are omitted, translates *string* to uppercase.

`TRUNC(number,n)`   Returns *number* with the numbers right of the decimal point truncated to *n* characters. The default value of *n* is 0.

`USERID()`   Returns the user-id.

`VALUE(name)`   Returns the value of *name*.

`VERIFY(string,ref)`   Returns 0 if all characters in *string* also appear in the string *ref*. Otherwise, returns the position of the first character in *string* that doesn't appear in *ref*.

`WORD(string,n)`   Returns the *n*th word in *string*.

`WORDINDEX(string,n)`   Returns the character position of the *n*th word in *string*.

`WORDLENGTH(string,n)`

Returns the length of the *n*th word in *string*.

`WORDPOS(string1,string2,start)`

Returns the word number of the first occurrence of *string1* in *string2*. If specified, the search begins at word *start*.

`WORDS(string)`

Returns the number of words in *string*.

`XRANGE(start,end)`

Returns a string consisting of all the characters between and including *start* and *end*.

`X2C(string)`

Returns the character equivalent of a hexadecimal string.

`X2D(string)`

Returns the decimal equivalent of a hexadecimal string.

Appendix D

Edit macro reference summary

This appendix summarizes the edit macro commands and assignment statements presented in this book. For each command, you'll find a complete format. If you need more information about any of these commands or statements, you can refer to chapter 9.

EDIT MACRO COMMANDS

The DELETE command

Format 1:

```
ISREDIT DELETE  [ALL] [range]  [{ X  }]
                                 { NX }
```

Format 2:
```
ISREDIT DELETE line-pointer
```

The INSERT command
```
ISREDIT INSERT line-pointer [count]
```

The LABEL command
```
ISREDIT LABEL line-pointer = .label [level]
```

The LINE command

Format 1:
```
ISREDIT (variable) = LINE line-pointer
```

Format 2:
```
ISREDIT LINE line-pointer = value
```

The LINE_AFTER command

```
                                  (DATALINE)   (value         )
                                  (INFOLINE)   (LINE          )
ISREDIT LINE_AFTER line-pointer = (MSGLINE )   (LINE pointer   )
                                  (NOTELINE)   (MASKLINE      )
                                               (TABSLINE      )
```

The LINE_BEFORE command

```
ISREDIT LINE_BEFORE line-pointer =  ⎧DATALINE⎫ ⎧value        ⎫
                                    ⎪INFOLINE⎪ ⎪LINE         ⎪
                                    ⎨MSGLINE ⎬ ⎨LINE pointer ⎬
                                    ⎩NOTELINE⎭ ⎪MASKLINE     ⎪
                                               ⎩TABSLINE     ⎭
```

The LINENUM command

```
ISREDIT (variable) = LINENUM label
```

The PROCESS command

```
ISREDIT PROCESS [DEST] [RANGE line-command]
```

The SEEK command

```
ISREDIT SEEK string [range]  ⎧NEXT ⎫ ⎧CHARS ⎫
                             ⎪PREV ⎪ ⎪PREFIX⎪
                             ⎨FIRST⎬ ⎨SUFFIX⎬
                             ⎪LAST ⎪ ⎩WORD  ⎭
                             ⎩ALL  ⎭

    [⎧X ⎫] [col-1 [col-2]]
     ⎩NX⎭
```

The SETMSG command

```
ISPEXEC SETMSG MSG(message-id)
```

The SHIFT command

```
ISREDIT SHIFT  ⎧)⎫  line-pointer  [cols]
               ⎪(⎪
               ⎨<⎬
               ⎩>⎭
```

EDIT MACRO ASSIGNMENT STATEMENTS

CHANGE_COUNTS

Returns two values representing the number of strings that were changed and the number of strings that could not be changed.

CURSOR

Returns two values representing the line and column position of the cursor.

DATA_CHANGED

Returns YES if the data has been changed since it was last saved, and NO if it hasn't.

DATASET

Returns the name of the current data set.

EXCLUDE_COUNTS

Returns two values representing the number of strings that were found and the number of lines that were excluded.

FIND_COUNTS

Returns two values representing the number of strings that were found and the number of lines where strings were found.

MEMBER

Returns the name of the current member.

RANGE_CMD

The line command that was used to mark a range.

SEEK_COUNTS

Returns two values representing the number of strings that were found and the number of lines where strings were found.

USER_STATE

Returns the current edit profile in an internal form that can be later restored.

Appendix E

ISPF dialog reference summary

This appendix summarizes the ISPF dialog manager commands and panel definition statements presented in this book. For each command, you'll find a complete format. If you need more information about any of these command, you can refer to chapter 10.

ISPEXEC COMMANDS

The DISPLAY command

```
ISPEXEC DISPLAY PANEL(panel-name)
```

The LIBDEF command

```
ISPEXEC LIBDEF    ⎧ISPPLIB⎫    ⎧DATASET ID(data set names...)⎫
                  ⎪ISPMLIB⎪    ⎩LIBRARY ID(ddname)           ⎭
                  ⎨ISPSLIB⎬
                  ⎪ISPTLIB⎪
                  ⎩ISPTABL⎭
```

The SETMSG command

```
ISPEXEC SETMSG MSG(message-id) [COND]
```

The TBADD command

```
ISPEXEC TBADD table-name [ORDER]
```

The TBBOTTOM command

```
ISPEXEC TBBOTTOM table-name
```

The TBCLOSE command

```
ISPEXEC TBCLOSE table-name
```

The TBCREATE command

```
ISPEXEC TBCREATE table-name    [ KEYS(key-name-list) ]

                               [ NAMES(name-list) ]

                               [ ⎧WRITE  ⎫ ]
                                 ⎩NOWRITE⎭

                               [ REPLACE ]
```

The TBDELETE command

```
ISPEXEC TBDELETE table-name
```

The **TBDISPL** command

```
ISPEXEC TBDISPL table-name  [PANEL(panel)]
```

The **TBGET** command

```
ISPEXEC TBGET table-name
```

The **TBMOD** command

```
ISPEXEC TBMOD table-name
```

The **TBOPEN** command

$$
ISPEXEC\ TBOPEN\ table\text{-}name\ \left[\ \left\{ \begin{matrix} \underline{WRITE} \\ NOWRITE \end{matrix} \right\} \ \right]
$$

The **TBPUT** command

```
ISPEXEC TBPUT table-name
```

The **TBSARG** command

$$
ISPEXEC\ TBSARG\ table\text{-}name\ [NAMECOND(name\text{-}cond\text{-}list)]
$$

$$
\left[\left\{ \begin{matrix} \underline{NEXT} \\ PREVIOUS \end{matrix} \right\} \right]
$$

The **TBSCAN** command

$$
ISPEXEC\ TBSCAN\ table\text{-}name\ [ARGLIST(name\text{-}list)]
$$

$$
[CONDLIST(cond\text{-}list)]\ \left[\left\{ \begin{matrix} \underline{NEXT} \\ PREVIOUS \end{matrix} \right\} \right]
$$

The **TBSKIP** command

```
ISPEXEC TBSKIP table-name [NUMBER(number)]
```

The **TBSORT** command

```
ISPEXEC TBSORT table-name
```

$$
FIELDS(variable\text{-}1, \left\{ \begin{matrix} C \\ N \end{matrix} \right\} ,\ \left\{ \begin{matrix} A \\ D \end{matrix} \right\}\ \ [variable\text{-}2...])
$$

The TBTOP command

```
ISPEXEC TBTOP table-name
```

PANEL DEFINITION STATEMENTS

Attribute definition

$$\text{TYPE}\left(\left\{\begin{matrix}\text{TEXT}\\\text{INPUT}\\\text{OUTPUT}\end{matrix}\right\}\right)$$

$$\text{INTENS}\left(\left\{\begin{matrix}\text{HIGH}\\\text{LOW}\end{matrix}\right\}\right)$$

$$\text{CAPS}\left(\left\{\begin{matrix}\text{ON}\\\text{OFF}\end{matrix}\right\}\right)$$

$$\text{JUST}\left(\left\{\begin{matrix}\text{LEFT}\\\text{RIGHT}\\\text{ASIS}\end{matrix}\right\}\right)$$

$$\text{SKIP}\left(\left\{\begin{matrix}\text{ON}\\\text{OFF}\end{matrix}\right\}\right)$$

$$\text{NUMERIC}\left(\left\{\begin{matrix}\text{ON}\\\text{OFF}\end{matrix}\right\}\right)$$

```
COLOR(color)
```

$$\text{HILITE}\left(\left\{\begin{matrix}\text{USCORE}\\\text{BLINK}\\\text{REVERSE}\end{matrix}\right\}\right)$$

The IF statement

```
IF (condition)
     statements
[ELSE
   statements]
```

The VER statement

```
VER (variable [,NONBLANK] [validation-test] [,MSG=value])
```

Validation tests for the VER statement

`ALPHA`	Contains alphabetic characters.
`NUM`	Contains numeric characters.
`ENUM`	Contains numeric characters or symbols used to format numeric values.
`HEX`	Contains hexadecimal characters.
`BIN`	Contains zeros and ones.
`LEN,operator,length`	Length matches the specified condition.
`PICT,string`	Data matches the picture string.
`NAME`	Contains a valid member name.
`DSNAME`	Contains a valid data set name
`RANGE,lower,upper`	Contains a number between the given range.
`LIST,value-1,value-2`	Matches one of the listed values.

.ZVARS assignment

```
ZVARS = '(var1,var2,...)'
```

Appendix F

Installation dependent information

This appendix provides space for you to record information that's unique to your installation, such as your logon-id and the procedures for accessing TSO. There are four copies of this information form, so you can record information about four systems.

MVS INSTALLATION DEPENDENT INFORMATION

Operating system

MVS version?

JES2 or JES3?

TSO/E version?

ISPF version?

Information required to access the system

TSO user-id:

Network access procedure:

DASD allocation information

Data set name high-level qualifier:

Eligible DASD volumes:

Frequently used data sets

User CLIST procedure library:

User REXX procedure library:

User ISPF panel library:

User ISPF table library:

Other installation dependent information

MVS INSTALLATION DEPENDENT INFORMATION

Operating system

MVS version?

JES2 or JES3?

TSO/E version?

ISPF version?

Information required to access the system

TSO user-id:

Network access procedure:

DASD allocation information

Data set name high-level qualifier:

Eligible DASD volumes:

Frequently used data sets

User CLIST procedure library:

User REXX procedure library:

User ISPF panel library:

User ISPF table library:

Other installation dependent information

MVS INSTALLATION DEPENDENT INFORMATION

Operating system

MVS version?

JES2 or JES3?

TSO/E version?

ISPF version?

Information required to access the system

TSO user-id:

Network access procedure:

DASD allocation information

Data set name high-level qualifier:

Eligible DASD volumes:

Frequently used data sets

User CLIST procedure library:

User REXX procedure library:

User ISPF panel library:

User ISPF table library:

Other installation dependent information

MVS INSTALLATION DEPENDENT INFORMATION

Operating system

MVS version?

JES2 or JES3?

TSO/E version?

ISPF version?

Information required to access the system

TSO user-id:

Network access procedure:

DASD allocation information

Data set name high-level qualifier:

Eligible DASD volumes:

Frequently used data sets

User CLIST procedure library:

User REXX procedure library:

User ISPF panel library:

User ISPF table library:

Other installation dependent information

Index

For professional programmers

Murach's Mainframe COBOL	$59.50
Murach's OS/390 and z/OS JCL	62.50
Murach's CICS for the COBOL Programmer	54.00
Murach's CICS Desk Reference	49.50
DB2 for the COBOL Programmer, Part 1 (Second Edition)	45.00
DB2 for the COBOL Programmer, Part 2 (Second Edition)	45.00
MVS TSO, Part 1: Concepts and ISPF	42.50
Murach's Java SE 6	$52.50
Murach's Java Servlets and JSP	49.50
Murach's C# 2005	$52.50
Murach's VB 2005	52.50
Murach's ASP.NET 2.0 Web Programming with VB 2005	52.50
Murach's ASP.NET 2.0 Web Programming with C# 2005	52.50
Murach's SQL Server 2005 for Developers	52.50

*Prices and availability are subject to change. Please visit our web site or call for current information.

Our unlimited guarantee...when you order directly from us

You must be satisfied with our books. If they aren't better than any other programming books you've ever used...both for training and reference....you can send them back for a full refund. No questions asked!

Your opinions count

If you have any comments on this book, I'm eager to get them. Thanks for your feedback!

To comment by

E-mail:	murachbooks@murach.com
Web:	www.murach.com
Postal mail:	Mike Murach & Associates, Inc.
	3484 W. Gettysburg, Suite 101
	Fresno, California 93722-7801

To order now,

 Web: www.murach.com

 Call toll-free:
1-800-221-5528
(Weekdays, 8 am to 4 pm Pacific Time)

 Fax: 1-559-440-0963

 Mike Murach & Associates, Inc.
Professional programming books